AF737600

Cybersecurity Education for Awareness and Compliance

Ismini Vasileiou
University of Plymouth, UK

Steven Furnell
University of Plymouth, UK

A volume in the Advances in Information Security, Privacy, and Ethics (AISPE) Book Series

IGI Global
DISSEMINATOR OF KNOWLEDGE

Published in the United States of America by
IGI Global
Information Science Reference (an imprint of IGI Global)
701 E. Chocolate Avenue
Hershey PA, USA 17033
Tel: 717-533-8845
Fax: 717-533-8661
E-mail: cust@igi-global.com
Web site: http://www.igi-global.com

Copyright © 2019 by IGI Global. All rights reserved. No part of this publication may be reproduced, stored or distributed in any form or by any means, electronic or mechanical, including photocopying, without written permission from the publisher. Product or company names used in this set are for identification purposes only. Inclusion of the names of the products or companies does not indicate a claim of ownership by IGI Global of the trademark or registered trademark.

Library of Congress Cataloging-in-Publication Data

Names: Vasileiou, Ismini, 1980- editor. | Furnell, Steven, 1970- editor.
Title: Cybersecurity education for awareness and compliance / Ismini Vasileiou and Steven Furnell, editors.
Description: Hershey, PA : Information Science Reference, [2019] | Includes bibliographical references.
Identifiers: LCCN 2018036338| ISBN 9781522578475 (h/c) | ISBN 9781522578482 (eISBN)
Subjects: LCSH: Business enterprises--Computer networks--Security measures. | Information technology--Security measures. | Employees--Training of. | Employee rules.
Classification: LCC HD30.38 .C93 2019 | DDC 658.3/124--dc23 LC record available at https://lccn.loc.gov/2018036338

This book is published in the IGI Global book series Advances in Information Security, Privacy, and Ethics (AISPE) (ISSN: 1948-9730; eISSN: 1948-9749)

British Cataloguing in Publication Data
A Cataloguing in Publication record for this book is available from the British Library.

All work contributed to this book is new, previously-unpublished material. The views expressed in this book are those of the authors, but not necessarily of the publisher.

For electronic access to this publication, please contact: eresources@igi-global.com.

Advances in Information Security, Privacy, and Ethics (AISPE) Book Series

Manish Gupta
State University of New York, USA

ISSN:1948-9730
EISSN:1948-9749

Mission

As digital technologies become more pervasive in everyday life and the Internet is utilized in ever increasing ways by both private and public entities, concern over digital threats becomes more prevalent.

The **Advances in Information Security, Privacy, & Ethics (AISPE) Book Series** provides cutting-edge research on the protection and misuse of information and technology across various industries and settings. Comprised of scholarly research on topics such as identity management, cryptography, system security, authentication, and data protection, this book series is ideal for reference by IT professionals, academicians, and upper-level students.

Coverage

- Tracking Cookies
- IT Risk
- Information Security Standards
- Data Storage of Minors
- Electronic Mail Security
- Privacy-Enhancing Technologies
- Network Security Services
- Device Fingerprinting
- Telecommunications Regulations
- Security Information Management

IGI Global is currently accepting manuscripts for publication within this series. To submit a proposal for a volume in this series, please contact our Acquisition Editors at Acquisitions@igi-global.com or visit: http://www.igi-global.com/publish/.

The Advances in Information Security, Privacy, and Ethics (AISPE) Book Series (ISSN 1948-9730) is published by IGI Global, 701 E. Chocolate Avenue, Hershey, PA 17033-1240, USA, www.igi-global.com. This series is composed of titles available for purchase individually; each title is edited to be contextually exclusive from any other title within the series. For pricing and ordering information please visit http://www.igi-global.com/book-series/advances-information-security-privacy-ethics/37157. Postmaster: Send all address changes to above address. Copyright © 2019 IGI Global. All rights, including translation in other languages reserved by the publisher. No part of this series may be reproduced or used in any form or by any means – graphics, electronic, or mechanical, including photocopying, recording, taping, or information and retrieval systems – without written permission from the publisher, except for non commercial, educational use, including classroom teaching purposes. The views expressed in this series are those of the authors, but not necessarily of IGI Global.

Titles in this Series

For a list of additional titles in this series, please visit: www.igi-global.com/book-series

Detection and Mitigation of Insider Attacks in a Cloud Infrastructure Emerging Research and Opportunities
T. Gunasekhar (Koneru Lakshmaiah Education Foundation, India) K. Thirupathi Rao (Koneru Lakshmaiah Education Foundation, India) P. Sai Kiran (Koneru Lakshmaiah Education Foundation, India) V. Krishna Reddy (Koneru Lakshmaiah Education Foundation, India) and B. Thirumala Rao (Koneru Lakshmaiah Education Foundation, India)
Information Science Reference • copyright 2019 • 113pp • H/C (ISBN: 9781522579243) • US $165.00 (our price)

Network Security and Its Impact on Business Strategy
Ionica Oncioiu (European Academy of the Regions, Belgium)
Business Science Reference • copyright 2019 • 350pp • H/C (ISBN: 9781522584551) • US $225.00 (our price)

Exploring Security in Software Architecture and Design
Michael Felderer (University of Innsbruck, Austria) and Riccardo Scandariato (Chalmers University of Technology, Sweden & University of Gothenburg, Sweden)
Information Science Reference • copyright 2019 • 349pp • H/C (ISBN: 9781522563136) • US $215.00 (our price)

Cryptographic Security Solutions for the Internet of Things
Mohammad Tariq Banday (University of Kashmir, India)
Information Science Reference • copyright 2019 • 367pp • H/C (ISBN: 9781522557425) • US $195.00 (our price)

Advanced Methodologies and Technologies in System Security, Information Privacy, and Forensics
Mehdi Khosrow-Pour, D.B.A. (Information Resources Management Association, USA)
Information Science Reference • copyright 2019 • 417pp • H/C (ISBN: 9781522574927) • US $285.00 (our price)

Handbook of Research on Information and Cyber Security in the Fourth Industrial Revolution
Ziska Fields (University of KwaZulu-Natal, South Africa)
Information Science Reference • copyright 2018 • 647pp • H/C (ISBN: 9781522547631) • US $345.00 (our price)

Security and Privacy in Smart Sensor Networks
Yassine Maleh (University Hassan I, Morocco) Abdellah Ezzati (University Hassan I, Morocco) and Mustapha Belaissaoui (University Hassan I, Morocco)
Information Science Reference • copyright 2018 • 441pp • H/C (ISBN: 9781522557364) • US $215.00 (our price)

The Changing Scope of Technoethics in Contemporary Society
Rocci Luppicini (University of Ottawa, Canada)
Information Science Reference • copyright 2018 • 403pp • H/C (ISBN: 9781522550945) • US $225.00 (our price)

IGI Global
DISSEMINATOR OF KNOWLEDGE

701 East Chocolate Avenue, Hershey, PA 17033, USA
Tel: 717-533-8845 x100 • Fax: 717-533-8661
E-Mail: cust@igi-global.com • www.igi-global.com

Editorial Advisory Board

William Caelli, *Queensland University of Technology, Australia*
Ronald Dodge, *Palo Alto Networks, USA*
Cynthia Irvine, *Naval Postgraduate School, USA*
Sokratis Katsikas, *Norwegian University of Science and Technology, Norway & Open University of Cyprus, Cyprus*
Jenny Radcliffe, *JennyRadcliffe.com, UK*
Awais Rashid, *University of Bristol, UK*
Kai Roer, *CLTRe AS, Norway*
Corey Schou, *Idaho State University, USA*
Eugene Spafford, *Purdue University, USA*
Merrill Warkentin, *Mississippi State University, USA*
Louise Yngström, *Stockholm University, Sweden*

Table of Contents

Detailed Table of Contents

The Cybersecurity Curricular Guidelines, a joint effort of the ACM, IEEE Computer Society, AIS SIGSAC, and IFIP WG 11.8, were created to provide developers of cybersecurity curricula with guidelines for material to include. The curricular guidelines have eight knowledge areas, broken down into knowledge units and topics. Underlying cross-cutting concepts provide linkages among the knowledge areas. Disciplinary lenses enable the developer to emphasize the knowledge units appropriate to the goals of the developed curricula. Each knowledge area also includes a list of essential concepts that all curricula should cover to an appropriate depth. The guidelines can be linked to workforce frameworks and certification criteria as well as academic curricula.

This chapter presents an implementation of a cybersecurity education program. The program aims to address some issues identified in current cybersecurity teaching in higher education on a European level, like the fragmentation of cybersecurity expertise or resource shortage, resulting in few higher education institutions to offer full degree programs. As a result of the Erasmus+ strategic partnership project SecTech, the program tries to overcome those issues by introducing collaborative development to cybersecurity education. SecTech lays the foundations for a collaborative education program, like the definition of a clear content, module and delivery structure, and the appropriate tool support to facilitate collaboration and content reuse. Additional effort is required to achieve long-term success, including the creation of a community that drives the content creation and maintenance, as well as an independent governance structure to steer the project in the long-term. While the project focuses on European collaboration, a global community is envisioned.

This chapter traces the evolution of cybersecurity skills requirements and development over the past 40 years, from the early days of computer security (Compusec) to the present day. The development of

Foreword

Incredible advances in computing technology have continued unabated since the 1950s. Society has reaped tremendous benefits from its increasing, wide-scale computer use enabled by these discoveries. Virtually every sector, including research, business, entertainment, communication, health care, and government have been vastly enhanced as they have adopted ever-advancing computing technologies. However, as we entrust more items of value to those computing systems, it has been no surprise that we are also experiencing an ever-increasing number of breaches of security, privacy, and overall threats to safety. The looming deployment of an order of magnitude more systems as part of the "Internet of Things" makes this even more troubling. It is clear that we want competent, well-informed people overseeing and maintaining these systems. Where do we find them?

It is inconceivable that any of us would board an airliner for a long flight if told that the chief pilot was "learning on the job." It is highly unlikely that we would want the electrical wiring in our homes installed by someone who "read some books and experimented at home." We would question the wisdom of entrusting our retirement savings to a stockbroker who entered the field after reading an excellent book on finance last week. In every field where there is a requirement of quality, and concern over potential losses, there is an expectation of having professionals on the job. Requiring a competent professional to perform tasks with significant implications for computing safety should be little different. It is therefore surprising how many organizations will unhesitatingly hire people to work in their computing enterprises – sometimes as part of the security and privacy teams – who have little more than a passing familiarity with the field overall; the ability of someone to write code that compiles or execute an attack against a poorly-defended system is sadly misjudged as sufficient evidence of overall competence.

This need for appropriately-skilled people is where the spectrum of activities in Awareness-Training-Education comes in. There is a large population of people who might work in the field of cyber, now and in the future, but they need to obtain the requisite knowledge skills. Having well-designed materials and exercises helps ensure that students gain a fundamental understanding of the field in which they will work. Additional training, both on and off the job, help to sharpen and refine the skills of everyone from the novice to the expert. Awareness activities help everyone understand fundamental issues and consequences, as well as gaining an appreciation for the expertise required — including how to differentiate a hobbyist from a professional when it is important to do so!

Computing as a discipline is less than 100 years old. The more specific field of cybersecurity/information assurance has only come into focus over the last few decades. The challenges of developing meaningful and effective awareness, training and education materials, processes, and evaluations are still fresh, and continually complicated by the on-going, rapid evolution of the field itself. That is why it is important to share and refine what we know, so that we can best provide for both the general good of those depending on safe computing, and to provide comprehensive foundations for people seeking to make a meaningful career in the field.

This volume contains chapters from many perspectives, each providing insight into some aspect of the problems and solutions in cyber education, awareness, and training. It contributes to the evolving toolkit that cybersecurity educators and professionals need. The problems we face in cybersecurity and privacy are legion, and everyone can play a part. This book is a valuable addition to the solution space.

Eugene H. Spafford
Purdue University, USA

Eugene H. Spafford *is a professor of Computer Sciences at Purdue University. He is also the founder and Executive Director Emeritus of the Center for Education and Research in Information Assurance and Security. He has been working in computing as a student, researcher, consultant and professor for over 40 years. Some of his work is at the foundation of current security practice, including intrusion detection, firewalls, and whitelisting. His most recent work has been in cybersecurity policy, forensics, education, and future threats. Professor Spafford is a Fellow of the AAAS, ACM, IEEE, (ISC)2, a Distinguished Fellow of the ISSA, and a member of the Cyber Security Hall of Fame -- the only person to ever hold all these distinctions. In 2012 he was named as one of Purdue's inaugural Morrill Professors -- the university's highest award for the combination of scholarship, teaching, and service. In 2016, he received the State of Indiana's highest civilian honor by being named as a Sagamore of the Wabash. Among other activities, he is a member of the Council of ACM and is editor-in-chief of the journal Computers & Security. More information: http://spaf.cerias.purdue.edu/narrate.html.*

Preface

THE NEED FOR CYBERSECURITY EDUCATION AND COMPLIANCE

Understanding of cybersecurity is vital to all users of IT systems and services, in order to protect themselves from threats and avoid unnecessary risks. However, despite years of experience in using an increasing array of technologies, this understanding is often found to be lagging behind or entirely lacking. It is particularly relevant in an organizational setting, where the lack of security awareness and compliance amongst staff is the root cause of many incidents and breaches. Unfortunately, while the problems are recognized, the actions to address them do not always follow to the level that one might expect.

In recognition of the related needs, it is now common to see the acronym SETA (Security Education, Training and Awareness) being used as an umbrella term for the efforts required to address the situation. Each of the underlying elements has a distinct meaning, and the US National Institute of Standards and Technology (NIST) has usefully distinguished them in a security context as listed below (Wilson et al., 1998):

- **Awareness:** To focus attention on security.
- **Training:** To produce relevant and needed security skills and competency.
- **Education:** To integrate all (security skills and competencies) into a common body of knowledge, adding a multidisciplinary study of concepts, issues, and principles.

As listed here, it is clear that the concepts build upon each other, and delivering layers of increasing depth (in terms of the detail, understanding and skill) for the recipients involved. Indeed, listing them in this order is more appropriate if we want to consider them as contributing towards different phases of an overall learning continuum. Having said this, while the definitions are useful to understand the distinctions, the terms often end up being used interchangeably in practice or thought of as synonyms (e.g., organizations might well respond to surveys and suggest that they have a security education program in place, when what they *actually* have is an awareness-raising activity).

Regardless of what we call it, there is often a gap when it comes to providing SETA support in a way that successfully enables participants to walk away with a clear understanding and acceptance of the issues and be in a position to comply with regulations and behaviors. If these are to be addressed then there needs to be adequate support and provision for effective training and education, that enables staff to know what is expected of them and have the necessary skills to follow it through. It is important to recognize the role of different audiences, from users through to management, and the importance of delivering education in a manner that goes beyond simply conveying knowledge and instead leads to a position that supports security compliance.

There are also frequent shortcomings at other levels, with a lack of staff with the specialized skills to support the design, deployment and management of cybersecurity. These individuals require a more fundamental education in the topic, as well as training to support the understanding and use of specific techniques and tools relating to their particular areas of responsibility.

With these needs in mind, this edited book takes the reader from appreciating the essentials of the cybersecurity literacy, through to understanding frameworks and models for delivering effective training and compliance.

THE ROLE OF THIS BOOK

The main objective of this book is to provide organizations (and relevant individuals within them) with a clear understanding of what security education is, the elements required to achieve it, and the means by which to link it to the wider goal of good security behavior and compliance. The discussion across the chapters is intended to address key perspectives that can contribute towards the overall goal, and they collectively develop the themes from appreciating the essentials of the cybersecurity literacy, through to understanding frameworks and models for delivering effective training and compliance.

Achieving the holistic approach requires attention and action from a number of directions. For the purposes of this book, four key perspectives are identified, which serve to inform the structure of the later chapters:

- **Users:** These are the people involved, and the ultimate targets of any awareness and education provision that may be made. It is their mindset and behavior that we are seeking to address, and so we need to identify the issues that need to be understood, and how we can position things to educate users most effectively. While people regularly use the related technologies on a personal basis, in many cases they also have a role as staff within an organizational setting, which links to the next perspective.
- **Organizations:** The party that typically feels the effect of awareness shortcomings, thanks to the incidents and breaches occurring as a result. They also have a role to play in delivering education and awareness activities and ultimately shaping the security culture of the staff concerned. At the same time, organizations face challenges in getting the skills that they need to support cybersecurity, as well as ensuring that staff at all levels understand and buy-into the aspects of security relevant to their roles.
- **Academia:** This represents a key perspective in terms of supporting the previous two, insofar as academic programs (particularly at the higher education level) will be the starting point for equipping the next generation workforce in dealing with cybersecurity, as well as with information technology more widely. However, in order for this to work effectively, cybersecurity needs to be recognized and appropriately delivered within the programs concerned, and therefore given appropriate emphasis within undergraduate and postgraduate qualifications.

- **The Profession:** Training and education helps to underpin and inform the cybersecurity profession more widely. This particularly links to how the profession itself views skills and competencies, and how people might go about acquiring them. The specialist cybersecurity workforce needs to ensure that it maintains relevant skills, and the profession needs to ensure that routes are available for them to do so, through both the recognition of the underlying skills and the certifications that support them.

The later chapters consider the role that each group should be playing, the challenges that they face, and the broad nature of what they should be doing about it. For example, organizations often face an awareness gap and a skills deficit, and so require several steps to raise themselves to a more appropriate level. Moreover, these steps are intrinsically linked to aspects arising from the other three areas, and so it is relevant for them to be considered holistically.

TARGET AUDIENCE

The book will be of interest to organizations wishing to achieve a security-compliant staff community. The content is relevant for managers and specialist staff such as Chief Information Security Officers in demonstrating the importance of awareness, training and education in supporting security compliance in everyday tasks. The material addresses security educators and the different contexts in which they work, recognizing that educational provision must be viewed at the level of both individuals and organizations, and that cybersecurity specialists may be supported through both academic qualifications and professional certifications. Considering the discussion overall will ideally enable each community to understand the perspective of the other. The content will also be of value to scholars seeking to understand the broader context in which cybersecurity education and skills can be fostered, alongside the underpinning principles for doing so.

With contributions from leading figures in both academia and industry, the chapters collectively draw upon both theoretical principles and practical experience in order to consider what must be done, and how to achieve it. The resulting volume thereby provides a relevant resource support overall strategy and practical decisions in the area.

CHAPTER STRUCTURE AND CONTENT

Reflecting the perspectives above, the material is split across four thematic sections, with 12 chapters collectively identifying and advising upon the different directions from which action is required.

Addressing the User

In the first section, the three chapters are concerned with the individuals who have to deal with and influence security as part of their day-to-day activities. In many cases they are non-specialists, but they nonetheless have a crucial role to play in maintaining protection.

Beginning the discussion, Furnell and Vasileiou present a holistic view of cybersecurity education requirements, recognizing the need for baseline cybersecurity literacy for individuals in order to support their use of systems and data on a personal basis and within the workplace. It also considers the requirements from the perspective of the organizations within which people are working, highlighting the problems that can be faced due to lack of awareness and considering how this can be addressed via effective SETA provision (including the desirability of tailoring the provision to individual needs). The discussion also identifies the need for individuals holding key cybersecurity responsibilities to have more specialized education and training and shows that difficulties can also be faced at this level due to a shortage of appropriately skilled individuals, as well as potential confusion in terms of the range of certifications that may be encountered in practice.

Although it is the users causing the problems, it is established that organizations have a key role in helping them to do better. With this in mind, Crumbaugh expands upon the importance of ensuring that the support provided to users is actually appropriate and effective. Drawing upon extensive experience as a cybersecurity practitioner, the author outlines a series of common mistakes that are often made in the delivery of awareness programs and the associated advice for avoiding them. The discussion also highlights some specific examples of user-facing threats that ought to be specifically emphasized as part of the SETA approach.

Having consider the mistakes that can be made, the chapter from Smyth et al. looks in more detail at the nature of the insider threats that SETA activities and compliance monitoring are often seeking to address. The discussion considers the nature of these insiders and the threats that they pose (both accidental and malicious), recognizing that some individuals essentially achieve insider status via subcontracting and outsourcing rather than being full employees. Education and awareness are seen to have a key role in tackling the issues, with the theme of tailored provision again emerging as a recommendation in order to more effectively reach the individuals that require support and guidance.

Addressing Organizations

With the prior chapters having established that organizations can be significantly affected if users are operating without appropriate SETA support, this section takes a broader view and looks at things that can be done from the organization's perspective.

Harris and Martin begin this discussion by looking at the promotion of cybersecurity compliance – this being the end result that organizations are looking to achieve from their staff. They start by presenting the landscape around cybersecurity governance, in terms of laws, regulations and external standards that organizations can find themselves needing to comply with. These in turn inform the policies facing the staff, and the associated need to measure and monitor compliance at the employee level. The discussion considers the approaches that can be used to achieve this, set alongside the theoretical backdrop of research that has been conducted in the compliance domain in order to provide the underpinning basis.

Having established compliance as the end goal, the next chapter considers how to position staff within the organization to achieve it. While SETA efforts have the individual effects of improving understanding and behavior, the collective effect within an organization is the development of a security culture, with staff recognizing their role in protection and operating in compliance with policies. Da Veiga's chapter provides an overview of security culture as an organizational concept and identifies the factors that could influence it. The discussion also presents a practical approach for assessing the culture within organizations, the output of which can then assist them in matching their SETA activities to support the areas that need it.

Building upon the discussion of security culture, Oldham and McAlpine present a discussion of techniques and tools that cybersecurity trainers and practitioners may use in order to achieve it in practice. Drawing upon direct experience in providing cybersecurity awareness and training services to industry, the authors reflect upon their experience of the approaches that work most effectively in practice and how these can be used and deployed in organizational settings. Particular attention is given to online training provision, as a means of reaching a wide audience of staff in a flexible manner, and the overall discussion offers a variety of valuable insights into what works and why.

Of course, while there are clear requirements to support staff in general, organizations also face the challenge of ensuring that their specialist cybersecurity capabilities are appropriately supported. While organizations may approach this in different ways – hiring in new people, developing existing staff, or outsourcing the provision – they still need to know the type and level of expertise that they are looking for. With this in mind, the chapter from Dhillon et al. discusses the need for organizations to identify and understand the core competencies involved in maintaining their overall cybersecurity capability. These competencies are described from strategic, exploitational, and supply perspectives – each of which is then further dissected in order to identify the key areas that organizations should be attending to if they are to keep their cybersecurity capability updated and effective.

Addressing Academia

An essential aspect of addressing cybersecurity education in a more substantive sense, particularly in relation to supporting aspiring IT and cyber professionals, relates to how it is handled in academic programs. As such, the third section gives specific focus to this perspective, with a set of chapters that collectively examine cybersecurity education in a higher education context.

In the first of these, Irons considers the requirements and challenges of delivering cybersecurity education effectively. This includes an examination of what effective education actually looks like in general terms, before homing in upon the cyber context more specifically. The discussion then outlines a range of delivery options, and then moves on to consider how subsequent assessment activities can be approached.

Having looked at the principles and approaches a broad level, the chapter from Bishop et al. provides some specific guidance on the content of cybersecurity curricula. Drawing upon recommendations arising from a collaborative effort between relevant professional bodies, the resulting CSEC2017 guidelines present a series of knowledge areas, units and topics that should be considered by those looking to implement specific cybersecurity courses. The chapter as a whole presents an overview of these aspects and illustrates how the guidelines can relate to different application areas and workforce frameworks.

The final chapter in this section, from Tokola et al., focuses upon a specific cybersecurity program example. It draws upon the work of a collaborative European project initiative – SecTech – that aims towards a cybersecurity program (and related content) that is developed and delivered in a collaborative manner. Relating the approach back to the CSEC2017 model as a reference, the discussion outlines the development, structure and delivery tools adopted by SecTech, with the program providing both an initial solution and a foundation for further collaborative development.

Addressing the Profession

Whether they took an academic route to get there or not, it is also important to recognize, develop and maintain the skills of cybersecurity professionals in the workplace. As such, the final section of the book gives specific consideration to what can be done at the professional level.

In Chapter 11, Fischer looks at the need to appreciate the distinct types of cybersecurity skills that are required within the profession, and for a related means to understand how they fit together. Following a brief historical perspective on the recognition of cyber skills, the mainstay of the discussion is focused upon a well-established Skills Framework from the Institute of Information Security Professionals (IISP). The text presents an outline of the security disciplines identified within the Framework, spanning business-level issues such as security management and governance through to more technically-focused skills such as implementation and digital forensic investigation. It also illustrates how the Framework has evolved through successive releases, providing an important indication of how cybersecurity skills themselves evolve (with knock-on implications for our education and training provision).

In the final chapter, Davis presents a perspective on the continuing cybersecurity education and training provision that professionals would expect to see in the workplace, highlighting the role and importance of security certifications. The discussion identifies the different forms of certification that exist, recognizing that they can vary in terms of both the content/coverage involved and the level of knowledge and skills that they aim to support. This in turn makes it important for both organizations and individuals to understand the role of any certifications under consideration and ensure that they are appropriately matched to their particular needs.

CONCLUSION

Awareness, training and education are vital aspects of an effective approach to cybersecurity and will represent an inevitable weak point in any organizational strategy if they are not given appropriate attention. Requirements exist across the breadth of users, from general employees in their day-to-day activities through to those engaged as specialists. However, the particular needs and how to serve them are notably different.

The book as a whole provides evidence of the challenges inherent in cybersecurity education, as well as offering the motivation to address them. While it is impossible to provide a one-size-fits-all solution, the chapters then offer pointers and directions that may help in individual circumstances, as well as enabling an understanding of the overall landscape that contributes towards effective SETA and compliance as a whole. As such, while some readers many not consider all sections and perspectives to be of equal relevance to their particular interests, all aspects nonetheless require attention as part of an overall, holistic approach.

Steven Furnell
University of Plymouth, UK

Ismini Vasileiou
University of Plymouth, UK

REFERENCES

Wilson, M., de Zafra, D. E., Pitcher, S. I., Tressler, J. D., & Ippolito, J. B. (1998). *Information Technology Security Training Requirements: A Role- and Performance-Based Model. NIST Special Publication 800-16*. Technology Administration, National Institute of Standards and Technology. doi:10.6028/NIST.SP.800-16

Section 1
Addressing the User

Chapter 1
A Holistic View of Cybersecurity Education Requirements

Steven M. Furnell
University of Plymouth, UK

Ismini Vasileiou
University of Plymouth, UK

ABSTRACT

This chapter sets the scene for the book as a whole, establishing the need for cybersecurity awareness, training, and education in order to enable us to understand and meet our security obligations. It begins by illustrating key elements that ought to form part of cybersecurity literacy and the questions to be asked when addressing the issue. It then examines the problems that have traditionally existed in terms of achieving awareness and education, both at the user level (in terms of lack of support) and the practitioner level (in terms of a skills shortage). The discussion highlights the importance of a holistic approach, covering both personal and workplace use, and addressing the spectrum from end-users through to cybersecurity specialists.

INTRODUCTION

From office applications to social media, from electronic business to global communications, the rise of information technology and the Internet has offered numerous benefits to individuals and organizations alike. With all the positives to point at, it is sometimes easy (and certainly convenient) to forget the downside – namely that the technology that we now take for granted (and often depend upon) comes with associated risks. Systems can be attacked. They can fail. Data can be lost or exposed. Users themselves can be targeted. At the same time, cybersecurity is often assumed to be someone else's problem, with the consequence that the very parties that ought to have a stake in it end up distancing themselves from it instead. For example, end users frequently seem to assume that their employer, their Internet Service Provider, or some other party (*any* other party!) is taking care of their security needs. In reality of course, they have a role to play as individuals, because no matter what steps may be taken elsewhere, there will be some threats that reach them directly. So, they will find themselves needing to make security-related

DOI: 10.4018/978-1-5225-7847-5.ch001

Copyright © 2019, IGI Global. Copying or distributing in print or electronic forms without written permission of IGI Global is prohibited.

decisions, and they clearly need a level of awareness and understanding in order to do so. Meanwhile, organizations may look at their employees and assume that they should already have acquired a level of general cybersecurity awareness from somewhere else. While this nicely excuses the organization from taking responsibility, it is often an entirely unrealistic stance. One of the key requirements is therefore for the various parties concerned to recognize their role and take ownership of it.

In fact, there is more to know at all levels of an organization, from the individuals who simply wish to use the technology, through to those that are tasked with providing the infrastructure and safeguards that enable them to do so securely. Indeed, a fundamental challenge is that we are not dealing with a one-size-fits-all situation. SETA needs exist at several levels, from users in personal settings, to users in a workplace context, and from technical specialists through to security professionals. As an illustration of how these levels may be split, and the requirements in each case, we can consider the following groupings:

- **Personal Users:** Need to understand how to protect their own data and use the associated technologies (devices and services) in a secure manner. They also need to be aware of why such protection is required.
- **Workplace Users:** Similar to the needs of personal users, other than the reason now relates to the need to protect workplace systems and data, in which they may not feel as directly invested.
- **Technical Specialists:** Refers to those responsible for designing, developing, implementing and running technology systems. There is a clear need for them to understand where security is required and how to deliver it.
- **Security Professionals:** Need a specific security skillset, which may be characterized and supported by specialist academic study and professional certifications.

These parties will develop and acquire their cybersecurity knowledge and skills in different ways and to different levels. Figure 1 presents a broad contrast between the paths that may be taken by general users versus those that become security professionals (noting that, for the cybersecurity professionals in particular, this is an illustration of a route rather than a prescription). For the former, one would hope that a general familiarity with cybersecurity issues would be developed during schooling, and then sup-

Figure 1. Contrasting the SETA pathways for general users versus cybersecurity specialists

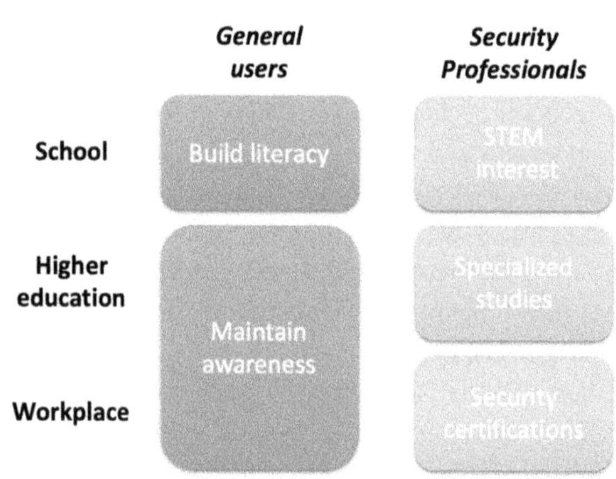

ported and supplemented by ongoing awareness-raising during any subsequent study and during their workplace life. This is intended to reflect that while they will not become in any way specialized in cybersecurity or technology more generally, they nonetheless need to have a credible understanding of the cybersecurity issues relating to them as individuals (and therefore require academia and employers to be playing their part in supporting this). Meanwhile, the path for security professionals is rather more focused. They would inherit the literacy and awareness aspects as lay users but would additionally be expected to have more specialized activities at each stage. For example, during schooling they may show a preference towards STEM (Science, Technology, Engineering and Mathematics) subjects, and then supplement this during higher education by opting for qualifications in subjects such as computer science or cybersecurity directly. Their workplace activity could then be supported by further specialized industry or professional certifications.

Of course, while this works from one perspective, it is certainly not a definitive view. In practice, there are numerous ways to cut this. For example, the need for awareness and the level of understanding required can also depend upon the individual's position within the organizational hierarchy, their responsibility for data and devices, and their role in the overall compliance structure. Taking their level within the organization as an example, typical staff members will inherit the needs of 'workplace users' in the previous list. Meanwhile, looking from a management perspective, local and departmental mangers will need to understand additional aspects in order to support them in making security-informed decisions in relation to people and processes for whom they are responsible. Meanwhile, at the leadership level of the organization, the understanding will need to reflect the relationship between security and issues such as business continuity and resilience, with the ability to factor security considerations into strategic planning. In parallel with this, an individual's responsibilities will help to inform any specific awareness or training that is needed in relation to the systems and data that they use or become responsible for. Finally, from the compliance perspective, the general staff require awareness and education in order to *be* security compliant, whereas the specialists require security understanding and skills in order to establish the framework that *enables* compliance (i.e. it is unlikely to be achieved if the organizations lacks staff with the knowledge and skills to put the right technologies and processes in place to support secure behaviors and practices).

Whichever way this issue is viewed, it ultimately leads to the questions of what needs to be done and the challenges that may be faced in doing it. This chapter consequently examines the situation in relation to supporting end-users, as well as in relation to the specialists needed to support cybersecurity. The discussion begins by considering what today's users need to know in terms of cybersecurity, and the extent to which they are supported to do so. This links to the impacts within the workplace context, and then broadens to consider the organization's needs more widely in terms of having appropriately skilled staff to define and manage their cybersecurity, alongside the general workforce being cyber-aware. In this sense, the chapter sets the scene on a range of topics that are explored more fully in later parts of the book.

CYBERSECURITY AWARENESS FOR END-USERS

Since the emergence of information technology, and particularly the widespread advent of personal computing in the late 1970s and early 1980s, there has been much reference to the need to foster and ensure *IT literacy* in our society. In more modern times, the parlance has become *digital literacy*, reflecting the fact that – for many people - IT has become embedded in virtually everything around them. Given the range of threats they are facing, it quickly becomes clear that citizens require *cybersecurity literacy* in order to safeguard themselves in their daily use of technologies and online services. As an example, some core areas of literacy are summarized in Table 1 (Furnell & Moore, 2014). For each topic there is an indication of what everyday users should understand and what they should be able to do as a consequence. Looking at the list, it is easy to see that many of the topics are unlikely to part of people's default knowledge and behavior, and so they need to learn the lessons from somewhere.

Such cybersecurity literacy is actually required in relation to both personal and workplace use, as we find ourselves confronted with related threats and vulnerabilities across a range of systems and devices, and in relation to both personal and workplace data. Some lessons are generic and span both contexts, whereas some are more specific to one or the other. For example, the core principles of selecting and safeguarding an appropriate password are the same regardless of where it is being used or what it is being used to protect. However, the specific rules and requirements (e.g. around length and composition) will often vary between systems. And so even at this level, ensuring the necessary knowledge and skills is a challenge. Users need to know what's expected of them, and they need to be equipped to do it. Additionally, there is also the small matter of getting them to accept that it's worth doing. Being able to reach that point requires action and support across a number of fronts.

In the context of their personal use, it is ultimately down to individuals to take a level of responsibility for themselves and to realize that it is in their own interest to do so. If they fail to understand the threats and take precautions it will primarily be their own systems and data that they are putting at risk as a

Table 1. Examples of baseline cybersecurity literacy

Topic	Users Should Understand ...	Users Should Be Able to ...
Authentication	The role of authentication in preventing unauthorized access.	Choose and use suitable passwords, and then follow good practice in terms of managing them.
Backup	The risks to systems and devices that may result in data loss, and the impact that such a loss may have for them.	Utilize appropriate means to backup their data and devices, and appreciate the need for these to be stored away from the original copies.
Malware protection	The potential impacts of malware and the possible routes for infection	Check that appropriate antivirus protection is installed and enabled.
Mobile devices	The risks that devices can face from both technical threats and the physical environment.	Employ available features for security and privacy, and take appropriate precautions to safeguard devices when on the move.
Privacy and data leakage	The sensitivity of different types of data, and the ways in which it could be misused (e.g. to support identity theft).	Configure privacy and access settings in contexts where personal data may be most readily shared (e.g. in social networks, between apps, or within cloud services), and make informed decisions about what to divulge.
Safe Internet access and web browsing	The existence of threats such as phishing, malicious sites, and unsafe downloads.	How to spot the signs of scams and social engineering, alongside recognizing the indicators that denote security and trustworthiness.
Secure networking	The risks posed by using unprotected or unknown networks.	Ensure that their own networks are protected, and make informed decisions about when it is safe to connect to others.
Software updates	The reason why software updates are released and the importance of patching vulnerabilities	Configure the system to handle updates in the most appropriate manner.

result (although even here it is not *exclusively* a risk to themselves - for example, a personal system that has become malware-infected because the owner did not understand or accept the need to protect it may end up affecting *other* users on the network if it starts spewing out spam or phishing messages, or starts to try to launch attacks against them). Of course, an individual's personal practices are quite likely to influence their default behavior when dealing with systems and data in the workplace as well. However, in the workplace the implications of an unaware and non-compliant user are immediately more significant, as they are now occurring in a context that has the direct potential to affect others and to impact upon the organization itself. Equally, in this scenario, it ought to be more obviously in the interests (as well as within the control) of the employer to support the staff in doing the right thing.

All of this leads to the obvious question of how aware and prepared the end-users actually *are*. Do they understand the problems and have the skills to deal with them? Of course, there is no single answer to this, because the situation is likely to differ according to personal circumstances and the degree to which cybersecurity issues have been promoted to them. If the user is in a country where there has been a sustained public awareness campaign, or where service providers have been proactive in pushing the messages and providing solutions, then they are likely to be better positioned than those that have not received such support. However, even where public awareness campaigns exist, they cannot be relied upon to be having as much impact as we would like. For example, in the UK, the Get Safe Online initiative has existed since 2006 as a public / private sector partnership to promote online safety and security advice to personal users and businesses (supported by the government as well as leading organizations in banking, retail, technology and other sectors). More recently it has been joined by the Cyber Aware campaign, a cross-government initiative that aims to drive cybersecurity-related behavior change amongst small businesses and individuals. In spite of these laudable efforts, a recent study from the UK Home Office determined that a large proportion of the public (along with Small and Medium-sized Enterprises) were underestimating the risk of cybercrime and feeling powerless in terms of protecting themselves against it (Home Office 2018). This in turn does not paint a picture of a confident and cybersecurity-aware user community, even where efforts had ostensibly been made to support them (or at least to make such support available via web guidance and resources).

Meanwhile, as an illustration of the position of users in the workplace, we can consider some findings from EY's Global Information Security Survey. This is a long-standing annual survey series and so looking at findings over successive years enables patterns and trends to be observed. The responses are drawn from executive and management level participants across EY's operating regions of EMEIA (Europe, Middle East, India and Africa), the Americas, Asia-Pacific, and Japan, with an average of over 1,600 respondents per annum across the surveys considered here (EY, 2017; EY, 2018). As such, they represent a fair sample from which to form an impression of how things stand in relation to end-users, and unfortunately, as we see from Figure 2, this impression is not a good one. Respondents were asked to indicate the top areas of vulnerability that were leading to increased risk exposure and what is notably clear is that 'careless or unaware employees' was consistently rated as the topmost area throughout this period. Perhaps unsurprisingly then, EY's 2017-18 survey report concluded with a number of key actions that all organizations should consider, and clearly listed amongst them is the advice to 'Focus on education and awareness' with recommendation that they should: *establish an education and awareness program, ensuring all employees, contractors and third parties can identify a cyber attack and are aware of the role they play in defending your business* (EY, 2017). Such advice leads to the clear question of whether organizations are *taking* such actions.

Figure 2. Top-rated areas of cybersecurity vulnerability in organizations (EY, 2017; EY, 2018)

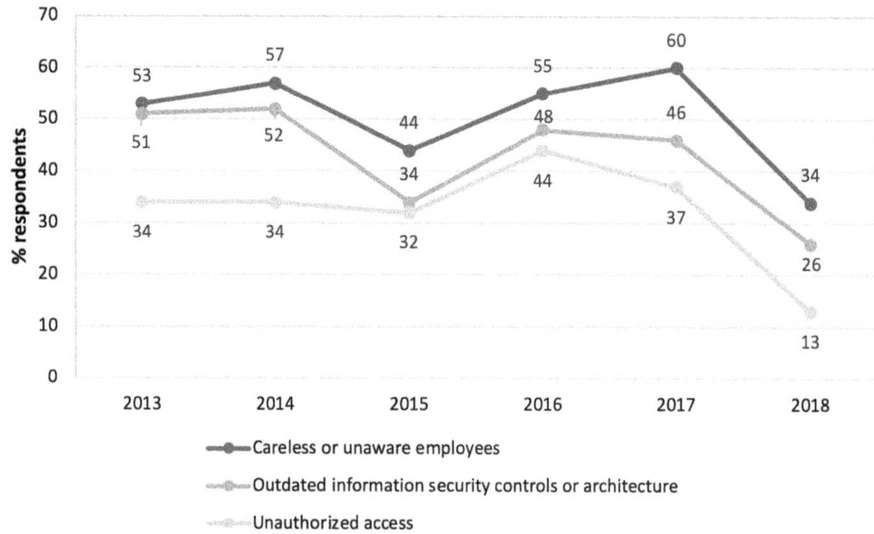

PROMOTING CYBERSECURITY IN THE WORKPLACE

The EY findings illustrate that organizations can find themselves with a problem. Regardless of the ups and downs of the specific figures, the undeniable message is that the employees represent the most significant area of vulnerability. Moreover, it is an aspect that is arguably preventable, to at least some degree. If the cause is employee unawareness, then supporting them in becoming aware ought to address the problem. In reality of course this is easier said than done, but organizations have at least *some* opportunity to influence their own fate in this area.

In terms of their staff community, they need to raise awareness, they need to educate them, and ideally, they need to build an overall cybersecurity culture. This latter point is somewhat aspirational and refers to security having become embedded within users' attitudes and activities. In this sense, it is the ultimate level of security-compliant behavior. Unfortunately, it is highly unlikely to be the norm, and most organizations are likely to find their staff operating across a spectrum of compliance levels, as illustrated in Figure 3 (Furnell & Thomson, 2009). These levels are briefly defined as below, with the first four reflecting different degrees of security compliance, while the remaining four then relate to non-compliant behavior:

- **Culture:** The ideal state, in which security is implicitly part of the user's natural behavior.
- **Commitment:** Security is not a natural part of behavior, but if provided with appropriate guidance/leadership then users accept the need for it and make an associated effort.
- **Obedience:** Users may not fully understand or buy into the principles but can be made to comply via appropriate authority (i.e. implying a greater level of enforcement than simply providing guidance).

Figure 3. Compliance and non-compliance behavior within an organization
(Furnell & Thomson, 2009)

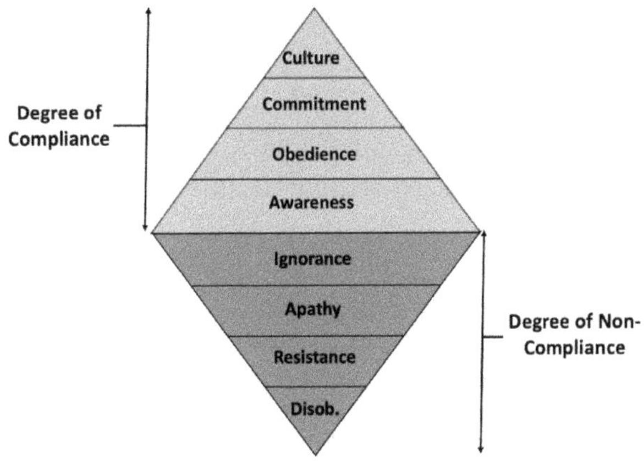

- **Awareness:** Users are aware of their role in information security but are not necessarily fully complying with the associated practices or behavior as yet.
- **Ignorance:** Users remain unaware of security issues and so may introduce inadvertent adverse effects.
- **Apathy:** Users are aware of their role in protecting information assets but are not motivated to adhere to good information security practices.
- **Resistance:** Users work against security, through factors such as laziness and disregard for known procedures.
- **Disobedience:** Users actively work against security, with insider abusers intentionally breaking the rules and circumventing controls.

A key point to recognize is that where staff are actually positioned within these levels will be closely linked to the efforts that the organization has made in terms of SETA-related activities. By default, the distribution is likely to be similar to that depicted in the Figure, with the majority of staff positioned within the middle categories, and relatively few staff at the extremes. Clearly, the objective of an effective SETA strategy would be to get as many staff into the higher levels as possible (albeit recognizing that those in the Disobedience category are unlikely to be reached via this route, and ought to be dealt with via disciplinary processes instead). Unfortunately, although it is a widely *recognized* issue, the extent to which cybersecurity education is actually *addressed* can at best be described as variable. Indeed, while organizations may readily see evidence of the need for it, following this up with action does not always appear to come naturally.

An Ongoing Lack of Provision

A look back at survey findings over many years suggests that lack of awareness is a long-standing and well-established problem. Consider, for example, the following selection of statistics taken from a range of past survey findings amongst UK organizations[1], each basically suggesting that only a third of organizations were making SETA provision:

- KPMG's Information Security Survey in 1998 found that 31% of organizations had security education and training programs (KPMG, 1998)
- In the Audit Commission's 2001 survey of IT abuse, 34% of the public and private sector respondents indicated that they had any form of computer security awareness training (Audit Commission, 2001)
- In its 2006 information security breaches survey, the Department of Trade and Industry found that an average of 35% of businesses utilized ongoing security training (DTI, 2006)

Of course, one may try to excuse these cases, because they were from many years ago when the role of technology was less prominent than it is today. However, aside from the fact that it *was* actually a problem even then, jumping forward to more recent findings unfortunately suggests little change. For example, looking at the UK's more recent Cyber Security Breaches Survey, we find that on average only 20% of the 1,500+ respondents indicated that their staff had attended "internal or external training, or seminars or conferences on cybersecurity in the last 12 months" (DCMS, 2018) – a picture that is also essentially unchanged from two prior years of the study (with the likelihood of provision increasing the larger the organization concerned). Moreover, the question is very broad and so positive answers could actually cover some quite dissimilar options, with notably differing impacts. For example, a member of the IT team having attended a cybersecurity conference is unlikely to have any direct effect upon general staff awareness, whereas an internal all-staff seminar on cybersecurity principles and practices would likely have a very positive effect. However, both scenarios would score a positive response to the question, and hence contribute to the 20% result overall. A more direct insight into the provision for employees in general came from a further question asking which types of staff had attended training. This revealed that while three quarters of directors or senior managers had attended or received training, only a quarter of general staff had done so. As such, the overall results portray a situation where only a minority of organizations are offering training, and then only a minority of those are doing so in a manner that reaches the general user community.

Of course, with the varying interpretations of what might be meant by training, there is arguably doubt about the accuracy of this picture. Organizations *could* still be doing things that help to promote security awareness, but without it falling into a class of activity that they would regard as 'training'. On this basis, it is worth looking at the responses to a further question from the same survey series, in which respondents were asked whether they were undertaking actions from the UK National Cyber Security Centre's *10 Steps to Cyber Security* (which have been advocated to UK businesses since 2012). One of these steps is 'User Education and Awareness', which is described as follows:

Users have a critical role to play in their organisation's security and so it's important that security rules and the technology provided enable users to do their job as well as help keep the organisation secure. This can be supported by a systematic delivery of awareness programmes and training that deliver security expertise as well helping to establish a security-conscious culture. (NCSC, 2015)

Figure 4 presents the claimed level of adoption by the Cyber Security Breaches Survey respondents, with the responses for the other nine steps also included for context. It is particularly notable that attention towards education and awareness is not only in the minority but is being omitted by organizations that clearly *have* addressed other aspects of security. It is also notable that the steps tending to receive

Figure 4. Attention towards the 10 Steps to Cyber Security (DCMS, 2018)

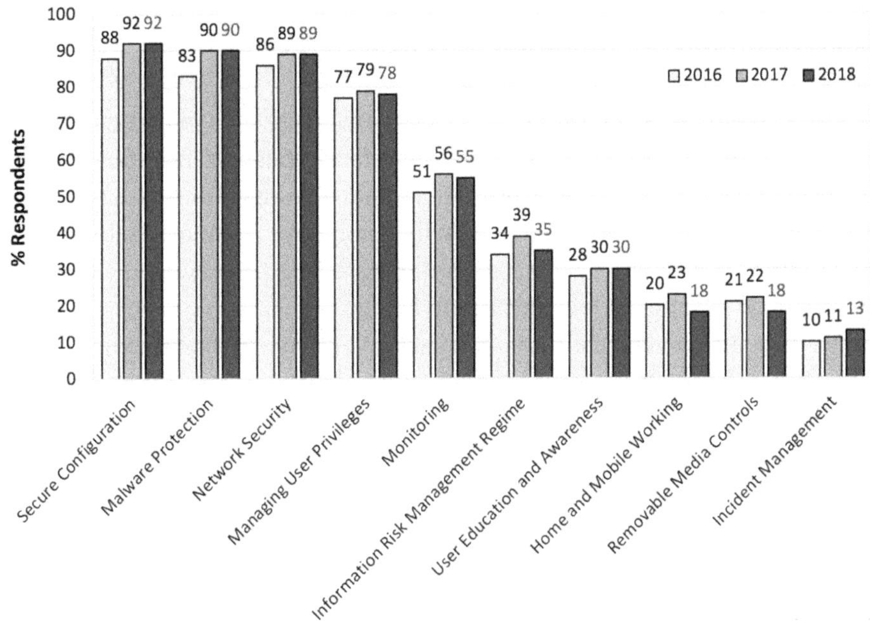

greater attention are those of a technical nature, where it is perhaps possible to automate or buy a product/tool that claims to do the job. Dealing with people does not fall as neatly into this category, and so related controls may assume a lower priority – not because they are less important, but because they are more difficult to do.

So, considering the results here, with 30% claiming to offer education and awareness, it is clear that the result is essentially no different to those previously listed above, from 10-20 years ago. Indeed, as a broad generalization, one might suggest that looking at almost any survey from any year is likely to reveal that no more than around a third of organizations are giving attention to SETA issues.

This all serves to raise the question of whether the lack of provision is simply because organizations are facing few problems, and do not feel they need it. Unfortunately, it takes little effort to disprove this theory. For a start, we have already seen the EY results showing unawares as a key area of perceived vulnerability. We can add to this from the Cyber Security Breaches Survey, where respondents cited both human error and lack of staff awareness as notable factors in their *most disruptive* breaches. Furthermore, looking at what respondents then did in the wake of such breaches, it becomes apparent that additional staff training or communications was one of the most prominent responses (it was actually the topmost response in 2017, from 28% of organizations, and second place in 2018 at 18%, just behind installing, changing or updating anti-malware protection at 22%). So, many of the organizations that had revealed a lack of awareness-raising were also suffering as a consequence and were only then making efforts to address the issue.

So, based on the above, a rather unfortunate picture appears to emerge – one of the main areas of vulnerability appears to center around people and their lack of security awareness, and yet the majority of organizations appear to persist in overlooking security awareness and education as an area for attention. Thus, while some commentators have dismissed security awareness as *a waste of time* (Schneier, 2013), it would seem naïve to think that the findings were not connected in some way!

Security Education: More Than Just a Policy

These days we are generally okay at pushing the message that security is important. Indeed, it would be relatively rare to find someone – at home or in the workplace - that does not know that it is something they *ought* to be concerned about. To that level then, awareness has been raised. Unfortunately, this does not get us very far in terms of something actually being done about it. Establishing cybersecurity as something of significance should be just the starting point, but risks being the end of the journey if users feel they cannot do it or do not feel the need to bother.

In the personal or home context, the user often has a choice about what to protect and to what level (e.g. whether to password-protect their device in the first place), whereas in the business setting they are more often going to be working at the behest of what the organization has prescribed. However, in either scenario, they still need to understand *what* they supposed to do, *how* to do it, and ideally *why* they ought to be doing it. Indeed, these questions potentially need to be addressed for any cybersecurity issue that we believe users should be aware of. Table 2 presents them in the order that they would most usefully be tackled, and explains the rationale behind each of them.

A bugbear in the provision of many security controls is that we will all too readily set rules and write policies, but then forget the need to support the people that are expected to abide by them. These people need more than just policies to be quoted at them; they need to be guided on how they are supposed to comply. Indeed, the distinction between *policy* and *guidance* is important, and is often a fundamental area in which the human aspect of cybersecurity falls down. Organizations are often good at setting policies, but typically less proficient following them up with meaningful support. Taking a somewhat

Table 2. Key questions when promoting cybersecurity to users

Issue	Related Questions	Rationale
Why	Why does this matter and why should I care?	Arguably the most fundamental issue, as it justifies why the issue matters and provides the foundation for the individual to buy into the subsequent points. If we have elected to make the individual aware of an issue, then we ought to ensure that they understand why.
Who	Whose concern is this? Is it something that I have a role in handling, or is someone else covering it for me? Do I just need to *know* about it, or do I have to *do* something?	The user needs to be clear on the role that they are expected to have in relation to the issue (again it will make them more attentive to absorbing later aspects of precisely what they then need to do as a consequence). There are, of course, some issues that users need to be aware of, even though no further action is required from them, and if a given issue is entirely for someone else to handle, then they can step out at this point, having been made aware that it exists and why it matters.
What	What am I supposed to do?	Having established that they have a role to play, the individual needs to know what it is. This is typically conveyed in the form of *policy*.
How	How do I do what I am supposed to do?	The obvious accompaniment to the previous issue, but often overlooked or under-supported. Conveyed to the individual in the form of *guidance*.
When / Where	When and where is it relevant? Does it apply all the time and to all systems?	Also covered as part of the *guidance* aspect, this is a further refinement that addresses the scenarios in which the security issue would be expected to be encountered. It should also cover whether there are any exception cases (e.g. situations where the desired practice cannot be followed due to technical limitations, or emergency scenarios where less secure alternatives are permitted).

cynical view, one might often suspect that this is because they need to be seen to have a policy in place in order to comply with expectations (or even regulations), and so by doing so they have ticked the box for compliance purposes. Additionally, by having a policy, there is something that staff can be held accountable against if an incident or breach occurs. Of course, while this may cover things from the perspective of the business, it's hardly fair from the perspective of those expected to follow the policy if they are expected to do so without further support.

Sometimes organizations may even be challenged to appreciate the distinction between policy and guidance in practical terms. So, as a brief illustration, let's consider a simplified example of the difference that might exist in relation to the theme of user authentication:

- **Policy:** Your device should be protected with suitable user authentication.
- **Guidance:** You should choose a password that is at least 10 characters long, and which includes letters, numbers and symbols. You should avoid using dictionary words or personal information that others may know about you.

Now, we could likely argue about many of the specifics here (including whether passwords are an appropriate form of protection in the first place!), and it is acknowledged that the guidance is not anywhere near comprehensive enough (e.g. nothing is mentioned about writing the password down and not sharing it with others, and we could further quibble about whether 10 characters is long enough or whether the user ought to be explicitly asked to use both upper and lower-case letters)! However, the point is hopefully already clear that policy and guidance are not the same thing. Policy raises awareness, while guidance aids understanding.

As an aside, there is also the potential to address another 'why' question here for the user. It is all very well telling them that they need to use at least 10 characters, and to avoid dictionary words, but the guidance could become more *explanatory* if it also indicated why this mattered (which, in case you are wondering, is primarily to reduce the vulnerability to compromise by password cracking tools that many attackers would be likely to use). Of course, some users might be suitably convinced simply on the basis of being told to do it, but for others the explanation will help them to make sense of it, and thereby improve the likelihood of their later acceptance and compliance.

What should be fairly readily apparent from the above is that none of this comes naturally. Cybersecurity is not an area in which people tend to be pre-equipped with the necessary knowledge and skills. They are not born with it, and historically they have not got much exposure to it through prior schooling. So, if we want people to know about it and practice it, then we need some way to get their attention and tell them. This, to differing degrees, is the role of cybersecurity awareness, training and education, and it provides the backdrop not only for this chapter, but in large part for the remainder of the book as a whole.

WHAT GOOD LOOKS LIKE

One question that possibly remains in the mind at this point is what are we seeking to achieve and what does a good approach look like? Is a more effective approach to SETA going to deliver any benefit? With this in mind, it is relevant to characterize what we should expect from a more effective approach to SETA issues. And, in short, it ought to be more compliant behavior from users, and a corresponding reduction in related security incidents.

As previously mentioned, cybersecurity awareness and education are often criticized as ineffective or even dismissed as a waste of time. And indeed, they *can* be – but it rather depends on how you do it. SETA is not just a question of repeatedly pushing a security policy at staff and annually testing them on it. Repeatedly telling people the same thing is not education. If they did not understand or agree with it the first time, then simply going around the track again is unlikely to have the desired effect. Similarly, achieving security compliance is not intended to be just box-ticking. We want to foster a cybersecurity mindset and culture that becomes embedded across the organization and the individuals within it.

The authors' own prior work has argued for a more personalized approach to SETA provision, which takes account of the individual circumstances of the learners concerned (Vasileiou and Furnell, 2019). Figure 5 presents the contrast between this and the traditional one-size-fits-all approach. While the left of the diagram depicts the typical provision, the righthand side suggests an approach that is tailored based upon factors specific to the individual concerned and denoting various factors that may influence both the SETA provision that is needed and the manner in which it may be best presented. For example, an individual's role within the organization will directly inform some of the aspects of security that they need to know about (perhaps emphasizing specific systems or data that they will come into contact with over and above the norm). Meanwhile, if we can take account of the individual's prior knowledge and existing predisposition towards dealing with security, then this could help frame the way that messages are targeted toward them. For instance, the way that we address someone who is risk averse and tends to be policy-compliant would ideally differ from the way in which we might approach someone who is security-resistant and risk tolerant (Pattinson and Anderson, 2005). Similarly, it may be helpful to recognize that people learn in different ways, and so presenting the materials in a manner matched to their preferred style could deliver better results. As an example, Fleming (2006) proposes the VARK (Visual,

Figure 5. Traditional and proposed modes of SETA provision
(Vasileiou and Furnell, 2019)

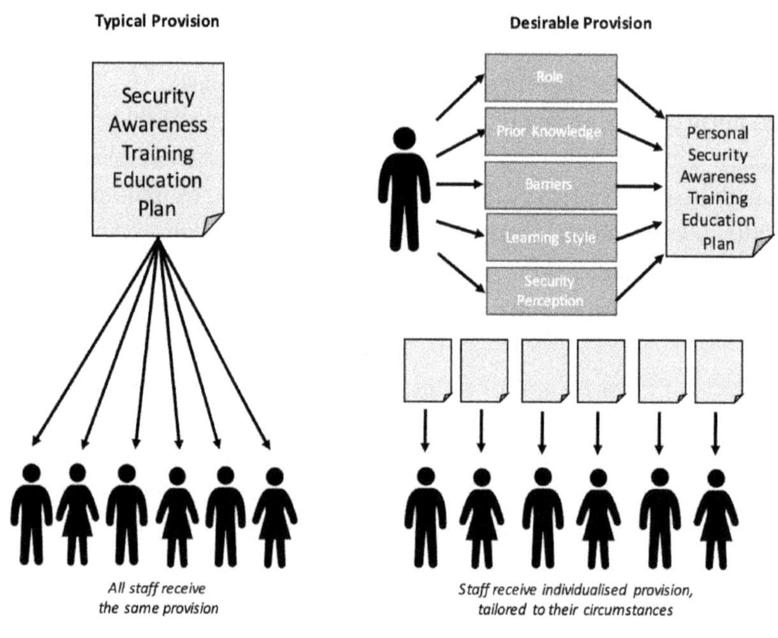

Aural, Read/write and Kinaesthetic) model, reflecting four sensory modalities that may be used for learning information (e.g. looking at diagrams rather than reading texts, or doing practical tasks rather than simply listening to presentation-style delivery). Finally, different people may face barriers to learning in terms of threshold concepts and troublesome knowledge that need to be understood, integrated and overcome before they are in a position to me make sense of other aspects (e.g. this could well be the case in a cybersecurity context if individuals are unfamiliar or uncomfortable with some of the surrounding IT knowledge that tends to underpin why security is required).

Of course, while this is easy to present in a diagram, it is far harder to achieve in practice. Enacting this approach would require information gathering in order to profile the individual needs and circumstances of each user. However, the associated effort here has the potential to deliver a far more tailored SETA experience, which ought to yield better results in terms of acceptance, understanding and compliance. Indeed, it is possible to go even further than this. For example, the ISF (2014) suggest that people/employees can be our strongest control, but simply delivering a training programme is not enough and that any security awareness training needs to target behaviour change by engaging people at personal level and setting realistic expectations. Linked to this, Gabriel and Furnell (2011) and Beris et al. (2015) both suggest the notion of security champions, where certain individuals are identified to lead a peer-learning approach, which aims to foster a community of good practice amongst colleagues within the workplace environment. This in turn aligns with Boud and Middleton (2003), who identify that learning in workplaces can take an informal format, encompassing a diverse range of people to work with. If the champions are well-selected and appropriately regarded amongst their peers, then they are well placed to guide and influence others towards the desired direction. The conceptual integration of this idea with the personalized plans is depicted in Figure 6, albeit recognizing that this represents more of an aspiration than a reality in the majority of cases.

Figure 6. Incorporating peer learning and security champions
(Vasileiou and Furnell, 2019)

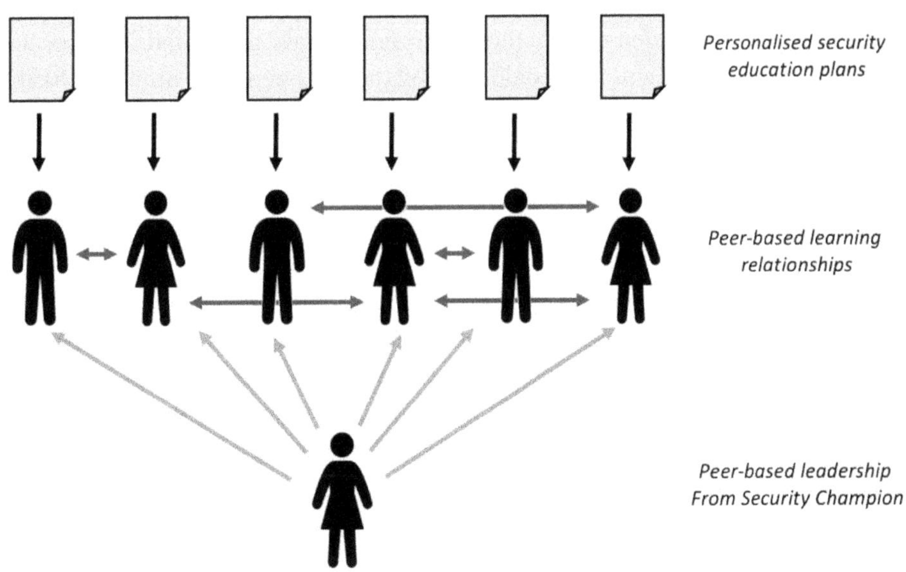

SPECIALIST CYBERSECURITY SKILLS FOR THE ORGANIZATION

Unfortunately, the requirement for cybersecurity education and training does not end with the users. It is also key for organizations in terms of supporting those responsible for implementing and running the security the protects everyone else. Security will not manage and direct itself, and if SETA provision is to be made for staff, then someone needs to lead and deliver it. And more generally, there needs to be appropriate people to handle the selection, deployment and management of other security controls as well. In order to do this, organizations need to have enough people with the right skills to do what is required. However, this is again an area in which many have historically been challenged, and there are actually two dimensions to this problem. Firstly, organizations need to realize that they *need* cybersecurity expertise to support them, and secondly, they need to be able to *find* it.

The realization aspect basically means recognizing and allocating cybersecurity responsibilities and putting the right people into roles. This may sound obvious, but there is ample evidence to show that it does not always happen. A common problem is that security is perceived to be an 'IT thing' and so the responsibilities are simply landed upon general IT staff to deal with. However, there is no guarantee that they will have any familiarity or interest in the area, risking the situation where security becomes half a job done badly (which in turn means that a credible level of security is unlikely to be achieved). What is actually needed is for security to be handled by people who understand the concept, the technologies and processes involved, and its relationship to the business, and have the skills and experience to enact it.

Looking again at the surveys considered in the earlier section, the UK Cyber Security Breaches Survey indicates that 70% of the 1,500 businesses surveyed agreed or tended to agree that the people dealing with cybersecurity in their organization had "the right cyber security skills and knowledge to do this job effectively". Although this is clear the majority, it this leaves almost a third of them in varying degrees of uncertainty or disagreement. Meanwhile, looking at the EY survey, only 8% of the respondents believe that their information security function *fully* meets the organization's needs, while more than a quarter directly indicate that the needs are not met, or that the function needs to be improved. A common cause of these gaps is found to be a shortage of skills to do the job, with 30% of respondents citing this as a reason. And so, in short, a lack of skills emerges as a common theme from both of the surveys.

This is turn leads to the question of why the organizations have a shortfall. Is it because they have not hired the right people, or because they could not find the right people to hire? The likely answer is a combination of both, and even if they have got themselves to the point of realizing that security-specific expertise is needed, organizations can find themselves challenged in terms of both a shortage of skilled practitioners in the market, as well as knowing what qualifications or certifications they should be looking for to match the skills they need.

While Table 1 summarized some areas of baseline cybersecurity literacy for the lay user, the skills needed from security practitioners need to go significantly beyond this. Unfortunately, one aspect resulting from an overall lack of security education is a lack of professionals skilled to handle and support it. This in turn causes knock-on problems for organizations wishing to address security concerns without the capability to do so. Indeed, the situation in the professional context is also challenging, and recent years have consistently provided evidence to indicate not only a skills shortage, but a significant level of shortfall. The following provide some examples of related forecasts, and while the specific numbers vary, the overall picture is essentially consistent (i.e. the industry is facing a situation of long-term under-supply):

- **2013:** The UK's National Audit Office suggested that it could take up to 20 years to bridge the cyber-skills gap (NAO, 2013).
- **2015:** Frost and Sullivan and (ISC)^2 concluded that there would be a global shortfall of around 1.5 million security practitioners by 2020 (Frost and Sullivan, 2015).
- **2016:** Foote Partners predicted that while global demand for cybersecurity talent would rise to six million by 2019, there would be a shortfall of 1.5 million professionals to fill the positions (Schneiderman, 2016).

This shortage of skilled practitioners has a resulting impact. For example, global findings from Intel Security and the Centre for Strategic and International Studies (CSIS) suggested that more than 80% of organizations considered there to be a shortage of cybersecurity skills, with almost three quarters suggesting that direct and measurable damage occurred as a consequence (Correa, 2016). Meanwhile, findings from Kaspersky Lab (based upon surveying over 4,000 companies) suggested that organizations lacking security skills can end up spending at least three times as much to recover from security breaches (Kaspersky, 2016). Moreover, half of those surveyed indicated that they had seen a growth in wages due to the talent shortage of talent, with similar proportions suggesting that they had experienced the shortage themselves and needed more security specialists. Adding a direct experience of their own to the findings, Kaspersky Lab indicated that they typically needed to interview 40 people in order to hire one expert.

Unfortunately, the supply issue is not the only challenge. Knowing that we *need* skills and specialists is one thing but knowing how to *identify* them is another matter. As discussion elsewhere in the book explores more fully, there is a range of providers (including CompTIA, EC-Council, ISACA, (ISC)^2 and SANS to name just a few of the leading and most recognized names), and each offers a range of related certifications to choose from. However, as one might expect, the range is there for a reason, with different certification options being available to suit different security specializations and levels of experience. Indeed, looking at the marketplace as a whole, we find a potentially bewildering array of certifications, with a study by Tittel et al. (2017) revealing over one hundred distinct offerings available (with 70 general, vendor-neutral certifications, 24 related to forensics or anti-hacking, and 10 other specialized options). Adding academic qualifications into the mix as well potentially muddies the waters even further, and so it is important to know what we are looking for in terms of both coverage and the level of depth. For example, do we want someone with a holistic understanding who can manage the overall cybersecurity provision, or do we need someone with specific expertise to handle a particular task or element of the technology? The needs are quite different and so the supporting qualifications/certifications should be matched accordingly. Figure 7 presents a way of looking at things, in terms of the different focus that may be given and the types of skills that may be developed as a consequence.

The key thing to realize here is that it is not a question of any of these options being right or wrong – all can have a relevant part to play – but it *is* important to recognize that they are *different*. As such, a qualification acquired at one level is unlikely to offer a natural substitute for another. This goes back to organizations needing to know what they need, and the later sections on academic and professional perspectives will help to provide further clarity.

Figure 7. Different levels of cybersecurity qualification and certification

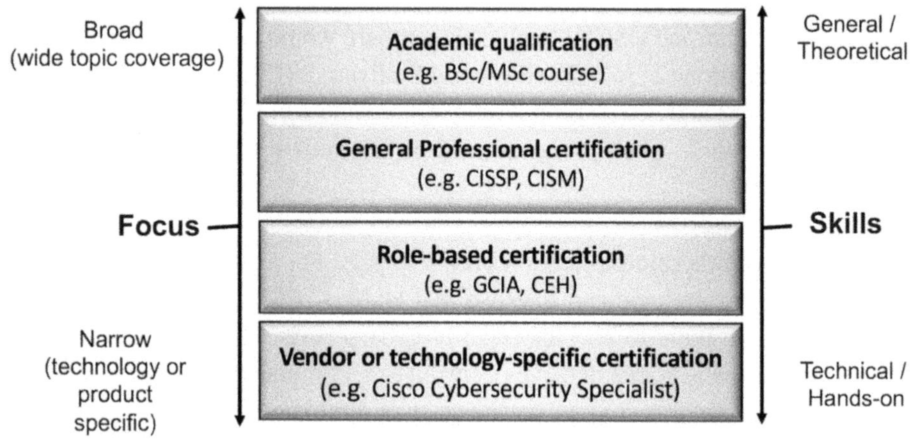

CONCLUSION

The overall message of this chapter, setting the scene for those that follow, is that SETA not only needs to be done, but needs to be done *well*. Unfortunately, there is no one-size-fits-all answer, and it requires action on several fronts. As such, like cybersecurity in general, it is not a simple problem to solve!

At the user level, there can currently be a great variance in who receives training and what they get trained in. Broadly speaking we need a better level of cybersecurity literacy coming through from general education in order to position people better for both workplace and personal use. At the organizational level, there is consequently a challenge to be faced in terms of ensuring an environment where the staff collectively operate within a coherent security culture. But the issue is wider than having a cybersecurity-aware workforce. It ideally needs people to be prepared prior to this, so that they are essentially cyber-ready by the time they get there. In this sense, it needs to be promoted in academic education – in schooling of the general populous in order to raise the baseline literacy early on, and then specifically in higher education for IT-related degrees (for the cybersecurity-specific skills).

Organizations can also suffer from a lack of specific cybersecurity expertise to set the agenda in the first place, and so this again depends upon support from academia to feed through appropriately qualified graduates, and from the profession more widely to support further skills development and certification. As such, cybersecurity needs to be promoted at the professional level. Indeed, it needs to be recognized *as* a profession, with the accompanying expectation for qualified and credible specialists to do the work.

The resulting situation is something of a jigsaw puzzle, and there are currently more pieces in some parts of the picture than others. However, recognition of the need is the first step towards addressing it, and the ultimate aim must be to ensure that cybersecurity awareness, training and education are appropriately provided all the way from general end-users through to cyber practitioners. The chapters that follow collectively draw upon both theoretical principles and practical experience in order to consider *what* must be done, and *how* to achieve it. The different sections suggest actions for different audiences, but collectively aim to enable an overall understanding of what is required and who can help us in trying to achieve it.

REFERENCES

Audit Commission. (2001). yourbusiness@risk – An Update on IT Abuse 2001. Audit Commission Publications.

Beris, O., Beautement, A., & Sasse, M. A. (2015). Employee rule breakers, excuse makers and security champions: Mapping the risk perceptions and emotions that drive security behaviors. *NSPW '15: Proceedings of the 2015 New Security Paradigms Workshop*, 73-84.

Boud, D., & Middleton, H. (2003). Learning from others at work: Communities of practice and informal learning. *Journal of Workplace Learning*, *15*(5), 194–202. doi:10.1108/13665620310483895

Correa, D. (2016). 82% of global IT pros admit to a shortage of cyber-security skills. *SC Magazine*. Retrieved from http://www.scmagazineuk.com/82-of-global-it-pros-admit-to-a-shortage-of-cyber-security-skills/article/512830

DCMS. (2018). Cyber Security Breaches Survey 2018. Main report. Department for Digital, Culture, Media & Sport.

DTI. (2006). *Information security breaches survey – technical report*. London, UK: Department of Trade and Industry.

EY. (2017). *Cybersecurity regained: preparing to face cyber attacks. 20th Global Information Security Survey 2017–18. EYG no. 06574-173Gbl*. EYGM Limited.

EY. (2018). *Is cybersecurity about more than protection? EY Global Information Security Survey 2018-19. EYG no. 011483-18Gbl*. EYGM Limited.

Fleming, N. D. (2006). *Teaching and learning styles: VARK strategies* (2nd ed.). Christchurch, New Zealand: Neil D Fleming.

Frost & Sullivan. (2015). *The 2015 (ISC)^2 Global Information Security Workforce Study*. Retrieved from https://iamcybersafe.org/wp-content/uploads/2017/01/FrostSullivan-ISC^2-Global-Information-Security-Workforce-Study-2015.pdf

Furnell, S., & Moore, L. (2014). Security literacy: The missing link in today's online society? *Computer Fraud & Security*, *2014*(May), 12–18. doi:10.1016/S1361-3723(14)70491-9

Furnell, S., & Thomson, K. (2009). From culture to disobedience: Recognising the varying user acceptance of IT security. *Computer Fraud & Security*, *2009*(February), 5–10. doi:10.1016/S1361-3723(09)70019-3

Gabriel, T., & Furnell, S. (2011). Selecting Security Champions. *Computer Fraud & Security*, *2011*(August), 8–12. doi:10.1016/S1361-3723(11)70082-3

Home Office. (2018). *A Call to Action: The Cyber Aware Perception Gap*. Retrieved from https://www.gov.uk/government/publications/cyber-aware-perception-gap-report

ISF. (2014). *From Promoting Awareness to Embedding Behaviours - Secure by choice, not by chance*. Information Security Forum. Retrieved from https://www.securityforum.org/uploads/2015/03/From-Promoting-Awareness-ES-2014_Marketing.pdf

Kaspersky. (2016). *Lack of Security Talent: An Unexpected Threat to Corporate Cybersafety*. IT Security Risks Special Report Series 2016, Kaspersky Lab. Retrieved from https://www.kaspersky.com/blog/security_risks_report_lack_of_security_talent/

KPMG. (1998). *Information Security Survey 1998*. London, UK: KPMG Information Risk Management.

NAO. (2013). *The UK cyber security strategy: Landscape review*. National Audit Office. Retrieved from https://www.nao.org.uk/report/the-uk-cyber-security-strategy-landscape-review

NCSC. (2015). *10 Steps: User Education and Awareness*. National Cyber Security Centre. Retrieved from https://www.ncsc.gov.uk/guidance/10-steps-user-education-and-awareness

Pattinson, M., & Anderson, G. (2005). Risk Communication, Risk Perception and Information Security. *Security Management, Integrity and Internal Control in Information Systems, Proceedings of IFIP TC-11 WG11.1 & WG11.5 Joint Working Conference*, 175-184.

Schneiderman, R. (2016). *Cyber Skills in High Demand Well Into The Future*. newswise. Retrieved from http://www.newswise.com/articles/view/660345/

Schneier, B. (2013). *On Security Awareness Training*. DARKReading. Retrieved from https://www.darkreading.com/risk/on-security-awareness-training/d/d-id/1139381

Tittel, E., Lemons, M., & Kyle, M. (2017). *Information security certifications: Introductory level*. TechTarget. Retrieved from http://searchsecurity.techtarget.com/tip/SearchSecuritycom-guide-to-information-security-certifications

Vasileiou, I., & Furnell, S. (2019). Personalising Security Education - Factors influencing individual awareness and compliance. In P. Mori, S. Furnell, & O. Camp (Eds.), *Information Systems Security and Privacy, Fourth International Conference, ICISSP 2018, Madeira, Portugal, Jaruary 22-24, 2018, Revised Selected Papers*. Communications in Computer and Information Science, Springer.

ENDNOTE

1 The situation is by no means unique to the UK but drawing upon past and present survey findings from the same region enables a level of consistency and continuity for comparison.

Chapter 2
Common Mistakes in Delivering Cybersecurity Awareness

Joshua Crumbaugh
PeopleSec LLC, USA

ABSTRACT

Human error is the cause of over 95% of data breaches and the weakest aspect of cybersecurity in nearly all organizations. These errors guarantee that hackers can easily gain access to almost any network in the world and take complete control of systems, data, and more. This chapter outlines the top mistakes organizations make in security awareness and why most companies are failing to properly prepare their users for cyber-attacks. Each point is accompanied by actionable data derived from real-world training program successes and failures.

INTRODUCTION

This chapter is written under two assumptions, which reads may consider to be self-evident, but others may not. First, the human element is the most significant element of cybersecurity. Second, educating and training employees, when done *right*, will improve performance. Each of these assumptions is useful to consider before moving onto the main thrust.

Cyber-security, just like physical-security, depends on layers or controls that prevent unauthorized access, especially policies, procedures, and technologies. Humans are involved at every layer. Humans write these policies. Humans carry out these procedures. Humans design, create, install, and maintain these technologies. Human, human, human.

As defensive technologies have improved, they have made it harder for criminals to gain unauthorized access to the networks behind these technologies, but so long as humans pervade every layer, there will be vulnerabilities. The author of this chapter has been hired as a penetration tester by organizations to help improve their security by breaking into their networks and helping them to plug the holes in their defenses. In the course of such penetration testing, humans are commonly targeted.

A vulnerability can be anything. When it comes to devices, it is often a flaw in its programming of some kind. These vulnerabilities are sometimes discovered and exploited by hackers before the equip-

DOI: 10.4018/978-1-5225-7847-5.ch002

Copyright © 2019, IGI Global. Copying or distributing in print or electronic forms without written permission of IGI Global is prohibited.

ment manufacturer even becomes aware of the problem. When manufacturers do become aware, however, they usually release new software to patch the vulnerability, but these are not always installed by the organizations who use the manufacturer's equipment in their network. That is how WannaCry crippled the UK's National Health Service and others (Smith et al. 2017): Known vulnerability. Patch available. Never applied.

In the author's work as a penetration tester, he was often asked by organizations to focus solely on their technical infrastructure. Sometimes it is because the requesting organization takes a piecemeal approach to improving their security, but it is also not uncommon for the company to purposefully ignore the human elements in their security, because they know they can be easily compromised that way, and they prefer to focus their efforts on improving their technologies.

One of the author's specialties as a penetration tester is social engineering, which is simply a fancy term for swindling, grift, confidence job, etc. In other words, social engineers fool people (usually by gaining their confidence) to manipulate their behavior. Sometimes this is done in person or on the phone or with a text or through social media, but most often it is done with an email, better known as a "phish". It is designed to fool someone into doing something they should not do. For example, one might be tricked into opening a malicious attachment or fooled by a message asking them to change their usernames and passwords.

These sorts of tricks are often much easier than snooping around a network looking for potential vulnerabilities to exploit. That is why phishing has become such a prevalent threat to individuals and organizations. From the safety of a remote location, criminals can quickly blast out thousands of these malicious emails, and all it often takes is just one person who gets fooled, and the door to a company's network is open.

Organizations typically combat these types of schemes with a variety of methods. That usually involves a combination of different technologies. In the case of email, that often means filters that look at incoming email for signs of known threats. This type of approach is usually reactionary, because it operates by blocking previously reported schemes. That is an important tool to have in the defensive arsenal to help prevent malicious emails from arriving in employees' inboxes, but they do not stop them all. Criminals are constantly coming up with new tricks to stay ahead of such defenses.

Another method that organizations use to fight against these tactics is to educate and train their employees. This usually covers typical tricks that criminals use to fool people. In the case of the more prevalent ones, like phishing, employees are often given training to help them spot and report suspicious emails. That is usually done by creating harmless phish, commonly referred to as "phishing emulations", to send to their employees to see who gets hooked. This serves as both a test to gauge risk and also an immersive form of training as successive campaigns of phishing emulations are sent to the workforce, which learns by doing.

There are many terms, phrases, and acronyms used to describe efforts to educate and train employees about cybersecurity. To keep it simple, this chapter uses the acronym SETA (Security Education Training Awareness) to encompass the overall domain. The next section outlines the many varieties of SETA that the author has seen in his career, highlighting strengths and weaknesses. This leads into the main contribution of the chapter, offering tips to practitioners to avoid common mistakes that reduce the effectiveness of their efforts.

A SEEMINGLY ENDLESS VARIETY OF SETA APPROACHES

Instances of security awareness programs vary widely across organizations. Some are created and conducted entirely in-house while others are fully outsourced. Most organizations, however, employ some mixture of in-house and outsourced resources, the latter especially being pre-made education and training content and tools.

Frequency, length, and medium of training are also factors that vary widely. Many organizations conduct SETA annually or biannually; fewer do it quarterly or monthly; fewer still do it more regularly. In some organizations, these sessions last all day, or sometimes it is a few hours. Some train their employees face-to-face, while others only use computer-based training. Other organizations employ a mix of the two.

Variety also exists in the content of the training. Many organizations take a one-size-fits-all approach, meaning all or most of their employees undergo the same training, regardless of role or responsibility. This content tends to be generalized and covers the most common potential threats that average employees might encounter. Other organizations take a more nuanced approach, targeting special classes of employees for role-specific education such as credit-card processing or confidential information handling or even executive training. A growing number of vendors exist today to supply this content, sometimes stand-alone, but increasingly the content is incorporated into Learning Management Systems (LMS) or proprietary platforms, the latter model often being Software as a Service (SaaS) also known as a do-it-yourself (DIY) tool.

COMMON MISTAKES

This section outlines the key areas that the author's experience has shown to be the most common failings in SETA approaches. These in turn have the potential to undermine the effectiveness of the resulting activities and can ultimately devalue the worth of attempting SETA in the first place.

You Lost My Attention

One of the reasons why education is not as effective as it can be is because it is boring and resented and seems unnecessary and is a distraction from one's job. Education often does not capture or keep their attention. Common complaints cite poorly done slide presentations and lectures or boring modules in computer-based training systems.

It is hard to educate someone who is unwilling to be educated, and that is even harder to do when you ignore some of the realities of being human. For example, most people have short attention spans. Designing courses that last hours require special techniques to capture and keep the attention of the students, but how many organizations task people with creating and delivering this content who don't have the right background. These people might be experts in cybersecurity and be able to talk ad nauseum about critical vulnerabilities and ways to prevent them, but if they have no experience in translating that to a lay audience or no experience in teaching, how effective do will it be?

What Was That Again?

One benefit of doing effective and engaging face-to-face training for several hours or even a full day is that it can help to kick-start a campaign to increase awareness and quickly change behavior in the short term. One might refer to this as "binge training", similar to cramming before a test or binging on some new 12-episode television series over the course of a wet and rainy weekend. Lots of things loaded into the short-term memory.

Most people, in the days following a cramming session or similar binge, will be able to recall and discuss things in great detail. As time passes, however, memory fades. A new joke has sprung up to describe this experience: *The great thing about binging a season of episodes is that you get to enjoy it twice* (the second time is when someone must rewatch the mostly forgotten first season before advancing to the next).

Now, binging a television show is something done for pleasure. It captures and holds interest, and it usually delights, something that really captured the interest and was enjoyed. How many employees might use words like "really enjoyed" or "delightful" to describe their experience learning about cybersecurity in a mandatory training? From this perspective, effective and efficient *ongoing* education and training is more likely to be retained and influence the behavior of a workforce. Consider an annual two-hour training session vs. 30 two-minute or 60 one- minute educational moments spread out over the course of a year. Which approach is more likely to have better retention? For that matter, which method is more likely to keep security top-of-mind?

Boring

At PeopleSec we informally survey customers and prospects and often convention goers to learn about their experiences with SETA. One of the most frequent things we hear from employees is that it's boring. We also hear that same feedback from many of the people who are in charge of conducting these SETA programs. In many cases, organizations tap technical people to develop the curriculum. These people don't always have the communication skills and knowledge of education and training that they need to do the job well. The product can often be content that is boring for employees, often unnecessarily technical. It's hard to get results if you can't capture and keep the attention of your students.

There are a number of remedies to this. One is to purchase high quality, pre-made content. The marketplace offers a lot of options, but for some organizations, it's not in the budget. Those organizations should look internally for employees that together have the requisite experience to create better curricula. Ideally, you'll want to put together a team with the following skill sets:

- Someone with the knowledge of common cybersecurity best practices and the most common and prevalent threats today
- Someone with a background in education and training to shape the aforementioned knowledge into a course or courses
- Someone with the skill to create learning materials for the course in whatever medium or media are to be used
- Someone with a background in psychology or organizational behavior to provide input so that the education and training will lead to changes in behavior

Inadequate and Underutilized Resources

Many organizations do not have or do not wish to have a dedicated human resource or a team to run a SETA program. For organizations first setting up such a program, they often tap one or more employees to build and do it in-house. They almost invariably have existing responsibilities, and those responsibilities are not always adjusted to make enough room for SETA. When that happens, quality often suffers, and results often fall short of what is desired.

Alternatively, many companies acquire a learning platform from a SaaS provider. Many of these platforms offer a lot of pre-made modules and tools, but these platforms are often not used to their potential. Common examples include:

- Person or people running SETA never learn to fully utilize the platform
- Person or people running SETA rarely have the time to fully utilize the platform
- Person or people running SETA don't have the background in education and training that they need to effectively use the platform. For example, how do I determine a user's risk-level? How do I adapt training for high risk users? How do I adapt training for low risk users?
- Person or people running SETA do not have the time to provide feedback to employees on their performance, especially personal feedback, which is often integral to behavior change.

Wrong Mix of Education and Training

The terms education and training are often used interchangeably. In most contexts, the distinction is not important. This is one of those contexts where it does matter. To illustrate the difference between these terms a memorable analogy on this subject.

If my daughter came home from school one day and told me that her class was learning about sexual education, I'd think that's a good thing. Less awkward conversations for me. If she came home, however, and told me they were doing sexual training, well, I'd call the police.

The education portion explains the concept, which helps to build awareness, but it does not necessarily lead to changes in behavior, which at the end of the day, is why organizations conduct SETA. They're after better security practices, not questions answered correctly on a test. Knowledge alone may help some people, but others may not know how to apply it. That is where training comes in. It is about putting that knowledge into action (i.e. learning by doing).

The education component of most SETA programs tends to be broad, and rightly so for such an expansive subject matter. Most curricula cover a wide variety of important subjects to help each employee get a better understanding of best cybersecurity practices. Not all topics, however, are equal. The most prevalent and immediate threats require more attention than other topics, and often they require training. In many cases, that is as simple as asking students to apply a concept they just learned. A quiz or test or discussion are easy ways to accomplish this. In other cases, when learning to defend against social engineering, more immersive training is required. That is especially the case with phishing, the subject of an upcoming section.

Education Is the Goal Whereas It Should Be Behavior Change

The chief aim of SETA is to change the behavior of an entire workforce to make the organization less susceptible to a security breach. Programs that only do education will often fall short of that goal. Creating awareness, therefore, is an important but preliminary step in the process. Awareness *alone* is not always enough to motivate changes in behavior. Consider people who smoke tobacco. Nearly all of them know that it is very bad for their health and often leads to cancer and other diseases, but that *knowledge alone is not enough* to get them to stop smoking.

This is a common mistake that many organizations make, especially those that task their technical employees with educating and training the workforce when they lack the experience and know-how to educate and train effectively. Without that proper background and experience, these types of organizations are more likely to make education the goal, expecting increased awareness and knowledge to magically lead to changes in behavior.

It is much the same when it comes to SETA. Employee may understand conceptually that a weak or reused password is a security risk, but they also might think that is something that other people need to worry about. *Who would want to hack me? What do I have access to?* This highlights another common mistake in SETA programs, namely the lack of relating what is being taught to each individual and his or her job.

If changing behavior is the goal, then security programs must move beyond teaching concepts in the abstract alone. Employees must be engaged in examining how these concepts relate to their day-to-day jobs. That begins with employees asking themselves basic questions after they learn new concepts. *If my user-account is compromised what sensitive or confidential information do I have access to? Do I really know or understand what is confidential or sensitive? How am I or should I be personally liable?*

It's in answering these types of questions and working to make things more secure based on this knowledge that one of the true benefits of security awareness education can be realized. The issue of relating training to each employee also relates to the medium of learning.

Medium Matters

In the previous section highlighted the importance of relating what is taught to the day-to-day job of each employee. That is a critical step in achieving behavior change, and one that many organizations fail to do. It is helpful to keep this example of mind when considering the medium (format) of learning.

SETA usually happens in-person or on the computer, sometimes both. In some cases, the learning might be equally effective regardless of format, though most computer-based systems tend to be more efficient and flexible. There are times, however, when face-to-face is better. Consider the following two scenarios:

1. As part of a computer-based learning session, John, an engineer, is asked to describe ways in which he might access or handle sensitive or confidential information in the course of a workday. A follow-up question then asks John to suggest improvements for accessing or handling this information. These suggestions are then sent to Alice, John's manager. Alice similarly receives suggestions from John's peers, and they are also sent to Ian in Information Security. Alice and Ian are then tasked with creating any new policies or procedures for Alice's team to make things more secure. They do this via email.

2. Following a computer-based learning session, Susan, a financial analyst, attends a mandatory face-to-face meeting with her co-workers and manager with remote workers participating via video conference. As a group, they discuss how their team accesses and handles all sensitive information, electronic or otherwise. Together, they brainstorm ideas for making things more secure and then mutually craft new policies and procedures for the team to put these ideas into action. They are helped through the process by Ian from Information Security.

Which is more likely to affect a behavior change that enhances security and why? The first scenario is efficient and flexible, both of which are desirable. John is able to learn at his own pace and according to his own schedule, and he can do it right from his desk. These are the strengths of computer-based learning.

The session is also engaging to some degree, because it is asking him to relate the concepts that he learned to his own job. After answering these questions, his boss Alice then gets his suggestions as well as the suggestions from his peers, and she works with Ian in InfoSec to translate any lessons learned into policies and procedures. The team is then thanked for their contributions (at least those who made suggestions), and new policies and procedures are handed down. They are expected to read, understand, and comply.

The second scenario is less efficient and flexible. The schedules of Susan and her co-workers and manager and Ian from InfoSec all must align for them to meet together. That is often not easy on a busy team with multiple projects, but not undoable. The interactive and cooperative nature of the meeting helps for a more thorough analysis, but it is slow.

It is especially helpful to have Ian from InfoSec on hand to throw out examples from his perspective of when this team touches sensitive data and how, but perhaps not the best use of his knowledge, since he's a highly paid specialist whose time is particularly valuable. As a non-technical finance team, they need assistance from someone who knows about their access and systems.

Progress is slow, and the group does not even finish discussing all of the ways that they handle sensitive data before time expires. A subsequent meeting is set up in which the team finally describes all of the ways that they touch sensitive data. The group then brainstorms ways to improve, and they mutually agree on a few key ways in which they can improve. They agree by consensus on new policies and procedures to adopt. Susan's manager and Ian from InfoSec make it official.

When considering these scenarios, which factors are more helpful to reach the end goal, i.e., changes in group-behavior that enhance security? The first scenario is efficient and flexible and therefore less disruptive to the organization overall. The second scenario is more disruptive, messy and slow, but it gives the matter a more in-depth consideration, and it makes everyone a part of the process, and the face-to-face element forces them all to be more engaged. Which is likely to achieve the desired end(s)?

Both of these scenarios involve organizations that are more mature on the security front than average, because they both seek to translate what has been learned into more secure ways of doing things.

Effectiveness Before Efficiency

Efficiency is always desired, but only as a second measure to effectiveness. Decisions on methodology should be enlightened by studies and surveys and statistics, but ultimately organizations must determine for themselves what goals to set and what they are willing to pay to achieve those. Some of those expenses might be straightforward, like the cost of buying pre-made education and training materials or developing them in house, but most will be murkier. What is an acceptable degree of disruption to the organization's day to day tasks to achieve these goals? What is the harm that might potentially be caused by different types of breaches that the organization might experience? How do those all add up for the organization? Many organizations fail to ask themselves these hard questions. Fewer still even try to answer them.

Not Enough Role-Based Training

SETA, if *properly* done, provides the right amount of education and training to individuals—in the form that is needed. Many employees, for example, may only need general education and training, but certain groups of employees will require very specialized treatment.

As an illustration of this, some indicative job functions with special needs would include the following:

- **Human Resources:** plays a critical role in Information Security, because humans pervade every layer of cybersecurity. Policies instituted by HR have teeth. For example, eligibility for promotions and bonuses and later moves can be made contingent on performance in SETA. Low risk employees may be made eligible for a slightly higher bonus, while high risk employees may be placed on an action plan.
- **Finance:** in short, anyone who has the ability to make a wire transfer of money is a potential target for cybercriminals.
- **Executives:** probably the single most important group for role-based training, as they make some of the most significant decisions and can also be amongst the most attractive targets.
- **Executive and/or Administrative Assistants:** This group is often overlooked, but in many organizations, they hold a lot of keys to the kingdom on behalf of the people they're supporting. They're also critical as helpers for security by virtue of their job function and access to executives.
- **Managers:** To help manage safe practices of employees such as storage of sensitive physical documents under lock and key when unattended, supervision of any removal of sensitive documents, workstation locking. Managers help build a culture of security, and they are also a first line of enforcement of policies. They also have close relations with their employees, so they are uniquely situated to be engaged in providing feedback.
- **Information Technology:** These staff have a clear role in selecting, deploying and configuring the technology used across the organization, and so need to be aware and mindful of security at each stage of the process.
- **Information Security[1]:** Both threats and defensive techniques are constantly evolving, so InfoSec personnel need to stay on top of trends as they develop, and they especially need education to understand how to combat the threats.
- **Software Developers:** Need to be aware that the code they write, and how they write it, has a crucial role in maintaining security. They need to know how to design and develop systems in a secure manner in order to minimize exploitable vulnerabilities.
- **Generally:** Any other job that handles sensitive information.

Would WannaCry have crippled the UK's National Health Service (NHS) had more employees received role-based training, especially executives? Ultimately, it was an executive decision not to spend the money to address the vulnerabilities. In retrospect, that was a poor decision. How did it come to be?

Did the decision-makers not get adequate information from Information Security personnel? It would likely be a waste of time to make employees in Information Security go through *general* SETA, but WannaCry exploited a widely known vulnerability that could have been prevented with an available patch, but many InfoSec personnel neglected to do so. Why? For many it seemed like an obscure and improbable vulnerability. Perhaps at the time, that was a reasonable perspective for them to have, but they may have looked at things differently at the time had they been adequately trained on vulnerabilities, especially from the point of view of the attacker. Criminals most often will go after low hanging fruit.

Incident Response Training

Cybersecurity breaches happen, but few organizations adequately prepare themselves for the possibility. When these breaches happen, a lot of people get involved, especially when severe. Some organizations are well prepared with policies and procedures in place that have been rehearsed by all hands for breaches small and large. Sadly, most are not.

Executive Training

One of the most important forms of role-based training involves executives, because, when done properly, it can have a quick and lasting change on an organization's culture. Before SETA, many employees tend to think of cybersecurity as something beyond their responsibility. That is something those tech people do. Executives are no different, but that type of thinking in an organizational leader tends to have a top down effect.

Every employee in a company plays a role in security, and increasingly more and more employees, even on the manufacturing floor, play a role in cybersecurity. In the course of an average day, many employees may deal with information that is sensitive. They all have a responsibility to keep it secure. That is even more so the case for managers and directors and executives. The higher up the chain you go, the more people are responsible for how their employees handle sensitive information.

If most people in an organization think of cybersecurity as someone else's responsibility, there is an excellent chance that the organization lacks proper policies and procedures for handling that sensitive data. After all, who better knows what is sensitive and not than those who deal with the data itself?

One important thing that many executives learn in their role-based training is that in many environments, they are given preferential treatment. Often, the same rules that apply to average employees are not applied to executives. This makes the organization far more vulnerable to social engineers who masquerade as executives to manipulate employees' behavior. You'd be surprised to learn how many people want to help executives and do things like give me credentials for domain administration right over the phone.

Lack of Difference Performance Requirements for Different Roles

Different job functions have varying degrees of access and authority within an organization. Inherently these job positions pose a greater potential risk to the organization than those with less access and authority. Here are a few examples to consider:

- Phillip, a sales manager, is pre-approved to make expenditures worth thousands of dollars.
- Susan in accounting has access to employees' tax records. She is also one of the few employees authorized to transfer funds.
- Tony, the building manager, has physical access to every part of company headquarters.
- Lucy, a network administrator, has access to every device on three windows domains.
- Dan, an administrative assistant, has access to everything that the executives he supports can access and do. In fact, it's his job often do handle things for them in their names.

Given their roles and permission, it would seem logical that their performance in SETA ought to be assessed to a higher standard than employees with less access and authority. However, it is very likely that in many organizations they would be managed within a one-size-fits-all provision.

Lack of Adjusting to Individual or Group Needs

Employee populations exhibit a wide variety of differences in knowledge of cybersecurity or security in general, in risk avoidance or acceptance, aptitude, retention, etc. More successful SETA programs adjust to these differences. That's especially the case with performance in the SETA program itself. The poorer the performance, the more risk is posed to the organization.

In the organizations that the author has dealt with in SETA, a very small number of employees are found to pose the majority of the risk to the company. The rest of the population is usually low risk, but organizations fail to either assign risk to each employee or to do it well, like basing it on a single test rather than cumulative performance over time. When they don't really know the risk posed by each employee, they are not in a position to conduct a more efficient training.

Simply put, high risk users need a lot of attention. They need more education and training and regular feedback. They also need to feel both watched and cared for. Some of that can be automated, but some of it requires human interaction to really affect positive changes in behavior. Low risk users, on the other hand, will probably get annoyed with extensive education and training that they continually demonstrate a mastery in. They would rightfully think it's a waste of their time.

How can you know which employee needs what level of attention if you're not measuring performance?

THREATS TO EMPHASIZE

Not all threats are equal, and neither are all user habits. What other types of attacks should receive emphasis for cybersecurity awareness programs? The short answer is whatever the industry is reporting as the most viable means of attack. This section considers some particular areas of cybersecurity that ought to be receiving particular attention, as a result of users' regular exposure to them and their clear and frequent tendency to make mistakes if not guided to do otherwise.

Phishing

Probably the largest failing of security awareness programs not focusing *enough* attention on the biggest threats. Too many provide a general education in cybersecurity, which is important, but some topics require greater emphasis than others, and none more so today than phishing. According to Verizon (2018),

96% of all successful targeted attacks began with a phish. Many organizations treat this annual study as a gospel, but how many adjust the content of their instruction to align with key statistics like this?

Phishing is a form of cyber-attack that most commonly happens through email. Would-be criminals design email messages that look like they are coming from your bank or credit card company or from your email provider. Many of these are very good, often near replicas. They are usually crafted to get recipients to click on a link in the email or open an attachment. Here is an example. An email is received that looks like it comes from PayPal, warning the recipient an attempt was made to access the account without authorization. *URGENT: Log into your account immediately to change your password.* Conveniently, a link or button is supplied for the recipient to click. Only, the link does not take the user to the real PayPal site, though the website seen certainly looks authentic[2]. The user, not suspecting that something is amiss, logs in by entering the required username and password. Voila! Their credentials have just been supplied to criminal.

Alternatively, the link might take the recipient first to a webpage that installs malware on the user's computer and then quickly redirects the user to the actual PayPal site. In this case, the goal is not to steal credentials but to use this scenario to convince someone to install the malware unknowingly. The variety of schemes is only limited by the imaginations and abilities of criminals.

Employees often wonder why their SETA programs at work contain such examples. *Why, after all, should my employer care if I get duped into giving my personal account to some criminal?* Well, there are a number of reasons, but two that should suffice to answer the question. First, many people use the same password for more than one account with sensitive access. If an employee uses the same password for PayPal as for work, then exposing the one endangers the other. Second, if an employee falls for something like this PayPal example, that employee is probably may more likely be susceptible to phishing and spear-phishing in particular.

When criminals phish an organization, such as with the PayPal-bait, they often send the same message to every email address that they can find or think of for the organization, many of which are already available in various places online, like the company website or at LinkedIn. At this stage, criminals are just seeing who they can get to take the bait. If a user gets hooked, he or she might subsequently be sent a spear-phish that is *specifically* targeting that individual. For example, a new email message arrives that appears to come from the IT department, possibly even stepping the user through a similar scenario, saying there has been suspicious activity detected, and asking for an urgent change to a password. The user clicks on the button in the email and is taken to a webpage that looks just like the company's email portal, and now the user really has given his or her work credentials to a criminal. Alternatively, the hacker doesn't bother with the spear-phishing part. Instead, he or she just uses the PayPal password along with the presumed username (usually discernible from the email address) to test if this is the password used for work.

To understand why phishing is so popular, we need to consider the perspective of the criminals themselves. First, phishing is relatively safe compared to other forms of crime. It does not require a physical presence. Second, the blackhat social engineer knows from experience that it's a numbers game. A certain percentage of recipients of phish will get hooked – and this percentage can be rather high. For example, Bursztein et al. (2014) found that the success rate ranged between 3% and 45%, with the average sitting at 13.7%. Third, attacks in email are insidious, because the vast majority of email messages people receive are totally harmless. Some may be unwelcome, but few are actually malicious. People get lulled into a false sense of security, especially when they think that things like spam filters, anti-virus, attachment scanning, blacklisted websites and the overall efforts of their IT or IS departments will keep them safe. It's that lack of suspicion that the social engineer exploits.

Here is a real-life example of successful spear-phishing by a criminal to a subsidiary of a larger American corporation. It convincingly looked like it came from the larger corporation. It was simply asking for copies of all of the W2s (tax forms) for people employed by a certain date. The unsuspecting recipient sent them on. It was only discovered later that this was spear-phishing. So what information was given to the criminals? Full legal names, social security numbers, income, home addresses, etc. With a little more information, a criminal could impersonate any one of these employees possibly to obtain a credit card, take out a loan or even a mortgage. Meanwhile, the resulting exposure of each employee cannot be easily remedied. Who will pay to change their names? Their social security numbers? How long will this exposure affect the lives of these employees?

Now, many organizations have tools in place to detect suspected phish and other forms of unwanted and potentially harmful email. These usually involve a variety of measures such as blacklisting known malicious websites, scanning email attachments, adding automated warnings into email messages to warn them to be careful, etc. When these tools are properly configured and maintained, they can be effective means of preventing potentially dangerous emails from arriving in users' inboxes, but they're not foolproof. They are often in part operating off lists of known tricks and websites that have been previously reported or they employ heuristics algorithms with varying degrees of success. Such tools are an important part of the cybersecurity mix, but they do not negate the need for employee training, especially for phishing. Some criminals are quite clever, and they are constantly changing their bait to keep ahead of these automated systems of protection[3].

To reduce an organization's susceptibility to phishing, a little bit of education is needed, and a lot of training. Regular phishing emulations should be conducted over time, based on the cumulative performance of each individual employees. People who fall for phish more often should receive more simulations. People who fall for phishing less frequently should get tested less frequently, but also with more difficult phishing messages, including spear-phishing. Crucially, employees must be trained to report *all* suspicious emails to some authority. The policy should be concise and clear and well known. All suspicious emails include phishing emulations.

Passwords

An area that needs a particular focus is in password-handling. It should not only teach best practices, but those practices should be required by company policy. Even when purchasing pre-made content, an organization's password policies need to be part of the education. The two biggest threats from passwords come from guessable and weak choices. Policies need to prohibit these.

Samples of guessable (or easily-crackable) passwords include the following, all of which users might nonetheless be tempted to choose if simply provided with the frequent minimal guidance to use a combination of upper/lowercase letters and numbers:

- Fall2018[4]
- Winter19
- Spring2019
- Password2019
- Password1

Weak passwords, such as eight characters with no capital letters, special symbols or numbers, pose a threat as well. If an attacker can gain access to the encrypted form of these passwords, then they can easily decrypt the password into its original value and elevate their access within the network. There is plenty of guidance out there about good password practice, and NIST (2017) has defined standards for what users should be required to do. The key issue is ensuring that this is communicated and understood by users, so that they have a chance to actually do it.

Social Media

Social media is being increasingly used by criminals. One obvious example is the proliferation of fraudulent charity sites that spring up following natural disaster. They dupe many generous donors to steal their contributions.

Looking at social media is part of the standard reconnaissance for most penetration testing teams on full scope engagements, and probably the same for hackers. Pentesting teams reconnoiter targets in all social media, but LinkedIn, Facebook, and Twitter are typical starting points, and it's often not necessary to explore other media. LinkedIn is particularly helpful, because it explicitly provides data related to employees at multiple organizations. Names, designations, and locations of offices are among the particularly helpful data that can be gleaned to create staff directories for social engineering attacks. Additionally, many employees tend to unwittingly disclose sensitive information about information systems and security controls within their job descriptions. This is invaluable for penetration testers, just as it is for hackers.

Few companies have comprehensive policies for social media, much less methods to enforce them, but it is an important component of SETA, especially because this attack vector is growing. Not only should social media be included in the content of education, it should also be the focus of immersive training.

One of the objectives for every organization after doing education and training on social media should be the creation of policies for social media use and also a means of enforcing them. For example, which employees have a business need to access social media? Few outside of marketing have this need. What's appropriate behavior for employees on personal social media? It only takes one employee to post a photo of their badge or ID card for a hacker to duplicate an almost exact replica that could give them access to whatever they want. This is an example of how a seemingly innocent post or tweet can expose an organization to risk.

CONCLUSION

It is clear that while SETA provision is important, simply doing something is not enough. It has to be done right if it is to deliver the expected results and be considered worthwhile. In fact, it is all too easy for efforts to be dismissed as a waste of time, without realizing that the reason that they are not working is that they were flawed in the first place.

The key message of this chapter to organizations wishing to address their staff with SETA initiatives is not to lose site of the main goal. The aim is to change the behavior of everyone in the organization and this needs to be reinforces over time by maintaining a security of culture. Each step that is taken should therefore be evaluated in terms of how it helps to accomplish that goal.

REFERENCES

Bursztein, E., Benko, B., Margolis, D., Pietraszek, T., Archer, A., Aquino, A., ... Savage, S. (2014). Handcrafted Fraud and Extortion: Manual Account Hijacking in the Wild. *Proceedings of the 2014 Conference on Internet Measurement Conference (IMC'14)*, 347-358. 10.1145/2663716.2663749

NIST. (2017). *Digital Identity Guidelines - Authentication and Lifecycle Management.* NIST Special Publication 800-63B. June 2017. doi:10.6028/NIST.SP.800-63b

Smith, S., Smith, S., Bailey, N., & Cahill, P. (2017). Why 'WannaCry' Malware Caused Chaos for National Health Service in U.K. *NBC News.* Retrieved from https://www.nbcnews.com/news/world/why-wannacry-malware-caused-chaos-national-health-service-u-k-n760126

Verizon. (2018). *2018 Data Breach Investigations Report* (11th ed.). Research Report. https://enterprise.verizon.com/resources/reports/DBIR_2018_Report.pdf

ENDNOTES

1. Information Security is not the same function of Information Technology. Although some of the skills of IT and IS personnel overlap, IT is essentially concerned with the technical infrastructure and making sure that it's available to employees. InfoSec, on the other hand, is a specialization of the security. https://www.csoonline.com/article/3225344/data-protection/information-security-is-not-information-technology.html
2. Some attacks get super crafty and purchase domain website addresses that look nearly identical to the real site. For example, one could replace the "L" in PayPal with an "I" and many won't see the difference. Paypal.com now becomes paypai.com, but when the attacker capitalizes the "i" it looks like a lowercase "l". Even suspicious and discerning users will likely be fooled by this.
3. The author's experience as a pentester suggests that phishing is almost always the easiest way in.
4. In organizations that require that employees change passwords every quarter, it is common to find examples of people combining the name of a season with the year tacked onto it.

Chapter 3
The Role of Education and Awareness in Tackling Insider Threats

Shaun Joseph Smyth
Ulster University, UK

Kevin Curran
Ulster University, UK

Nigel McKelvey
Letterkenny Institute of Technology, Ireland

ABSTRACT

Insider threats present a major concern for organizations worldwide. As organizations need to provide employees with authority to access data to enable them to complete their daily tasks, they leave themselves open to insider attacks. This chapter looks at those who fall into the category which can be referred to as insiders and highlights the activity of outsourcing which is employed by many organizations and defines the term insider threat while pointing out what differentiates an accidental threat from a malicious threat. The discussion also considers various methods of dealing with insider threats before highlighting the role education and awareness plays in the process, the importance of tailoring awareness programs, and what the future holds for insider threats within organizations.

INTRODUCTION

In the early 1990s the United States saw a drive in the growth of business because of telecommunications networks and the Internet. Despite this growth, the dependency placed upon these networks placed the U.S. in a precarious position as it also increased their vulnerability to cyber exploitation and by the end of the twentieth century the U.S. had become the most vulnerable nation to cyber-attacks aiming to disrupt or interfere with essential services (McConnell, 2002).

DOI: 10.4018/978-1-5225-7847-5.ch003

Copyright © 2019, IGI Global. Copying or distributing in print or electronic forms without written permission of IGI Global is prohibited.

Organizations, worldwide regardless of their size or form have all accepted that an increase in the development of their existing services is essential if they are to improve and gain a much-needed advantage over their fellow competitors. In their quest to achieve this goal organizations understand that a greater dependence is placed upon the need for information technology (IT) for them to compete successfully in the world of modern-day business (Abawajy, 2014). Businesses are already connected with the bulk of transactions taking place in an electronic format the consequence of which is a constant rise in the quantity of both personal and sensitive data produced and later collected. Sensitive data is looked upon as one of the many assets of any organization as many appreciate its significance, considering it to be the lifeblood of the processes and procedures which take place within their business (Sarkar, 2010). As many of today's organizations compete in lively and fast-moving environments which are constantly developing, they produce a large volume of sensitive data in a bid to achieve their goals which include lower prices, higher quality of products and services and a rapid development. However, the provision of new opportunities coupled with the globalization of activities in both businesses and organizations combined with the swift growth of ICT has given rise to a new problem in the form of threats (Stavrou et al. 2014).

Organizations can find themselves on the receiving end of threats as their information security is susceptible to dangers from a wide variety of sources which present in many different formats varying from the less complicated spam emails to the more structured and complex form of attack such as malwares (malicious software) which can steal or contaminate data and ultimately produce enough damage to leave systems in a condition where they are inoperable (Abawajy, 2014).

One such threat includes that caused as a direct result of online social networking (OSN) which has recently experienced a sudden rise. Certain employees within organizations are accountable for information and are later responsible for the leakage of this same information to outside parties. Careless use of social media has a harmful influence on organizations placing networks and systems at risk of malware which can result in many negative issues including copyright and defamation issues, reduced productivity which significantly affect the organization's reputation and future income (Molok et al. 2011).

Modern-day information systems are challenged by a wide range of threats and even though attacks which are started from outside such as viruses and hacking receiving much publicity the insider threat however, presents a considerably higher level of danger (Theoharidou et al. 2005). This view is shared by Baracaldo and Joshi (2012), McCormac et al. (2012), and Warkentin and Willison (2009) who all point out that Insider attacks are still one of the most dangerous threats organizations can face today.

The insider threat comes from the trusted organizational member and they can cause the greatest harm as they have access to the organization's greatest asset 'information'. Those individuals employed within an organization have the capability to either damage or destroy sensitive information using uncomplicated noncompliance of security policies, negligence, the absence of motivation in the protection of sensitive data, careless actions within the workplace or insufficient training. Including reduced productivity and revenue such actions result in the failure to protect the confidentiality of the organization, its associates, customers and ultimately the reputation of the organization's information system. This problem is often referred to as the 'endpoint security problem' as the employee is the last point of contact or endpoint of the information system (IS) and its network. It is often said that the weakest link or greatest security problem within a network lies between the keyboard and the chair (Warkentin, and Willison, 2009).

Organizations are faced with an ever-growing task in relation to computer security and face persistent attacks from both external and internal sources as there are many different threats which are all keen to breach organizational security defenses with a noticeable increase in the vulnerability to threats posed by the insider because of the worryingly high increase in the possession of privileged access to the network which they enjoy and require to carry out their jobs (Nurse et al. 2014; Martinez-Moyano et al.2008).

This view is also expressed by Claycomb and Nicoll (2012) as they highlight that insider threats are both a constant and ever-increasing problem. The insider attack presents a much greater risk to organizations, the main reason for this however is not solely due to the advantage which the insider currently enjoys by already holding secure access to the network but it is also due to the fact that the majority of network security procedures direct their attention to the prevention of external attacks from those who are outside the network perimeter the consequence of which is a reduction in the importance assigned to the safeguarding of network components against malicious access internally from within the actual network itself from management/employees who already have network access and certain privileges inside the network itself (Nurse et al.2014; McCormac et al. 2012). Martinez-Moyano et al (2008) also emphasize that the growing dependence of organizations on technological infrastructures has placed organizations in a position where they are exposed to an increased vulnerability from insider threats.

The rest of this chapter looks at those individuals who can be classed as insiders and offers a definition for the term 'insider threat' looking at their frequency of occurrence and the different causes. The practice of non-compliance within the workplace is examined highlighting some reported breaches of security by organizational employees and the reported damage caused to those organizations due to the practice of insider threats. Also covered within this chapter are the roles which both education and awareness can play in dealing with the growing problem of the insider threat within an organizational setting including the possibility of reducing the issue or eradicating it completely as organizations now place more emphasis on external threats and their prevention than they do on the insider threat which can be equally if not more dangerous to an organization.

BACKGROUND

The cost incurred to businesses worldwide due to security breaches and computer viruses has been a total of $1.6 trillion a year and 39,363 human years of productivity (Ula and Fuadi, 2017). This highlights the importance placed in the ability for organizations to protect their assets and why the security of information is such a major concern in organizations. The potential for attacks from hackers is such a worry that many are forced to employ services in a bid to protect against viruses and malware and the likelihood of an attack from an outsider. However, although protection from external attacks is an important concern it is also essential not to dismiss the possibility of attacks which occur closer to home as much evidence suggests that internal breaches have been the cause of many significant, costly attacks and security incidences in both government and organizational sectors (Sarkar, 2010). A similar view is shared by Chinchani et al. (2005) as they highlight that many organizations concentrate solely on external attacks as techniques and tools are now available to help in finding and fixing such weaknesses, unlike the internal threat which is not yet fully understood, difficult to calculate and there is an absence of available tools and techniques which are able to help with such a situation.

Insider attacks are a well-recognized problem with the threat they offer being acknowledged as far back as the 1980s (Chinchani et al. 2005). However, for years organizations have wrestled with this internal issue of defending themselves from individuals which they should trust in the day-to-day running of their business. Such individuals are referred to as 'insiders' which include employees, freelance workers, consultants and others who have the privilege of having access to vital areas within an organization which ultimately enables them to access important organizational information. Individuals in such positions however may exploit the trust bestowed upon them for their own personal gain and pose as a serious threat to confidentiality within the organization, the organization's significant assets and ultimately the organization's reputation (Liu et al. 2008).

Insiders worldwide are accountable for many such incidents with reports of insider threats by those granted the privilege of access to information within organizations where they have been employed. Many such incidents however, go unreported to protect the reputation and good name of the organization yet many still make the headlines such as the following:

- Over a period of months in 1996 two credit union employees working together altered credit reports for monetary gain. Both employees had authorization as part of their normal duties to update information received by the company however these two individuals misused their authorization by removing negative credit indicators and adding fabricated indicators of positive credit in exchange for money. The total amount of fraud because of these activities surpassed $215,000 however, the risk associated with the credit union as a result was immense (Randazzo et al. 2005).
- Sarkar (2010) highlights how the UK government hit the headlines in 2008 when a Home Office contractor lost a USB stick which held details of all 84,000 prisoners within Wales and England resulting in the end of a £1.5 million contract with a management consultancy firm.
- An international financial services company fell victim to a logic bomb in 2002 deleting 10 billion files in the company and affecting servers of over 1300 companies throughout the United States. The company suffered losses totaling $3million needed to repair damage and recreate the deleted files. Investigations later revealed that the logic bomb was planted by a frustrated employee who quit the company over a dispute regarding the amount of his annual bonus (Randazzo et al. 2005).

The incentive to work on insider threats varies from country to country as the U.S. interest appears to be centered more around events which cause damage to national security such as the case of Robert Hanssen, an FBI insider who was arrested in 2001 for stealing and selling secrets to the Russians and more recently, the case of Bradley Manning an American soldier and insider who revealed many confidential U.S. government documents. When compared to the $7billion fraud committed against the French bank Societe Generale by one of its own traders, Jerome Kerviel the difference is obvious (Hunker and Probst, 2011).

WHO ARE INSIDERS?

A reliable definition of an insider is difficult to obtain and as such it hampers the detection of threats from this group of individuals. The assumption of a perimeter around an organization such that those within the perimeter can referred to as insiders is not practical with the increase in mobile computing and outsourcing (Bishop and Gates, 2008). Similarly, an insider can have wireless connectivity and have a physical presence far away from an organization while likewise individuals can be physically present within an organization but have no authorization to use the computation infrastructure (Chinchani et al. 2005). Despite the arguments which surround an insider's physical location, many descriptions of what constitutes an insider are however offered. One such definition includes that proposed by Magklaras and Furnell (2005) who explain that the insider is an individual who has legitimately been given the ability to access one or several elements of the IT infrastructure using one or more authentication mechanisms. It is the use of the word legitimately which differentiates between the insider who enjoys a certain level of trust and advantages in comparison to the external hacker who must spend extra time and effort in obtaining a point of entry to the computer system an advantage which the insider already enjoys. As Sarkar (2010) highlights the insider can be an employee who has the required privileges such as keys, log on details for the network and suitable network access to enable them to fulfil his/her duties in their place of work on a day-to-day basis. This is a view which is shared by Greitzer et al. (2008) who define the insider as a person who is now or was on some earlier occasion granted the authority to access the organization's information system, data or network and such authorization is indicative of a high level of trust in that individual.

Hayden (1999) who also explains that insiders who can be employees, contractors or service providers or somebody with valid access to a system however, stresses that the issue of trust is an important factor regarding insiders as the more privileges they enjoy on the system, the greater will be their level of knowledge and access on the system and ultimately, they pose a higher potential threat.

Probst et al. (2010) describe an insider as the following:

- An insider is an individual who has rightful access to resources.
- An insider is an individual or company which the organization trust.
- An insider is the user of a system who can use their privileges for the wrong purpose.
- An insider is an individual who despite having authorized access may use this benefit to damage or remove organizational assets or help outsiders in carrying out such acts.

Probst et al. also highlight how the following definition for an insider has been proposed:

An insider is a person that has been legitimately empowered with the right to access, represent, or decide about one or more assets of the organization's structure. (Probst et al. 2010)

Despite this proposed definition of insiders, there are however, insiders which are not necessarily always friendly in nature helping organizations in their day-to-day functions as some may present as threats posing a danger to organizations and their resources namely their private data/information (Park and Ho, 2004). In defining the insider Anderson (1999) looks at the intent of the insider classifying them into three categories which include Normal – Abnormal – Malevolent. Anderson (1999) explains each of these three categories further highlighting the intent of each of three insider types as follows:

- **Normal:** This category of insider is likely to carry out insider activity which is unlikely to present a threat.
- **Abnormal:** The insider activity by this group may consist of routine errors which may cause issues in a weak system causing private information to be accidentally revealed
- **Malevolent:** This includes insider activity which presents a threat as it is carried out with mischievous intent.

McConnell (2002) highlights that everybody connected to the Internet is a possible insider within an organization and ordinarily in an environment which is non-computing the authority to access information is based upon distinct roles which relates to users and the access privileges they have. However, within the modern computing environment roles often change and, in many instances, are less well-defined.

The greatest threat to computer security is symbolized by insiders as these individuals understand fully the commercial side of their organization and the workings of the computer system and they possess confidentiality and the legitimate access to the network which enables them to carry out insider attacks (Nguyen et al. 2003)

THE INSIDER THREAT

The subject of the insider threat is not a new issue as documented reports of this problem date as far back as the 1980s (Chinchani et al. 2005) and as Miller and Maxim (2015) stress it is the responsibility of organizations to face up to the fact that insider threats pose a significant threat and are increasing in difficulty. The task of achieving a conclusive definition for the insider threat is both challenging and complex as so many varied opinions on this subject exist (Humphreys, 2008). Despite this fact there are however, many different definitions presented on this subject some of which including the following:

Cappelli et al. define the insider threat as:

Individuals who were, or previously had been, authorized to use the information systems they eventually employed to perpetrate harm. (Cappelli et al. 2004)

Bishop and Gates explain how the insider threat can be defined with respect of these two primitive actions:

1. violation of a security policy using legitimate access violation of a security policy using legitimate access

2. violation of an access control policy by obtaining unauthorized access (Bishop and Gates, 2008)

Finally, the definition offered by Greitzer et al. differs again as they say:

The insider threat is manifested when human behavior departs from compliance with established policies, regardless of whether it results from malice or a disregard for security policies. (Greitzer et al. 2008)

Greitzer and Frincke (2010) also highlight that despite the vast amount of research which has been carried out on the insider threat, especially in the studies of both the psychology and motivation of insiders, the prediction of insider attacks however still proves exceedingly difficult. The insider threat has commanded a serious amount of attention and it is referred to as the most difficult security problem to deal with because the insider has information which is unknown to outside hackers and as a result, they are able to inflict serious damage (Hunker and Probst, 2011). Internal attacks take place when authorized individuals including trusted employees within an organization execute specific actions in the organization abusing the trust and privileges, they have thus causing harm to the organization (Baracaldo and Joshi, 2012; Chinchani et al. 2005; Greitzer et al. 2008; Blackwell, 2009). As Greitzer et al. (2008) point out insider threats begin when the behavior of humans deviates from compliance with established policies whether it is a result of malicious intent or just a complete disregard for security policies

Trying to escape such threats from insiders is a frightening task as it is essential that employees receive privileges to enable them to carry out their jobs in an efficient manner. However, the provision of too many privileges to an employee can have detrimental effects if they are misused in either an intentional or unintentional fashion (Baracaldo and Joshi, 2012). Greitzer and Frincke (2010) claim that only a small number of employees take part in the type of behavior which could be described as that of an insider threat as the rest of the working population is made up of individuals who are classed as both honest and hard-working. Worryingly however, they also highlight that a report by the U.S. Department of Defense in 1997 confirmed that 87% of those intruders into the Department of Defense which were recognized included either employees or others who were internal to that organization.

The main motivational factor behind many insider attacks is pure and simple financial gain as highlighted by Cappelli et al. (2004) as they claim that carrying out insider attacks for any other purpose is simply not worth the risk. Financial gain can be achieved through different formats depending on the type of organization in which the insider threat takes place. In financial establishments such as banks, the value lies in customer account records and company accounts which give a direct route to funds while other types of organizations such as software companies do not offer such immediate financial rewards as the real value lies in the branded software code (Chinchani et al. 2005). Monetary losses incurred because of insider attacks range in value from five hundred dollars to tens of million dollars with approximately 75% of organizations experiencing a negative impact to their business and 28% reporting a negative influence on their reputations (Baracaldo and Joshi, 2012). All commercial sectors are troubled by the insider threat for several reasons including the following:

- Personal gain and profit (scams, fraud or theft of information and other assets).
- Taking part in reckless behavior whether it was intended to cause harm or not.
- Malicious damage/sabotage which was intended to inflict harm.

Martinez-Moyano et al. (2008) clarifies that data analysis carried out by CERT/CC (coordination center for the computer emergency response team) stresses that the three different insider threats which organizations face include 1) Long term, 2) Sabotage, 3) Espionage or information threat. Franqueira et al. (2010) also highlights that other classifications of the insider threat concentrate solely on the intentions of the insider and likewise organizes them into three separate categories which include the following:

- Theft of information also referred to as espionage when individuals steal private or personal from the organization.
- IT sabotage which occurs when somebody damages the organization or any individual within it.
- Finally, the third category refers to fraud which occurs when someone acquires unwarranted services or property from the organization.

Franqueira et al. (2010) point out however, that there is a connection between these three classifications as impersonators are in a better position to execute fraud while trespassers or those who carry out a lawful action in an illegal or improper manner are in a better place for the execution of sabotage and espionage. According to Greitzer and Frincke (2008) there are many different types of crimes associated with insider threats include Espionage, Sabotage, Terrorism, Embezzlement, Extortion, Bribery and Corruption. Even though insider threats have a higher success rate, they occur less often than outsider attacks as displayed in table 1. They pose a greater risk than their counterparts and have an immediate advantage by having legitimate access to the system (Chinchani et al. 2005).

MALICIOUS/ACCIDENTAL THREATS

The very mention of an insider threat invokes the image of an unhappy employee who is planning to take revenge or a malicious employee who is looking to achieve financial gain. Every organization is afflicted by employees who unintentionally put their employers and the organization itself in danger. Such insider threats however, are not deliberate and take place due to basic unfamiliarity or inexperience (Sarkar, 2010). All insider threats are not the same, as highlighted by Miller and Maxim (2015). There are several different types of insider threats which include the malicious insiders who are current or former employees or even trusted partners of the organization who abuse their positions and their legitimate access to the organization's network system/data making decisions fully aware that their actions will cause damage to the organization and have a full understanding that their actions will have a negative effect on the organization they attack. Such actions include - but are not restricted to - theft of information, fraud and sabotage. In comparison to this there are the insiders who are exploited by outside groups and influenced into carrying out actions which they see as reasonable but will result in damage to the organization. Finally, there is the category of insiders who, despite having privileges, are careless in security responses or cause a security breach through incorrect handling of the organization's main asset, 'information' on the network (Miller and Maxim, 2015; Cole, 2015; Glasser and Lindauer, 2013). Since few employees take part in insider threat activities the task of predicting insider attacks is made more difficult and experts have realized that a character who is despondent in his or her place of work and current job situation signifies the characteristics displayed by a would-be insider threat (Greitzer and Frincke, 2010).

Sarkar (2010) highlights that the largest security threat comes from those individuals with extended privileges and authorized access as great emphasis is placed on the importance of understanding the psychology of those individuals who are involved in insider activity, both malicious and non-malicious. Hunker and Probst (2011) list that there are psychosocial signs which highlight that an individual has the potential to be a malicious insider, some of which include the following:

- Disgruntled
- Accepting feedback
- Anger management

Table 1. Percentage of Insider attacks against outsider attacks

Year	2004	2005	2006	2007	2008	2010
Insider Attacks	29%	20%	32%	31%	34%	27%
Outsider Attacks	71%	80%	68%	69%	66%	73%

(Zawalge et al. 2013)

- Disengagement
- Disregard for authority
- Performance issues

The detection of malicious insiders presents an enormous task as Azaria et al. (2014) explain that initially the quantity of malicious insiders who have been exposed inside any given organization is normally very small, normally only amounting to a mere handful over the space of a decade thus creating an imbalanced data set of more than 99.9% honest users and less than 0.1% of malicious insiders which is not ideal for machine learning algorithms as they naturally assume data is balanced and the use of imbalanced data usually results in high accuracy for the majority class. Azaria et al. (2014) are also keen to point out that detection of malicious insiders is hindered further due to the lack of a publicly available data set for the insider threat as many companies are unwilling to share such data to protect their reputation.

Colwill (2009) emphasizes that the insider threat is constantly present revealing itself in many different formats and that the malicious insider can cause more harm to an organization as it has more advantages than the outside attacker. Colwill (2009) also highlights that those individuals who carry out malicious insider actions have a casual experience or mechanism which influences their motivation and ultimately leads to betrayal. Such experiences can be classified into three main sources which include:

- Rising, intensified or unaddressed dissatisfaction with their role or worth within an organization.
- Recruitment by unfriendly outside individuals or groups.
- The penetration of a malicious threat actor to a trusted position.

Neumann (2010) points out that despite the vast amount of attention which the intentional malicious misuse achieves it would however be considered irresponsible to overlook the acceptable accidental misuse as there is a likelihood that once this type of activity is accepted it could encourage malicious misuse later.

OUTSOURCING

Worldwide communications offer the chance to outsource tasks which were previously carried out within the organization in the home country to sites almost anywhere in the world. Such moves can involve transporting organizational activities to areas which have a favorable taxation structure which is more profitable with lower labor and set-up costs involving companies abroad which offer services at prices which are inexpensive and can deliver skills which are in limited supply. As a result, the move by organizations to outsourcing has become such an attractive proposition that the practice of outsourcing has become universal throughout the public and private sectors (Jones and Colwill, 2008). The quantity of third-party employees who are granted the privilege of long-term access to company systems and information comparable to that of full-time employees is increasing rapidly and as such the position of large volumes of outsider third party personnel is changed to insiders creating confusion over the difference between full-time company employees and third-party personnel (Jones and Colwill, 2008; Munshi et al. 2012).

While the subcontracting and outsourcing of certain tasks offers many benefits such as leading to improvements in efficiency, monetary gains, cheaper labor costs and other potential advantages it does however present the issue of the movement of organizational boundaries where security defenses could have been placed (Gollmann, 2011). As the growing tendency within organizations favors the use of mobile computing, working from home and outsourcing it also increases the probability of insider attacks. Outsourcing increases the possibility of confidential data being breached as information is moved beyond the organization's control and this data is made available to these third parties (Ophoff et al. 2014).

Despite the obvious difficulty of organizations ensuring that the confidential information they share while outsourcing stays confidential and no data breaches occur, outsourcing is however, not without its own difficulties. As highlighted by Colwill (2009) who firstly explains that the language differences can present issues such as misinterpretation misunderstanding at all stages and secondly outsourcing approaches can create further complications as many permanent staff witness roles being outsourced leading to feelings of alienation within the organization and employees are fearful of job security in case their roles within the organization are next in line for outsourcing. Colwill (2009) also highlights that provision of effective education in outsourced locations to the same level as it can be delivered within an organization is difficult due to the numbers of employees hired each month and due their physical location.

With many companies outsourcing many functions to external service providers, possibly in other countries allowing them to avail of the financial benefits, technical issues such as auditing the part of a business process which is being outsourced become difficult. Data protection and collection laws vary from country to country and outsourcing the task of auditing itself can be challenging as protection of the valuable confidential data already collected is of supreme importance and data should be as anonymous as possible so that it does not relate back to a particular individual revealing only the required data which the auditor needs to get results but prevents them from access to data they do not require and as a results prevents them from drawing unwanted conclusions from the data they have access to (Probst et al. 2010).

STOPPING INSIDER THREATS

An extensive and successful insider threat mitigation approach must include the motivational factors and behavior of humans beside organizational factors such as policies, procedures, hiring, training practices and technical weaknesses along with the best practices for avoidance or the early detection of unauthorized insider activity (Greitzer et al. 2008). Most mitigation strategies concentrate on how incidents are performed, detected and how the insider's identification is revealed. Even though such methods are successful in stopping insiders and their activity this occurs only when significant damage has already happened. Monitoring networks, email accounts and the log in activity of employees and their everyday work pattern may find irregularities here or there without causing suspicion. However, by the time these irregularities begin to add up and it is time to act on these findings it is in many cases too late as the insider has already acted and the damage has already been performed (Puleo, 2006).

As organizations develop, they become reliant on information technology with growing importance placed upon information security which was initially viewed as a technology problem which could be tackled using complex hardware and software solutions. However, the increasing number of security breaches has since disproved this theory, proving that it is in fact mainly a people problem as failure by the end users to recognize and follow the technological controls creates a concern as systems are compromised as a result (Yayla. 2011). With the issue of the insider threat growing in difficulty Sarkar

(2010) also highlights that technical solutions are not adequate for this issue as insider threats are essentially a people issue while Whitman (2003) emphasizes that technologists often ignore the human solutions opting instead for technology solutions when in fact it is essential that the human factor must firstly be discussed and incorporate technology for support when needed to achieve the required human behaviors. Colwill (2009) highlights that there is no disputing that the least technical controls for the prevention of insider attacks should include the following:

1. Encryption;
2. Access control;
3. Smallest possible privilege;
4. The use of monitoring, auditing and reporting

Colwill (2009) also points out that standard security policies and procedures are needed, and organizations must enforce said policies showing clearly what is expected of their employees. One method employed is the strict enforcement of company policies and excluding the personal use of any company assets within the workplace. As Colwill (2009) however, highlights that for such a measure to be successful it would need networks to be closed to all but essential business applications thus avoiding access to websites which are not work related and prevent time wasting and the risk of malware infections.

One method of detecting insider misbehavior is to adopt the use of monitoring as a suitable system can substantially reduce the potential of insider attacks and give an alert for the presence any suspicious behavior on the system so that the user's privileges can be restricted and prevent a possible insider attack (Baracaldo and Joshi, 2012). Even though research revealed that 70% of fraud is an insider issue 90% of security controls and monitoring are still focused on the external threat (Colwill, 2009). However, Greitzer and Frincke (2010) point out that although monitoring employees is an important activity in the fight against the prevention of possible insider threats they also highlight that employees could take offence when they learn that the very organization they work hard for each day is monitoring their very activity as only a minority of employees actually engage in insider activity which could possibly harm the organization.

As Flynn, et al. (2003) however, points out the use of monitoring should not just limit itself to individuals within the organization as the growing trend is leaning towards an increase in a mobile workforce who have the potential to cause an insider threat through the malicious use of the many mobile devices which this section of the workforce employ has also increased the potential for malicious use. Organizations need to be aware of the functionality of these mobile devices and in some cases the use of privately-owned mobile devices can be prohibited completely as they could be used to seize sensitive information and remote access to privileged data should be limited to a certain number and keep a log of when users use remote access for further inspection.

The Implementation of strong passwords is strongly recommended as is the practice of precise account management policies (Greitzer and Frincke, 2010; Randazzo et al. 2005). Even though the practice of good password management is strongly recommended within organizations, Randazzo et al. (2005) point out however that active practices such as compulsory password protection and change policies and the use of password-protected screen savers should be encouraged as this reduces the opportunity of insiders carrying out an attack using a fellow employee's computer or account. The importance of effective password practice is also highlighted by Cappelli et al. (2009) who explain that however vigilant an organization is in trying to prevent insider threats, if there is a possibility that their computer accounts can be compromised then the opportunity to side-step manual and automated controls exists and for this reason, password management practices and policies should apply to all employees to ensure that all the activity on any account is attributed to the account holder and only the account holder. If for any reason an employee's employment, consulting or contracting contract needs to be stopped then the immediate deactivation should take place of all their computer accounts, authorization on the system, remote access and privileges within the organization (Randazzo et al. 2005; Flynn et al. 2003)

Organizations should apply separate policies which privileged users should sign as they can cause the most harm having the greatest access to systems, networks and applications and they can log into the system as another user and have greater technical ability. Organizations should also employ techniques which only enable online activity to be attributed to one single employee thus disabling the privileged user from carrying out online activity under the guise of another employee. As with other employees if the privileged user's contract had to be ended then the organization should disable their access to the system at once to prevent an insider attack from a former employee (Flynn et al. 2003).

Organizations should investigate methods by which employees feel they can report suspicious behavior. Occurrences such as the sharing of passwords, trying to access information which an employee does not need to fulfil their duties or trying to gain access to unauthorized information or showing a complete disregard for the organization's safety policies and noncompliance with policies which are in place to protect the organization and the information it safeguards. Encouraging employees to engage in this type of practice will alert security personnel to the noncompliance with policies, thus providing them with the opportunity to investigate the issue before it becomes a major problem (Randazzo et al. 2005).

EDUCATION AND AWARENESS

In many organizations, the bulk of their security budget and time is devoted to placing defenses at the system boundary to protect the information and assets stored from outsiders including thieves and hackers who were engaged in the practice of economic espionage and other illegal activities. The everchanging environment has resulted in major technological advances offering employees the ability to make the most of the opportunity to communicate with the organization's network while still enjoying better mobility and this growth in remote working, home working and the decision to include outsourcing further complicates the issue with an increase in the number of personnel who have access to insider privileges resulting in organizations being exposed to an increased number of insider threats (Jones and Colwill, 2008). Appropriate employee education is a significant contributor to improving the durability of an organization and essential for the effective management of insider threats (Eggenschwiler et al. 2016). In the world of cybercrime Insiders have become one of the most extensively mentioned offenders as numbers increased with the past decade alone seeing a steady rise in the volume of attacks which have been reported as a direct result of insider activity (Eggenschwiler et al. 2016).

Technical solutions can offer valuable protection against security threats in the form of technology which offers a method for both the regulation and control of access to information and helps with the monitoring and detection of malicious activity. They are however unable to deliver a complete solution to the problem as it is the working environment and the human element which deliver the true foundations for success as the activities of cyber criminals takes on many different formats. It is for this very reason that the practice of user awareness and ongoing education are both recognized activities considered crucial in the mitigation of cyber threats (Colwill, 2009; Choo, 2011). Colwill (2009) also points out that the greatest non-technical methods accessible for both human issues and security are possibly education, training and awareness. Eggenschwiler et al. (2016) also emphasize the importance of educational measures, employee training and awareness campaigns highlighting the crucial part they play in the quest for insider threat recovery as they stress that encouragement of relevant education for employees within organizations is essential as the practice of such behavior not only contributes greatly to the strength of an organization but it is vital as it contributes considerably to the provision of an effective insider threat management.

Probst et al. (2010) highlight that employing the use of suitable training and awareness-building education will inspire the preferred security culture which an organization is looking for, while Furnell and Clarke (2005) emphasize that both awareness and understanding of security are prerequisites for the establishment of an effective security culture within an organization. Hunker and Probst (2011) highlight the importance of staff security awareness as they emphasize that it should be regarded as an essential factor for any comprehensive plan and the three levels of user awareness which should exist include the following:

- **Perception:** The user can detect treats in the environment.
- **Understanding:** The user can combine information from different sensors, understand them and the resulting knowledge allowing them decrease risks in the environment.
- **Prediction:** The user can predict future attacks and alter their own behavior to reduce or remove the risk completely.

The roles of awareness, training and education are also recognized by Whitman (2003) who highlights that one of the essential roles performed by an organization's security should be the implementation of a security education, training and awareness (SETA) program. Such programs seek to inform employees of the significance of security and its application in the day-to-day operation of an organization and by pairing this education program with a successful awareness program the desired result can be achieved, namely that employees will be able to recall the information provided, remembering organizational security and be conscious of this security as they deal with important information as they carry out their daily tasks in the workplace.

It is through the implementation or non-implementation of security countermeasures such as technology for monitoring purposes and SETA programs that organizations can prove their level of commitment to security. The awareness of employees along with the identification of the level of commitment shown by organizations will ultimately influence behavioral intent (Aurigemma and Panko, 2012). Siponen (2000) points out that information security awareness refers to a state where employees are aware and truly committed to the organization's security mission and although increased awareness should in theory decrease user related faults and improve the effectiveness of security techniques and procedures. This however is not always the case as in many instances despite creating security awareness amongst employees the true effectiveness of information security techniques and procedures is however lost as many end-users either misuse, misunderstand or simply do not employ the end-user security guidelines. Siponen et al. (2006) highlights that since the main threat to IS (information system) security is created by employees, alternative measures need to be adopted to deal with this issue as it is not enough for employees to be aware of IS security principles but there is a need for them to learn the IS procedures. The use of training sessions, presentations, newsletters, emails and screen savers in the promotion of IS security awareness in organizations is strongly supported as is the use of posters, brochures and newsletters in increasing the IS security messages within organizations. Kyobe (2005) emphasizes the importance of both education and awareness, highlighting that in order to achieve a better understanding of both security principles and application of technology policies in an organization it is fundamental to educate, train and generate security awareness.

Jones and Colwill, (2008) point out that security and awareness programs should be utilized to generate a better understanding of threats which exist both from insiders and outsiders emphasizing the methods employed to gain information or data access including malicious attacks and the direct consequences which can be suffered by an organization as a direct result of failure of controls. Such programs may also have an influence in creating a better level of trust between the employee and their employer as they offer the employee a better understanding and reason for the security policies and protocols which have been put in place as highlighted by Jones and Colwill (2008) and (Colwill, 2009). Employing such training updates also helps increase staff awareness of the organization's security cultural values and an improved staff awareness should realize a reduction in the probability of accidental breaches and a rise in the volume of malicious activity which is detected and reported (Jones and Colwill, 2008). A similar opinion is shared by Anderson (1999) who claims that in many cases the simple employment of measures such as security awareness, education, detection and reaction measures will often help with the insider problem which plagues many organizations.

TAILORING AWARENESS PROGRAMS

The recommendation for organizations whether large or small is the implementation of a security, education, training and awareness program to achieve an effective insider threat management. Although many ideas within cybersecurity awareness are common worldwide each organization should however tailor the training programs appropriately to specifically deal with the policies and meet the needs of their own organization (Cone et al. 2007). Each employee is an individual and when commencing an awareness program within an organization this should be taken into consideration as their different personalities will govern how they deal with compliance in relation to cybersecurity policies and when dealing with SETA programs a one size fits all approach should not be adopted as it is recommended that organizations instead provide a cybersecurity training and influential messages which are modified accordingly to meet the distinctive elements of each employee's personalities (Mc Bride et al. 2012).

Third parties are usually present at some point within processes as outsourcing is commonplace within many of today's organizations and as such, they may need education which is equivalent to that of the organization's full-time employees. It is important to offer solutions which not only develop but also preserve trust and relationships over time with the focus fixed on education and the creation of a better attention to security and support for employees and third parties. Delivering an effective education also presents a difficult hurdle which must be conquered, and ongoing education and awareness should support changes to meet the needs of employees especially in outsourced environments as providers are constantly increasing in numbers and many new employees are hired each month (Colwill, 2009). While the continuation of ongoing awareness programs is necessary especially in settings which have large turnovers of staff, Colwill (2009) expresses that finding out the success of programs in such areas can however prove difficult.

FUTURE RESEARCH DIRECTIONS

The insider threat is a problem which has the potential to cause significant damage, has been increasing in frequency in earlier years and it is a problem which is expected to grow in years to come. Many organizations are not fully aware of the seriousness of the problem that the insider threat poses, and it is essential that the future needs to ensure that all organizations are fully aware of the situation and apply company-wide policies to guarantee that all assets stay protected from the risks that they are constantly facing (Humphreys, 2008). With the increased number of organizations outsourcing tasks it is necessary that those carrying out outsourced tasks are receiving efficient education and awareness training like that of full-time insider employees as those in outsourced environments are regarded in many cases as insiders as they are offered the same privileges and access to information to enable them to carry out their duties.

Cone et al. (2007) highlights that an organization which receives effective security awareness training can greatly improve the confidence an organization has in their information although keeping the attention of a trainee for a satisfactory time span which is long enough to convey the required information is a challenge especially when the targeted audience view the topic as unexciting. New methods of delivering information in awareness training exercises are needed in the future and one such method which engages the target audience is the use of video games as they are involving and keep the attention of those for whom it is designed for (Cone et al. 2007).

Previous studies have concentrated on insider attacks which have already occurred and reactive issues such as what happens post insider attack and as Azaria et al. (2014) points out the detection of past attacks is not a serious problem and interest should be placed on what type of attack will be used in the future if the situation should arise where insider threats are prevented completely. Sarkar (2010) highlights that many professionals refer to the insider threat as a time bomb and the belief is that insider threats are more extensive than the figures which are recorded as many organizations do not divulge figures on the frequency of breaches and how often they occur as it could ultimately damage the reputation of the organization.

CONCLUSION

While awareness and education can both prepare the groundwork, the actual alteration in the behavior of individuals however, involves ceasing the practice of old habits and forming new ones through targeted training. To obtain the greatest benefit this needs to involve more than simply repeating security policies and veer towards building understanding along with development of knowledge of circumstances which cause security risks and the behaviors and reactions which are needed (Colwill, 2009). The insider threat is a well-established security issue and without adequate techniques, there is little that can be done to counteract the problem of the insider threat (Chinchani et al. 2005) and Hunker and Probst (2011) point out that the insider is already present within the system in some shape or form. The threat from insiders physically exists and is increasing in size and according to Miller and Maxim (2015) it is the duty of organizations to come to the reality that the insider threat could strike at any time and they should adopt a more aggressive standpoint in fighting the insider threat and avoid 'the run for cover' attitude.

The issue of the insider threat is an exclusive dilemma which can never be completely eradicated (Miller and Maxim, 2015; Sarkar, 2010; Hunker and Probst, 2011; Chinchani et al. 2005) and it can only be managed by employing mitigation strategies although due to the complexity of employees, contractors, suppliers, consultants outsourcing and the mobility of workforces this is an ongoing challenge for organizations (Sarkar, 2010). The worrying aspect is that although employees should be made aware of the difference between acceptable and unacceptable behavior in the workplace and from firms surveyed only 20% propose to increase awareness in the future and only 40% now offer constant awareness training to employees (Colwill, 2009).

REFERENCES

Abawajy, J. (2014). User preference of cyber security awareness delivery methods. *Behaviour & Information Technology*, *33*(3), 237–248. doi:10.1080/0144929X.2012.708787

Anderson, R. H. (1999). *Research and Development Initiatives Focused on Preventing, Detecting, and Responding to Insider Misuse of Critical Defense Information Systems (No. RAND-CF-151-OSD)*. Rand Corp.

Aurigemma, S., & Panko, R. (2012). January. A composite framework for behavioral compliance with information security policies. In *45th Hawaii International Conference on System Science (HICSS)* (pp. 3248-3257). IEEE.

Azaria, A., Richardson, A., Kraus, S., & Subrahmanian, V. S. (2014). Behavioral analysis of insider threat: A survey and bootstrapped prediction in imbalanced data. *IEEE Transactions on Computational Social Systems*, *1*(2), 135–155. doi:10.1109/TCSS.2014.2377811

Baracaldo, N., & Joshi, J. (2012). A trust-and-risk aware RBAC framework: tackling insider threat. In *Proceedings of the 17th ACM symposium on Access Control Models and Technologies* (pp. 167-176). ACM. 10.1145/2295136.2295168

Bishop, M., & Gates, C. (2008). Defining the insider threat. In *Proceedings of the 4th annual workshop on Cyber security and information intelligence research: developing strategies to meet the cyber security and information intelligence challenges ahead* (p. 15). ACM.

Blackwell, C. (2009). A security architecture to protect against the insider threat from damage, fraud and theft. In *Proceedings of the 5th Annual Workshop on Cyber Security and Information Intelligence Research: Cyber Security and Information Intelligence Challenges and Strategies* (p. 45). ACM. 10.1145/1558607.1558659

Cappelli, D., Moore, A., Trzeciak, R., & Shimeall, T. J. (2009). *Common sense guide to prevention and detection of insider threats 3rd edition–version 3.1*. Published by CERT, Software Engineering Institute, Carnegie Mellon University. Retrieved from http://www. cert. org

Chinchani, R., Iyer, A., Ngo, H. Q., & Upadhyaya, S. (2005). Towards a theory of insider threat assessment. In *Proceedings. International Conference on Dependable Systems and Networks, 2005 (DSN 2005)* (pp. 108-117). IEEE. 10.1109/DSN.2005.94

Choo, K. K. R. (2011). *Cyber threat landscape faced by financial and insurance industry. Trends & issues in crime and criminal justice No. 408*. Canberra: Australian Institute of Criminology.

Claycomb, W. R., & Nicoll, A. (2012). Insider threats to cloud computing: Directions for new research challenges. In *IEEE 36th Annual Computer Software and Applications Conference (COMPSAC)* (pp. 387-394). IEEE.

Cole, E. (2015). *Insider threats and the need for fast and directed response*. SANS Institute InfoSec Reading Room, Tech. Rep.

Colwill, C. (2009). Human factors in information security: The insider threat–Who can you trust these days? *Information Security Technical Report, 14*(4), 186–196. doi:10.1016/j.istr.2010.04.004

Cone, B.D., Irvine, C.E., Thompson, M.F., & Nguyen, T.D. (2007). A video game for cyber security training and awareness. *Computers & Security, 26*(1), 63-72.

Eggenschwiler, J., Agrafiotis, I., & Nurse, J. R. (2016). Insider threat response and recovery strategies in financial services firms. *Computer Fraud & Security, 2016*(11), 12–19. doi:10.1016/S1361-3723(16)30091-4

Flynn, L., Huth, C., Trzeciak, R., Buttles, P., & Nations, A. (2013). *Best Practices Against Insider Threats in All Nations. Technical Note CMU/SEI-2013-TN-023*. Software Engineering Institute.

Franqueira, V. N., van Cleeff, A., van Eck, P., & Wieringa, R. (2010). External insider threat: A real security challenge in enterprise value webs. In *International Conference on Availability, Reliability, and Security 2010 (ARES'10)* (pp. 446-453). IEEE. 10.1109/ARES.2010.40

Furnell, S., & Clarke, N. (2005). Organisational security culture: Embedding security awareness, education and training. *Proceedings of the 4th World Conference on Information Security Education*, 67-74.

Glasser, J., & Lindauer, B. (2013). Bridging the gap: A pragmatic approach to generating insider threat data. In IEEE Security and Privacy Workshops (SPW), 2013 (pp. 98-104). IEEE. doi:10.1109/SPW.2013.37

Greitzer, F. L., & Frincke, D. A. (2010). Combining traditional cyber security audit data with psychosocial data: towards predictive modeling for insider threat mitigation. In *Insider threats in cyber security* (pp. 85–113). Boston, MA: Springer. doi:10.1007/978-1-4419-7133-3_5

Greitzer, F. L., Moore, A. P., Cappelli, D. M., Andrews, D. H., Carroll, L. A., & Hull, T. D. (2008). Combating the insider cyber threat. *IEEE Security and Privacy, 6*(1), 61–64. doi:10.1109/MSP.2008.8

Hayden, M. (1999). *The Insider Threat to U.S. Government Information Systems* (NSTISSAM-INFOSEC/1-99). National Security Agency.

Humphreys, E. (2008). Information security management standards: Compliance, governance and risk management. *Information Security Technical Report, 13*(4), 247–255. doi:10.1016/j.istr.2008.10.010

Hunker, J., & Probst, C. W. (2011). Insiders and Insider Threats-An Overview of Definitions and Mitigation Techniques. *Journal of Wireless Mobile Networks, Ubiquitous Computing and Dependable Applications, 2*(1), 4–27.

Jones, A., & Colwill, C. (2008). Dealing with the malicious insider. *Australian Information Security Management Conference*, 52.

Kyobe, M. (2005). Addressing e-crime and computer security issues in homes and small organizations in South Africa. *European management and technology conference on the integration of management and technology*, 1-13.

Liu, D., Wang, X., & Camp, J. (2008). Game-theoretic modeling and analysis of insider threats. *International Journal of Critical Infrastructure Protection*, *1*, 75–80. doi:10.1016/j.ijcip.2008.08.001

Magklaras, G. B., & Furnell, S. M. (2005). A preliminary model of end user sophistication for insider threat prediction in IT systems. *Computers & Security*, *24*(5), 371–380. doi:10.1016/j.cose.2004.10.003

Martinez-Moyano, I. J., Rich, E., Conrad, S., Andersen, D. F., & Stewart, T. R. (2008). A behavioral theory of insider-threat risks: A system dynamics approach. *ACM Transactions on Modeling and Computer Simulation*, *18*(2), 7. doi:10.1145/1346325.1346328

McBride, M., Carter, L., & Warkentin, M. (2012). *Exploring the role of individual employee characteristics and personality on employee compliance with cybersecurity policies*. RTI International-Institute for Homeland Security Solutions.

McConnell, M. (2002). Information assurance in the twenty-first century. *Computer*, *35*(4), supl16-supl19.

McCormac, A., Parsons, K., & Butavicius, M. (2012). *Preventing and profiling malicious insider attacks (No. DSTO-TR-2697). Defence Science and Technology Organisation Edinburgh*. Command Control Communications And Intelligence Div.

Miller, R., & Maxim, M. (2015). *I Have to Trust Someone.... Don't I?* CA Technologies.

Molok, N. N. A., Ahmad, A., & Chang, S. (2011). Information leakage through online social networking: Opening the doorway for advanced persistence threats. *Journal of the Australian Institute of Professional Intelligence Officers*, *19*(2), 38.

Neumann, P. G. (2010). Combatting insider threats. In *Insider Threats in Cyber Security* (pp. 17–44). Boston, MA: Springer. doi:10.1007/978-1-4419-7133-3_2

Nguyen, N., Reiher, P., & Kuenning, G. H. (2003). Detecting insider threats by monitoring system call activity. In *Information Assurance Workshop*, 2003. *IEEE Systems, Man and Cybernetics Society* (pp. 45-52). IEEE. 10.1109/SMCSIA.2003.1232400

Nurse, J. R., Legg, P. A., Buckley, O., Agrafiotis, I., Wright, G., Whitty, M., ... Creese, S. (2014). A critical reflection on the threat from human insiders–its nature, industry perceptions, and detection approaches. In *International Conference on Human Aspects of Information Security, Privacy, and Trust* (pp. 270-281). Springer. 10.1007/978-3-319-07620-1_24

Park, J. S., & Ho, S. M. (2004). Composite role-based monitoring (CRBM) for countering insider threats. In *International Conference on Intelligence and Security Informatics* (pp. 201-213). Springer. 10.1007/978-3-540-25952-7_15

Probst, C. W., Hunker, J., Gollmann, D., & Bishop, M. (2010). Aspects of insider threats. In *Insider Threats in Cyber Security* (pp. 1–15). Boston, MA: Springer. doi:10.1007/978-1-4419-7133-3_1

Puleo, A. J. (2006). *Mitigating insider threat using human behavior influence models (No. AFIT/GCE/ENG/06-04)*. Air Force Inst Of Tech Wright-Patterson Afb Oh School of Engineering And Management.

Randazzo, M.R., Keeney, M., Kowalski, E., Cappelli, D.M., & Moore, A.P. (2005). *Insider threat study: Illicit cyber activity in the banking and finance sector*. Academic Press.

Sarkar, K. R. (2010). Assessing insider threats to information security using technical, behavioural and organisational measures. *Information Security Technical Report*, *15*(3), 112–133. doi:10.1016/j.istr.2010.11.002

Siponen, M., Pahnila, S., & Mahmood, A. M. (2006). A new model for understanding users' is security compliance. PACIS 2006 Proceedings, 48.

Siponen, M. T. (2000). A conceptual foundation for organizational information security awareness. *Information Management & Computer Security*, *8*(1), 31–41. doi:10.1108/09685220010371394

Stavrou, V., Kandias, M., Karoulas, G., & Gritzalis, D. (2014). Business Process Modeling for Insider threat monitoring and handling. In *International Conference on Trust, Privacy and Security in Digital Business* (pp. 119-131). Springer. 10.1007/978-3-319-09770-1_11

Theoharidou, M., Kokolakis, S., Karyda, M., & Kiountouzis, E. (2005). The insider threat to information systems and the effectiveness of ISO17799. *Computers & Security*, *24*(6), 472–484. doi:10.1016/j.cose.2005.05.002

Ula, M., & Fuadi, W. (2017). A Method for Evaluating Information Security Governance (ISG) Components in Banking Environment. *Journal of Physics: Conference Series*, *812*(1), 012031. doi:10.1088/1742-6596/812/1/012031

Warkentin, M., & Willison, R. (2009). Behavioral and policy issues in information systems security: The insider threat. *European Journal of Information Systems*, *18*(2), 101–105. doi:10.1057/ejis.2009.12

Whitman, M. E. (2003). Enemy at the gate: Threats to information security. *Communications of the ACM*, *46*(8), 91–95. doi:10.1145/859670.859675

Yayla, A. A. (2011). Controlling insider threats with information security policies. *European Conference on Information Systems*, 242.

KEY TERMS AND DEFINITIONS

Compliance: The certification or confirmation that the person performing an action such as an employee does so in a manner which meets company rules and policies and the activity is carried out meeting standards and guidelines as per the conditions of a contract.

Cyber-Attacks: A cyber-attack refers to an assault against a computer system, network, or internet-enabled application or device. Hackers employ a wide range of devices to carry out such attacks. They include malware, ransomware and many other approaches.

Cybercrime: This refers to any illegal activity involving a computer, networked device or a network. Many cybercrimes take place purely for financial gain although some take place against computers or devices to impair them or disable them and others use computers to spread malware, illegal information, images, or other types of data.

Espionage: This is the act of acquiring private information without the authorization from the owner of the confidential information and it is often referred to as spying or obtaining secret information which can be political, military, or industrial in format.

Fraud: This refers to deception, wrongful or criminal misdoings which are solely intended to result in either financial or personal gain.

Malware: This is short for malicious software which is designed purposely with the focus of initiating damage on a computer, server, or computer network. Malware causes damage once it is implanted or introduced in some manner to the target computer in the form of executable code, active content or other software while the user is still unaware that their system has been compromised.

Mitigation: This is the action involved in reducing the force, severity, intensity or painfulness of something and as a result the seriousness or grief experienced from something unpleasant is therefore decreased.

Organizations: This refers to a group of people such as that found in an institution or association who collectively work together in an organized way to achieve a shared purpose or to successfully undertake and achieve collective goals.

Outsider: This is a person or individual who does belong to or who is not involved or included within a specific group of people or organization.

Sabotage: This is a deliberate action whose goal is to weaken an organization by causing disruption, obstruction or destruction. Those that engage in this process are referred to as saboteurs and they usually hide their identities due to the result of the penalties inflicted because of their actions.

Spam: Unwanted or inappropriate messages sent via the Internet normally to a large volume of Internet users usually for advertising purpose or to entice individuals to reveal personal information or spreading malware.

Section 2
Addressing Organizations

Chapter 4
Promoting Cybersecurity Compliance

Mark A. Harris
Augusta University, USA

Ronald Martin
Augusta University, USA

ABSTRACT

In a global online economy, organizations are tasked with protecting their cybersecurity assets. Penalties from failing to protect assets, such as customer data, can severely harm an organization and even lead to bankruptcy. Cybersecurity governance programs need to be aware of the laws and regulations affecting their organizations and use applicable standards or frameworks to develop appropriate cybersecurity polices and controls. Compliance programs then need to monitor policy compliance on a continuing basis. This chapter discusses the laws, regulations, and standards that are used to create cybersecurity polices and the typical tools used to measure compliance. In addition, theoretical cybersecurity compliance research is reviewed to highlight supplementary techniques to improve compliance.

INTRODUCTION

In 2014, Walgreen's Inc. was held liable for $1.4 million due to a pharmacist revealing confidential patient information (HHS, 2018) in violation of the United States (U.S.) Health Insurance Portability and Accountability Act of 1996 (HIPAA). The decision set a precedent by which companies could be held liable for an employee's actions regarding HIPAA compliance (Evans, 2014). Inaction in securing patient health information can also violate HIPAA. In 2017, CardioNet, Inc. reached a $2.5 million settlement for leaving a laptop with patient information unsecured that was consequently stolen (Day, 2017). These are examples from just one of many laws and regulations affecting organizations today. In a violation of the Sarbanes-Oxley Act of 2002, Morgan Stanley paid a $1 million penalty in 2016 for inaction that allowed 730,000 customer account's information to be stolen. The U.S. Securities and Exchange Commission (SEC) claims the company "failed to adopt written policies and procedures reasonably designed to protect customer data" (SEC, 2016). In another Sarbanes-Oxley violation involving

DOI: 10.4018/978-1-5225-7847-5.ch004

Copyright © 2019, IGI Global. Copying or distributing in print or electronic forms without written permission of IGI Global is prohibited.

the loss of customer data, investment advisor R. T. Jones Capital Equities Management paid a $75,000 fine for also failing to adopt written policies and procedures to protect customer data (SEC, 2016). In a violation of the Children's Online Privacy Protection Rule (COPPA), the company VTech was penalized $650,000 for failing to encrypt their Web site's customer data in transit, failing to notify parents of data collected from children, and failing to verify those creating parent accounts were actually adults.

The potential loss from violating laws and regulations requires organizations to establish policies and other governing documents outlining the expectations for employees' behavior regarding adherence to all appropriate laws, regulations, and industry standards. The process of ensuring an enterprise establishes and deploys appropriate controls is generally referred to as cybersecurity governance. The National Institute of Standards and Technology (NIST) defines governance as "the process of establishing and maintaining a framework and supporting management structure and processes to provide assurance that information security strategies are aligned with and support business objectives, are consistent with applicable laws and regulations through adherence to policies and internal controls, and provide assignment of responsibility, all in an effort to manage risk" (Bowen, 2006). The part of the governance definition discussed in this chapter is the adherence to policies and internal controls, often referred to as compliance.

ISACA (n.d.), formerly the Information Systems Audit and Control Association, defines compliance as "adherence to, and the ability to demonstrate adherence to, mandated requirements defined by laws and regulations, as well as voluntary requirements resulting from contractual obligations and internal policies." The enterprise demonstrates compliance with applicable cybersecurity requirements through the creation, deployment and enforcement of cybersecurity policies. Policies are documents that record a high-level principle or course of action indicating the intention and direction management has determined (ISACA, n.d.-a). To help with implementing broad-level policies, organizations often develop accompanying standards, guidelines, and procedures (Nieles et al., 2017). NIST's SP 800-12 states that standards and guidelines specify technologies and methodologies and that procedures detail steps to accomplish tasks. Policy standards, guidelines, and procedures are specific to the organization, but are often informed by externally recognized standards and frameworks.

The content of the policies will be driven by a variety of factors. For instance, certain industries have specific requirements defined by congressional action via legislation and commensurate regulations. HIPAA in the medical field and Sarbanes-Oxley in the financial industry are examples of industry specific legislation requiring cybersecurity related activities. Other influences on policy creation include a desire by an organization to be seen as adherent to externally recognized cybersecurity standards, such as the ISO 27000 series.

Once an organization has cybersecurity policies in place, users are required to abide by them. Users typically are the organization's employees and contracted workers. Users are often informed about the organization's cybersecurity polices through a security education, training, and awareness program. Such programs may have face-to-face trainings, web-based trainings, security awareness posters, and more that take place on a periodic schedule. Once polices are created and users are aware of them, organizations need to ensure compliance. There are many tools available for measuring compliance with cybersecurity polices and some can be automated. For example, firewalls can be configured to block certain sites to maintain compliance. Software scanners can be scheduled to scan the network and equipment for vulnerabilities and configuration issues. Penetration testing can be used by an authorized team to actually exploit weaknesses. Beyond tools, organizations use internal and external auditing to help ensure compliance. Some laws and regulations require periodic auditing, such as HIPAA.

The purpose of this chapter is to explain the motives for an organizational-wide cybersecurity compliance program and to discuss the latest research for improving compliance. The next section explains prominent laws and regulations that influence cybersecurity governance, followed by a section discussing external standards and their influences on cybersecurity governance. Following is a section describing the need for cybersecurity policies and the influences of laws, regulations, and standards. General deterrence theory, the most widely used theory in compliance research, is discussed next, followed by a section describing the findings of theoretical compliance research. The last section concludes the chapter.

COMMON LAWS AND REGULATIONS

Organizations and cybersecurity professionals need to be aware of the many laws and regulations that affect their organizations. In the U.S., there are many federal, state, and local laws. With a world economy, organizations must also be aware of international laws and regulations. Within certain industries, organizations need to be aware of the laws and regulations that are specific to those industries. Below are some of the most influential laws and regulations.

The U.S. Federal Information Security Modernization Act (FISMA) of 2002 created the requirement that all federal agencies develop, document, and implement an agency-wide cybersecurity program (FISMA, 2018). This law only applies to federal agencies and emphasizes a risk-based policy for cost-effective security. Agencies within the federal government are required to: (a) plan for security; (b) ensure appropriate officials are assigned security responsibilities; (c) periodically review the security controls in their systems; and (d) authorize system processing prior to operations and, periodically, thereafter (FISMA, 2018). FISMA publications are developed and published by the National Institute of Standards and Technology (NIST).

The Health Insurance Portability and Accountability Act (HIPAA) provides protections over medical information through the establishment of two primary rules, the privacy rule and the security rule. The security rule "requires appropriate administrative, physical and technical safeguards to ensure the confidentiality, integrity, and security of electronic protected health information" (HHS, 2013). The privacy rule establishes rights for patients over their health information and sets rules and limits on those viewing and receiving their health information (HHS, 2013). The privacy rule also requires appropriate safeguards to ensure the privacy of patient's health information (HHS, 2013). HIPAA establishes the requirement that a covered entity must implement the mechanisms and methods necessary to accomplish the requirements espoused in both rules. Penalties for violations range from \$100 to \$50,000 capped at \$1.5 million per year per violation type. There is no allowance for ignorance or accidental release of confidential patient information (HHS, 2013).

The Family Educational Rights and Privacy Act (FERPA) is a federal law established to protect the privacy of student education records (USDE, 2018). Parents have certain rights over their children's education records until those rights are transferred to the student at age 18, then known as an eligible student. Privacy and protection of the student's record is essential. The school typically needs to "have written permission from the parent or eligible student in order to release information from the student's record" (USDE, 2018). Disclosure of student information to unauthorized entities is a violation of FERPA, but the penalties are a little different than HIPAA. Instead of a monetary fine that requires payment, FERPA violators risk losing federal funding (Hlavac and Easterly, 2015).

In another regulation, the safeguards rule in the Gramm Leach Bliley Act (GLB) requires financial institutions under the jurisdiction of the U.S. Federal Trade Commission (FTC), their affiliates, and service providers to have measures in place to ensure the safety of customer information (FTC, 2018a). Some organizations may not be aware that they are covered by GLB because of the broad definition of "financial institutions," which is anyone engaged in providing financial products or services. This includes the obvious institutions, such as banks and mortgage brokers, but also covers the less obvious, such as ATM operators, professional tax preparers, and real estate appraisers.

The Children's Internet Protection Act (CIPA) requires "qualifying schools and libraries to have an Internet safety policy that includes technology protection measures. (FCC, 2017). Schools and libraries subject to CIPA are required to have a policy that addresses: (a) access by minors to inappropriate material; (b) safety and security of minors using electronic communications; (c) unauthorized access by minors; (d) unauthorized disclosure, use, and dissemination minor's personal information; and (e) measures restricting minor's access to harmful material (FCC, 2017).

In other regulation regarding minors, the Children's Online Privacy Act (COPPA) addresses the collection of information from children under the age of thirteen. COPPA imposes data collection requirements on Web sites and online services that are directed to children under 13 and those that are aware of data being collected from children under 13. Common steps taken include asking the age of the site visitor, getting verifiable parental consent, posting COPPA compliant privacy policy information, notifying parents directly about information collected from children, honoring parent's rights regarding collected information, and implementing reasonable procedures to protect the security of children's information (FTC, 2018b).

The United States is not the only country to impose laws which govern the protection and /or dissemination of personally identifiable information. The European Union's (EU) General Data Protection Regulation (GDPR) codifies privacy rights as well as restrictions on the use of personal information. Some of the prominent rules include the need to: (1) have privacy policies written in clear and straightforward language; (2) have users give affirmative consent before a business can use their data; (3) allow users to move their data to another social media platform; (4) allow users to access their collected data; (5) allow users the right to have their data erased; and (6) notify users without delay about a data breach (EU, n.d.-a). The enforcing authorities can impose penalties to organizations up to 20 million Eurodollars or 4% of the company's worldwide turnover (EU, n.d.-b).

Losses from violations of laws and regulations such as these can significantly impact an organization. The losses resulting from violations can potentially bankrupt a small or medium sized business. The monetary penalty or loss of federal funding are not the only losses organizations need to consider from a violation or breach. There are also typically losses associated with a reduction in reputation, customer loyalty, future lost revenue, stock price loss, and the cost of detecting and mitigating the problem that caused the violation. For those reasons, organizations not explicitly covered by a particular law or regulation would still benefit by adhering to a recognized applicable cybersecurity standard. Since cybersecurity standards enhance security, the ability of an organization to declare and demonstrate they are taking appropriate steps to ensure the protection of their cyber assets can be a valuable differentiator among competitors (Scarfone, Benigni, & Grance, n.d.).

CYBERSECURITY STANDARDS

ISACA defines a standard as "a mandatory requirement, code of practice or specification approved by a recognized external standards organization…" (ISACA, n.d.-a). Standards are adopted by organizations to give formal policies credibility and direction. The ISACA definition is specific to external standards, but an organization may choose to create their own internal standards by either modifying an appropriate external standard or simply creating one that fits their organization. The word "standard" and the work "framework" are often used interchangeably and will be in this chapter. For example, a definition of a framework is "a series of documented, agreed and understood policies, procedures, and processes that define how information is managed in a business, to lower risk and vulnerability, and increase confidence in an ever-connected world" (Wild, 2018). Whether it is called a standard or framework, if an organization adopts it and it becomes mandatory, then it must be complied with. This section focuses on some of the more common external standards. There are several common sources of external standards, including entites such as The International Organization for Standardization (ISO), the National Institute of Standards and Technology (NIST), the Center for Internet Security (CIS), and ISACA.

The ISO 27000 series is a collection of more than a dozen standards that help organizations manage the security of financial information, intellectual property, employee details, and information entrusted to the organization by third parties (ISO, n.d.). The 27001:2013 standard focuses on the requirements for establishing, implementing, maintaining and continually improving an organization's cybersecurity management system (ISO, 2013). In order to ensure wide acceptance and relevance, the requirements are generic and are intended to be applicable to organizations of all sizes and industries (ISO, 2013). An organization that achieves ISO 27001 accreditation will be recognized as following industry best security practices.

NIST has defined over one hundred cyber related standards and guidelines listed as special publications (SPs). While these SPs are aimed at federal systems, they are well suited for adoption by any organization. Of particular interest is SP 800-53, Security and Privacy Controls for Information Systems and Organizations. SP 800-53 is a comprehensive set of safeguarding measures for all types of computing platforms, including general purpose computing systems, cyber-physical systems, cloud and mobile systems, industrial/process control systems, and Internet of Things (IoT) devices (NIST, 2017). The safeguarding measures include security and privacy controls to mitigate risks to organizations.

The Center for Internet Security has identified 20 cyber-defense controls that provide detailed defensive actions against cyber-attacks (CIS, n.d.). The controls are developed by leading cybersecurity experts, including the NSA red and blue teams, the U.S. Department of Energy nuclear energy labs, law enforcement organizations and some of the nation's top forensics and incident response organizations (SANS, n.d.-a). The CIS controls map to most major compliance frameworks such as the NIST Cybersecurity Framework, NIST 800-53, ISO 27000 series and regulations such as PCI DSS, HIPAA, NERC CIP, and FISMA (CIS, n.d.). This means and organization is able to select a framework or standard more specifically applicable to its enterprise and use these 20 controls in conjunction with the chosen framework. The controls are effective because they are created to thwart the most common attack patterns described in the leading threat reports (SANS, n.d.-a).

ISACA created a framework for information technology governance called Control Objectives for Information and related Technology (COBIT), but it now just goes by the name COBIT. COBIT's latest version helps businesses develop, organize and implement strategies around information management and governance (White, 2017). COBIT focuses specifically on security, risk management, and information governance and works well with aligning business and IT goals (White, 2017). COBIT was derived from the expertise of over 140,000 governance, security, risk and assurance professional in 187 countries. (ISACA, n.d.-b). COBIT is generic and can be used in organizations of all sizes, whether public, not-for-profit, or commercial (ISACA, n.d.-b).

While these standards are primarily associated with cybersecurity and governance, there are also industry standards, such as the Payment Card Industry Digital Security Standard (PCI-DSS). PCI-DSS is meant to protect cardholder data and applies to all entities that store, process or transmit cardholder data (PCI, 2010). The standard requires that entities demonstrate adherence to twelve requirements which include installing and maintaining a firewall, encrypting data transmissions over open networks, and maintaining a policy that addresses information for all personnel (PCI, 2010).

These are a few of the common frameworks and standards that are available to help organizations govern their cybersecurity programs. Some are narrow in focus, such as CIS and PCI-DSS, and others are quite elaborate and detailed, such as COBIT. Many of the privacy and security controls and processes described in these standards overlap with one another, so it makes little sense for an organization to adopt all of them. However, because organizations can be very different from one another, many that adopt these frameworks mix-and-match controls to fit their organization. This is the hybrid approach. When an organization is writing a security policy, it makes sense to investigate many of these standards and choose the best combination of controls. Those standards that are used to develop the security policy should then be referenced in the policy itself. This gives credibility to the developed security policy.

POLICIES

In order to properly govern cybersecurity within an organization, security leaders need to be aware of the laws and regulations that affect their organization, business objectives, and organization specific requirements. A primary way of achieving compliance with these objectives is through cybersecurity policies. Security leaders creating policies should also be aware of standards and frameworks that can be used to help address their needs. Many security professionals use these as starting points for creating policies.

While standards identify certain required actions, the demands are not specific to a technology or methodology. The specifics of implementation are determined by the needs of the enterprise within the governance framework and espoused via policies. According to ISACA, policies are "a document that records a high-level principle or course of action that has been decided on" (ISACA, n.d.-a). The principle or course of action described here are those established by the laws, regulations, or adopted standards associated with the enterprise. The SANS Institute, a cyber-related cooperative research and education organization, defines a cybersecurity policy as "a document that outlines specific requirements or rules that must be met" that are usually point-specific, covering a single area (SANS, n.d.-b).

NIST's SP 800-12 defines three types of policies: (1) program policies; (2) issue-specific policies; and (3) system-specific policies (Nieles et al., 2017). The creation of a program policy is the first step in establishing any kind of effective cybersecurity framework for an organization. The program policy creates the cybersecurity program, sets the strategic direction for security within the organization, and assigns resources for implementation (Nieles et al., 2017). Issue-specific policies address a variety of concerns that are important to the organization and can be quite numerous. For example, acceptable use of cyber-related technology, email and Internet privacy, and the establishment and maintenance of a cyber-security education, training, and awareness program are all issue-specific policies. Program and issue-specific policies are high level and have a broad scope because they are written to encompass the entire organization (Nieles et al, 2017). System-specific policies, however, are narrowly focused as they give direction on actions permitted or not permitted on specific systems (Nieles et al., 2017). For example, workstation configuration, firewall configuration, and server configuration are all considered system-specific policies.

The SANS Institute supports a program called the Security Policy Project. The goal of the project is to offer everything needed for the rapid development and implementation of cybersecurity policies (SANS, n.d.-b). In support of this goal, over two dozen security policy templates have been created and published for public consumption. Regardless of policy type, there are several sections within the policies that are consistent: (1) the purpose and the scope of the policy; (2) a link to any standards or frameworks that were used to inform the policy; and (3) compliance. Defined within the compliance section, SANS (n.d.-b) identifies the requirement to measure and determine compliance, list potential exceptions to the policy, list who may approve exceptions, and list the consequences for non-compliance. Not only should a policy establish a directive, but must also define what it means to have correctly complied with the directive.

Once policies are created, controls are used as a means of enforcing the policies and checking and measuring compliance (ISACA, n.d.-a). Controls are typically classified as physical, technical, or administrative (also called procedural). Physical controls are those that exist in the physical world (e.g., locks, doors, and cameras). Technical controls are typically devices or software services (e.g., firewalls and intrusion detection systems). Administrative controls deal with developing and ensuring compliance with policy and procedures. They tend to be documentary in nature and state things that employees may do, must do, or cannot do (SANS, n.d.-b).

Compliance becomes a matter of identifying, implementing, and adhering to the controls. Selecting the proper controls to implement policies can be informed by many factors, such as stakeholder needs and concerns, business mission needs, standards and frameworks, best practices, laws and regulations, executive orders, and directives (NIST, 2017). Implementation of the selected controls will often be a straight forward technical endeavor, however there are other considerations to compliance. For example, if the policy states a firewall must be deployed to ensure a safe demarcation between the internal network and the Internet, simply purchasing an off-the-shelf device does not fulfill the requirements of the policy. The policy may include additional requirements, such as how the device is to be configured. It is important to verify all requirements have been met before compliance can be declared.

Validation of a control's correct configuration, implementation, and operation is often accomplished through auditing. Auditing can be a simple evaluation of a list of requirements in the form of a checklist or it can be a complex exercise like a penetration test (pen-test). A pen-test is the attempt to gain access to a resource without having knowledge of usernames, passwords, and other typical means of access (Northcutt et al., 2006). Pen-tests are often used to verify security on firewalls, networks, and important systems.

It is a reasonable assertion that the creation and implementation of policies and standards implies the expectation of compliance by covered entities, whether persons or corporations. Some laws and regulations, such as HIPAA and Sarbanes-Oxley, require periodic compliance auditing by independent third-party auditors to demonstrate adherence. Regulations require that certain actions are performed or certain issues are addressed, however, they do not specify how accomplish those requirements. This creates a problem since adherence to "federal, state, and international privacy and security laws and regulations often is more an interpretive art than an empirical science…" (Holmes, 2007). A study conducted by the Poneman Institute (2017) found that organizations tend to "invest in compliance activities because of laws and regulations and not necessarily to improve their security posture." This is probably due to the uncertainty created by a fluid interpretation of regulatory expectations combined with the devastating penalties for non-compliance. The issue leads to a business posture where "doing the right thing means doing what's right for the bottom line, not necessarily what's right in terms of the regulation or even what's right for the customer" (Holmes, 2017). One can also imagine the business case where the cost of compliance is simply more expensive than the penalty for non-compliance. The most pressing issue emanating from this situation is that businesses can get sidetracked pursuing accreditation and lose sight of the overall goal, which is achieving a robust and resilient cybersecurity posture.

Many organizations are not willing to accept the risk associated with non-compliance and will instead conduct frequent self-assessments to determine their standing in relation to governing regulations. A self-assessment can gain greater reliability through the adoption of recognized standards by which to compare implemented controls. The National Checklist Program (NCP) sponsored by NIST is an example. The NCP is a publicly available U.S. government repository of security checklists that provide detailed guidance for configuring operating systems and applications (NIST, n.d.). Adopting rigorous standards allows an organization to proactively identify and address potential problems rather than wait for third-part auditors to find compliance issues.

Once controls are implemented and validated, the need to maintain compliance becomes the focus. Compliance is a continuous process that needs to become more efficient, effective, and adjust to environment changes. Laws and regulations change, which affects standards and policies. Business priorities and processes change, which also affects policies. When policies change, the controls and procedures associated with those policies need to adjust. Auditing and self-assessments also need to adjust to measure compliance with the new policies. Large organizations often have a compliance team that is responsible for these tasks.

Cybersecurity education, training, and awareness programs are often used to explain policies to users. However, even the most efficient and effective organizations at creating policies and relaying that information to users can expect less than 100% compliance. There will always be accidental and intentional non-compliance. Some users may understand the policy, but choose non-compliance for a particular reason, such as the policy interferes with productivity. Others may be bad actors and intentionally choose non-compliance to harm the organization. Still others may be non-compliant because they are not aware of a policy or the policy is not clear. While 100% compliance is an unrealistic expectation, organizations should strive to get as close as possible. The next few sections discuss theories and compliance research that may help organizations achieve a higher rate of compliance.

DETERRENCE THEORY

There have been many theoretical studies that investigated compliance with cybersecurity policies. These studies used multiple theoretical backgrounds, such as the use of deterrence theory, social bond theory, the theory of planned behavior, protection motivation theory, and the theory of reasoned action. It is beyond the scope of this chapter to discuss all of these theories in detail. However, it is prudent to discuss deterrence theory because it is the most common theory used in compliance research.

Deterrence Theory can formally be traced back to the 1700's in the criminology writings of Cesare Beccaria and Jeremy Bentham (Tomlinson, 2016). Informally, the principles of deterrence theory can be traced back to the beginning of civilization. There are three basic principles, the first of which is that a message must be relayed to a target group, such as being found guilty of stealing from another will lead to imprisonment. Second, the target group receives the message and perceives it as a threat. The last principle is the target group makes a rational choice based on the information and avoids engaging in the activity that leads to punishment. The easiest of these principles to achieve is principle one, relaying the punishment information to the target group. In cybersecurity, this can be accomplished with cybersecurity education, training, and awareness. Principles two and three are more problematic (Tomlinson, 2016). Some individuals might not be threatened by the sanctions and others might not make choices that the general society considers rational. Research has shown that rational choices can become less rational when an individual is under the influence of drugs and/or alcohol (Chapman & MacKenzie, 2010). This may also be true when individuals are having problems at home, such as marriage or financial difficulties.

Deterrence theory has two major uses, specific deterrence and general deterrence. Specific deterrence posits that individuals that commit crimes and are caught and punished will be deterred from committing future crimes (Tomlinson, 2016). A sanction placed against someone "is theorized to reduce the probability of that individual committing the same offense again" (Harris, 2012). General deterrence is focused on reducing deviance in the general population by society witnessing others getting caught and punished. It is theorized that "individuals in society are deterred from deviant activities because of their fear of punishment and that fear is reinforced by their knowledge of others getting punished" (Harris, 2012). Specific deterrence is more prevalent in cybersecurity research.

Punishment in deterrence theory is divided into three main factors: severity of the punishment, certainty of getting punished, and the celerity of the punishment. Severity is the painfulness or unpleasantness of a sanction. Certainty is the probability that a deviant behavior will be detected and punished. Celerity, also known as swiftness, is the quickness to which the punishment follows the crime. Most of the deterrence theory research is on the effects of severity and certainty of punishment in deterring undesirable behavior and there has been little research on the effect of celerity. Severity of punishment was once thought to be the main deterrent, but overcrowded prisons and other research suggest otherwise (Tomlinson, 2016). In research by Schneider & Ervin (1990), the authors concluded that people who had been punished more severely actually engaged in more deviant behavior. The authors surmised that severe punishments caused chain reactions that reduced the individual's opportunities for normalized behavior. Certainty of punishment has had mixed results in research for its deterring effect. Kleck et al. (2005) found that perceived certainty of sanctions has very little effect on individuals reoffending. Other research had contradicting findings where the certainty of sanctions worked on some individuals, but not others (Matthews & Agnew, 2008). Swiftness of punishment is the least researched factor and most research indicated that it was a relevant factor in deterring deviant behavior (Tomlinson, 2016).

Deterrence theory has evolved in the last 30 years, particularly when Stafford and Warr (1993) introduced the deterring effect of avoiding punishment and exposure to others avoiding punishment. Doing something wrong and getting away with it reduces the deterring effect. Witnessing others doing something wrong and getting away with it also reduces the deterring effect. An expanded Stafford and Warr (1993) model has four categories of experience: (1) direct experience of punishment; (2) direct experience of punishment avoidance; (3) indirect (vicarious) experience of punishment; and (4) indirect (vicarious) experience with punishment avoidance. This new model adds a new dimension of perceptual influence from others (Harris & Furnell, 2012). For example, indirect punishment avoidance would posit that an employee may perceive less risk in violating a policy if they witness others violating policies with no consequences. The opposite of that would suggest that the perception of risk would increase if an employee witnesses other violating policies and suffering consequences (Harris & Furnell, 2012). An employee that breaks the rules set by policy and gets away with may actually increase deviant behavior due to reduced perceived risk (Stafford and Warr, 1993). An employee that sees others breaking policy rules and getting away with it again will perceive less risk in breaking policy rules. On the other hand, the opposite may be true for an organization that enforces sanctions on those violating policy rules. Specific deterrence may come into play when someone breaks a policy rule and is punished. They may be deterred from breaking future policy rules. Also, an employee may be deterred from breaking policy rules if they witness others breaking policy rules and getting punished. An organization that enforces sanctions on policy violators may have greater compliance.

Sanctions are often classified as either formal sanctions, such as losing one's job or going to jail, and informal sanctions, such as shame, guilt, and embarrassment. Formal sanctions are typically imposed by law enforcement, governing entity, or workplace, where rules are established and offenses are punished. However, more recent literature (Pogarsky & Piquero, 2004, Nagin & Pogarsky, 2001) has investigated the deterrent effects of informal sanctions. These types of sanctions often exceed those of formal legal sanction threats (Grasmick & Bursik, 1990). For example, the informal sanction of shame and embarrassment for a sex offender conviction is often more severe than the legal penalties issued through the judicial system. Informal sanctions can last must longer than formal legal sanctions.

OTHER THEORETICAL COMPLIANCE RESEARCH

Research in deterrence theory and compliance with cybersecurity policy has yielded mixed results. In a study that investigated deterrence theory and user's adherence to cybersecurity policies, D'Arcy et al. (2009) found that perceived severity of sanctions was more effective in reducing IS misuses than certainty of sanctions. Users were more concerned with the severity of the sanction than the certainly of being caught. In trying to explain the insignificance of certainty of sanctions, the authors suggest that as users become more aware of security policy, they might also become more aware of the difficulty in detecting violations. In addition, this study found three practices that deter information systems misuse: user awareness of security policies; security education, training, and awareness programs; and monitoring (D'Arcy, et al., 2009). These findings suggest that it is effective for security education, training, and awareness programs to make users aware of the security policies and the sanctions for violations.

In other research investigating severity, Cheng et al. (2013) found that the severity of the sanctions was a significant factor in determining one's intentions to violate security policy. Finding significance in the severity of sanctions is contradictory to typical findings in sociology and criminology (Cheng et al., 2013). Also contrary to typical findings, the authors found that the certainty of sanctions was not a significant factor.

While these studies found that the severity of sanctions were significant factors, multiple studies contradict those results. Herath and Rao (2009) found that perceived certainty of punishment was the most effective in shaping behavior, and that severity was not. Surprisingly, severity of punishment actually had a negative effect and reduced compliance (Herath and Rao, 2009).

In other research using deterrence theory and rational choice theory, Li et al., (2010) also found a negative effect of severity of sanctions, where there was a reduction of compliance. In addition, the researchers also measured severity against one's personal norms, which are the expectations people have for themselves about doing what is considered right and avoiding what is considered wrong. The authors found that severity of sanctions was influential only to those with low personal norms, which was 4% of their participants. For those with moderate or high personal norms, severity had a negative effect. This finding indicates that severity of sanctions gets to a certain point with employees with moderate and high personal norms where the sanctions become too severe and compliance is reduced. Both of these studies found significance in informal influences, which are discussed later.

In another study that investigated deterrence theory and cybersecurity policy compliance, Chen et al. (2018) dug deeper into the mixed results of previous studies. The authors introduced several mediating and control variables to see how they interacted with the significance of the severity of sanctions. The researchers found that none of the new variables interacted with sanction severity and the intentions to comply with policies (Chen, et al., 2018). However, with these other variables considered, the severity of sanctions was no longer a significant factor. Investigating further, the researchers concluded that an employee's choice to comply or not comply with policies is primarily based on informal sanctions and personal capability and not formal sanctions. The informal sanctions investigated included social disapproval, such as condemnation by peers, and self-disapproval, such as moral beliefs (Chen, et al., 2018). Personal capability refers to general computer self-efficacy or one's overall confidence in their ability to use a computer, application, or complete specific information systems tasks. Condemnation of peers, self-disapproval, and self-efficacy were found to be more significant than formal sanctions. The authors suggest that organizations provide employees with an environment to learn organizational values and develop their personal capabilities.

Herath and Rao (2009) also investigated informal sanctions and the intent to follow security policies. They found that both intrinsic and extrinsic motivators influenced intentions more than certainty and severity of punishment. Intrinsically, if employees found their security behavior had a positive impact on the organization, they were more likely to follow policies. The most significant influence was extrinsically, where employees were influenced by the expected beliefs of their superiors, IT management, and peers. If they thought these groups embraced security policy, then they were influenced to also embrace security policy. These findings suggest that creating on organizational wide security culture is important.

Also investigating informal sanctions, Harris and Furnell (2012) measured user's reactions to anticipated shaming by their organization for policy non-compliance. Users were presented a scenario where they were trained on the proper way of complying with a cybersecurity policy, but failed to do so after training. They were given various potential punishments that involved typical punishments, such as getting a verbal warning all the way up to being fired. They were also given various anticipated shaming punishments, such as having their names and photos emailed to co-workers and having their names called out over the loud speaker. Users ranked potential responses from least severe to most severe. The results showed the five least severe potential responses to their non-compliance were all non-peer shaming punishments, with the most severe of those five as being written up by management. The next more severely ranked punishment was having their names emailed to co-workers, followed by being asked to stand at the next corporate meeting. Considered yet more severe was losing 10% of a week's wages, followed by having their names called out over a loud speaker when only employees can hear. Continuing up the list of severity, next was having their names and photos emailed to co-workers. The non-peer shaming punishment of getting demoted was next, followed by having their names and photos placed on employee bulletin boards and in break rooms. The most severe punishment was getting fired. An interesting finding is that getting demoted was considered less severe than having their names and photos put on bulletin boards and in break rooms. While this research is interesting, it should be not be used in practice without careful consideration. Peer shaming employees may lead to discontent and a toxic work environment. If peer shaming is to be considered, it is recommended management start with less severe methods.

Cheng et al. (2013) used social bond theory to investigate employee's intentions to violate cybersecurity policy. According to the theory, individuals that possess stronger social ties are less likely to engage in deviant behavior (Cheng, et al., 2013). The first of four components of the theory is attachment, which refers to the affection and respect that an individual has with significant others (Hirschi, 1969). The authors investigated employee's attachment to their immediate supervisors, co-workers, job, and organization. They found that attachment to one's immediate supervisor and co-workers had no effect on policy violations intention, but the attachment to one's job and organization were significant (Cheng et al., 2013). This implies that the more someone cares about their job and organization, the more likely they are to follow policies. The second component of social bond theory is commitment, which refers to the aspiration of attaining a high status job (Cheng et al., 2013). The third component is involvement, which refers to the amount of time one spends on conventional activities, such as job related tasks or organizational activities. The fourth component is beliefs, which refers to the degree to which individuals believe and accept a conventional value system, such as a society's value system of following rules (Cheng et al., 2013). The authors found that commitment and belief both had significant effects on individual's policy violation intention, but involvement was not significant. From the four components of social bond theory, the authors concluded that attachment to one's job and organization, as well as their desire for attaining a high status job, were all the most significant indicators of one's policy violations intent.

Cheng et al (2013) also investigated social pressure and peer behavior for policy violations intent. Social pressure in the cybersecurity context refers to the individual's pressure to meet significant other's and organizational expectations. Significant others may refer to supervisors, co-workers, friends, and family. Peer behavior refers to the behavior of co-workers in regard to following policies. The authors concluded that social pressure and peer behavior were both significant. The expectations of their immediate supervisor, co-workers, organization, and family have a great influence on employee's policy violation intentions (Chen et al., 2013). Also, the perceived behavior of co-workers also had a significant impact. This part of the authors study crosses over general deterrence theory's indirect view of punishment and the anticipation of shaming.

Safa et al. (2016) used social bond theory and involvement theory to investigate compliance. Involvement theory refers to the energy, time, and participation in a particular activity (Lee et al., 2004). Involvement influences attitude and can manifest in various forms (Safa et al., 2016). In this research, involvement refers to cybersecurity knowledge sharing, collaboration, intervention, and experience of the employee. The researchers found that all of these had a significant effect on employee's attitude towards compliance. So the more an organization can get their employees involved with cybersecurity, such as awareness, training, and education programs, the better for policy compliance. Like Chen et al., 2013, the authors found that commitment influenced one's intention to comply with policies. Attachment was defined by these researchers as the respect and affection that an individual has with significant others (Safa et al., 2016). Attachment was found to be insignificant, which conflicts with the findings of Chen et al., 2013, where they found social pressure and peer behavior was influential.

Drawing from psychology research, Han et al. (2017) investigated the intent to comply with policy with a concept known as psychological contract. Psychological contract is defined as "an individual's belief about the mutual obligations existing between an individual and his/her organization" (Rousseau, 1995 as cited by Han et al., 2017). Breaches of psychological contract occur when and employee feels what was promised was not received, creating a negative imbalance. Such breaches from the employee's perspective reduces their contributions to the organization (Han, et al., 2017). Employees that receive more from the organization than they were promised perceive a positive imbalance and increase their contributions to the organization. A model was created that investigated perceived benefit and perceived cost of compliance and the intention to comply. For example, the cost of changing one's password monthly is time consuming and demands effort, while the benefit of doing so could be increased security (Han, et al., 2017). This cost benefit analysis is done for each policy an employee makes a compliance decision about. The researchers used psychological contract as a mediating variable between perceived cost of compliance and the intention to comply. They found that managers were influenced by psychological contract and non-management employees were not. The authors suggest these mixed results are due to differing employee investment in the organization. More importantly, the researchers also found that both groups were influenced by the perceived benefit of polices and not influenced by perceived cost. This suggests that educating employees about the benefit of policies is a way to increase compliance.

Also drawing from psychology research, Vance et al (2013) used the theory of accountability to investigate access policy violations. The authors found that increased identifiability, monitoring awareness, evaluation awareness, and social presence led to an increase in the accountability of the user's actions and thus a reduced intention to violate access policies. The authors suggest that system design artifacts that increase accountability will reduce access policy violations. In a follow-up study, Vance et al. (2015) applied the hypothetical scenarios from the first study to an actual user interface design on a records system in a large organization with professional users. The authors demonstrated that their user interface artifacts substantially increased accountability and reduced the intent to violate access policies. While the theory of accountability is related to deterrence theory's certainty of punishment, the theory differs from deterrence theory in that the theory of accountability's central mechanism is self-image preservation and social approval and not a cost-benefit analysis (Vance et al., 2015).

While much of compliance research focuses on deterrence, there has been little research investigating the influence of rewards on cybersecurity compliance, especially tangible rewards like financial incentives. The rewards research to date has yielded mixed results. In a research paper by Siponen et al., 2010, the authors investigated the intention to comply with cybersecurity policies and the actual compliance with policies using protection motivation theory and deterrence theory. Of particular interest in this study is the inclusion of rewards, both intrinsic (intangible) and extrinsic (tangible). Intrinsic rewards can be praise from peers and extrinsic rewards may be money, gold stars, and metals (Siponen et al., 2010). Results showed that deterrents had significant influence on actual compliance and rewards did not. The authors suggested that management should deemphasize using tangible and intangible rewards. However, the research did show that normative beliefs and self-efficacy had significant affects.

In another study that also investigated deterrence theory and rewards, Chen, Ramamurthy, and Wen (2013) had contradicting results. The authors found that the level of reward had a significant affect on compliance intention. This means the better the reward, the more likely they were to comply. The authors also concluded that the severity and certainty of punishment also had significant affects. The interaction of reward levels and punishment was also investigated and the researchers found that the impact of punishment on the intention to comply with security policies was greater when reward was low than when reward was high (Chen, Ramamurthy, and Wen, 2013). Rewards had very little impact, whether low or high rewards, when punishment severity was high. This indicates that the best situation for implementing a reward program is to do so with low severity punishments.

CONCLUSION

Due to the potential severe penalties, both legal and non-legal, from failing to secure organizational cybersecurity assets, organizations must run a strong cybersecurity governance program. Cybersecurity professionals need to be aware of the laws and regulations that affect their organization, as well as the business mission, and organization specific needs. With the guidance of standards and frameworks, cybersecurity professionals need to create a strong cybersecurity program and strong cybersecurity policies. Compliance with these policies is essential to the vitality of the organization. Typically, organizations use cybersecurity education, training, and awareness programs to inform employees about cybersecurity policies. It is also typical for organizations to use tools and auditing to ensure compliance with policies, laws, and regulations. However, no organization can expect 100% compliance, but should instead continuously improve their compliance programs with the goal of getting as close as possible. This is where the technical aspects of auditing and monitoring for compliance can be mixed with the social aspects from theoretical research to improve compliance.

Deterrence theory, the primary theory used in compliance research, suggests that people breaking the rules and getting away with it and those seeing others breaking rules and getting away with it have reduced perceptions of risk that can lead to increased policy violations (Strafford and Warr, 1993). Cybersecurity professionals should be diligent at enforcing sanctions for those violating policy. However, research also shows that most users move toward non-compliance once sanction severity gets to a certain point (Li et al., 2010). This suggests that organizations impose sanctions and hold users accountable for violations, but limit the severity of the sanctions. The severity of sanctions also affects the use of rewards systems for compliance. For example, research suggests rewards can be effective, but only when coupled with low severity punishments (Chen, Ramamurthy, and Wen, 2013). Once the severity of punishment reached a certain point, rewards became ineffective.

More important than sanctions were intrinsic and extrinsic motivators. Social and peer pressure were significant factors in increasing compliance (Cheng et al., 2013). Users were influenced more by the expected beliefs of their peers and superiors than by sanctions. Creating a cybersecurity culture that propagates a strong security message from the top down can increase compliance (Herath and Rao, 2009). Also based on intrinsic motivators, the theory of accountability suggests that specific user-interface designs can increase accountability and decrease the intent to violate policies (Vance et al., 2015).

Research also indicates that organizations can do more to increase cybersecurity compliance by investing more in their employees. For example, research shows organizations should help users learn organizational values and develop their personal capabilities (Chen et al., 2018). Self-efficacy is important, so training users on the use of computing devices and applications can lead to increased compliance (Chen et al., 2018). In addition, organizations can invest in their employees by creating environments where employees feel respected and have a sense of belonging. Research shows this attachment to the organization increases the likelihood of complying with policies (Cheng et al., 2013). Organizations should also create paths for career advancement. Research demonstrates that employees with higher levels of investment and those seeking advancement in the organization are more likely to comply with policies (Cheng et al., 2013). Research also demonstrates that employees that feel the organization is fair to them are more likely to comply with policies, while those that feel the organization is unfair are less likely (Han et al., 2017). This fairness can come in many forms, such as wages and opportunities for advancement.

Cybersecurity education, training, and awareness programs are also essential to increasing compliance (Safa et al., 2016). Not only do users learn about the policies, but they should also learn about the benefits of policy compliance. Research indicates there is an increase in compliance when users are aware of the policy and see the connection between the policy and the benefit to the organization (Han et al., 2017), as well as the sanctions for non-compliance (D'Arcy et al., 2009).

In order to maximize compliance, organizations should continuously monitor and adjust their compliance programs to take advantage of the latest technologies and compliance research. Some combination of technologies and theoretical concepts may prove to be most effective.

REFERENCES

Bowen, P., Hash, J., & Wilson, M. (2006). *NIST Special Publication 800-100: Information Security Handbook: A Guide for Managers*. Retrieved July 9, 2018 from https://nvlpubs.nist.gov/nistpubs/Legacy/SP/nistspecialpublication800-100.pdf

Chapman, S., & MacKenzie, R. (2010). The global research neglect of unassisted smoking cessation: Causes and consequences. *PLoS Medicine*, *7*(2), e1000216.

Chen, X., Wu, D., Chen, L., & Teng, J. (2018). Sanction severity and employees' information security policy compliance: Investigating mediating, moderating, and control variables. *Information & Management*, *55*(8), 1049–1060. doi:10.1016/j.im.2018.05.011

Chen, Y., Ramamurthy, K., & Wen, K. (2013). Organizations' information security policy compliance: Stick or carrot approach? *Journal of Management Information Systems*, *29*(3), 157–188. doi:10.2753/MIS0742-1222290305

Cheng, L., Li, Y., Li, W., Holm, E., & Zhai, Q. (2013). Understanding the violation of is security policy in organization: An integrated model based on social control and deterrence theory. *Computers & Security*, *39*, 447–459. doi:10.1016/j.cose.2013.09.009

CIS. (n.d.). *CIS controls frequently asked questions (FAQ)*. Retrieved from https://www.cisecurity.org/controls/cis-controls-faq/

D'Arcy, J., Hovav, A., & Galletta, D. (2009). User awareness of security countermeasures and its impact on information systems misuse: A Deterrence Approach. *Information Systems Research*, *20*(1), 79–98. doi:10.1287/isre.1070.0160

Day, J. (2017). *$2.5 Million Settlement Reached as HIPAA Crackdown Continues on Unsecured Portable Devices*. Retrieved from www.jdsupra.com/legalnews/2-5-million-settlement-reached-as-hipaa-64406/

EU. (n.d.a). *European Commission: 2018 reform of EU data protection rules*. Retrieved from https://ec.europa.eu/commission/priorities/justice-and-fundamental-rights/data-protection/2018-reform-eu-data-protection-rules_en, Accessed July 11, 2018.

EU. (n.d.b). *European Commission: A new era for data protection in the EU: What changes after May 2018?* Retrieved from https://ec.europa.eu/commission/sites/beta-political/files/data-protection-factsheet-changes_en.pdf

Evans, T. (2014). $1.44M HIPAA award upheld after Walgreen pharmacist shared patient data. *Indianapolis Star*. Retrieved from www.indystar.com/story/news/2014/11/14/m-award-upheld-walgreen-pharmacist-shared-patient-data/19035783/

FCC. (2017). *Children's Internet Protection Act: CIPA*. Retrieved from https://www.fcc.gov/consumers/guides/childrens-internet-protection-act

FISMA. (2018). Retrieved from https://csrc.nist.gov/Projects/Risk-Management/Detailed-Overview

FTC. (2018a). *Financial institutions and customer information: Complying with the safeguards rule*. Retrieved from https://www.ftc.gov/tips-advice/business-center/guidance/financial-institutions-customer-information-complying

FTC. (2018b). *Federal Trade Commission: children's online privacy protection rule: a six-step compliance plan for your business*. Retrieved from https://www.ftc.gov/tips-advice/business-center/guidance/childrens-online-privacy-protection-rule-six-step-compliance

Grasmick, H., & Bursik, R. (1990). Conscience, significant others, and rational choice: Extending the deterrence model. *Law & Society Review*, *24*(3), 837–861. doi:10.2307/3053861

Han, J., Kim, Y., & Kim, H. (2017). An integrative model of information security policy compliance with psychological contract: Examining a bilateral perspective. *Computers & Security*, *66*, 52–65. doi:10.1016/j.cose.2016.12.016

Harris, M., & Furnell, S. (2012). Routes to security compliance: Be good or be shamed? *Computer Fraud & Security*, *2012*(12), 12–20. doi:10.1016/S1361-3723(12)70122-7

Harris, M. A. (2012). Shaming as a technique for information security policy and training adherence. *Proceedings of the Southern Association for Information Systems Conference*, 92-97.

Herath, T., & Rao, H. (2009). Encouraging information security behaviors in organizations: role of penalties, pressures and perceived effectiveness. *Decision Support Systems, 47*, 154-165.

HHS. (2013). *HIPAA administrative simplification, u.s. department of health and human services office for civil rights*. Retrieved from https://www.hhs.gov/sites/default/files/ocr/privacy/hipaa/administrative/combined/hipaa-simplification-201303.pdf?language=es

Hirschi, T. (1969). *Causes of delinquency*. Berkeley, CA: University of California Press.

Hlavac, G., & Easterly, E. (2015). *Ferpa primer: The basics and beyond*. Retrieved March 3, 2019 from https://www.naceweb.org/public-policy-and-legal/legal-issues/ferpa-primer-the-basics-and-beyond/

Holmes, A. (2007). *Your guide to good-enough compliance*. Retrieved from https://www.cio.com/article/2439324/risk-management/your-guide-to-good-enough-compliance.html

ISACA. (n.d.). Retrieved July 7, 2018 from https://www.isaca.org/about-isaca/Pages/default.aspx

ISACA. (n.d.a). Retrieved from https://www.isaca.org/Pages/Glossary.aspx

ISACA. (n.d.b). Retrieved from https://cobitonline.isaca.org/about

ISO. (2013). *International Organization for Standardization, ISO/IEC 27001: 2013, information technology, security techniques, information security management systems, Requirements*. Retrieved from https://www.iso.org/obp/ui/#iso:std:iso-iec:27001:ed-2:v1:en

ISO. (n.d.). *ISO/IEC 27000 family - information security management systems*. Retrieved from https://www.iso.org/isoiec-27001-information-security.html

Kleck, G., Sever, B., Li, S., & Gertz, M. (2005). The missing link in general deterrence research. *Criminology*, *43*(3), 623–660. doi:10.1111/j.0011-1348.2005.00019.x

Lee, S., Lee, S.-G., & Yoo, S. (2004). An intergrative model of computer abuse based on social control and general deterrence theories. *Information & Management*, *41*(6), 707–718. doi:10.1016/j.im.2003.08.008

Li, H., Zhang, J., & Sarathy, R. (2010). Understanding compliance with internet use policy from the perspective of rational choice theory. *Decision Support Systems*, *48*(4), 635–645. doi:10.1016/j.dss.2009.12.005

Matthews, S. K., & Agnew, R. (2008). Extending deterrence theory: Do delinquent peers condition the relationship between perceptions of getting caught and offending? *Journal of Research in Crime and Delinquency*, *45*(2), 91–118. doi:10.1177/0022427807313702

Nagin, D., & Pogarsky, G. (2001). Integrating celerity, impulsivity, and extralegal sanction threats into a model of general deterrence: Theory and evidence. *Criminology*, *39*(4), 865–888. doi:10.1111/j.1745-9125.2001.tb00943.x

Nieles, M., Dempsey, K., & Pillitteri, V. (2017). *NIST Special Publication 800-12 Revision 1: An introduction to information security*. Retrieved from https://nvlpubs.nist.gov/nistpubs/SpecialPublications/NIST.SP.800-12r1.pdf

NIST. (2017). *Draft special publication 800-53, r5. Security and privacy controls for information systems and organizations*. Retrieved from https://csrc.nist.gov/CSRC/media//Publications/sp/800-53/rev-5/draft/documents/sp800-53r5-draft.pdf

NIST. (n.d.). *NIST: national vulnerability database*. Retrieved from https://nvd.nist.gov/ncp/repository

Northcutt, S., Shenk, J., Shackleford, D., Rosenberg, T., Siles, R., & Mancini, S. (2006). *SANS Institute, penetration testing: assessing your overall security before attackers do*. Retrieved from https://www.sans.org/reading-room/whitepapers/analyst/penetration-testing-assessing-security-attackers-34635

PCI. (2010). *PCI security standards council, PCI DSS quick reference guide*. Retrieved July 13, 2018 from https://www.pcisecuritystandards.org/documents/PCI%20SSC%20Quick%20Reference%20Guide.pdf

PCI. (2010). *PCI security standards council, PCI DSS quick reference guide*. Retrieved from https://www.pcisecuritystandards.org/documents/PCI%20SSC%20Quick%20Reference%20Guide.pdf

Pogarsky, G., Piquero, A., & Paternoster, R. (2004). Modeling change in perceptions about sanction threats: The neglected linkage in deterrence theory. *Journal of Quantitative Criminology*, *20*(4), 343–369. doi:10.100710940-004-5868-z

Ponemon Institute. (2017). *The true cost of compliance with data projection regulations*. Retrieved from https://www.globalscape.com/resources/whitepapers/data-protection-regulations-study

Rousseau, D. (1995). *Psychological contracts in organizations: Understanding written and unwritten agreements*. Sage Publications.

Safa, N., Von Solms, R., & Furnell, S. (2016). Information security policy compliance model in organizations. *Computers & Security*, *56*, 70–82. doi:10.1016/j.cose.2015.10.006

SANS. (n.d.a). *CIS critical security controls*. Retrieved from https://www.sans.org/critical-security-controls

SANS. (n.d.b). *SANS Institute, information security policy templates*. Retrieved from https://www.sans.org/security-resources/policies

Scarfone, Benigni, & Grance (n.d.). *Cyber Security Standards, NIST.* Retrieved March 4, 2019 from https://ws680.nist.gov/publication/get_pdf.cfm?pub_id=152153

Schneider, A. L., & Ervin, L. (1990). Specific deterrence, rational choice, and decision heuristics: Applications in juvenile justice. *Social Science Quarterly*, *71*(3), 585–601.

SEC. (2016). *SEC: Morgan Stanley failed to safeguard customer data*. Retrieved from https://www.sec.gov/news/pressrelease/2016-112.html

Siponen, M., Pahnila, S., & Mahmood, A. (2010). *Compliance with information security policies: an empirical investigation.* IEEE Computer Society.

Stafford, M. C., & Warr, M. (1993). A reconceptualization of general and specific deterrence. *Journal of Research in Crime and Delinquency*, *30*(2), 123–135. doi:10.1177/0022427893030002001

Tomlinson, K. (2016). An examination of deterrence theory: Where do we stand? *Federal Review*, *80*, 3.

USDE. (2018). *U.S. Department of Education: Family Educational Rights and Privacy Act (FERPA)*. Retrieved from https://www2.ed.gov/policy/gen/guid/fpco/ferpa/index.html

Vance, A., Lowry, P., & Eggett, D. (2013). Using accountability to reduce access policy violations in information systems. *Journal of Management Information Systems*, *29*(4), 263–289. doi:10.2753/MIS0742-1222290410

Vance, A., Lowry, P., & Eggett, D. (2015). Increasing accountability through user-interface design artifacts: A new approach to addressing the problem of access-policy violations. *Management Information Systems Quarterly*, *39*(2), 345–366. doi:10.25300/MISQ/2015/39.2.04

White, S. (2017). *What is COBIT? A framework for alignment and governance*. Retrieved from https://www.cio.com/article/3243684/methodology-frameworks/what-is-cobit-a-framework-for-alignment-and-governance.html

Wild, J. (2018). *Five most common security frameworks explained, origin security*. Retrieved from https://originit.co.nz/the-strongroom/five-most-common-security-frameworks-explained/

Chapter 5
Achieving a Security Culture

Adéle Da Veiga
University of South Africa, South Africa

ABSTRACT

A security culture can be a competitive advantage when employees uphold strong values for the protection of information and exhibit behavior that is in compliance with policies, thereby introducing minimal incidents and breaches. The security culture in an organization might, though, not be similar among departments, job levels, or even generation groups. It can pose a risk when it is not conducive to the protection of information and when security incidents and breaches occur due to employee error or negligence. This chapter aims to give organizations an overview of the concept of security culture, the factors that could influence it, an approach to assess the security culture, and to prioritize and tailor interventions for high-risk areas. The outcome of the security culture assessment can be used as input to define security awareness, training, and education programs aiding employees to exhibit behavior that is in compliance with security policies.

INTRODUCTION

The protection of information in an organization is a combined effort of technological, procedural as well as human-related controls (ENISA, 2017). Management that understands the behavioral and cultural aspects of their organization can use it to reduce the risk end-users could pose to information protection (Whittman & Mattord, 2012). One of the human or behavioral controls that organizations can focus on is to inculcate a strong security culture (AlHogail, 2015; ENISA, 2017; Geeling, Brown, & Weimann, 2016). A strong security culture is a culture where information is protected throughout its lifecycle when employees process and interact with it, introducing minimal risk from accidental or ignorant behavior as part of everyday practice in the organization (Da Veiga & Martins, 2015a).

A strong or positive security culture in an organization is essential to mitigate risk from a human perspective in order to secure information (AlHogail, 2015; ENISA, 2017). This will contribute to reducing the risk of employee misbehavior, increase the overall security policy and regulatory compliance, improve the organization's security stance and aim to minimize financial loss due to security incidents or breaches related to employee behavior (Mahfuth, Yussof, Baker & Ali, 2017; Van Niekerk & Von

DOI: 10.4018/978-1-5225-7847-5.ch005

Copyright © 2019, IGI Global. Copying or distributing in print or electronic forms without written permission of IGI Global is prohibited.

Solms, 2010; Verizon, 2017). It is critical to evaluate the security culture continuously and to address identified gaps to improve employees' compliance with security policies and requirements. Organizations can achieve this by regularly conducting an assessment of the security culture, monitoring the change and implementing corrective actions to influence the culture positively (Da Veiga & Martins, 2015a).

This chapter defines the concept of a security culture in the context of an information security and cybersecurity culture. An overview of the development of it in an organization is discussed, focusing on the internal factors that could potentially influence the security culture. A security culture assessment approach is discussed with practical advice to roll out such an assessment in an organization. The emphasis is on understanding what the as-is security culture is in order to implement corrective actions to influence it positively. Examples are given of how to analyze the data, which management can use to define change management plans using methods such as awareness, training and education.

Defining a Security Culture

A security culture can be seen as the unconscious manner in which things are done in an organization to secure information. Every organization has a security culture, which is a subculture of the wider organizational culture (Da Veiga & Martins, 2017; Hayden, 2016; Schlienger & Teufel, 2003; Van Niekerk & Von Solms, 2005). The security culture can be explained as the "way things are done" in the organization to secure information. The way things are done by employees are underpinned by their assumptions, values, beliefs and attitudes (Schein, 1985, Van Niekerk & Von Solms, 2005), which is described as, "the way an organization functions as a sort of collective unconscious for the organization" (Hayden, 2016, pp. 44).

The manner in which employees undertake to protect information when they process it, is based on their shared tacit assumptions, as formed by their beliefs and values, and relates to the motivation for their decisions (Da Veiga & Eloff, 2010; Van Niekerk & Von Solms, 2006). The espoused values such as honesty and fairness form over time and relate to what employees believe should be done to protect information (Da Veiga & Martins, 2015b; Van Niekerk & Von Solms, 2006). The security culture of an organization is visible in tangible aspects of the organization, which are referred to as artifacts, underlined by the values of the organization. These tangible aspects could relate to the security policies and related training sessions, an incident-reporting or helpline, monthly awareness e-mails, the use of technology such as digital certificates for e-mail and so on (Okere, Van Niekerk, & Carroll, 2012; Schein, 1985; Schlienger & Teufel, 2003).

SECURITY CULTURE IN AN ORGANIZATIONAL CONTEXT

The Difference Between a Security Culture and a Cybersecurity Culture

The concepts of cybersecurity culture and information security culture both refer to the concept of a culture related to security, but from a different context. Cybersecurity can be seen as a subset or a component of information security (ISACA, 2017; B. von Solms & R. von Solms, 2018). In the same manner a cybersecurity culture is a subset of an information security culture. The distinguishing factors are the format of the information, the technology and the human element involved, as explained below.

Cybersecurity is concerned with the safeguards that must be implemented to protect information in a digital format from threats that emanate from a global network, like the internet (ISACA, 2017). Information security, on the other hand, includes threats to information across the architecture and in various formats, including hardcopy documents as well as verbal or visual communications (ISACA, 2017, C. P. Pfleeger, S. L. Pfleeger, & Margulies 2015). The cybersecurity culture is therefore described as the way things are done by users to protect information in cyberspace, whereas the information security culture is the way users do things to protect information throughout its lifecycle and in various formats, typically in the context of an organization or entity. From an organizational perspective the cybersecurity culture forms part of the wider information security culture in an organization. For example, the risk that employees introduce by downloading malicious files from the internet will pertain to the cybersecurity culture as well as the information security culture, whereas leaving confidential client documents in open office areas relates only to the context of information security culture.

A cybersecurity culture has been defined formally as, "the knowledge, beliefs, perceptions, attitudes, assumptions, norms and values of people regarding cybersecurity and how they manifest in people's behavior with information technologies" (ENISA, 2017, pp. 5). This definition is in line with the aim of cybersecurity culture being, "to instill a certain way to 'naturally behave' in daily life, a way that subscribes to certain [cybersecurity] assumptions" (Gcaza et al., 2015, pp. 3). The definition of cybersecurity includes three distinct concepts, namely the protection of digital information and information system resources in cyberspace as well as the protection of the end user using cyberspace (Da Veiga, 2016b; Von Solms & Van Niekerk, 2013). A cybersecurity culture can therefore not be confined to people in organizations, but extends to the individual in his/her work and home environment, the national and international context which includes organizations and even governments (Da Veiga, 2016b) who should define action plans and strategies on all levels to mitigate risks from cyberspace (Luiijf, Besseling & De Graaf, 2013). In contrast, an information security culture focuses on the organizational environment and what the organization, as the accountable party, should do to protect organizational information, which includes a focus on the behavior of employees who process the information.

The information security culture includes what employees do on a routinely basis that is accepted as the norm when processing information across the security architecture of an organization. The information security culture also extends to the behavior of employees relating to physical security, disaster recovery and business continuity (Da Veiga & Eloff, 2010). The scope of information security culture therefore focuses specifically on the culture of employees of an organization, which could include permanent staff, contractors, temporarily staff, consultants and third parties. In the context of this chapter the term "security culture" will be used when referring to an "information security culture", which is inclusive of a cybersecurity culture in the context of an organization.

Dominant and Sub Security Cultures in Organizations

The security culture in an organization often manifests in a dominant security culture with related sub security cultures (Da Veiga & Martins, 2017). The dominant security culture reflects the common perceptions of the majority of the employees of how information should be secured in line with the fundamental information security requirements. The subcultures are reflected in groups of employees that have common perceptions as a result of residing in a certain region, being in different departments or having different demographical traits related to age, gender, race or educational backgrounds (Da Veiga & Martins, 2017; E. C. Martins & N. Martins, 2016). A subculture might transpire in a department where employees believe the protection of the confidentiality of information is less important and where the emphasis is on meeting deadlines and sharing information quickly. The dominant security culture can be leveraged to influence the sub security cultures and to aid in directing beliefs and behavior of a sub security culture with the aim of aligning it with the dominant culture (E. C. Martins & N. Martins, 2016). Having a dominant security culture and various sub security cultures in one organization has the result that the same approach cannot be followed to change or influence the security culture, as the perceptions and non-compliance behavior across the subcultures might vary. A tailored and focused approach for the dominant and sub security cultures is therefore required to institute effective change in each. A security culture assessment can aid management to understand the security culture across the organization and to match the interventions to the needs.

The Desired Security Culture

The information security culture in an organization can be compared with an ethics culture as defined by Rossouw and Van Vuuren (2013). They name four categories of strategies for an ethical culture, namely reactive, compliance, integrity and totally aligned, which can also be applied to a security culture, figure 1. Management should aim for a totally aligned strategy for a security culture. In such a security culture management proactively engages with employees and deploys resources to direct the security culture. The organization's strategy and vision accommodate security, and positive reinforcement is used to reward compliance behavior. The totally aligned security culture can be seen as a strong or positive culture where employees value information and process it securely throughout its lifecycle. The incidents related to employee errors and negligence are minimized in the totally aligned security culture and employees have a thorough understanding of what is expected of them when processing information.

A reactive strategy towards security culture is the opposite of the aligned strategy. Organizations that are reactive focus on equipping employees on an ad-hoc basis, often after data breaches or security incidents occurred. An organization has an integrity strategy towards the security culture when it proactively implements strategies to minimize incidents, such as employee training and awareness, and data-loss prevention strategies; however, the approach is neither proactive nor integrated with the overall strategy of the organization. A compliance strategy focuses on compliance with regulatory and industry standards, as well as on the organization's policies and procedures. In this environment management typically performs self-assessments, monitoring and audits. For the compliance strategy the approach is rule-based and not an integral part of the operations across the organization.

Security Culture and Small and Medium-Size Enterprises

A security culture applies to large organizations as well as small- and medium-size (SMEs) enterprises (organizations). In the same way that an organization has an organizational culture, each organization has a unique security culture. While the concept also applies to SMEs, one needs to take cognizance of the fact that SMEs might not process the same volumes of information, have the same governance structures or level of information security policies in place, but are exposed to the same information security and cyber risks as large organizations. SMEs experience different challenges to large organizations in that they often do not have sufficient resources to invest in information security such as having a lack of skills, budget and time (Dojkovski, Lichtenstein & Warren, 2010). It is, however, also important for SMEs to ensure that they have a strong security culture to aid them in mitigating the risk from a human

Figure 1. Security culture strategies

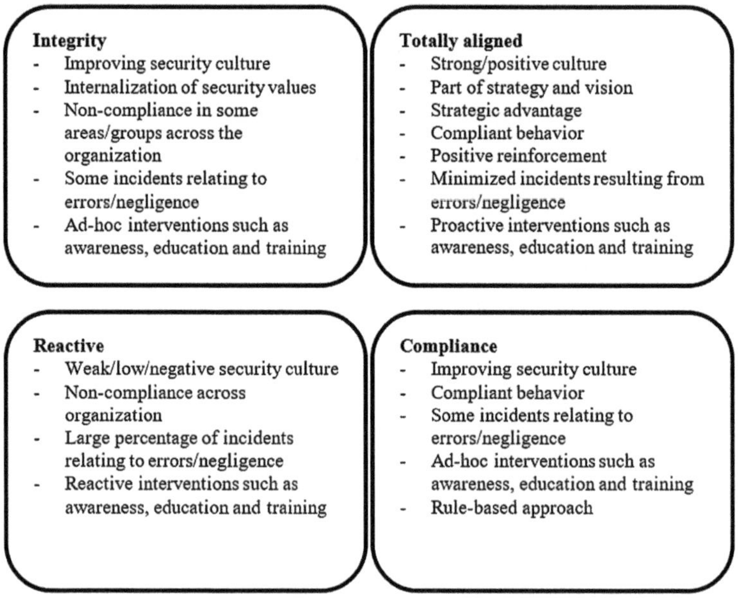

perspective. SMEs should also concentrate on addressing the factors discussed in the next section that influence a security culture as it is part of the foundational elements to implement information security. Whilst it is important to assess the security culture in SMEs, it is important to ensure that SMEs use their resources to implement the necessary technology and process controls for information security and progress to focus on training, awareness and education of employees to further strengthen the security culture.

FACTORS THAT INFLUENCE A SECURITY CULTURE

Security culture is regarded as a subset of the organizational culture (Schlienger & Teufel, 2003; Van Niekerk & Von Solms, 2005). One can therefore refer to the development of an organizational culture to understand what influences the development of a security culture has in an organization. Hellriegel, Slocum and Woodman (1998) explain the development of an organizational culture as a process over time, initiated by the strategy and vision of senior management in an organization. Their direction is conveyed through policies and procedures in the organization, which influence employee behavior. Over time the employee behavior becomes part of the organizational culture and as such also the way in which information is processed and secured, being the security culture. Figure 2 illustrates the development of a security culture with the embedded cybersecurity culture and related dominant or subcultures. The security culture is not rigid and can be influenced by a number of external and internal factors.

Factors external to the employee and organization play a role in influencing the security culture in an organization, such as regulation (AlHogail, 2015) and the national culture (G. Hofstede, G. J. Hofstede & Minkov, 2010). Internal factors such as the personality of the employees and their perceptions can also contribute to influence their behavior and in turn influence the security culture (Padayachee,

Figure 2. Developing and influencing a security culture
(adapted from Da Veiga & Martins, 2017)

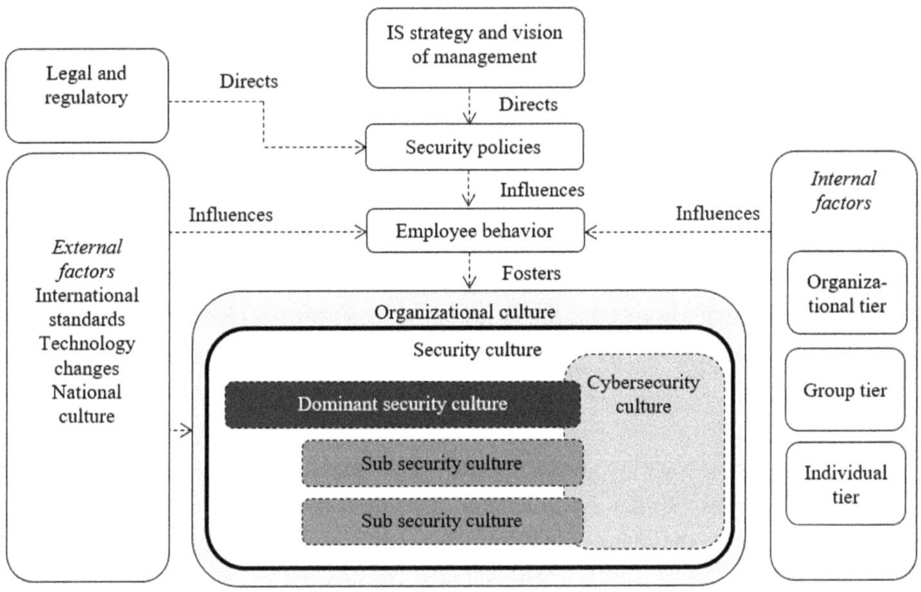

2012). Organizations need to ensure that the external and internal factors are considered as part of the security program to ensure that a holistic approach is followed to promote compliance in a consistent and effective manner.

Internal Influences

The internal influences refer to factors internal to the organization. They can be grouped under the organizational tier where formal structures are defined, the group tier where employees operate in groups and the individual tier where individuals each have a unique personality, background and traits. The next section gives an overview of each.

Organizational Tier

Formal structures that influence employee attitude and behavior are added on the organizational tier (Robbins, 2001). These could relate to formal roles assigned to the board of directors, executive management, senior management and security practitioners to govern security in an organization (ISACA, 2017). Executive management defines the manner in which security is managed in the organization, with top management leading by example to enable employees to follow (ISACA, 2017; Mohelska & Sokolova, 2015). According to ISACA (2017) top management should endorse security requirements and follow through on disciplinary action where employees do not comply. Their expectations should be communicated through various channels, including awareness and education programs. To further direct the security culture, executive management should provide the necessary resources such as cybersecurity practitioners with sufficient skills and experience as well as sufficient financial resources to implement security requirements and to educate employees.

Group Tier

There are various compositions of groups in organizations, each with unique views and ways of functioning (Robbins, Odendaal & Roodt, 2003). These groups relate to the composition of subcultures that are evident in organizations and could include members of a group in a department, a committee, a certain age group, gender or educational background (Robbins, 1997). The Chief Security Officer (CSO) should ensure that awareness programs specifically target groups of employees that exhibit behavior that are not in compliance with the security policy or that is not aligned with the expected security culture.

Individual Tier

Employees (individuals) have various characteristics that vary in terms of their demographics, background, nationality, age, personalities, attitudes and assumptions (Robbins, 2001). The characteristics of individuals could influence the manner in which they behave and comply with security requirements in an organization (Robbins et al., 2003). The security awareness programs of organizations should therefore also make provision for individual training and education.

External Influences

External influences on the organization relate to factors that can influence the security culture from outside the organization such as competitors, changes in the economy, new technological developments, national culture, industry standards and legal requirements. For example, organizations with offices in jurisdictions with data protection regulation have to implement controls to protect personal information and ensure compliance with the processing requirements of the respective privacy laws. Employees will be expected to process personal information according to the organization's privacy policies and necessary legal requirements. Offices in jurisdictions without data protection legislation will not be required to adhere to the same strict legal requirements for the processing of personal information and as such the culture towards privacy might vary from highly, moderated to low, across jurisdictions (DLA Piper, 2018). New technology also influences the manner in which employees share and process information that could either contribute to the protection of information or introduce risk. New technology like the Internet of Things (IoT), Bring Your Own Device (BYOD), cloud computing, and social media usage introduce new risks to the integrity, confidentiality and availability of information. Employees have, for example, been found to share too much information over social media and in some cases confidential information, which can lead to litigation (He, 2012). While external factors emanate from outside the organization, it often has an impact on a strategic and operational level in an organization where internal policies have to be formulated to minimize risks from external factors.

As the focus is on the security culture from within the organization and what management can do to direct it purposefully, the next section will discuss the internal factors – referred to as the foundational elements – that form the cornerstone of a desired security culture in an organization.

THE FOUNDATIONAL ELEMENTS FOR A DESIRED SECURITY CULTURE

Figure 3 outlines the foundational elements of a security culture. While all these elements and external factors play a role to influence and direct the security culture, it should be noted that security training, education and awareness are among the most critical elements. The security culture of employees who have attended or who have been exposed to either security training or awareness has been found to be higher or more positive compared to those employees who were not (Da Veiga, 2016a). However, the elements such as the role of leadership and change management are also critical to embed security values in the organization.

Leadership and Governance

Management and leadership in security are required to cultivate a strong security culture (Glaspie & Karwowski, 2018). Management should set the strategic direction, policy principles, lead by example, provide the necessary resources to implement security across the organization, and implement appropriate governance structures to support the security culture on the organizational level (Glaspie et al., 2018). Top management support, buy-in and direction can positively influence the security culture (Alnatheer, 2012; Dojkovski et al., 2010; Kraemer & Carayon, 2005). Top management also plays a role in creating awareness amongst employees regarding what is expected to protect information in line with the desired security culture (Dojkovski et al., 2010). Their expectations are typically documented in the security policies as the "overall intention and direction as formally expressed by management" (ISO/IEC, 2013 pp.13). To further govern security in the organization, management should display their commitment by giving clear direction and explicitly assigning roles and responsibilities while also acknowledging their security responsibilities (ISO/IEC, 2013).

Policies and Procedures

Security policies and procedures are regarded as critical success factors for an information security program (ISO/IEC, 2013). However, creating a security policy alone neither ensures employee aware-

Figure 3. Foundational elements of a security culture

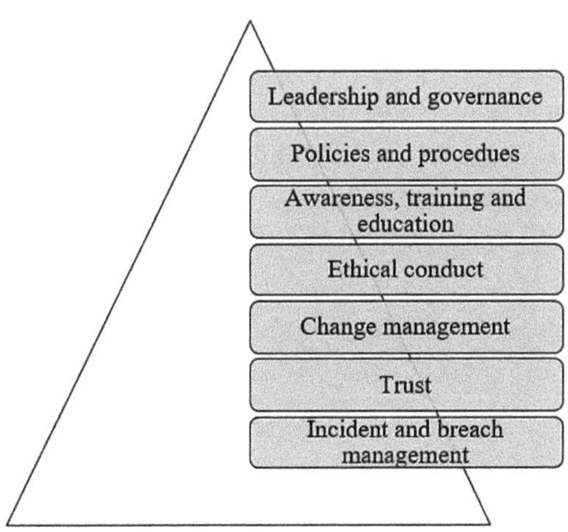

ness nor compliance (Glaspie et al., 2018). The ISO/IEC 17799 (2013) international standard includes the distribution of guidance about the policies as well as appropriate awareness, training and education as critical success factors to implement information security in an organization. The positive impact of being aware of the security policy contents is illustrated by research that have found that the security culture is more positive (or stronger) for employees who have read the security policy, as opposed to those who have not (Da Veiga, 2016b).

Encouragement to comply with the security policies have also been found to improve security across the organization (Tang, Li & Zhang, 2015). It has been found that compliance levels to policies are influenced by rewards as well as punishment for non-compliance (Chen, Ramamurthy & Wen, 2015; Whittman & Mattord, 2012). The same approach can however not be used for all organizations as each organization's security culture is unique. For example, in a security culture case study conducted in a bank, only 55.4% of employees indicated that security requirements should be part of their performance appraisal; however, in an audit and tax firm, 79.3% of employees were comfortable with incorporating security requirements in their performance appraisal with the aim of improving security policy compliance.

Awareness, Training, and Education

Security awareness, training and education (SETA) are aimed at empowering employees through knowledge, skills and guidance to protect information (Whitman & Mattord, 2017). Awareness activities focus on ensuring that employees remain conscious of information security requirements (Whitman & Mattord, 2019). Security education focuses on a formal delivery of security requirements while security training is training tailored for employees to use the organizational resources in the context of their job role (Whitman & Mattord, 2019).

Security education (Al Hogail, 2015) and training (Glaspie et al., 2018) are critical to creating a security culture (Chen & Wen, 2015). Similarly, security awareness is regarded as one of the most important factors to create a strong security culture (Al Hogail, 2015; ENISA, 2017; Ruighaver, Maynard, & Chang, 2007), which has also been emphasized by the Organization for Economic Cooperation and Development (OECD, 2002). Security awareness is regarded as focusing on "what" as opposed to "how", which relates to training (Herold, 2011). Security awareness is typically less formal than training, with a variety of delivery methods (e.g. posters, e-mails, newsletters, speakers, logos, banners, promotional items) and is conducted on a continuous basis by the organization to update employees about security policy requirements (Herold, 2011).

Targeted SETA programs are required to address the "human error or failure" effectively (Whitman & Mattord, 2019, pp. 268). A security culture assessment can be used to identify the job levels or departments that require SETA as well as the most preferred method of delivery. This can aid management to direct the SETA programs effectively to match the needs of the employees and to address the gaps identified. While the security culture assessment can inform SETA programs, it is key to use a holistic approach whereby the effectiveness of SETA programs is also assessed by using different techniques. Whitman and Mattord (2019) recommend an approach whereby awareness outcomes can typically be assessed with true/false or multiple-choice scales, training outcomes can be assessed through applied learning, and educational outcomes can be assessed through essay-style questions relating to interpretive learning. It is important to note that a security culture assessment does not measure the learning outcomes of SETA programs, but rather the perception and attitudes of employees towards security in the organization.

Ethical Conduct

In the information security field, information security professionals are guided by codes of ethics such as those of the Association for Computing Machinery (ACM, 2018), the Information Systems Security Association (ISSA, 2018) and the Information Systems Audit and Control Association (ISACA, 2018). All employees are not necessarily guided by these codes of ethics. They will typically be guided by the ethics code of the organization. However, employees from different nationalities or countries could have different perceptions towards ethics (Whitman & Mattord, 2012). To complicate the matter even more it has been found that attitudes towards ethics in the use of computer resources differ among individuals in the same country or even in one organization (Whitman & Mattord, 2012). Whitman and Mattord (2012) emphasize that education can be used to overcome the challenge of diverse ethical attitudes. It is therefore critical for the organization to understand the perceptions and attitude of their workforce in order to identify employee groups whose attitudes and perceptions are not in line with the organization's code of ethics and security policies. The information security culture assessment as discussed in this chapter can be used to identify such groups and to establish what interventions are required.

Change Management

Change management is important to instill a strong information security culture (Ashenden & Sasse, 2013; Ruighaver et al., 2007). A formal change management approach should be followed to direct the security culture purposefully. Change can only be initiated through a formal process during which the security culture is assessed to gain an understanding of it (Berry & Houston, 1993; Byars & Rue, 1997; Herold, 2011). The assessment serves as an organizational diagnosis to identify the as-is security culture and any prevailing issues or risks in the dominant culture or subcultures with the objective of improving or directing the culture. The data can be used to "stimulate and guide desirable changes" (Martins, 2017, pp. 1) in the security culture. Security culture changes should be implemented in such a manner that the changes are embedded and over time become part of the overall organizational culture. Change management approaches such as Prosci's ADKAR (Hiatt, 2006) change management model have been applied successfully in projects (Kazmi & Naarananoja, 2014; Kiani & Shah, 2014; Sheperd, Harris, Chung & Himes, 2014) and can also be applied to conduct the security culture assessment and to implement related changes.

The ADKAR change management model includes five phases, namely awareness (about the necessity for change), desire (to be part of and to support the change), knowledge (of how to bring about the change), ability (to be capable of implementing changes) and reinforcement (to maintain the implemented changes). These phases can be used to implement the change management actions as identified from the security culture assessment. Knowledge of the survey data and findings can be used to create awareness amongst stakeholders and employees for the need to change, which will also support the desire to change. Knowledge of how to change can be derived from the survey data by focusing on the most negative concepts and groups as identified in the data. The ability to change should be supported by management resources that also extend to a follow-up assessment to monitor the change and impact of the actions, which can be used to reinforce changes. Interestingly, in the security culture case studies conducted employees indicated their willingness to change and preparedness to accept some inconvenience to change. For example, in one of the financial organizations, 96% of employees indicated that they were prepared to change their working practices in order to secure information assets, with another 97% indicating that they were willing to accept inconvenience to secure important information. This might, however, not be the case in all organizations and a structured change program can aid management to implement security changes in a constructive manner.

Trust

When implementing security in an organization, a trusting relationship should be in place between management and employees so that compliance with security policies is facilitated and commitment to information security is illustrated by management – especially, as trust is regarded as one of the fundamental characteristics of leadership (Robbins, 1997; Flowerday and Von Solms, 2006). Trust is necessary in organizations to facilitate the sharing of knowledge (Rossouw & Van Vuuren, 2013), which also relates to knowledge of how to secure information. To facilitate an environment of knowledge-sharing through security training, education and awareness, a trusting relationship should be in place to contribute to the development of a strong security culture. Trust as a construct is also assessed during the security culture assessment to establish if it could be hampering the development of a totally aligned security culture.

Incident and Breach Management

Incident and breach management relates to the plan of the organization to respond in the event of a security incident or data breach in terms of the detection, reaction and recovering (Whitman & Mattord 2019). From the employees' perspective it is important that they know what a security incident is, who to report it to and what to do in the event of such an incident. In previous security culture assessments conducted in organizations, employees indicated in many of the case studies that they did not know who to report security incidents to and also did not know what an incident is. Table 1 portrays the results of one of these case studies in which employees were asked who they should report security incidents to. In this case study the majority believed they should report to the Group Information Security Officer, followed by their manager, where in actual fact they were required to report security incidents to the Helpdesk. In this same case study 72.1% of employees knew what a security incident is. In the follow-up surveys this improved to 87.6%, following targeted interventions.

Table 1. Reporting security incidents responses

Response Option	Frequency	Percentage of Responses
Helpdesk	206	9.5%
Immediate manager	1 287	59.6%
Group information security officer	1 596	73.9%
Human Resources	61	2.8%
Information Technology	225	10.4%
I don't know	92	4.3%
Whistle-blowing process	138	3.6%

A PROCESS TOWARDS CHANGING THE SECURITY CULTURE IN AN ORGANIZATION

There are various reasons why organizations might want to conduct a security culture assessment. They might need data to prove a suspicion that the behavior of employees in a certain department or biographical group is not in line with the expected culture. The organization might want to identify aspects of risk in the security culture to prioritize and tailor interventions, or to monitor the impact and success of change after the implementation of interventions. One benefit of the security culture assessment is that the data can be used to inform the content and focus of awareness, training and education programs. Follow-up assessments can provide management with data to benchmark and compare progress to further identify awareness, training and education needs.

The Security Culture Assessment Approach

Organizations that embark on a security culture assessment project can use the approach outlined in figure 4 as a guideline to conduct the assessment. This approach has four phases to conduct the assessment in a planned, structured and organized manner with the objective of obtaining valid and reliable data that management can use for strategic decisions to improve the security culture. It is a quantitative approach whereby a questionnaire is deployed in an organization by using a survey strategy. Questionnaires work well when deployed to assess attitude towards and opinions about an organizational practice (Saunders, Lewis & Thornhill, 2016), such as the security culture. The results can be generalized across the organization if a statistical representative sample is used and surveys are also a cost-effective approach (Saunders et al., 2016). A mixed method approach can also be used, such as incorporating documentary research where communications, contents of security policies and audit reports are reviewed. More in-depth information can be obtained if interviews or focus groups are used to confirm data from

Figure 4. Security culture assessment approach

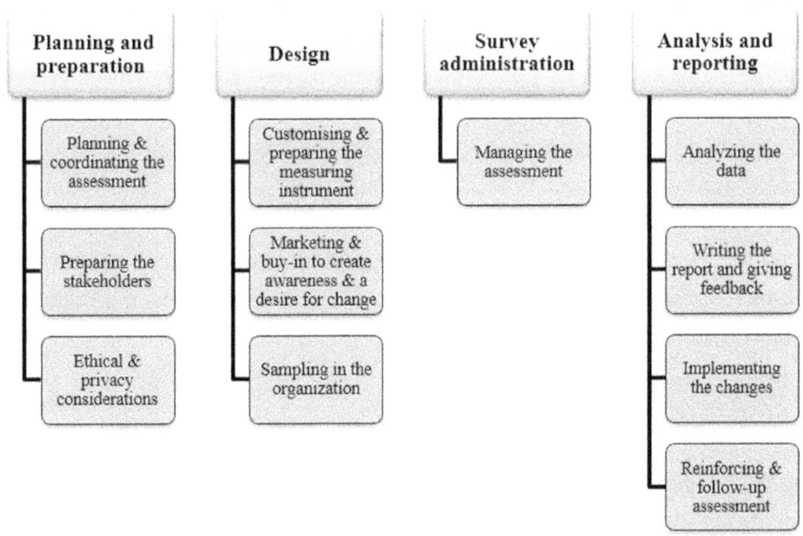

the security culture survey, for example to explore reasons for certain answers provided by the various demographical groups. The steps in each of the four phases are discussed below to give organizations a high-level overview of how to conduct the security culture assessment.

Planning and Coordinating the Assessment

There are a number of aspects to consider when planning the security culture assessment, such as the objective of the assessment, the scope, data protection legislation and project management. Firstly, management should identify the objective of conducting a security culture assessment. Usually, the two most common reasons for assessments are to measure and to change (Borg & Mastrangelo, 2008). The objective could relate to understanding the current security culture to integrate the findings as part of the risk profile of the organization, or to follow up on audit findings in certain business units or regions where employee behavior resulted in security incidents or breaches, or to identify what the content and focus of the security awareness program should be for various departments. Ultimately, the objective is to purposefully change the security culture to the desired culture in which less incidents and data breaches are occurring owing to employees' behavior.

Management should also agree on the scope of the project, such as whether all the organization's offices in the various regions and countries should be included. It should also be determined whether all employees have access to computers to be able to access and complete the questionnaire electronically, and/or whether paper-based questionnaires will be required. Another factor to consider is whether the questionnaire should be translated into more than one language, especially if offices in other countries are included.

Many organizations prefer to host the survey internally, while others make use of third parties or consultants. When third parties or consultants are used, organizations usually have to engage in a third-party contract process and agree on the privacy and security requirements of the data. This could take some time to negotiate and agree on, especially if different data protection regulations are to be considered for cross-border transfer of the data. For example, if the offices of the organization are located across the United States as well as Europe, the employees' biographical data, as captured in the questionnaires, will be saved in the third-party database, which could reside in the United States. The General Data Protection Regulation (GDPR) (European Parliament, 2016) requirements for cross-border transfer of European citizens' data must then be considered and applied in the survey process.

The assessment process does not only relate to sending out the questionnaire and analyzing the data. The project should be managed using aspects of project management principles, such as defining specific tasks and assigning roles and timelines to them. For example, the timeline of activities; the survey timeframe (typically not during a holiday or year-end as the response rates will be lower); the stakeholders to include; the different roles; the budget; which tasks can run concurrently; planning the feedback method and timeframe for feedback to management, employees and stakeholders; and so on should be determined (Martins, 2017).

Preparing the Stakeholders

The management of stakeholders in the security culture assessment is critical and often impacts on the success of organizational diagnoses projects. Ledimo (2017) emphasizes that the stakeholders should be identified upfront and engaged with to manage resistance and concerns. A number of stakeholders, which include the Information Security Officer (ISO) or Chief Information Officer (CIO) and departments in the organization, such as training or human resources, should be part of the team to increase the success of the project (ENISA, 2017).

The ISO or CIO is often the security culture assessment project sponsor that either drives the project or allocates the responsibility to someone in his or her team. When an organization conducts an assessment, the output will result in change plans that have to be implemented (Ledimo, 2017). The stakeholders tasked with implementing the change should therefore be involved from the start. These stakeholders could relate to the marketing and communications team that designs and delivers awareness material, the training team that might need to compile and deliver customized and focused training based on the results, the Information Technology Department that might need to work with the training team to assist in defining the training content or to implement/revise technological controls, and the risk and compliance team that might need to follow up on high-risk departments or integrate the findings in their reports. In some instances, trade union representatives should be included as they might need to give input for the planning and should receive feedback on the results as it could impact their members.

The stakeholders comprising individuals or committees (e.g. Risk and Compliance Committee) should be identified upfront and their buy-in should be obtained. This could be done by presenting the project to them and discussing the benefits and potential use of the results to institute change. The board or executive representation might also be required to support the security culture assessment project (ENISA, 2017).

Ethical and Privacy Considerations

Questionnaires usually include a section where demographical data is collected in order to segment the data for comparison purposes and to identify priority groups across the organization to target interventions. While the questionnaires should be anonymous, personal identifiable data such as department name, age, job level, language, years of employment and gender is still collected. When these data fields are combined, it might be possible to identify individuals especially in demographical groups in which there are only a few staff members. Ethical and privacy requirements should therefore be considered, as listed below in alphabetic order (Da Veiga, 2017):

- **Autonomy:** Employees' decision to participate or not to participate in the security culture assessment should be respected (Mitchell & Jolley, 2007; Oates, 2012; Saunders et al., 2016).
- **Best Interest:** The participants should be informed of the security culture assessment through a proper communication channel such as a meeting, e-mail of informed consent agreement where their interests and role are described (HPCSA, 2008).
- **Benevolence:** A risk assessment can be conducted to evaluate the type of personal identifiable information and attitude, or opinion information that will be collected to ensure that the rights of participants are respected, and that confidentiality and privacy requirements are met. Ultimately the benefits should outweigh the risk of the assessment (Miller & Brewerton, 2003, Saunders et al., 2016).
- **Compassion:** The organizations should illustrate compassion if participants from vulnerable groups, such as those with disabilities, are included. Measures should be implemented to enable them to participate (HPCSA, 2008).
- **Confidentiality:** The personal identifiable information and all responses should be treated as confidential by all parties, including any third parties involved in the planning, hosting, data cleans-

ing, statistical analysis and report writing (Miller & Brewer, 2003; HSRC, 2017; Oates, 2012; Saunders et al., 2016). Adequate security measures should be in place to protect the electronic survey data when sent across the organizational or third-party networks, in the database as well as when being e-mailed or statistically analyzed.

- **Consent:** Employees should give consent for their data being transferred cross-border, or if their data will be used for other purposes (European Parliament, 2016; Oates, 2012; Saunders et al.; 2016).
- **Excellence and Competence:** The questionnaire should be validated statistically to ensure that the data and findings are reliable and valid (ISACA, 2016; HPCSA, 2008; HSRC, 2017).
- **Honesty:** The project team should ensure that the data used in reports and feedback sessions is reported on in an honest and accurate manner (Miller & Brewerton, 2003; Singapore Statement, 2010, Saunders et al., 2016).
- **Human Rights:** The human rights of all participants and stakeholders should be considered, for example to have fair selection criteria representing all groups across the organization when defining the selection criteria if a sampling approach is used (HPCSA, 2008).
- **Impartiality and Independence:** The stakeholders involved must declare any conflicts of interest, such as being a shareholder of the company that will host the data (ALLEA, 2017).
- **Integrity:** The assessment must be conducted in line with the organizational values considering fairness, honesty and quality of the data collection, analysis and reporting (Singapore Statement, 2010; HPCSA, 2008).
- **Justice:** The project team and stakeholders must treat all the participating employees with respect, sensitivity and fairness, especially if the employees are compensated to participate (HSRC, 2017; HPCSA, 2008).
- **Objectivity and Independence:** The project team should conduct the assessment in line with their organizational codes of ethics and professional codes of ethics (Babie, 2004; ALLEA, 2017; ISACA, 2016). If the project is audited or monitored, the reviews should be conducted independently from the project team. Objective decisions should be made based on the data and facts and not on opinions.
- **Transparency:** The participants must be informed of the survey objective, any possible risks and expectations. Results should be communicated to the relevant stakeholders to ensure transparency (Mitchell & Jolley, 2007).

Customizing and Preparing the Measuring Instrument

There are a number of security culture questionnaires available, which can be used for the assessment of security culture. The most prominent ones are listed below in alphabetical order:

- AlHogail (2015) proposed the Information Security Culture Framework (ISCF), which comprises five dimensions, namely strategy, technology, organization, people and environment (STOPE). Four domains of human behavior factors (preparedness, responsibility, management, and society and regulations) are assessed in each of the dimensions. This questionnaire has a reliability score (Cronbach alpha) of 0.619 to 0.928.
- The Information Security Culture Assessment (ISCA) questionnaire has been designed to assess the as-is security culture in an organization (Da Veiga & Eloff, 2010). The questionnaire is based

on the Information Security Culture Framework (Da Veiga & Eloff, 2010) and comprises ten dimensions, namely change management, information asset management, information security leadership, information security management, information security policies, information security program, trust, user management, training and awareness, and privacy perception. The reliability score (Cronbach alpha) is between 0.764 and 0.877 (Da Veiga & Martins, 2015b). This questionnaire was used successfully in five financial institutions in South Africa, in a mining organization as well as consumer market organization. In one of the financial institutions the questionnaire was deployed across twelve countries at four different occasions during a period of eight years to monitor the impact of the interventions and change on the information security culture (Da Veiga & Martins, 2015a, 2015b, 2017) and in another it was deployed twice. Furthermore, it was implemented in a government parastatal and in an audit, tax and advisory firm. The results obtained from these assessments were found to be valid and reliable to facilitate changes in employee attitude and related behavior, and to inculcate a positive information security culture.

- In a book Lance Haydon (2016) published he included a security culture survey with ten questions to measure security culture. He proposes that a security culture can be defined as the Competing Security Cultures Framework (CSCF), being either a process culture (with tight control and internal focus), a compliance culture (with tight control and external focus), a trust culture (with loose control and internal focus) or an autonomy culture (with loose control and external focus). The objective is to assess and identify the cultural traits and values relating to security in the organization in order to map the culture in one of the four quadrants of the CSCF. This approach follows a survey method.
- Schienger (Schlienger & Teufel, 2003; 2005) developed an information security culture questionnaire and corresponding tool. He defined questions focusing on the individual's attitude, the organization's attitude and the possible solution where after the results are triangulated. The questionnaire is currently available in German as part of Schlienger's consulting services of Tree Solution (2018).

In this chapter the ISCA questionnaire is used for illustration purposes as it is statistically validated and produced positive results in case studies, which were published. The full questionnaire is available in a 2018 publication by Da Veiga, titled "An approach to information security culture change combining ADKAR and the ISCA questionnaire to aid transition to the desired culture" in the Information and Computer Security Journal.

The theoretical questionnaire dimensions (constructs) are as follows (Da Veiga & Martins 2015a, Da Veiga & Martins 2015b):

1. **Information Asset Management:** Assesses users' perceptions of the protection of information assets
2. **Information Security Management:** Assesses management's perceptions of information security management
3. **Change Management:** Assesses the perceptions about change and the willingness of users to change in order to protect information
4. **User Management:** Assesses user awareness and training with regard to the requirements to protect information

5. **Information Security Policy:** Assesses whether users understand the information security policy and whether communication thereof was successful
6. **Information Security Program:** Assesses the effectiveness of investing in information security resources
7. **Trust:** Assesses the perceptions of users regarding the safekeeping of private information and their trust in the communications of the organization
8. **Information Security Leadership:** Assesses users' perceptions of information security governance (e.g. monitoring) to minimize risks to information
9. **Training and Awareness:** Assesses employees' perception of additional needs for information security training
10. **Privacy Perception:** Assesses employees' perception of privacy principles

While this questionnaire's questions are defined, it is important to customize the terminology and perhaps add or remove one or two questions that might be relevant/not relevant in the background section of the questionnaire, and include specific biographical questions relating to the structure of the organization and profile of the employees. It is advisable not to change too much of the questionnaire as it affects its reliability and validity. Should this be the case, statistical analysis, such as the Cronbach Alpha and factor analysis should be conducted to validate the questionnaire again (Martins & Ledimo, 2017).

The questionnaire can be developed in an online tool such as SurveyTracker (Scantron, 2018), SurveyMonkey (2018) or Qualtrics (2018). These tools include electronic distribution of the questionnaire, automatic data capturing and also the analysis and exporting of the data.

Marketing and Buy-in to Create Awareness and a Desire for Change

It is important to market the security culture survey to the employees and stakeholders in order to get enough responses for the survey across the organization. The questionnaire can be accompanied by an invitation or cover letter from management such as the Chief Information Officer or the Chief Information Security Officer, explaining the objective, why to participate, how long it will take, confidentiality and anonymity and any further instructions. This is typically sent via e-mail with the hyperlink to the electronic questionnaire. Regular reminder emails help to obtain responses; so do incentives such as receiving a small gift on completion, or standing a change to win a prize (Martins & Ledimo, 2017b).

Sampling in the Organization

Various sampling techniques, such as simple random, stratified, clustered, convenience or snowball sampling can be used (Cresswell, 2014; Oates, 2012; Saunders, Lewis, & Thornhill, 2016). If the objective is to obtain insight into the dominant and subcultures, all employees can be invited to participate, thereby including the entire organization as the sample. The method of Krejcie and Morgan (1970) can be applied to obtain a 95% confidence that the results can be generalized across the organization. Using this method an organization can calculate how many responses are required for the overall results, as well as per biographical group such as a department, as long as the organization can determine the number of employees in each department. For example, an organization with 100 employees requires a response rate of 80, an organization with 500 employees requires a response rate of 217, an organization with 1 000 employees require a response rate of 278 and an organization with 10 000 employees require a response rate of 370. If an organization with 10 000 employees calculate the response rate per job level or department, the overall responses required will be more than 370 as the responses should be calculated separately per department, which will add up to more than the overall figure. Where sufficient responses are not obtained, the results can be validated with interviews or focus groups.

Managing the Assessment

The security culture assessment should be managed by tracking the responses received on a weekly basis, identifying departments or groups with insufficient responses, sending out reminders and establishing if additional communication is required to motivate employees to respond. The various stakeholders, such as the technical team hosting the survey, the communication team that might post notices on the intranet or that sends out reminders require updates on the progress. The process for the completion of paper-based questionnaires should also be planned and managed, for example if facilitators will be used and for data capturing.

Analyzing the Data

It is advisable to use a statistical analysis program such as IBM SPSS Statistics (IBM Analytics 2018) to analyze the data. A Likert scale is used for the ISCA questions. Scores below a mean of 4.00 (Da Veiga & Martins 2015a) can be flagged for improvement, as indicated in figure 5.

The security culture data can be analyzed by conducting the following as a minimum:

- The number of responses (frequencies) for each of the biographical groups should be calculated, as well as whether a representative response rate was obtained. Table 2 gives an example of the responses received per job level in one of the security culture assessments. In the last column the means for all the security culture questions are listed, showing a close resemblance between the job levels.
- The means of each of the statements in the ISCA can be calculated. These can be listed from the highest to the lowest to identify the most positive and most negative statements to prioritize interventions. Scores below a mean of 4.00 can be flagged for improvement where actions plans should be defined. Table 3 illustrates the top five results of a security culture assessment comparing the means for four of the surveys conducted. The "*" indicates a significant improvement from the 2010 to 2013 data.

Figure 5. Likert scale application for the ISCA

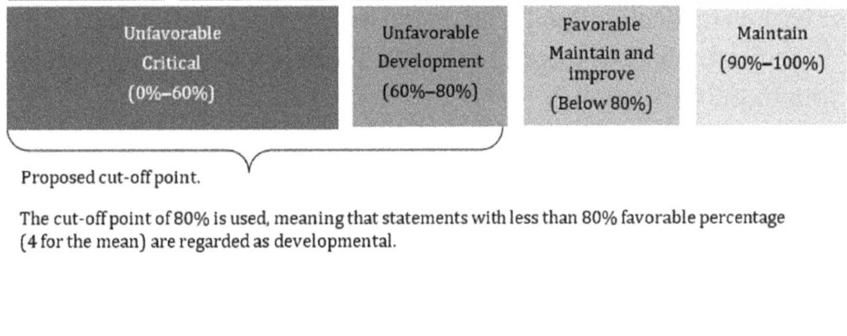

Table 2. Responses and means per job level

Response	Percentage of Responses	Means
Executive	2.4%	3.94
Manager	20.8%	3.90
Non-managerial employee	76.5%	3.89
No response	0.3%	N/A

Table 3. Five most positive statements

Statements	Dimension	2013	2010	2007	2006
It is important to understand the threats (e.g. theft of equipment, alterations or misuse of information) to the information assets in my division.	Information asset management	* 4.53	4.48	4.48	4.43
I accept that some inconvenience (e.g. changing my password regularly, locking away confidential documents or making back-ups) is necessary to secure important information.	Change	4.43	4.40	4.43	4.37
I am aware of the information security aspects relating to my job function (e.g. how to choose a password or handle confidential information).	User management	* 4.44	4.36	4.36	4.22
I believe it is necessary to commit people to information security.	Information security program	* 4.38	4.33	4.33	4.26
I am prepared to change my working practices in order to ensure the security of information assets (e.g. computer systems and information in paper or electronic format).	Change	4.30	4.29	4.25	4.20

- The means of each of the ten dimensions can be calculated. The dimensions with the lowest mean score should be prioritized for interventions.
- T-tests and analysis of variance (ANOVA) tests can be conducted to identify significant differences among biographical groups such as departments or age groups. This will give management an indication of which group to prioritize for the interventions as well as how to customize interventions for each group based on the specific aspects that scored low as identified in the data. Figure 6 presents the data of one of the security culture assessments where the data was segmented among employees in the Information Technology (IT) department, compared with employees who are not working in IT. The t-tests indicated that there was a significant difference between the means of these groups. For example, in 2013 the IT group, with a mean of 4.15, was significantly more positive than the non-IT group with a mean of 4.09. The implication is that the non-IT group should be prioritized if management plans interventions, which would typically be defined where means are below 4 for the mean.

T-tests can also be used to identify significant improvements from one survey to the next as indicated in table 4. The "*" indicates that the means of the 2013 statements were significantly more positive when compared with the 2010 means.

- If the survey was repeated, comparison analysis can be done to identify improvement or changes from the previous results. The means per dimension for each of the years when the survey was

Figure 6. Means for IT and non-IT employees

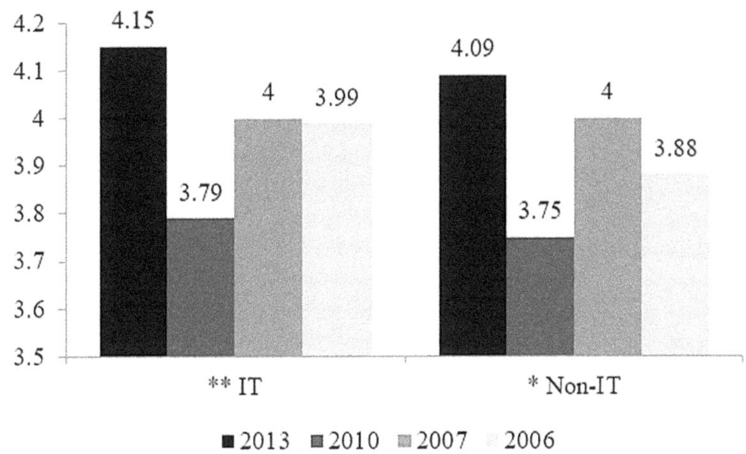

conducted can be displayed on a radar chart as depicted in figure 7. The overall mean for 2013, 4.10, indicates an improvement from the 2010 overall mean, 3.76. The ten dimensions of the ISCA questionnaire, used in this specific case study, are displayed with the means of the questions for each dimension. For most of the dimensions, the same trend is visible with awareness and training being the dimension where the most intervention and improvement is required compared to the information access management dimension that remained one of the most positive dimensions. The privacy dimension was only included in the 2010 and 2013 survey and hence no data is available for the other two years.

The advantage of the longitudinal analysis is to track and monitor the change over time to establish if interventions were successful and where corrective action is required. This type of analysis can be done per department, job level or office area to also track over time whether the security culture is improving or if not, and where intervention is required. The data can also aid management to motivate for budget aimed at awareness, training and education initiatives or to showcase success of corrective actions.

Table 4. Significant differences for individual statements

Statements	Dimension	2013	2010
My division clearly outlines what is expected of me with regard to information security.	Information security leadership	* 3.82	3.66
I believe employees adhere to the information security policy.	Information security leadership	* 3.81	3.66
The contents of the information security policy were effectively communicated to me.	User management	3.73	3.69
I am informed in a timely manner as to how information security changes will affect me.	Change	3.75	3.71
The contents of the information security policy are easy to understand.	Information security policies	* 3.81	3.76

Figure 7. Means per dimension for four assessments

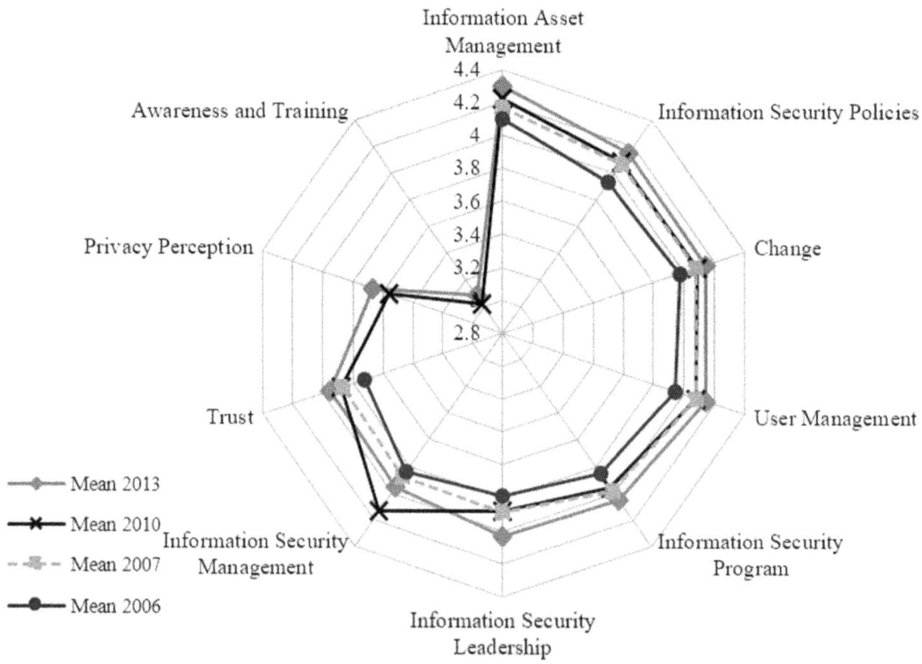

Writing the Report and Giving Feedback

Once the data analysis is complete, the next step is to compile a report of the results with the recommendations. Typically the report should include aspects such as the security culture assessment (survey) objective, the methodology followed, the number of responses received compared to the sample sizes required, the overall results per dimensions, the results per statement, the results per biographical group (positive and negative results), recommended action plans and an implementation plan (Martins, 2017). The report can also be summarized in PowerPoint to be presented to the various stakeholder groups. Feedback should also be given to employees to ensure transparency and for employees to understand the necessity to change where improvement is required.

Table 5 gives an extract of recommendations that were made in one of the security culture assessments. For more examples please refer to the article "Defining dominant and sub security cultures", in *Computers & Security* by Da Veiga and Martins published in 2017.

Implementing the Changes

The security culture assessment results provide management with a view of the security culture and which aspects or groups require change to improve the culture. A change management process such as that of ADKAR can typically be used to implement the change. Awareness about the change can be created through the feedback to stakeholders, focusing on the offices or groups that scored the lowest. The desire to change can be motivated by illustrating aspects that require improvement which, for example,

Table 5. Example of recommendations

Intervention	ISCA Finding	Recommendation
Communication about the sharing of passwords	Employees believe they can share their passwords with (2010): Helpdesk Managers Secretaries Colleagues	**Action:** Communicate to employees that no passwords should be shared **Demographical group:** Non-IT employees and non-managerial **Method:** E-mail, presentation and web-based training (in order of method preferred by employees)
Communication of the security policy	31.9% of respondents believe that the security policy was not explained and communicated to them effectively 38.9% of respondents have not read the security policy 32.2% of respondents do not know where to get a copy of the security policy	**Action:** Conduct additional policy communication and awareness **Demographical groups:** Non-IT department, South Africa, United Kingdom and Australia **Method:** Develop a security policy brochure with content overview and link Send out monthly e-mails with policy content messages Conduct face-to-face policy overview presentations

can be discussed in focus groups. This can be reinforced through the use of role models, change agents in departments, incorporating security aspects in performance appraisals or incentives. The transition phase includes the focus of education, training and awareness for employees in the aspects identified in the ISCA assessment, starting with the priority audiences. Organizations should ensure that they have the necessary resources and ability to change, such as training the ISO and CISOs, or making use of external consultants to implement some of the changes required. Reinforcing the change can be facilitated by conducting a follow-up ISCA survey.

Reinforcing and Follow-up Assessment

The follow-up ISCA assessment can be used to monitor the implemented changes and to identify where the results improved. Additional data in the organization can also be used, for example to track the number of incidents related to employee error and negligence prior to and after interventions.

CONCLUSION

In this chapter the concept of a security culture was discussed as being the unconscious manner in which things are done in an organization to secure information. The security cultures vary among organizations and even within an organization with dominant and sub security cultures that emerge. The intrinsic and extrinsic factors that influence a security culture are discussed in this chapter, emphasizing the importance of education, training and awareness.

This chapter further outlined a process to assess the security culture by discussing the key aspects to consider – from identifying the stakeholders to the report writing and feedback phase. The Information Security Culture Assessment (ISCA) instrument was discussed as a questionnaire that can be used to establish the level of the security culture with the objective of identifying biographical groups or areas, such as business units or age groups in the organization where intervention is required to direct the security culture purposefully through interventions that can be conveyed by training, awareness and education.

The importance of focusing on the human element is emphasized to aid with security policy compliance and ultimately to establish a strong security culture. An information security culture will be evident in employees that exhibit compliance behavior and have coherent values towards protecting information, thereby minimizing the threat the human element poses to the protection of information. The aim is to achieve a totally aligned security culture.

REFERENCES

AlHogail, A. (2015). Design and validation of information security culture framework. *Computers in Human Behavior*, *49*, 567–575. doi:10.1016/j.chb.2015.03.054

AlHogail, A. (2015). Cultivating and Assessing an Organizational Information Security Culture: An Empirical Study. *International Journal of Security and Its Applications*, *9*(7), 163–178. doi:10.14257/ijsia.2015.9.7.15

All European Academics (ALLEA). (2017). *The European Code of Conduct for Research Integrity.* Retrieved from https://ec.europa.eu/research/participants/data/ref/h2020/other/hi/h2020-ethics_code-of-conduct_en.pdf

Alnatheer, M. (2012). Understanding and Measuring Information Security Culture in Developing Countries: Case of Saudi Arabia. In *Proceedings of the Pacific Asia Conference on Information Systems (PACIS)*. Ho Chi Minh City, Vietnam: Association of Information Systems.

Ashenden, D., & Sasse, A. (2013). CISOs and organizational culture: Their own worst enemy? *Computers & Security*, *39*, 396–405. doi:10.1016/j.cose.2013.09.004

Association for Computing Machinery (ACM). (n.d.). *ACM code of ethics and professional conduct.* Retrieved from www.acm.org/about/code-of-ethics

Babie, E. (2004). *The practice of social research* (10th ed.). Belmont, CA: Thomson Wadsworth.

Berry, M. L., & Houston, J. P. (1993). *Psychology at work.* Brown and Benchmark Publishers.

Borg, I., & Mastrangelo, P. M. (2008). *Employee surveys, tools and practical applications. Employee surveys in management: theories, tools and practical applications*. Cambridge, MA: Hogrefe.

Byars, L. L., & Rue, L. W. (1997). *Human resource management* (5th ed.). Boston: McGraw-Hill.

Chen, Y., Ramamurthy, K., & Wen, K. (2015). Impacts of comprehensive information security programs on information security culture. *Journal of Computer Information Systems*, *55*(3), 11–19. doi:10.1080/08874417.2015.11645767

Cresswell, J. W. (2014). *Research design – Qualitative, quantitative, and mixed methods approaches* (4th ed.). Los Angeles, CA: SAGE Publications.

Da Veiga, A. (2016a). Comparing the information security culture of employees who had read the information security policy and those who had not: Illustrated through an empirical study *Information &. Computers & Security*, *22*(24), 139–155. doi:10.1108/ICS-12-2015-0048

Da Veiga, A. (2016b). A cybersecurity culture research philosophy and approach to develop a valid and reliable measuring instrument. In *Proceedings of 2016 Science and Information Computing Conference* (SAI2016) (pp. 1006-1115), London: IEEE. 10.1109/SAI.2016.7556102

Da Veiga, A. (2017). Ethical and privacy considerations for research. In N. Martins, E. Martins, & R. Viljoen (Eds.), *Organizational Diagnosis: A guide for practitioners* (pp. 273–298). Randburg, South Africa: Knowledge Resources.

Da Veiga, A., & Eloff, J. H. P. (2010). A framework and assessment instrument for information security culture. *Computers & Security*, *29*(2), 196–207. doi:10.1016/j.cose.2009.09.002

Da Veiga, A., & Martins, N. (2015a). Improving the information security culture through monitoring and implementation actions illustrated through a case study. *Computers & Security*, *49*, 162–176. doi:10.1016/j.cose.2014.12.006

Da Veiga, A., & Martins, N. (2015b). Information security culture and information protection culture: A validated assessment instrument. *Computer Law & Security Review*, *31*(2), 243–256. doi:10.1016/j.clsr.2015.01.005

Da Veiga, A., & Martins, N. (2017). Defining and identifying dominant information security cultures and subcultures. *Computers & Security*, *70*, 72–94. doi:10.1016/j.cose.2017.05.002

DLA PIPER. (2018). *Data protection laws of the world.* Retrieved from https://www.dlapiperdataprotection.com/index.html

Dojkovski, S., Lichtenstein, S., & Watten, M. J. (2010). Enabling information security culture: Influences and challenges for Australian SMEs. *Proceedings of the Australasian Conference on Information Systems, (ACIS).*

European Union Agency for Network and Information Security (ENISA). (2017). *Cyber security culture in organizations.* Retrieved from doi:10.2824/10543

Flowerday, S., & Von Solms, R. (2006). Trust an element of information security. In *Proceedings of Security and Privacy in Dynamic Environments (IFIP/SEC2005)* (pp. 87–98). Boston: Kluwer Academic Publishers. doi:10.1007/0-387-33406-8_8

Gcaza, N., & Von Solms, R. (2017). A strategy for a cybersecurity culture: A South African perspective. *The Electronic Journal on Information Systems in Developing Countries*, *80*(1), 1–17. doi:10.1002/j.1681-4835.2017.tb00590.x

Geeling, S., Brown, I., & Weimann, P. (2016). Information systems and culture – a systematic hermeneutic literature review. In *Proceedings of the International Conference on Information Resource Management (CONF-IRM)* (paper 40). South Africa, Cape Town: Association for Information Systems.

Glaspie, H. W., & Karwowski, W. (2018). Human Factors in Information Security Culture : A Literature Review Human Factors in Information Security Culture : A Literature Review. In *Proceedings of Advances in Intelligent Systems and Computing* (pp. 269–280). Springer.

Haydon, L. (2016). *People centric security – Transforming your enterprise security culture*. McGraw-Hill Education.

He, W. (2012). A review of social media security risks and mitigation techniques. *Journal of Systems and Information Technology*, *14*(2), 171–180. doi:10.1108/13287261211232180

Health Professions Council of South Africa (HPCSA). (2008). *General Ethical Guidelines for the Health Professions Council of South Africa, Annexure 12*. Retrieved from http://www.hpcsa.co.za/conduct/Ethics

Hellriegel, D., Slocum, J. W. Jr, & Woodman, R. W. (1998). *Organizational behavior* (8th ed.). Cincinnati, OH: South-Western College.

Herold, R. (2011). *Managing an information security and privacy awareness and training program* (2nd ed.). Boca Raton, FL: Taylor and Francis Group.

Hiatt, J. M. (2006). *ADKAR: A Model for Change in Business, Government and our Community*. Loveland, CO: Library of Congress.

Hofstede, G., Hofstede, G. J., & Minkov, M. (2010). *Cultures and Organizations: Software of the mind* (3rd ed.). The McGraw-Hill Companies.

Human Sciences Research Council (HSRC). (2018). *Code of Research Ethics*. Retrieved from http://www.hsrc.ac.za/en/about/research-ethics/code-of-research-ethics

IBM Analytics. (2018). *IBM SPSS Statistics*. Retrieved from https://www.ibm.com/analytics/data-science/predictive-analytics/spss-statistical-software

Information Systems Audit and Control Association (ISACA). (2017). *Cybersecurity Fundamentals Study Guide* (2nd ed.). ISACA.

Information Systems Audit and Control Association (ISACA). (2018). *Code of Professional Ethics*. Retrieved from http://www.isaca.org/certification/code-of-professional-ethics/pages/default.aspx

ISO/IEC. (2013). *ISO/IEC 27002: Information technology – security techniques – code of practice for information security management*. BSI.

Kazmi, S. A., & Naarananoja, M. (2014). Collection of change management models – an opportunity to make the best choice from the various organizational transformational techniques. *GSTG International Journal on Business Management*, *3*(3), 71–79.

Kiani, A., & Shah, M. H. (2014). An application of ADKAR change model for the change management competencies of school heads in Pakistan. *Journal of Managerial Sciences*, *VIII*(1), 77–95.

Kraemer, S., & Carayon, P. (2005). Computer and Information Security Culture: Findings from two Studies. In *Proceedings of the Human Factors and Ergonomics Society Annual Meeting* (pp. 1483-1487). Orlando, FL: Human Factors and Ergonomic Society. 10.1177/154193120504901605

Krejcie, R. V., & Morgan, D. W. (1970). Determining Sample Size for Research Activities. *Educational and Psychological Measurement*, *30*(3), 607–610. doi:10.1177/001316447003000308

Ledimo, O. (2017). Preparing and involving all stakeholders. In N. Martins, E. Martins, & R. Viljoen (Eds.), *Organizational Diagnosis: A guide for practitioners* (pp. 25–38). Randburg, South Africa: Knowledge Resources.

Luiijf, E., Besseling, K., & De Graaf, P. (2013). Nineteen national cyber security strategies. *International Journal of Critical Infrastructures*, *9*(1/2), 2–31. doi:10.1504/IJCIS.2013.051608

Mahfuth, A., Yussof, S., Baker, A. A., & Ali, N. (2017). A systematic literature review: Information security culture. In *Proceedings of the International Conference on Research and Innovation in Information Systems* (ICRIIS) (pp. 456-463). Langkawi, Kedah, Malaysia: IEEE. 10.1109/ICRIIS.2017.8002442

Martins, E. C. (2017). Planning and coordinating an organizational diagnosis. In N. Martins, E. Martins, & R. Viljoen (Eds.), *Organizational Diagnosis: A guide for practitioners* (pp. 1–23). Randburg, South Africa: Knowledge Resources.

Martins, E. C., & Ledimo, O. (2017). Developing and sourcing assessment instruments. In N. Martins, E. Martins, & R. Viljoen (Eds.), *Organizational Diagnosis: A guide for practitioners* (pp. 39–83). Randburg, South Africa: Knowledge Resources.

Martins, E. C., & Ledimo, O. (2017b). Survey administration process. In N. Martins, E. Martins, & R. Viljoen (Eds.), *Organizational Diagnosis: A guide for practitioners* (pp. 85–112). Randburg, South Africa: Knowledge Resources.

Martins, E. C., & Martins, N. (2016). Organizational culture. In S. P. Robbins, A. Odendaal, & G. Roodt (Eds.), *Organizational Behaviour* (3rd ed.; pp. 606–641). Cape Town, South Africa: Pearson Education.

Martins, N. (2017). Survey administration process. In N. Martins, E. Martins, & R. Viljoen (Eds.), *Organizational Diagnosis: A guide for practitioners* (pp. 1810–202). Randburg, South Africa: Knowledge Resources.

Miller, R. L., & Brewerton, J. D. (2003). *The A-Z of Social Research*. London: Sage Publications. doi:10.4135/9780857020024

Mitchell, M. L., & Jolley, J. M. (2007). *Research design explained* (6th ed.). London: Thomson Wadsworth.

Mohelska, H., & Sokolova, M. (2015). Organizational culture and leadership – joint vessels? *Procedia: Social and Behavioral Sciences*, *171*, 1011–1016. doi:10.1016/j.sbspro.2015.01.223

Oates, B. J. (2012). *Researching Information Systems and Computing*. London: SAGE Publications, Inc.

Okere, I., Van Niekerk, J., & Carroll, M. (2012). Assessing Information Security Culture: A Critical Analysis of Current Approaches. In *Proceedings of the Information Security for South Africa Conference (ISSA)* (pp. 136-143). IEEE. 10.1109/ISSA.2012.6320442

Organization for Economic Co-Operation and Development (OECD). (2002). *Guidelines for the security of information systems and networks. Towards a culture of security*. Retrieved from http://www.oecd.org/internet/ieconomy/15582260.pdf

Padayachee, K. (2012). Taxonomy of compliant information security behavior. *Computers & Security, 31*(5), 673–680. doi:10.1016/j.cose.2012.04.004

Pfleeger, C. P., Pfleeger, S. L., & Margulies, J. (2015). *Security in Computing* (5th ed.). Upper Saddle River, NJ: Prentice Hall.

Qualtrics. (2018). *Qualtrics Research Core*. Retrieved from https://www.qualtrics.com/research-core/

Robbins, S. P. (1997). *Essentials of Organizational behavior* (5th ed.). Upper Saddle River, NJ: Prentice Hall.

Robbins, S. P. (2001). *Organizational behaviour* (9th ed.). Prentice Hall.

Robbins, S. P., Odendaal, A., & Roodt, G. (2003). *Organizational behaviour – Global and Southern African perspectives*. Cape Town, South Africa: Pearson Education.

Rossouw, D., & Van Vuuren, L. (2013). *Business ethics* (5th ed.). Oxford University Press.

Ruighaver, A. B., Maynard, S. B., & Chang, S. (2007). Organizational security culture: Extending the end-user perspective. *Computers & Security, 26*(1), 56–62. doi:10.1016/j.cose.2006.10.008

Saunders, M., Lewis, P., & Thornhill, A. (2016). *Research methods for business students* (7th ed.). Pearson Education Limited.

Scantron. (2018). *SurveyTracker*. Retrieved from http://www.scantron.com/software/survey/surveytracker-plus/overview

Schein, E. H. (1985). *Organizational culture and leadership*. San Francisco: Jossey-Bass Publishers.

Schlienger, T., & Teufel, S. (2003). Analyzing information security culture: Increased trust by an appropriate information security culture. In *Proceedings of the International Workshop on Trust and Privacy in Digital Business (TrustBus 2003) in conjunction with the 14th International Conference on Database and Expert Systems Applications (DEXA 2003)*. Prague: IEEE. 10.1109/DEXA.2003.1232055

Schlienger, T., & Teufel, S. (2005). Tool supported management of information security culture. In *Proceedings of IFIP 20th International Information Security Conference proceedings* (pp.65-77). Springer. 10.1007/0-387-25660-1_5

Sheperd, M. L., Harris, M. L., Chung, H., & Himes, E. M. (2014). Using the Awareness, Desire, Knowledge, Ability, Reinforcement Model to build a shared governance culture. *Journal of Nursing Education and Practice, 6*(4), 90–104.

SurveyMonkey. (2018). Retrieved from http://www.surveymonkey.com

Tang, M., Li, M., & Zhang, T. (2015). The impacts of organizational culture on information security culture: A case study. *Information Technology Management, 17*(2), 1–8.

The European Parliament. (2016). *The European Council. General Data Protection Regulation (GDPR), Regulation (EU) 2016/679*. Official Journal of the European Union.

The Information Systems Security Association (ISSA). (2018). *ISSA code of ethics*. Retrieved from www.issa.org/?page=codeofethics

The Singapore Statement on Research Integrity. (2010). Retrieved from www.singaporestatement.org

Tree Solution. (2018). *Sicherheitskultur*. Retrieved from http://www.treesolution.ch/10-0-Smart-Tools-fuer-mehr-Sicherheit.html

Van Niekerk, J. F., & Von Solms, R. (2010). Information security culture: A management perspective. *Computers & Security*, *29*(4), 476–486. doi:10.1016/j.cose.2009.10.005

Verizon. (2017). *Data breach investigations report* (10th ed.). Retrieved from http://www.verizonenterprise.com/verizon-insights-lab/dbir/2017/

Von Solms, B., & Von Solms, R. (2018). Cybersecurity and information security – what goes where? *Information and Computer Security*, *26*(1), 2–9. doi:10.1108/ICS-04-2017-0025

Von Solms, R., & Van Niekerk, J. (2013). From information security to cyber security. *Computers & Security*, *38*, 97–102. doi:10.1016/j.cose.2013.04.004

Whitman, M. E., & Mattord, H. J. (2012). *Principles of information security* (4th ed.). Course Technology Cengage Learning.

Whitman, M. E., & Mattord, H. J. (2017). *Management of information security* (5th ed.). Course Technology Cengage Learning.

Whitman, M. E., & Mattord, H. J. (2019). *Management of information security* (6th ed.). Course Technology Cengage Learning.

ADDITIONAL READING

Da Veiga, A. (2018). An approach to information security culture change combining ADKAR and the ISCA questionnaire to aid transition to the desired culture. *Information and Computer Security Journal*, *2018*(5). doi:10.1108/ICS-08-2017-0056

Geert Hofstede. (2018). *Geert Hofstede*. Retrieved September 14, 2018, from https://geerthofstede.com/

Hofstede, G., Hofstede, G. J., & Minkov, M. (2010). *Cultures and Organizations - Software of the Mind*. New York, USA: McGraw-Hill.

Hofstede Insights. (2018). *Hofstede Insights*. Retrieved September 14, 2018, from https://www.hofstede-insights.com/

Keil Centre. (2018). *Keil centre*, chartered psychologists and ergonomists, Retrieved September 14, 2018, from http://www.keilcentre.co.uk/products-services/safe-people/safety-culture/safety-culture-maturity-model/

Minkov, M., & Hofstede, G. (2013). *Cross-cultural analysis – The science and art of comparing the world's modern societies and their cultures*. California, USA: Sage Publications. doi:10.4135/9781483384719

KEY TERMS AND DEFINITIONS

Cybersecurity Culture: The cybersecurity culture is the unconscious way things are done by users to protect information in cyberspace. This culture extends to home users, employees in organizations or entities, users in communities as well as users from a national or international context.

Information Security Culture: The information security culture is the unconscious way things are done by employees to protect information throughout its life cycle and in various formats, typically in the context of an organization or entity. The information security culture includes cybersecurity culture in the context of an organization.

Information Security Culture Assessment (ISCA): A validated security culture questionnaire with ten constructs to assess the security culture in an organization.

Security Culture: A security culture can be seen as the unconscious manner in which things are done in an organization to secure information. The security culture is synonymous with the information security culture and includes cybersecurity culture in the context of an organization.

Chapter 6
Techniques and Tools for Trainers and Practitioners

Melanie Oldham
Bob's Business, UK

Abigail McAlpine
Bob's Business, UK

ABSTRACT

If the material is to be delivered effectively, organizations need to understand the human side of cyber security training. In this chapter, the authors draw upon over a decade of experience in creating and adapting training and resources with the help of industry professionals and feedback from clients, which has led to a successful and highly acclaimed approach to cybersecurity education. The resulting discussion considers how to adopt the right approach to cybersecurity training for organizations, with training modules that cater to end users, and which are designed to ensure maximum retention of information by presenting short, humorous, animated scenarios that are relatable for the target audience.

INTRODUCTION

For organizations looking to meet compliance requirements or develop a security conscious workforce, this chapter can be used to provide insight into the different approaches to educating the workforce and the different tools and techniques to help develop an established awareness campaign. Understanding and assessing the needs of an organization is essential for the ongoing engagement of learners' interest in cybersecurity. While awareness campaigns are now becoming more commonplace in organizations many see the information as guidance rather than rules, some may even see it as a tick box exercise and cumbersome to integrate into staffs' roles, also possibly perceived as negatively affecting the performance in their tasks and activities.

As well as communicating the fundamental teachings of cybersecurity it is also necessary to understand how learners take in information. This chapter presents hints and tips on how to differentiate, plan and manage training sessions, courses and modules to best fit the organization's needs and those of its learners. This tactic allows more informed decisions about how to approach cybersecurity training and

DOI: 10.4018/978-1-5225-7847-5.ch006

Copyright © 2019, IGI Global. Copying or distributing in print or electronic forms without written permission of IGI Global is prohibited.

the benefits and problems with each tactic. Organizations can utilize combinations of different tactics to teach learners how to be safe and secure when engaging with the digital environment.

It is vital to provide factual and critical information when educating the workforce in the correct attitudes and behaviors to conduct within the organization. Cybersecurity training will also provide skills to navigate themselves more securely online with broader society. Adequate training is more than just providing the facts, and how to apply them, the most effective training changes how learners change their attitudes and behaviors in the long-term, it changes how the individuals engage with others online, their self-awareness and their ongoing interest in the education of cybersecurity. Cybersecurity awareness should not stop once a learner leaves an educational environment. Great training inspires and encourages learners to develop an inquisitive mind, not just for organization security but their personal security and those around them.

All organizations have the opportunity to become cyber secure; this is known as Cybersecurity Culture (CSC) which refers to people's behavior, knowledge, perceptions, attitudes, assumptions, norms and values interacting with technology and devices. Good CSC should encompass an understanding of the current culture within an organization and the gap before the ideal culture. The European Union Agency for Network and Information Security (ENISA) states that CSC should:

Encompasses familiar topics including cybersecurity awareness and information security frameworks but is broader in both scope and application, being a concern with making information security considerations an integral part of an employee's job, habits and conduct, embedding them in their day-to-day actions (ENISA, 2018).

This chapter provides practical help and support towards establishing the needs of learners and readers will be asked to consider, reflect and re-evaluate their teachings with feedback from learners. Whether organizations are at the start of the journey of educating their workforce, or part way through, and whether they are handling the training internally or externally, the chapter aims to provide the information required to create an efficient and effective learning plan.

WHY TEACH CYBERSECURITY ONLINE?

Learning is sometimes more useful as an isolated activity; many learners enjoy learning flexibly at their own pace, others prefer to learn in a social context. Using the courses provided by Bob's Business as an example, the aim is to combine the best of both, with online learning being accessible in the office or on the go. Training can be in a group environment, and post-training discussion is encouraged with extra learning re-enforcements and resources.

Although there is a now a recognized, established and growing need for cybersecurity training for organizations there is a fundamental lack of understanding of how to treat and educate workforces. An active CSC will drive changes in policy, procedures and everyday activities; the motives for different organizations to conduct cybersecurity training are different across the board. Cyber threat awareness campaigns are not sufficient to protect organizations and individuals from cyber threats independently. Cybersecurity awareness campaigns should be in tangent with business processes and everyday activities.

Humans are often the weakest link in cybersecurity; training should be sufficient and engaging enough for the workforce to feel that they work in an open and communicative organization and think that they know and understand how to raise cybersecurity threats in a positive environment that does not scrutinize employees for not spotting a warning earlier. Employees should not feel that they are unable to do their job and demonstrate cybersecurity awareness at the same time.

CSC should be adopted across the organization through all members of staff from top down. Security considerations should manifest themselves naturally in people's everyday activities, behaviors and attitudes as an integral part of an individual's role. CSC should be resilient but responsive to new threats and technologies; it should be implemented in new processes and procedures as time and tasks move forward.

Tools and practices must be tailored to the specific needs and circumstances of an organization. Matured and well-established CSC practices already implemented by organizations specifically cater to the different needs of their business, in some cases, the training should be individually tailored to the different audiences within their organization which helps provide a clear and structured approach to the development of a strong CSC.

Knowledge leadership ensures an evidence-based approach that builds CSC policies, programs and strategies tailored to the organization. The implementation of a secure CSC is to provide alignment with an organizations policies or daily processes. Bringing together a new approach to cybersecurity must be done in harmony with changes to organization policies as well as training. Maximizing the adoption of a new CSC requires support from all levels of an organization, core members of the workforce including management and senior management need to champion the change and push the tailoring of company-wide policies to support the training. Developing a robust cybersecurity culture requires repetitive ongoing engagement, this is not a simple on-off activity.

To successfully teach cybersecurity online training requires the adoption of many different training and education methods to provide open and flexible learning that suits the learners individual learning styles and supports the retention of information. The settings of a formal course where organizations must push employees into a meeting room or venue at the cost of their typical working day can be cast aside in favor of more adaptable online training. Training should be both initiated by management but also championed by them, CSC should be initiated at the top-level, mid-level and bottom-level of an organization.

An example drawn from the authors' own experience occurred during feedback discussion with a client organization regarding the success of a prior cybersecurity simulation course. The organization mentioned an authentic discussion caused because of the training. Specifically, one member of staff had posted in the organization's group messaging service that he had received a phishing email which directed him to the 'Think Before You Click' training course. The employee stated how doing the training was a waste of his time and he was too busy. His peers commented that his conduct was the reason for the training, as the exercise would not have launched without him interacting with a phishing email that could have been a scam. In this instance, his peers understood the need for the training and how vulnerable their organization was because of members of their organization not considering their attitudes and behaviors of engaging with the online environment and potential cybersecurity risks. The employee's dismissiveness reinforced the message that this training was needed as a result of employee conduct. It also created authentic conversations in the workplace that encouraged better cybersecurity awareness.

Successful CSC requires a complete change in mindset across an organization, regardless of which sector the organization sits in, its size or structure. Senior management often drives the culture change within organizations regarding cybersecurity, contextually with the introduction of stricter General Data Protection Regulation (GDPR) legislation many in senior management positions have taken note of the highly promoted fines for non-compliance with GDPR. This approach has forced a changing of goals, policies, objectives, processes, structures and management in an entire range of industries.

Technology opens the opportunity to upskill the standards of staff's cybersecurity knowledge to meet the needs of an organization to protect against the latest threats and vulnerabilities. For the best retention of information, learners need courses that are suited to their learning needs, not just the industry norms. Some employees may have a better understanding of the digital environment where others may have been within an organization before Internet use daily was the social norm. Cybersecurity courses must not assume a level of cybersecurity understanding. It is essential to assess needs for an organization before purchasing or creating cybersecurity training, while industry level training may meet the industry tick boxes, it may not meet the immediate knowledge, skill gaps and requirements of the learners or the organization.

One view of online courses is that they open the opportunity and ability for information access for all. It can be an opportunity to deliver existing course material online. However, this content would have to be adapted to support the alternative learning styles and needs. The discussion explains the need to assess the cybersecurity knowledge gaps of learners as well as the organization.

E-learning is often unsuccessful due to poor engagement rates, forcing learners to sit through hours of courses is not beneficial as learners struggle to take in the amount of information expected. E-learning can adopt the social benefits by rolling out company-wide campaigns that encourage communication and discussion that allows learners to discuss how the training can be utilized in their day to day role. A month by month approach is sufficient as it allows learners to absorb information at their pace while completing it in sync with the rest of the organization.

PREPARING TO TEACH ONLINE

Before developing cybersecurity training, organizations need to create an itinerary of needs to consider the correct methods to approach the training efficiently. These questions will help to design or purchase cybersecurity that will provide the best education and retention for the workforce:

- Why does your organization need cybersecurity training?
- What are the organizational risks?
- What makes an excellent training experience?
- What makes training stick?
- What reinforces learning?
- How to develop training that encourages ongoing conscious learning?
- What makes good engagement?
- Does it meet standards or legislation?

Once the organization has the answers to these questions, it should consider what would provide the opposite experience and then what would only provide an average experience. There are not necessarily right or wrong answers to these questions. This method is merely an opportunity to establish the expectations of training before considering the learning content.

There are many barriers created when training does not meet learners' levels of understanding, training can become tedious, patronizing or make learners feel insecure or stupid for their lack of knowledge.

Pushing out training that is not catered to different learner levels can build a wall between learners and their understanding of the course and the lessons the training is communicating. This information is pivotal to understand and utilize in the event of a cybersecurity breach.

The authors' approach to cybersecurity training is an all-inclusive approach for every member of staff, no matter their level within the organization, no assumptions should be made on the level of understanding, and no learner should feel alienated or stupid because of the training. It also includes creation of bespoke training for organizations, as understanding how brand values and imagery function within an organization and communicate issues in a way that employees will understand and buy into is essential for many larger organizations. Learners should be provided with the skills to enable them to conduct themselves appropriately and safely inside and outside of the organization.

When delivering a training campaign to all learners, careful consideration should be made to understand the motivation for the training in the first place. Is the training simply a tick box exercise that names and shames individuals who later go onto fail when put under pressure, or alternatively is it a learning journey where individuals are given ample time, resources and support to learn how to prevent cybersecurity failures, what to do in the case of an attack and how to report it in line with legislation and organizational policies? Obviously, the latter is the more likely route to actually support the learner.

Creating a bespoke approach can require essential changes to branding, style and language changes to suit an organization, of course when creating a course with specific organizations in mind it becomes easier to add in exact details for contacts or where organization policies and procedures can be found.

Regulation can impose additional costs to an organization as the subsequent needs of designing, documenting and updating CSC policies, practices and responsibilities of organization can be cost heavy, the alternative consequence for ill preparation for a data breach or attack can be catastrophic.

The Directive on Security of Network and Information Systems (2016) and GDPR legislation state that those who fail to abide by security requirements entirely may result in fees or penalties for non-compliance. Reasonable care should be implemented to reinforce the importance of maintaining and updating policies within the organization. The structure should be enforced to remind individuals of the costs and personal responsibilities they must adhere to.

When planning a course, it requires careful consideration of disability access for all learners. The truth is that this is often something missed when organizations choose to build their training in-house, vitally missing the opportunity to train all employees equally. Good online courses adapt for a range of needs and provide the option of all learners to be:

- Independent and indiscriminate of any users of ICT
- Can match the needs of all audiences and learners
- Can help all learners reflect critically and evaluate their learning and training

Accessible training is not about providing special privileges to those with disabilities, it is about providing the equal opportunity and access to all learners to take in the same content in that benefits and supports them.

Through developing and researching learner needs across the years, the authors have developed and embraced the ways to make training more accessible and though often this requires extra design, feature building and testing, it has resulted in courses that are more engaging, interactive and retainable for learners.

Not making training accessible results in organizations identifying employees who would not be able to take the E-learning and provide a face-to-face alternative. Accessibility is not just for those who have disabilities, there are various barriers to the enjoyment and retention of information and adapting training to those with visual, audio or motor impairments adds to quality and value that is offered to learners, as employees learn in different ways.

The W3C has a published guide of recommendations for accessibility benchmarks for those developing online sites, programs or resources. The Web Content Accessibility Guidelines (WCAG) (Web Accessibility Initiative, 2018) not only provide great guidance for the inclusivity of content but also following these guidelines raise the levels of engagement across the board as there are less barriers for every learner.

The WCAG require courses to be screen reader compatible, and there are plenty of screen readers available on the market. The authors have encountered many organizations that require full reports of testing the courses for accessibility as a part of the educational tender and contract.

Long-term training should have a full breakdown of learning objectives and a summary of education that will be taught. Training should not be conducted in one session or a short amount of time. Not all learners can take in all the training at the same rate. It is essential to consider the amount of time that a piece of training will last for. It is important to consider readability metrics when writing cybersecurity training, communications and guidance. The comprehension of training for end-users can depend upon their understanding of the terminology and readability of the content (Alkhurayyif, 2017). When developing cybersecurity guidance, it is essential to consider the following points:

- Can the language in the course be simplified?
- Should additional steps be added to the instructions?
- Can the course be changed into an alternative format?

Considerations need to be made about how to introduce the material to the employees and get them used to the online course system. As learners get used to resources, it is then easy to gradually introduce language and concepts that are more difficult to memorize. The demographics of audiences change so training needs to be adapted to all needs.

At the end of the course, learners should be able to define and describe the critical vocabulary. Learners should know the ways to identify potential threats and understand the consequences of not identifying these threats. Finally, they should understand how to operate tactfully in the future by following or creating policies and procedures that deal with the specific topics covered in training. A final bonus of this training would be the ongoing learning of the student out of their interest and the transferal of the cybersecurity education into their personal lives.

Bloom's Taxonomy of Educational Objectives (Bloom, 1956) considers that many learners should be successful in their studies if provided with sufficient time and support. Bloom's Revised Taxonomy (Anderson, 2002) demonstrates an arrangement method theorizing that learners should be judged against clear objectives rather than competitive systems which categorize learners as successful or unsuccessful based on where their scores lie in comparison with others doing the same course. This approach means that the emphasis is on the learners understanding of a subject rather than their ability to memorize facts and figures.

Bloom's Revised Taxonomy (Anderson, 2002) categorizes taxonomies into three domains, 'Cognitive', 'Affective' and 'Psychomotor'. This theory has inspired decades of texts and educational theory about the levels of cognitive challenge with merely remember and reciting knowledge provided in courses being the lowest cognitive skill.

- **Remembering:** The ability to retrieve, recognize and recall information from the course. A simple quiz can prove this. Remembering what to do if a data breach occurs means that they know how to handle the situation, how to escalate and report it further.
- **Understanding:** The ability to construct meaning from the course and interpret, classify, summarize, compare or explain teachings from the course. Knowledge can be proven by the learner being able to show a full table of advantages and disadvantages. Do they appreciate the damage to reputation and impact a breach may have on the organization?
- **Applying:** The ability to use their knowledge such as in a defined situation or simulation. This ability can be confirmed by the learner being able to identify the appropriate methods to deal with possible cybersecurity scenarios. Do the learners take precaution? Do they lock their desktops and devices? Do they watch out for tailgaters? Are they building this into their normal daily activities?
- **Analyzing:** Can break material up into parts and understand how these parts interact with each other to provide an overall purpose. They can compare and ascertain how specific case studies are similar or dissimilar and why their results were different. Can they assess and analyze a situation? Do they click on links unthinkingly and in a rush? Can they identify cybersecurity vulnerabilities in their peer's behaviors?
- **Evaluating:** Can make judgements based on the information and standards provided. The learner should be able to create a model, table or method of comparison to understand how to support or disprove concepts and demonstrate findings. Are the learners able to identify issues that cause cybersecurity vulnerabilities by staff circumnavigating policies and procedures? Do systems need to be re-visited to become more cyber secure?
- **Creating:** Can put elements together to form a full concept of a topic, including the planning, generating of ideas and production. Learners should be able to provide a detailed plan of how the future of cybersecurity may be. Are they able to create a better cybersecurity culture? Are they able to develop security policies and procedures in future projects?

Learners can showcase all manners of cognitive skills listed in Bloom's taxonomy, some will only demonstrate one or two skills, but all learners should ultimately be encouraged to take an interest in cybersecurity as this will result in a behavioral change about any future cyber challenges or threats. Learning must be incremental, start simple and build confidence and increasing in complexity, consideration must be taken for learners' time to take the course and take in the information provided, from the research and experience of the authors, the full ideal course time should take between 8-12 minutes for optimum retention of information.

To assemble the perfect approach to company-wide adoption of new CSC policies and practices it is essential to consciously build commitment and champions of CSC from the different disciplines within the organization. It is also important to note that just because the technical team deal with the cybersecurity of the organization on a daily basis, they may not be the best communicators of the issues and challenges that cybersecurity creates.

Senior Management should be signaling support and ownership of the campaign for better CSC, by helping to embed the changes into organizational strategy. Cybersecurity enhancement should be an interest to senior management because of the fines and penalties for non-compliance with GDPR and the Data Protection Act from the ICO.

The IT Department or Tech Team should be able to offer and expand their expertise in the core competencies of CSC in an organization to implement and support cyber secure behavior and manage risk awareness. They are also key to developing a swift procedure, policy and response to how any incidents or breeches are handled and responded to. They should align IT and cybersecurity goals to the new legislation and provide a clear and concise breakdown of the expectations of individuals within an organization.

Human resources (HR) are essential to facilitate training, communications, awareness and in some cases to establish how staff should be monitored and handled in the case that an evaluation or disciplinary sanction need to be implemented. HR can also help to provide resources for incentives should the organization choose to do so for positive CSC relations.

Legal need to ensure that all policies and procedures meet and contribute to full compliance within the legislation the organization operates within. For example, legal obligations are not the same in different international countries, so consideration should be made for meeting international legislation. This includes the requirement that suppliers meet GDPR compliance. Legal are also responsible for making sure that expectations of employees are established and what monitoring/accountability should be managed in line with the law.

Marketing and Communications need to communicate a change in mindsets, perceptions and knowledge internally throughout the company, but they are also required to instill customer and business partner trust in the organization as the importance and relevance of CSC grows. The skill of these teams should be used to market cybersecurity in a way that is made attractive to all staff in a similar way they would market products and services.

There are many factors behind the successful adoption of a secure CSC program. How an organization accepts a behavioral change or adaptation, it is dependent on the workforce's collective beliefs, actions, values and attitudes towards cybersecurity. The CSC must work in tangent with everyday processes to avoid the possibility of employees circumnavigating the cybersecurity changes to the policy if they become cumbersome.

Upon starting Think Before You Click in 2015, one of the authors' biggest clients had a phishing rate of 43% in their initial baseline exercise. By 2018, this had decreased to 10.6%, a 75% reduction in phishing rate since the beginning of training. This clearly demonstrates the change in behavior that is promoted by phishing campaigns that focused heavily on communication, collaboration, trust and transparency.

The Internet allows the access to online courses; however, this does not mean that putting all learning materials online is sufficient for the learner. In face-to-face training, the trainer can teach learners through a combination of approaches and real-time feedback from the learners.

The use of alternative methods of teaching demands the course content adapts to a variety of learning styles and needs. Where some would assume that providing one course for many would limit the time-demands on trainers, it can result in higher demands and expectations to monitor and mentor learners through more stimulating instructional and supportive methods of training.

TOOLS AND TECHNIQUES

One of the problems facing Chief Information Security Officers (CISOs) is getting people to engage with an information security awareness campaign. Typically, engagement with E-learning is usually low if the course is made mandatory. This can be improved is by leveraging social influencing within an organization. Using the power of people to influence others to complete training because they want to be seen to be doing the right thing and following the herd.

By implementing companywide campaigns that include the whole organization (including the senior management team) it encourages ongoing social influencing. An effective way to achieve this is to run a campaign concentrating on one cybersecurity topic per month – for example: January - Perfect Passwords, February - Mastering Malware and supporting this with discussions on social forums.

It is important to use marketing techniques to help with companywide engagement. By delivering content in a way that attract people's attention whilst also delivering key messages in language and context that they understand, all of which is important to the success of an awareness campaign.

Another typical failing of in-house awareness campaigns, developed by the compliance or technical teams, is when training courses are in a language used by technical individuals. When course content is in a language that the majority of learners will not understand learners develop a fear of the unknown and therefore become more resistant to listen to the teachings of the course.

It is imperative that communication is at the heart of all information security training courses, what makes users more susceptible to information security threats are the very things that make them human: personality, emotions and motivations. It is impossible to understand what motivates and influences people if communication is poor or does not exist.

In the event of an information security breach organizations will want to encourage and ensure that the individual knows how to prevent putting themselves or the organization at risk, and that they know who to turn to for help and support to minimize the impact in the timely and effective manner. However, if individuals have a fear of those in technical positions and communication barriers exist then it is important to break these down.

The language and tone used should be inclusive, friendly and easy to understand. The more complicated it is, the more disengaged people become. The use of jargon and acronyms should be avoided, and messages should be kept simple and to the point. People learn more effectively when things are concise and in less than 10 minutes chunks.

Analogies and stories are a really effective way to help people to understand and have empathy with a given situation, if people can actually understand something, they are more likely to adopt measures to prevent the negative situations occurring.

One of the criticisms of information security is that it is a dry and quite dull subject it is important to consider where entertainment plays a part in education and the way that people absorb information. The more entertaining and humorous we find things the more we retain information that we are presented with. Making campaigns fun and engaging will consequently increase the retention rate of the information that is provided and enhance the overall experience.

Gamification is another really effective way of ensuring engagement and reinforcement of information. Humans are competitive by nature and strive to be the best. By introducing an element of gamification, where individuals are rewarded for their efforts and can see their progress in relation to their peers, can in turn increase their engagement.

Individuals also possess a fear of missing out (FOMO), so when competing for a title marketing can deliver an effective winners' campaign that will emphasize the importance of engaging with the training. It will also increase pressure amongst peers to compete with the opportunity to be rewarded or receive credit for completing training so that other individuals aspire to achieve the same accolade.

Interaction in training and education can be fundamental to fueling learning. Quizzes, questions and hotspot test learner's knowledge and provide instant recognition of their learning and newfound cybersecurity culture. How a learner takes in information relies on some factors.

Interaction fuels gratification – there are three forms:

1. Instant
2. Delayed
3. None

Instant validation of learning and knowledge helps the learner to retain information to pass on to others. This positive reinforcement for learners encourages them to positively recite and interact with the course content.

Simulated training exercises where users are presented with the impact of their actions at the point at which it occurs are more effective at changing behavior. This is because users are presented with the errors of their ways immediately and therefore can empathize. One way in which the authors have achieved this is that if simulated phishing emails have been delivered and recipients have clicked on the link, they are presented with an educational landing page highlighting the fraudulent and dangerous aspects of the email.

It's important when running simulations that adequate thought is given to the emotions the user may experience, and to avoid any negative reactions and ensure the success of the campaign. By providing individuals with an indication that the training exercise is going to happen and how to react in the event of such an incident and who is on hand to support this, again helps any organization to ensure an effective reaction in the event of a breach as there is barriers of fear and anxiety will be removed.

Simulations are a great way to conduct 'mock attacks' which take several forms, these can be conducted in a number of ways including smishing, phishing, vishing contact made with staff to test how individuals would deal with potential threats. This can also be applied offline with social engineering where individuals attempt to gain access to the office, computers or company files through malicious means. This approach tests whether staff adhere to correct procedures and policies regarding cybersecurity and also helps to identify any weaknesses. For example, if the office has a lot of outsourced staff and new faces, some members of staff are less likely to see new faces as a threat.

GENERAL CONSIDERATIONS

Learning is done by the learner; it is impossible to force them to learn no matter what teaching methods or tactics are utilized. The saying 'you can lead a horse to water, but you cannot make it drink' is the same as trying to teach employees something they have no interest in. However, there's an opportunity with cybersecurity to turn the tables on those who ordinarily tune out employment training

Cybersecurity is not just relevant at work; most people have a small level of understanding of the risks of the online environment for them at home. If organizations can get learners to see how a lack of cybersecurity awareness can put themselves, their friends and their family at risk it provides the opportunity to teach knowledge that sticks in their minds every time they go to click a link in an email, connect to public Wi-Fi or reply to an email from an unknown sender. It is easy to learn what is required or expected to tick boxes and memorize answers without developing a personal understanding of the subject, the key to cybersecurity training is to make it personal and that in turn makes it memorable. We need to let go of the idea of standing at the front of the room with a slideshow presentation and provide the opportunity for learners to learn in a way that benefits them.

Trainers and training can have an immediate and lifelong impact on learners, and the policies that an organization chooses to communicate through its training could have a lasting influence over the interest of those that participate.

Cybersecurity training should:

- Enable learners to reach their full potential
- Teach change right from the start
- Encourage ongoing interest in cybersecurity
- Make training enjoyable
- Encourage them to evaluate their habits at work and home
- Make training relatable

Most learners already work with new technologies such as smartphones, tablets and laptops. Applications open new opportunities to enhance the learning experience in a virtual learning environment.

Online courses mean that the role of the trainer changes entirely, the required knowledge for a course can be crowdsourced from a range of professionals in the industry to develop the best experience for learners. With bespoke or tailored online courses the role of the trainer can change significantly as more time is required to create, review and write content for the course.

It is essential to consider the design of the course and which learning aims and objectives need to be covered in the course. There is a subtle difference between goals, objectives and outcomes of a course. What is essential when developing a CSC course is a clear outline of what needs to be covered and how these points could be made in the most effective way for the learner to retain the information.

Learning aims, and objectives state a brief and basic idea of what level of education organizations want learners to achieve and what they should know by the end of the course. Specific interactive elements should be designed to support the learning of these key aims. The learning aims are likely to be very general summaries of a broader topic and bridging the knowledge gap between the two often requires a series of learning activities as stepping stones.

An excellent online course should not solely be theory or practical. Some courses only provide a combination approach in the way that they provide a method-based teaching course then conduct a quiz or test at the end. A good course should try to intertwine these approaches more effectively by utilizing these tactics throughout the course rather than separating the two into sections.

The theory may be demonstrated through rationale or demonstrative examples that discuss the various learning objectives or attributes that are necessary to meet the expectations of learners or the industry standards. Delivering these materials online require training providers to pick, plan and prepare appropriate course materials for the digital environment.

Technology drives the development of training delivery tools. The Internet as a delivery tool has some pros and cons which will be discussed later in this chapter. Consideration for structuring and pacing must be taken when building cybersecurity courses, long-winded sessions do not benefit learners, especially if learners spend a significant amount of time trying to figure out where they were the last time they were doing the training.

On paper, online training is more cost-effective, but considerations should be made about continuous expenses of making training more up to date and effective by putting potential cost savings into the tailoring content and courses to suit an organization.

Development of a successful CSC program within an organization requires full adoption across the board, the change in culture requires a nuanced approach with the support of influential employees and management as well as a sufficient training program. This education should shape norms, attitudes and behaviors within an organization.

Different departments within an organization compete for finite funds, allocation of financial and time resources into a CSC program need to be taken seriously as it is easy to waste resources on ineffective training.

Delivery costs such as making the course material and keeping it up-to-date, sometimes special software and licenses need to be purchased to create the course content. It is good to compare the costs of face-to-face training with online delivery, the latter of which could save substantial money but cost to host the training online. Venue costs in face to face delivery can add a significant sum to the total amount for the training.

Set-Up costs associated with setting up the training and collating the correct information about cybersecurity could be considered for those looking to build their training, the time cost and investment can be extensive. The development of training also requires a level of understanding of the subject or the purchasing of such information, certificates and education. When paying for trainer's organizations are paying to upskill employees with intellectual capital owned by the trainer. Trainers incur extra costs when needing to add or review and revise the courses to meet expectations and latest legislation such as GDPR (General Data Protection Regulation) or DPA 2018 (Data Protection Act).

Educational and training courses are a means of business and utilized for generating income. However, the standard of these courses is not necessarily the same across all suppliers; different trainers would break down resources and training into separate products.

If organizations wish to cut costs and corners with training, it is easy to provide large documents that explain all the essential information, but ultimately this does not adapt to the different learning types, and excessive clicking and scrolling will result in dissatisfaction from the learners, and the material will be ignored.

There are costs associated with providing a training service that is often absorbed by the trainers, such as materials costs, travel, accommodation, venues and course building. For the learner, there are often costs associated with training that is often left unconsidered.

Loss of working hours leaving them to catch up with their regular workload around their usual hours or catch up in overtime, stretching the workforce manhours to incorporate training can put extra stressors on employees and leave them vulnerable to burning out or making mistakes, training must not add too much stress on employees.

Organizations looking to build an interactive course internally will incur software or building costs; however, often it is far more beneficial to create bespoke training for the organization as it helps learners to imagine themselves in the same scenarios.

E-learning courses are a ready-made solution, but engagement stats are often low. To ensure an active adoption effort must be applied to create an implementation plan which will be adopted and supported by stakeholders and effectively communicated and executed. Face to face training tends to be more successful since it can separate the user from the working environment and the destructions of inbound communications and colleagues wanting attention. To compete learning must be engaging and immersive to eliminate distraction and keep the learner focused. However, blended learning allows the best of both opportunities, as it allows the learner to learn in an immersive way whilst the course content helps to reflect and allows discussion of subjects in a group environment.

There are benefits to any organization who are wishing to upskill their workforce with cybersecurity training. The online material in an Internet environment opens the opportunity to protect anyone from putting the organization at risk while also not at the significant cost of inflexibility.

It is feasible that there will be an increase in enrolment because of the courses being accessible online and on the go. If training is adequately developed and constructed course providers can provide instant feedback that help learners feel that their needs and opinions are satisfied and valued. The economic costs of breaches to an organization can encompass a range of financial and intellectual property costs as well as loss of reputation. Losses to an organization can take on multiple forms including the loss or compromise of confidential information, fines for personal data breaches, downtime of systems or services, disruptive costs to revenues, as well as damage the reputation and business.

Investment into developing better cybersecurity technology and practices can significantly reduce and prepare an organization against costs and losses; it also allows the opportunity to maintain and establish competitiveness by embracing security control that helps to alleviate the security risks of engaging with the online environment. Raising the immunity of the workforce to a security breach or infection can slow the spread of infection within an organization.

Learners are more connected to their phones, so they are more likely to complete the training in their own time willingly. If training is in a more comfortable format for learners, they are more likely to complete the training. The authors own experience has observed a trend in learners achieving their training before 9am, from 12pm to 2 pm (i.e. lunchtimes) and during weekends.

The structured nature of the training gives learners a view of the content as a professional in the industry would learn it, the ability to provide phishing simulations affords real-life experience which aids the learning experience. Online and flexible learning stimulates learners and promotes positive learning attitudes and behaviors towards education.

Online learning should provide the learners with the ability to login to learning at any time and provide feedback that can directly and positively affect the progression of the training programs. The ability to work on the course at any time convenient to the learner improves their motivation and ability to work on the training on the go. Bespoke training and tailored solutions allow for individualized instruction making it more relevant to the learner's environment.

Teaching spaces are not limited to online learning, it opens enrolment opportunities for more students to participate in learning the course content, and everyone receives the same experience every time, this means that any recognition for the course as an education or training leader such as awards and certification can be the same experience and training replicated for each learner.

Fundamental changes for an organization require evident involvement and responsibilities require everyone in the organization to foster a level of ownership of its success and motivation to commit to a change in CSC rather than simple tick box exercises to prove compliance. CSC is practical if all employees understand their role within it and the tools, skills and knowledge required for successful adoption. Learning should be done in a safe environment to prevent dismissive attitudes to CSC, dialogue should be encouraged to optimize learning. The opportunity to ask questions and receive responses that allow the reinforcement and motivations to be secured within the organization. Incentives can be created to align individuals closer to the new policies.

Cybersecurity extends beyond the workplace as employees can work on their own devices, travel from work and home and use some of the same identifying information in their personal and professional lives, education and utilization of this knowledge strengthen the organization's protection from cyber threats.

DEVELOPMENT AREAS

All teaching and training must consider learners, and learning styles dictate the relationships between education and learning. It is critical to understand the need to facilitate all learning styles so as not to alienate any learners. Some learners may find the use of computers scary or threatening and others may find it enjoyable and comfortable to utilize. Consideration must be made to explain how to make the most out of training and how to navigate the training for those who are less computer-literate.

Working through courses online can be a massive frustration for learners who face issues with the technology of the course if something goes wrong learners want to talk to people, not computers. It is essential that learners understand who they can contact if there is something wrong with the training. Recognition of progress is a positive reinforcement to learning, being able to promote new knowledge online can be a great way to reward hard work. The ability to encourage completed courses on LinkedIn and portfolios can be a great promotional tool for the training provider too.

Trainers who generate relatable concepts to aid learners in understanding and lead to positive learning experiences and outcomes. A good starting point for learners is a personal experience, learners who can relate to brilliant case studies or scenarios have a better chance of retaining information. This type of approach provides learners with the opportunity to self-reflect and analyze their actions in the workplace. By selecting scenarios that learners can relate to, the learning lasts long-term and can be seen and experienced in the learner's environment. Learners then adapt their cybersecurity education to their environment later. This approach is something that the authors have utilized in training courses, and it has helped learners to apply the skills demonstrated in courses in their real environments.

Stories are good because they create a visual picture; you are appealing to a human being, not a robot. Stories help to promote employee best practice with the relevant scenarios and advice. Learning material can help employees identify with the cybersecurity threats, they can also feature a response to threats and what measures and employee could take to prevent them from actualization. Stories can be communicated through online learning videos, posters, infographics and more.

Videos can communicate the correct response to cyber threats, but so can interactive tasks or gamification in online training. Games engage a learner to actively interact with the course, which facilitates participation with the training rather than watching a video play. Gamification can work as an online workshop that allows the learner to play around with different aspects of scenarios.

Accents, looks, prejudices all distract attention from the presenter rather than the content being told; cartoon characters work because people do not have the same prejudices against characters.

Cybersecurity training can be delivered in several online methods, as well as offline materials and hybrid learning. Hybrid learning provides an opportunity to raise the strength of CSC within an organization. The method of training should be delivered in the best way for the organization. Consultation of organizational resources should be made so that the implementation of the program is achievable.

Encouraging learners to reflect on their education is essential for them to develop their understanding of their habits, attitudes and behaviors. Change does not happen if participants cannot identify the questionable practices that may leave them vulnerable to exploitation or cyber threats.

Reflection enables learning to be more dynamic, it encourages critical thinking skills, to analyze their work and life situations and to imagine different scenarios and people these cybersecurity threats could exploit. This reflection helps to develop their skills and practice of the training they have been taught.

The privacy paradox (Barth & Jong, 2017) demonstrates major discrepancies between users and employees attitudes to cybersecurity and privacy and their actual behavior, mainly that whilst they may claim to be very concerned about their privacy they are very unlikely to take any actions to prevent or protect the disclosure of their personal data.

Simplifying layers of complexity in cybersecurity training is essential to communicate information and education to everyone; it is not productive to believe that all learners will understand the cyber risks, threats or consequences. Building on fundamental principles, some learners may realize the underlying cybersecurity concept, they may not know what they mean. When progressing from primary cybersecurity education to more complex concepts, it is best to lead learners through a story that links to their background so that they can relate it to their own life.

Some online courses or websites suffer the fatal flaw of inadequate or unclear navigation; this means that learners get frustrated or give up on learning due to difficulties in getting where they want to be. Not only is it essential to consider users understanding of how to navigate the learning platform but to track or beta test the learner's journey. Beta testing should be done by users who had no place in the design or development of the course for an accurate reflection of user experience. Explanations of how to navigate the learning platform should be readily available and explained to all learners.

Emails are a simple method of contacting everyone within an organization as they can deliver cybersecurity messaging directly to all members of staff, it also makes training more accessible at a later date so that staff can revisit the staff training portal. It is also easy to track click through rates of staff who take the training and can further help identify risks associated with attitudes and behaviors of staff within an organization. It can also be beneficial to ensure that access to training is found on the organization's intranet.

Training is often created by techies or legislation people. However, the best people to design courses are the marketing team who are great at communication; cybersecurity should be marketed internally,

Teaching cybersecurity courses online can be a perfect medium, a variety of strengths. The Internet is a vast area for growth and exposure for courses; material can be designed instructional to meet the needs of learners best. Humans can control and interact with the program themselves providing opportunities to interact kinesthetically. However, this has some failings as it requires learners to have reasonable access to the Internet to stream content, there can be the possibility of technology errors that lead to courses not being completed.

Adopting courses to the digital environment can be difficult for trainers who need to alter their teaching style, Course and training providers also need to boost or utilize their credibility and reputation as a provider of quality cybersecurity training.

LEARNING REINFORCEMENTS AND RESOURCES

Selecting and developing resources to provide stimulating context and structure to the learning experience fosters strong reinforcement to the learning objectives.

With each of the resources it is critical to consider the following points:

- How firmly does this resource support the key learning objectives?
- Is the language meeting learners reading ages?
- Is the design clear to navigate?
- Have you had others beta test or review the resources?
- Are the questions used to make learners consider the key learning points?
- Does it cater to a broad range of learners?

The more entertaining or funny it is, the more memorable the training is likely to be. Communication awareness training allows fast reactions rather than barriers. IT team need to be approachable and referenced in communications. To support more extensive and continuous learning, it is beneficial to bring cybersecurity back to the forefront of the workforce minds. Encourage members of the workforce to bring business cases to report on.

Reinforcement of training includes carrying out research into cybercrime and cybersecurity in the sector with reports, news articles and statistics about the organization's own industry. Managing cybersecurity risk projects, a robust unified approach to CSC. Behavioral change to develop cyber secure culture is not something that happens overnight. It is something that happens with continued reinforcement and it is therefore imperative that operational procedures and policies have information security at its center. Providing guidance, tools and advice on how to react in the event of an incident and the best practice behavior will benefit the organization immensely.

Reinforcement of key messaging via digital and physical resources such as posters, screen displays, floors stickers and web banners are effective in aiding cognitive recognition if the design, text and tone of voice are consistent, as the human brain subconsciously recognises and pieces together common aspects. Meanwhile, another method of reinforcement is to have the IT department collect evidence of log files presenting successful or unsuccessful attacks upon the organization. These should highlight the potential damage these attacks could present to the organization. This acts as a feedback tool to influence the next line of defense against security issues.

The adoption of a new CSC extends beyond a simple 'Cybersecurity Awareness' campaign. Learners should understand a clear concept of how they will be assessed on a regular basis. This concept may change how they approach cybersecurity risks as they become more alert to any potential examinations. There are however some assessments in cybersecurity that can be done best with a level of deception. This approach is not only practical to assess how high the cybersecurity risk is to an organization but also a learning opportunity for individuals who fall foul of the tests.

Monitoring and target setting, many online courses focus entirely on the outcomes of the end of course tests and quizzes. However, in cybersecurity, the real test comes when utilized in the right situations and learners keeping this education at the front of their mind when dealing with the potential cyber threats.

Activities and outcomes also fall under the greater umbrella of assessment as they are closely intertwined and should be considered in the broader evaluation of the cybersecurity course.

- **Activities:** What will learners do? What tasks will they interact with? Are there interactive knowledge checks or assessments?
- **Outcomes:** What questions will they be able to answer? What knowledge will they have a result of the cybersecurity training?
- **Assessment Criteria:** What are the key criteria points that will let trainers know that learners have taken information in? To what extent?

The best activities are easy to describe, use prompts to help learners understand the tasks, aid learning the critical points of the training and use a combination of stories, analogy, mystery and common interest and help learners to sustain interest in the discipline.

Evaluate learning with short summaries which help learners to remember key points. Users are presented with an oversaturation of information on so many varying forms of media that it has reduced the amount of time that they will concentrate on any one given thing; therefore, it's important the key messaging to be short sharp in order for the user not to be switched off. Recapping the key points from the lesson help to reflect on learning and summarize the courses.

Determining the need for a stronger CSC can be difficult as building a strong business case for the training relies on staff to be honest in relating the aspects of their attitudes, awareness and behavior when interacting with the online environment. IBM conducted a Cybersecurity Intelligence Index report which exposed that 95% of cybersecurity breaches are due to human error (Powers, 2018). Perceptions of staff in regard to cybersecurity can be quite problematic as even a positive attitude towards cybersecurity in organizations has related to risky cybersecurity behaviors (Hadlington, 2017) both attentional and motor impulsivity were both significant positive predictors of risky cybersecurity behaviors.

However, it is not a probable that individuals will be honest or understand the terminology used in self-completion questionnaires, there are a number of bias with self-reporting including the motive of providing desirable responses or misunderstanding of causality.

In research conducted on over 1,000 members of organizations just over half of the respondents (58%) stated that they were aware of security threats and the risk they pose to corporate information, whilst 39% of the respondents thought that it was the company's responsibility to protect data (Muncaster, 2017).

Almost two-thirds of the same respondents (62%) stated that they thought their behavior had a low to moderate impact on the corporation's security and just under half of the respondents (48%) claimed they were not bothered about their corporate security policy as they did not believe it affected their role (Muncaster, 2017).

There are seven core dimensions of security culture using the Security CLTRe Framework (da Veiga, 2010) and these can be used to measure the human factors that contribute to CSC.

1. Behaviors
2. Attitudes
3. Cognitions

4. Compliance
5. Communication
6. Norms
7. Responsibilities

The benefit to creating a business case for online CSC training is that it helps provide insight to the current cybersecurity weaknesses within an organization and it also enables key insights into any patterns of behavior within certain areas of the business. This approach also helps to provide a starting point for key metrics of improvement after implementation of the training. Pre and post measurements would be ascertained to prove a need for the training and the success of the program.

Commonly it is a combination of behavior or attitudes towards CSC that can cause the most human factor damage to an organization. By selecting metrics on attitudes and behaviors it becomes easier to understand and overcome the causal effect on the success of CSC programs and allow the future modification of the training to combat any issues that arise. Creating a report on the current CSC situation allows the reflection of specific contextual or situational security issues, it can also help to identify stronger and weaker groups or department within an organization or identify any patterns that may emerge.

CONCLUSION

There are many benefits to a business or organization getting involved in initiatives to build cybersecurity skills. These include providing individuals and employees with the skills and capabilities to identify and manage a cybersecurity risk effectively. This will benefit the organization as the financial cost to the business can be extremely high and the cost in consumer confidence can cripple a business. Investment into these skills are both essential and cost effective for organizations.

This also provides organizations the opportunity to prioritize, influence and reward employees for developing cybersecurity skills, knowledge and experience that they may pass on to others. It can also help to inspire a more diverse range of talented cybersecurity specialists within the business and beyond and finally it will increase awareness of the career opportunities that are offered, and loyalty to those organization, amongst those wishing to recruit and retain staff (HM Government, 2018).

After the points covered in this chapter, it may seem obvious that implementing a positive change to strengthen CSC in organizations to a sufficient cyber secure workforce would be beneficial to any organization. However, understandably all departments within an organization are competing for funding from a limited fund of financial resources. Some may be required to develop a strong business case for funding the input into CSC.

Recommendations for the successful adoption of a secure CSC is to:

- Secure at all levels of an organization – a full commitment to CSC is essential for the successful adoption across the business, this includes higher levels of the organization who are expected to champion the new cybersecurity policy.
- Implement a CSC plan and policy across the organization that provides a guide for anyone within an organization to follow

- To show successful metrics of companywide adoption and overcome any barriers is essential to assess where the organization currently sits in respect of its CSC and build a report centered around the implementation, goals, success criteria and target audience of the training. This will help provide the measurement of impact.
- Draw upon guidance provided by the industry blogs, resources and white papers.

The manner of communicate with learners and organizations requires a specific understanding of who are learners might be and what the organization want to achieve. Communicating training effectively does not just mean what is said about cybersecurity training but how it is presented. It is the language used, the construction of sentences, the sound of the delivery, and the personality of the trainers all have an influence.

If organizations engage effectively and positively with staff regarding cybersecurity education, then in the event of a breach they are more likely to understand that the organization is a safe environment in which they can report the incident, enabling a quicker response that can minimize the damage done.

REFERENCES

Alkhurayyif, Y. &. (2017). Evaluating Readability as a Factor in Information Security Policies. *International Journal of Trend in Research and Development*, 54-64.

Anderson, L. W. (2002). *Revising Bloom's taxonomy.* Ohio State University.

Barth, S., & Jong, M. D. (2017). The privacy paradox – Investigating discrepancies between expressed privacy concerns and actual online behavior – A systematic literature review. *Telematics and Informatics*, *34*(7), 1038–1058. doi:10.1016/j.tele.2017.04.013

Bloom, B. S. (1956). *Taxonomy of educational objectives*. New York: Longmans, Green.

da Veiga, A., & Eloff, J. H. P. (2010). A framework and assessment instrument for information security culture. *Computers & Security*, *29*(2), 196–207. doi:10.1016/j.cose.2009.09.002

ENISA. (2018). *Cyber Security Culture In Organisations*. Retrieved from ENISA: https://www.enisa.europa.eu/publications/cyber-security-culture-in-organisations/at_download/fullReport

Government, H. M. (2018). *Cyber Security Skills: A guide for business*. Retrieved from HM Government: https://assets.publishing.service.gov.uk/government/uploads/system/uploads/attachment_data/file/386248/bis-14-1276-cyber-security-skills-a-guide-for-business.pdf

Hadlington, L. (2017). Human factors in cybersecurity; examining the link between Internet addiction, impulsivity, attitudes towards cybersecurity, and risky cyber security behaviours. *Heliyon (London)*, 00346.

Muncaster, P. (2017). Cisco: Complacency and Ignorance Make Staff Major Security Threat. *Infosecurity Magazine*. Retrieved from https://www.infosecurity-magazine.com/news/complacency-and-low-awareness/

Powers, C. (2018). *Are hackers targeting your industry? Find out in the 2015 Cybersecurity Intelligence Index.* Retrieved from IBM: https://www.ibm.com/developerworks/community/blogs/81c130c7-4408-4e01-adf5-658ae0ef5f0c/entry/Are_hackers_targeting_your_industry_Find_out_in_the_2015_Cyber_Security_Intelligence_Index?lang=en

Web Accessibility Initiative. (2018). *Web Content Accessibility Guidelines (WCAG) Overview.* Retrieved from Web Accessibility Initiative: https://www.w3.org/WAI/standards-guidelines/wcag/

Chapter 7
Ensuring Core Competencies for Cybersecurity Specialists

Gurpreet Dhillon
The University of North Carolina at Greensboro, USA

Kane Smith
The University of North Carolina at Greensboro, USA

Karin Hedström
Örebro University, Sweden

ABSTRACT

Within an organization, it is critical that all employees possess a security awareness and thus play a part in the protection of said organization's information assets. Some employees will have key roles and responsibilities and require specific skills to support them. However, organizations can face challenges in regard to recognizing the required specialized skills as well as where to obtain them. For this reason, whether an organization chooses to hire new staff, developing existing staff, or outsource the activities altogether, it is necessary to know the type and level of expertise required. To this end, this chapter discusses the need for organizations to understand and identify the essential skills related to cybersecurity in order for their employees to develop core competencies in these areas.

INTRODUCTION

Due to globalization, increased competition, accelerated technological advancements, and lightning quick communications, today's businesses are redesigning their organizational structures (Dhillon and Backhouse 1996; 2001; Dhillon and Kolkowska 2011). There has been a dramatic shift in the model of rigid organizational structures toward more loosely coupled networks. In this environment, Information Systems (IS) security gains new prominence and becomes one of the most important issues businesses face. In this new environment, a simple technical expertise alone is not enough. For IS security to be truly effective organizations need to hire skilled and knowledgeable people, develop effective informa-

DOI: 10.4018/978-1-5225-7847-5.ch007

Copyright © 2019, IGI Global. Copying or distributing in print or electronic forms without written permission of IGI Global is prohibited.

tion security processes, and synthesize the two into a seamless system (Dhillon and Backhouse 1996; 2001; Dhillon and Kolkowska 2011). Therefore, technical expertise needs to be coupled with a thorough understanding of organizational processes and human behavior in order to meet today's challenges of an increased focus on an information society (Dhillon and Kolkowska 2011).

The face of the business is constantly changing. This is due to both the globalization of today's commerce, and technological innovations in communication and information exchange fields, the standard business model has moved away from closed, bureaucratic structures towards loosely coupled networks (Dhillon and Backhouse 1996; 2001). These networks exchange information through a complex system of formal and informal channels. This is much different from the hierarchical exchange of information between internal business units, as was typical in the past. The opportunities provided by the opening of the countries' borders, together with rapid advances in information systems have changed the way in which businesses collect, store, use and exchange critical and valuable information. As technology developed and allowed companies to analyze data in a much more effective and extensive manner, the value of this data increased drastically (Dhillon and Kolkowska 2011). Simultaneously, the same technological advances have made information available to a wider audience. This new reality greatly expanded and changed the context in which IS security is considered.

There has been extensive research done in order to determine what the principles of managing information systems' security are. Dhillon and Backhouse (2000) quote two sets of security principles as the ones that, when combined, create a comprehensive framework for IS security management. The first set of principals refers directly to IS systems and their physical security. The first set delineates confidentiality, integrity and availability (CIA) as the three major principles ensuring secure IS. Confidentiality refers to the prevention of unauthorized disclosure of information, integrity deals with the prevention of unauthorized modification to data, and availability refers to the prevention of unauthorized withholding of data or resources. However, these principles are highly limited and perceive IS solely as data stored on a computer or in a database therefore, the second set of principles (RITE) complements the first one by focusing on the organizational aspects of information flow and exchange within and among organizations.

RITE includes the principles of responsibility, integrity, trust and ethicality. Responsibility requires that all members of an organization understand their roles and responsibilities. The principle of integrity requires individuals to acknowledge and accept their membership in the organization. Trust is seen as a counterweight, to external supervision and control, and thus requires self-control from individual members of the information exchange network. In addition, the principal of trust requires that individuals accept and acknowledge responsibility related to the information they access and process. The last principle of RITE refers to ethicality, as opposed to rules, and expects both individuals and the organization as a whole, to act in accordance with commonly accepted ethical practices.

DEFINING ORGANIZATIONAL COMPETENCIES

Organizational competence is needed for harnessing the full power of Information Technology, especially in the context of IS security (Lado and Wilson 1994; McGrath et al. 1995; Dhillon 2008). Hence, the role of IS security can only be exploited effectively by an organization if it has developed a set of core competencies, yet as the role of IT changes so do the required competencies related to IS security (Lado and Wilson 1994; McGrath et al. 1995; Dhillon 2008). These required competencies can be divided into three categories: Strategic, Exploitational and Supply (See Table 1). Each core organizational competency encompasses a different aspect of IS security and will therefore require a different set of skills to execute. However, before these competencies can be explored, it is first important to understand what is meant by organizational competence.

In the literature (Lado and Wilson 1994; McGrath et al. 1995; Dhillon 2008), two major paradigms are used to explain organizational competence; The first draws upon the concept of industrial organization economics, which traditionally emphasizes barriers to competition, in particular some industries are attractive because they contain 'structural impediments to competitive forces' and thus allow its firms to maintain competence in their respective area. The second says that firms are fundamentally distinctive and develop unique combinations of resources that allow them to ingrain individual competencies within themselves. These resources are a long-lived productive ability that allows an organization to gain strategic advantages because of its special competencies. Organizational resources may be physical or intangible and a resource is strategic when it results in a significant portion of the investment base of the firm and is not freely available in a competitive resource market (see the works of Weick 1979; 1995). However, as there are few 'structural impediments' for buying IT, it is generally considered to be a key resource of the organization and it is organizational competence that is required to exploit IT (Dhillon 2008). Therefore, IS security should be regarded as an organizational competence that is necessary to fully exploit the benefits of IT within an organization in this new era (Lado and Wilson 1994). Organizational competence for harnessing these benefits can then be developed through two necessary components: First, and improvement of individual know-how and skills and Second, institutionalization of purposeful prudent interactions. The following sections explore the three necessary categories of organizational competency in the context of IS security.

Strategic Competency

The importance of customer needs and management vision and support are important factors in the strategic use of IT. An innovating organization's understanding of technological and business aspects increases the probability that it will introduce competitively significant enhancements and sustain their

Table 1. Core organizational competencies and corresponding cybersecurity requirements

Competence Category	Cybersecurity Competence
Strategic	The Competency to Create Adequate Business Processes, The Competency to Clearly Define Roles, The Competency to Recognize the Importance and Scope of IS Security Concerns, The Competency to Identify Internal Threats to IS Security, The Competency to Develop IS Security Processes, The Competency to Implement IS security Policies, The Competency to Maintain Policy Flexibility, The Competency to Regulate the Flow of Information, The Competency to Communicate the Necessity for IS Security Procedures, The Competency to Facilitate Informal Communication About IS Security, The Competency to Monitor Adequately
Exploitational	The Competency of Managers to Lead and Influence Others Awareness, The Competency of Continuing Personal Development, The Competency to Work in Teams, The Competency to Maintain Ethical Behaviors and Engender Loyalty, The Competency to Maintain Good Hiring Practices
Supply	The Competency to Sustain Technical Expertise, The Competency to Synthesize Technical and Business Knowledge,

advantage despite copying by rivals (Dhillon 2008). Competence to exploit an opportunity is influenced by the prevailing management culture, experience, and employee satisfaction (Dhillon 2008). The presence of first-mover benefits provides the basis for the sustainability of advantage and in addition to this benefit, innovators may achieve continued advantages even after the technology or skill set is widely diffused (Dhillon 2008). Therefore, Strategic competence is the ability of the organization to understand and appreciate the strategic use of IT and to consider future options affecting the way an organization works (the argument is drawn from the works of Weick & Roberts 1993 and McGrath et al 1995).

Specifically, understanding IS security as it relates to an organization's ability to protect its information assets is a critical necessity for maintaining a competitive edge in any industry. While IT assets may become ubiquitous throughout an industry, the processes, policies and business practices as well as organizational commitment to them will not. Business leaders will require the ability to look, introspectively, at their organization to identify opportunities for improvement in an open and honest manner. These leaders will need to foster an environment that inculcates new and current members alike with a security-oriented mindset as well as provide clear roles and responsibilities for all employees as it involves IS security. However, simply developing goals and outlining responsibilities will not be sufficient from a policy standpoint, organizations must also develop and retain competency with them in order to obtain a competitive advantage.

Exploitational Competency

The use and exploitation of IT has shown that a unique combination of the firm's resources provided a way to maintain high performance levels. The strategic importance of a resource will depend on the extent to which it is competitively available, hence if the resource is unique, it is likely that resource owners will be able to appropriate some of the benefits. Thus, organizations can only sustain competitive advantage if their resources cannot be expanded freely or imitated by other firms (Dhillon 2008). Therefore, the exploration and enhancement of unique sources of practice, know-how and culture at an organizational level can then be the source of sustained advantage. Hence, firms must develop new competencies and new ways of combining resources that are difficult for their competitors to appropriate.

While strategic competency deals with the development of policy, their execution requires skilled managers who can execute on a broader vision while retaining competency in specific IS security skills or tasks. This is a difficult task and managers with this competency take years to develop within an organization. However, once they exist, they represent a huge competitive advantage for an organization. These possess the competency to influence others, engender teamwork and foster a culture of continued personal development and ethical behavior, helping create new managers and leaders with these desired skills (see Orton & Weick 1990). When dealing with IS security, employees look to leadership for guidance in these areas and competent managers will inspire them to act in a manner that is secure and thusly beneficial to the organization.

Supply Competency

A competitive advantage for an organization depends on the interaction between industry conditions and its ability to identify and exploit opportunities. An examination of cases of IT-based competitive advantage showed that sustained superior performance requires the interplay of the environmental conditions and internal competencies (Dhillon 2008). Hence, under no circumstances can IT alone be regarded as the firm's motivation in producing strategic applications[1]. Organizations require a set of skills, which can react effectively to various changes in the business environment. Therefore, an understanding of the potential strategic impact of IT and its integration with business processes may lead to sustainability of competitive advantage.

In today's environment, data analytics and data in general is becoming the tool used for improving competitive advantage within all industries. However, when a firm fails to properly develop the skills and competency around IS security within that organization, the results can lead to disaster. Often times a lack of technical expertise or the inability to synthesize business and technology leads to failures in IS security. When IS security gets in the way of or prevents an employee from doing their job to the best of their ability, security will fall by the wayside. Organizations must recognize and anticipate the varying and ever-changing skill sets necessary to properly protect their organization and integrate those new skills with current business practices.

The three core organizational competencies listed and discussed above comprise the necessary ingredients to develop and sustain a competitive advantage in today's era of information technology. Specifically, IS security, viewed in the context of a competitive advantage, must be explored and developed in all three areas by organizations. However, neither an individual's skills, nor the procedures or routines within an organization defines competency. Competency is a marriage of individuals' skills with adequate established, business processes that allow an organization to execute and exercise those skills advantageously. Hence, a company's abilities to perform the tasks necessary to ensure IS security can be translated directly into organizational competencies, as they consist of both the talent and expertise of individuals synthesized with properly designed business procedures to form core organizational competencies in cybersecurity. The following sections explore each core organizational competency in the context of cybersecurity and define key competencies within each category that can be exploited by firms for a competitive advantage in IS security.

STRATEGIC COMPETENCIES FOR CYBERSECURITY

The Competency to Create Adequate Business Processes

When discussing business settings, organizational structure and knowledge, it is important to precisely define, design and then communicate a company's strategic goals and business processes. Properly designed and defined business processes are universally thought to be the foundation for effective IS security. Organizations must be able to realize their strategic objectives and create effective business processes in accordance to those objectives. It is then on those clear and cohesive business processes that all security strategies can be built.

The Competency to Clearly Define Roles

Effective IS security is impossible to achieve without clear, consistent business processes. However, an equally important step toward securing IS lies in the organization's ability to clearly define the roles and responsibilities of all its' members as the definition of various employee functions is critical for the health of any organization's structure. All members of an organization need to fully understand the purpose and the scope of their distinctive roles. It is in every organization's interest to not only assign roles in accordance with business processes, but to also explain the purpose of each role, and clarify individual responsibilities. IS security design should take into account roles distributed throughout the organization, and always support, rather than limit, the execution of duties related to these roles. In particular, IS security design must carefully consider each role's required access to information. In organizations where roles are clearly and precisely defined and employees understand their positions contribution to the company's overall strategy, security issues are much easier to manage. In addition, in organizations that are IS security aware in this manner, many threats to IS are mitigated and problems tend to be solved before they become serious.

The Competency to Recognize the Importance and Scope of IS Security Concerns

Security processes must be designed in accordance with an organization's strategic and business goals. No security system will be effective unless it follows business processes. For successful and effective IS protection to be developed, top management must acknowledge how crucial IS security is to business success and understand how severe the outcome of a security breach could be. Once this realization is in place it is much easier for the company to commence its journey toward design, development and implementation of an effective IS security plan.

For example, IS security tools should never be standardized. All security procedures and tools should always follow specific business processes and be adjusted to fit specific business settings and operations. Thus, for a company to properly develop its security policies, controls, and procedures top management, responsible for development of guiding principles, needs to be able to identify major threats every IS faces. It is crucial that those in charge preparing a structure to protect the IS must be qualified for the task. They must possess the knowledge of security issues, current trends and solutions. However, security managers knowledge cannot be limited to technological issues, they need to keep in mind the company's core business and understand the company business processes.

The Competency to Identify Internal Threats to IS Security

Within an organization it is necessary to distinguish between employees committing unintentional breaches of information system security, and the malicious, conscious acts that aim to steal, tamper with or destroy information possessed by an organization. Both of these threats are real, and both can result in severe consequences. However, each demands a slightly different approach when developing security controls and protection tools. When designing information security systems every organization must be cognizant of the need to prevent both malicious acts, and unconscious giving away or destroying information, and they must be able to protect their information from both types of security breaches.

Accidental acts that result in security breaches can be avoided only if the organization acknowledges the possibility of the occurrence of such acts. Therefore, organizational competencies that are critical, in this context, consist of company's ability to anticipate and prevent situations, in which information can be endangered by unconscious announcement of sensitive and confidential information or unintentional deletion of data. To be able to predict all possible, undesirable scenarios, organization needs to possess in-depth knowledge of the reality in which its business processes are performed. Only by possessing this knowledge can companies create security systems that would be robust to unintentional abuse or deletion of information.

Aware acts or deliberate sabotage of information is yet another threat every company must be aware of when designing its information security system. Here, ability to conduct accurate risk analysis is one of the most important competencies an organization may possess. Ignorance of the need to, or negligence of implementing necessary precautions to protect data theft, and information sabotage, may seriously jeopardize both the financial stability of a company, and its competitive position in the industry. Ability to foresee all possible situations in which information security could be breached is certainly a base for proper design of protection systems. However, the ability to actively execute controls, policies and regulations, and constant monitoring are, on the business level, one of the most important competencies an organization must possess to protect itself from individuals consciously breaching information security.

The Competency to Develop IS Security Processes

To design a robust and effective security system organizations must possess competencies allowing them to predict dangers coming from both aforementioned directions. However, the competency of analyzing ongoing business processes to predict threats for information systems is not sufficient to protect company from these threats. Capability to assign proper resources to develop effective processes preventing and protecting information systems is equally important. Policies, controls and processes designed by any organization must be the result of management knowledge of organizational, business, and technical aspects of information flow and exchange. Regulations, which maximize the protection of information systems, should never disrupt the execution of business process. The ability to find the right balance between control and protection procedures, and the facilitation of business processes is the most important competency an organization should possess when formulating information security systems. This requires an organization to understand its own specific needs, as well as possess an understanding of human behavior and how it may affect their implementation and execution.

The Competency to Implement IS Security Policies

Undeniably, organizations need to possess the competency of designing functional and effective IS security policies. However, this competency is not sufficient, and it must be complemented by the organization's ability to execute these policies. Organizations need to be able to actively enforce their procedures with controls that are specific to their own industry and organization. Too often organizations expend effort and resources to design security regulations and policies, pat themselves on the back for a job well done, and fail to execute these policies properly and scrupulously. Policies and controls are useful only if organization is able to devote the time and resources necessary to utilize them properly. Enforcement of security procedures is equally vital in the context of technological security and managerial controls. In addition, even if business processes and IS security controls are compatible, the end user must be kept in mind. If processes are cumbersome, employees are likely to skip them or bypass them to make their jobs easier, unaware of the potential for damage. For example, bank tellers not logging off the computer every time they step away from the terminal because customers are waiting, they are very busy and it takes too long to log back on, and/or a supervisor's key is required.

Similarly, from a managerial standpoint, competent individuals should perform managerial controls and monitoring actively and with devotion. In addition, the entire organization must have a clear understanding of the lines of command, and know who should perform which control procedures, and know to whom suspicious behaviors should be reported. Furthermore, every employee should be able to report suspicious behaviors to an individual outside of their department, who does not report to the same supervisors.

The Competency to Maintain Policy Flexibility

Despite obvious necessity to design effective and strong protection systems, flexibility of established security systems, controls and procedures is also required. Flexibility in this context is understood as the ability of the rule makers in the organization to revise established rules and procedures. IS security management needs to be able to accept suggestions/criticisms from the members of the organization. Organizations do not operate in a perfect world. Unanticipated problems are likely to arise. Therefore, the organization should have a method of evaluating and if necessary, revising its security system to adapt to and meet the changing needs of the organization.

The Competency to Regulate the Flow of Information

A frequent issue, directly contributing to the security of IS, is the limitation of access to sensitive information. This issue is directly related to the issue of role definition discussed earlier. Access to information should be assigned accordingly to those roles. Employees should have access only to that information that is required for them to fulfill their duties. Employees' should be prevented from accessing information and features that are not necessary for them to fulfill their duties.

The Competency to Communicate the Necessity for IS Security Procedures

IS security is not only the domain of the top management. It is true that those responsible for core business tasks, need to understand the importance and the scope of information protection. However, at the same time, those assigned to protect information systems, employees, must understand the organizational processes and business goals of their organizations, and provide protection along the entire course of the information flow. Therefore, an organization must have the ability to convey the criticality of maintaining IS security throughout the whole organization. Top management has to be willing to provide the resources necessary to develop effective security systems, while employees need to be convinced of usefulness and importance of these systems.

As stated earlier, the biggest threat to information security comes from inside the company. It is also important to acknowledge that this threat can be as much a result of a conscious act, as a result of unintended acts that are due to unawareness, lack of knowledge or simply ignorance. One of the most important barriers to creating an effective IS security plan, is the lack of awareness of the consequences uncontrolled information exchange can cause. Prevention is far more important than crisis management. Therefore, managers need to be able to conduct accurate and relevant risk analysis. A "Big picture" approach is critical for effective risk analysis, as what may seem to be an insignificant mistake or innocent information exchange, can, in reality, have much further reaching effects than the organization could anticipate. Any information handled, processed or passed over should always be handled with the understanding that it could potentially be misused or stolen. General awareness of company's business processes and goals is critical to ensure information security. It is also important for the employees to understand both the purpose and the scope of IS security policies, controls and protections.

In this context, company's ability to facilitate communication between company's employees at all levels, joins the list of most critical competencies ensuring IS security. Communication is critical for employees, at all levels, to be aware of what can happen if the security will be breached, and to understand what material falls under the IS security realm. Organizations should have the ability to convince their employees that access to the information goes hand in hand with a corresponding level of liability. The ability to communicate this level of personal accountability, and the willingness to continually remind employees of this rule will make them less likely to demand unlimited access to data.

The Competency to Facilitate Informal Communication About IS Security

Competency to facilitate communication between management and employees should be present at both the formal and informal levels of the organizational environment. Written policies are the most formal form of communication across the organization. Training is an integral part of formal communication, although organizations must also encourage interaction and opinion exchange on the informal level. In many organizations, formal levels of communication are in place. However, they are rarely supported by management's ability to develop informal settings that would facilitate interaction between management and employees, leading to effective understanding of the security issues. Informal level of communication is therefore, the often lacking, but equally important link, of communication competency.

Communication is one of the most important means to increase employees' awareness of IS security issues. When we talk about competency to communicate issues of IS security more than just the manner and channels an organization chooses to use to communicate with their employees are critical. It is also important to understand what kind of information should be communicated. The ability to provide employees with proper content, through effective channels, as often as necessary is a combination of skills and processes that constitutes what we define as a competency in internal communication.

The Competency to Monitor Adequately

The ability to track and monitor business role execution is the last step, on a business level, that is critical to the security of IS systems. This phase should never become routine. The process of monitoring should always be conscious and thorough. The process of monitoring should be performed by competent employees able to verify the accuracy and correctness of all the procedures conducted upon the monitored employee.

Monitoring should be a multilevel process. Employees who, due to their roles, or external liaisons, could have interest in breaching security rules and norms (e.g. those in direct contact with clients, or competition), should be monitored closer than those who are detached from external temptations. Stoppage or prevention of security breach is not the only advantages of the monitoring system. Monitoring can be extremely useful in recognizing employees' behavioral patterns. This information should be used to update or redesign security processes.

EXPLOITATIONAL COMPETENCIES FOR CYBERSECURITY

The Competency of Managers to Lead and Influence Others Awareness

The ability lead, as opposed to just holding a supervisory position, is yet another competency required from managers, and recognized as an important contributor to IS security. A mix of knowledge and enthusiasm create a leader. Managers must be well versed in the company policies. They are also the ones who have to be able to clearly communicate requirements, policies and expectations. Those managers are the first line support, example givers, and role models for the rest of the staff. Their approach to protection of IS will set the example for other employees, and thus increase both security awareness and obedience of security rules.

The awareness of information security issues must be raised so it is on all employees' minds. The ability to influence IS security awareness should never be limited to computer users. Integrity, trust, and ethics are expected of all employees. Managers within organization should possess abilities to influence employees' awareness of security issues. They should not only have verbal and written skills to communicate with their employees. They should also have a will and drive to "sell an action plan" to the content of all organization members.

The Competency of Continuing Personal Development

This competency refers to individual's willingness to improve qualifications and to continue to learn on a daily basis. However, this willingness to provide advantages needs to find support in the organization. There should be structures in place that would encourage and reward further personal development. One of the most basic, personal development tasks, so critical for security issues, is computer literacy. It is in every organization's interest to attract motivated and eager to learn individuals, who will be able to understand and incorporate the fast-changing technological solutions that security of IS will require.

The Competency to Work in Teams

The ability to share ideas, opinions and experience with other members of the organization builds a sense of community and motivates teamwork. To create strong team, members of the organization need to possess skills, knowledge and the will to contribute to the quality, efficiency or even just atmosphere of work. This contribution creates sense of belonging and common cause. This is important because those who consider themselves as members of a team, are more willing to actively seek systems protection, and are more eager to alert the organization of potential problems. In addition, they are less likely to be disenfranchised and disgruntled and therefore less likely to try to problematic in terms of security.

The Competency to Maintain Ethical Behaviors and Engender Loyalty

Having honest employees and creating an environment that fosters company loyalty is crucial. Unfortunately, there is no proven formula for finding and hiring only honest employees, and there is no guarantee that even the most employee centric business practices will ensure employee loyalty. However, company policies that stress honest and fair dealings, and stress integrity and confidentiality when it comes to sharing company critical data with others can help significantly. Employees must be trustworthy; morality must be ingrained into culture. Nevertheless, the culture should be based on: be a "watchdog", always be alert mentality. Ensuring that everyone understands and obeys the company's policy for IS security must start with managers setting the example. Not all fraud by unethical personnel can be prevented. However, properly designed, and well-communicated, ethical guidelines incorporated into company culture, can still be effective in controlling less than ethical behaviors.

The Competency to Maintain Good Hiring Practices

Vetting candidates is an important business process, however very few companies systematically did so in a reliable manner. Many firms have policies for vetting potential employees, but they often do not follow through, or systematically check references, employment histories etc. Some companies may de-facto accept a professional license as proof of a job candidates' integrity. Hiring people of only high ethical capability is certainly the goal of most managers. Vetting of all new hires through calling references, a criminal background check, and hair drug testing (where legal) can help to minimize risk. Companies need to put effort into "hiring smart", finding trustworthy, professional, and ethical employees. It was argued that these are the type of people who will provide much better support, and respect IS security policies, even after they leave the company.

SUPPLY COMPETENCIES FOR CYBERSECURITY

Surprisingly, a low level of concern related to the technological aspects of IS security exists among many organizations. However, it should not be concluded that this issue is not important. While there are functional tools available to provide technical support for data and information protection, the issues discussed in two preceding parts of this chapter are often considered more troubling to organizations, as they are often neglected or underestimated by many firms. Institutionalizing a method to handle and develop the other competencies is also much more difficult to do, as they are also much less clear-cut issues.

The Competency to Sustain Technical Expertise

Those who are responsible for the technical side of information protection obviously need to possess knowledge of security tools available through hardware and software products. Internet firewall, anti-virus protection on servers and workstations, password security, file access security, physical security, security monitoring, are all security related components. IT personnel responsible for IS security must be versed in the available up-to-date products that are designed to protect data and assets. Knowledgeable IT department personnel must be able to configure IS to flag suspicious activities, and to limit access to data at different levels, depending on the business roles assigned to those who access the data. IT specialists must keep the IS system up-to-date. This task requires not only knowledge and expertise on novelties available on the market, but it also requires the ability to convince top management to assign proper resources to purchase, install, and maintain IS systems.

The Competency to Synthesize Technical and Business Knowledge

As stated earlier, security systems need fit in with business process. Therefore, customization or adoption of technological solutions to individual business processes is a key to a secure IS. Managers must be aware that one of the first steps to secure IS is to use high-level technology that is easy to implement and operate. IT managers who are responsible for the design of security systems and processes need to understand the company, its goals and business processes. Thcy need to understand not only what processes the organization has in place, but also what goal these processes are designed to achieve and who are the people who execute these processes. Knowledge of all of these aspects of business, combined with technical knowledge creates a solid competency to develop useful, effective and robust security system.

CONCLUSION

Due to globalization, increased competition, accelerated technological advancements, and lightning quick communications, today's businesses are redesigning their structures. There has been a dramatic shift in the model of organizational structures toward loosely coupled networks. In this environment, Information Systems (IS) security gains new prominence and becomes one of the most important issues businesses face. In this new environment, a simple technical expertise alone is not enough. For IS security to be truly effective organizations need to hire skilled and knowledgeable people, develop effective information security processes, and synthesize the two into a seamless system. As technology developed and allowed companies to analyze data in a much more effective and extensive manner, the value of this data increased drastically. Simultaneously, the same technological advances have made information available to a wider audience. This new reality greatly expanded and changed the context in which IS security is considered.

Hence, within an organization, it is critical that all employees possess a security awareness and therefore play a part in the protection of said organization's information assets. Some employees will have key roles and responsibilities and require specific skills to support them. However, organizations can face challenges in regard to recognizing the required specialized skills as well as where to obtain them. Hence, whether an organization chooses to hire new staff, developing existing staff or outsource the activities altogether, it is necessary to know the type and level of expertise required. To this end, this chapter discussed the need for organizations to understand and identify the essential skills related to cybersecurity in order for their employees to develop core competencies in these areas.

REFERENCES

Backhouse, J., & Dhillon, G. (1996). Structures of responsibility and security of information systems. *European Journal of Information Systems*, *5*(1), 2–9. doi:10.1057/ejis.1996.7

Dhillon, G. (2008). Organizational competence for harnessing IT: A case study. *Information & Management*, *45*(5), 297–303. doi:10.1016/j.im.2008.01.008

Dhillon, G., & Backhouse, J. (2000). Technical opinion: Information system security management in the new millennium. *Communications of the ACM*, *43*(7), 125–128. doi:10.1145/341852.341877

Dhillon, G., & Backhouse, J. (2001). Current directions in IS security research: Towards socio-organizational perspectives. *Information Systems Journal, 11*(2), 127–153. doi:10.1046/j.1365-2575.2001.00099.x

Dhillon, G., & Kolkowska, E. (2011). Can a cloud be really secure? A Socratic dialogue. In *Computers, privacy and data protection: an element of choice* (pp. 345–360). Dordrecht: Springer. doi:10.1007/978-94-007-0641-5_16

Handley, S. M. (2012). The perilous effects of capability loss on outsourcing management and performance. *Journal of Operations Management, 30*(1), 152–165. doi:10.1016/j.jom.2011.10.003

Lado, A. A., & Wilson, M. C. (1994). Human resource system and sustainable competitive advantage: A competency-based perspective. *Academy of Management Review, 19*(4), 699–727. doi:10.5465/amr.1994.9412190216

McGrath, R. G., MacMillan, I. C., & Venkataraman, S. (1995). Defining and developing competence: A strategic process paradigm. *Strategic Management Journal, 16*(4), 251–275. doi:10.1002mj.4250160402

Orton, J. D., & Weick, K. E. (1990). Loosely coupled systems: A reconceptualization. *Academy of Management Review, 15*(2), 203–223. doi:10.5465/amr.1990.4308154

Weick, K. E. (1979). *The social psychology of organizing* (2nd ed.). Reading, MA: Addison-Wesley.

Weick, K. E. (1995). *Sensemaking in organizations.* Beverly Hills, CA: Sage Publications.

Weick, K. E., & Roberts, K. H. (1993). Collective mind in organizations: Heedful interrelating on flight decks. *Administrative Science Quarterly, 38*(3), 357–381. doi:10.2307/2393372

ENDNOTE

1 Because IT alone could not provide any strategic advantage, it has often been the reason for its outsourcing. See arguments by Handley (2012).

Section 3
Addressing Academia

Chapter 8
Delivering Cybersecurity Education Effectively

Alastair Irons
University of Sunderland, UK

ABSTRACT

This chapter draws on current research and best practice into teaching in cybersecurity in higher education. The chapter provides a theoretical and pedagogical foundation for helping tutors make decisions about what topics to include and approaches to teaching and assessing the cybersecurity curriculum. There are of course a range of potential stakeholders in cybersecurity education ranging from government, policy, and law makers to all members of society. However, for the purposes of brevity, this chapter will focus on learners and those creating and delivering cybersecurity education in the higher education (HE) sector.

INTRODUCTION

The chapter discusses the opportunities for different and innovative ways of learning about cybersecurity – designed to provide deep learning and thus a greater understanding of principles, theories and applications of cybersecurity. The purpose of the chapter is to explore the differences between the delivery of cybersecurity education and the delivery of other computing-based subjects in Higher Education. Whilst the delivery of cybersecurity will utilize good practice from the delivery of computing, computer science and other subjects in HE the discussion in this chapter attempts to emphasize and examine the issues from a cybersecurity perspective.

In recent years, computing technology and computer systems have experienced dramatic growth. The growth in the number of systems (communications, information systems, Internet systems and e-commerce) and the advances in the scale, the functionality and the usability of systems have provided opportunities for malicious users to exploit insecure and non-robust systems. The pace at which companies and their customers have embraced technologies such as cloud computing, smart devices, mobile technologies, and the Internet of Things (IoT) has created an environment that is changing faster than organizations

DOI: 10.4018/978-1-5225-7847-5.ch008

Copyright © 2019, IGI Global. Copying or distributing in print or electronic forms without written permission of IGI Global is prohibited.

and legislators can keep abreast of. It's not only systems that are changing – the way people use the systems and the expectations of speed and convenience means that cybersecurity can often be relegated in importance. Allied to the growth in systems technologies is the growth in the amount of data that is provided and the huge variety of ways in which data is collected, manipulated and stored.

The range of systems and technologies and the speed of implementation and adoption provide opportunities for cybercriminals to exploit. In addition to chance to take advantage of vulnerabilities in systems the advances in technology give computer criminals the opportunity to conceal their activities, to cover their tracks and attempt to destroy evidence of their actions. The ability to prevent cybercrime attacks and cybersecurity breaches that have taken place and the resultant requirement to examine the cybertrail have raised the need to develop specialists in cybersecurity – a set of practitioners who have the methods, skills and techniques to prevent, detect, recover and restore systems and data in the event of an attack.

The global news headlines frequently present cybersecurity attacks, vulnerabilities or failures, illustrating that there is an increasing loss of control over the cyber-threats to business. Recent years have seen high profile attacks to major corporations such as Tesco Bank, Talk Talk, Daimler Chrysler. In 2017 the NHS in the UK (along with 160 other organizations) were rocked by the "Wannacry" attack. Other headlines have reported belief and fear that the recent U.S. elections could be manipulated by a foreign power and speculation over whether development in artificial intelligence could lead to cyber attacks perpetrated by machines, without any human motivation.

The changing technology environment and the growth in threats and potential threats means that the role of cybersecurity is increasing in importance. As society and business becomes more reliant on cybersecurity the efficiency of cybersecurity education – what we teach and how we teach it – becomes an important objective. Similarly, there is a need to consider the learners, what they need and want to learn as well as how they learn as in integral part of cybersecurity education.

McGettrick (2013) argues for the need for cybersecurity education as opposed to cybersecurity training. In this chapter the focus is on cybersecurity education – but as tends to be the case with discussion on any aspect of cybersecurity there is overlap between the categories, so some aspects of training come in to the consideration of cybersecurity education. Part of the rationale for looking at this topic is because there are so many different providers offering a range of different cybersecurity learning products claiming to deliver education and training.

It is worth asking the question as to why there should be consideration given to examining the ways in which to deliver cybersecurity education. Cybersecurity is a complex and wide-ranging topic (or series of topics) to consider. The complexity associated with cybersecurity means that there is a need to consider different teaching approaches to enable cybersecurity learning. Rashid et al (2018) argue that "the foundational knowledge on which the field of cybersecurity is being developed is fragmented, and as a result, it can be difficult for both students and educators to map coherent paths of progression through the subject". There are many topic domains in which we potentially have interest in cybersecurity including (but not limited to) information security, systems security, network security and Internet security each with a set of fundamentals and principles and different theories and applications. In addition, there is an interesting mix of technical, policy, governance, ethical and human / society subjects which require different approaches to teaching and learning. As far back as 1997, Pfleeger et al (1997) suggested a broad range of sub topics making up the cybersecurity knowledge base, including "security policy, privileges, authentication, correctness and auditing", and how these relate "trusted systems, operating systems, database management systems, distributed systems, cryptography, protocols, system correctness, intrusion detection and mobile code". Hallet et al (2018) raise questions about the number of cybersecurity curriculum frameworks and indicate concerns about lack of equivalence across the different frameworks. The breadth of subjects to include makes the delivery of cybersecurity education even more complex.

Teaching cybersecurity as a subject in its own right is complicated enough. However, there is a further complicating factor because there is an additional expectation that cybersecurity is taught as part of the curriculum across the computing / computer science family of disciplines. Irons et al (2016) argue that embedding cybersecurity into computing science degrees presents a real opportunity to ensure that everyone involved in creating the digital economy – especially the technology underpinning it – understand the threats, vulnerabilities and mitigations that need to be managed. Embedding cybersecurity, and contextualizing cybersecurity, in other computing subjects such as programming, databases, and networks is important in the development of those subjects. The challenges in teaching cybersecurity in these disciplines runs in parallel with the effective teaching of cybersecurity as a specialist subject in its own right. Cybersecurity has recently (2017) been added to the components of the BCS accreditation criteria, reflecting the importance placed on cybersecurity and the expectation that all computing graduates should have knowledge and skills in cybersecurity as they move towards chartered status.

Cybersecurity is a rapidly changing and rapidly evolving discipline. This means that anyone involved in cybersecurity to a greater or lesser extent, from a technical to a managerial, from an organizational to an individual level needs to constantly review and update their knowledge on cybersecurity. This in itself presents a challenge for efficient cybersecurity education.

Anyone working or seeking to work in cybersecurity needs to develop a range of abilities and competencies in addition their technical knowledge of cybersecurity. For example, cybersecurity practitioners will come across situations where they are required as professionals to be able to make judgments when faced with uncertainty. Linked to this is the need to be able to have the confidence to react quickly to situations with robust and reliable solutions. Cybersecurity practitioners will need to be able to work both as part of a team and independently. Teaching these competences has an impact on the way that we seek to teach cybersecurity efficiently and effectively.

Invariably when we look how to teach cybersecurity education effectively there will be consideration given to the topics covered elsewhere in this book. Where appropriate there will be cross-reference to materials and topics covered other sections. In particular we will look at the links between the other chapters relating to cybersecurity curricula and the education program.

The remainder of this chapter covers the challenges in cybersecurity education; what to teach; how to teach effectively; approaches to learning and teaching cybersecurity; balance between theory and practice; use of technology in teaching; assessing cybersecurity knowledge, understanding and skills; and the need for continued professional development.

CHALLENGES IN CYBERSECURITY EDUCATION

There are many challenges in cybersecurity education, and these are discussed in this section. Understanding and overcoming the challenges in education will enable cybersecurity education to be delivered effectively. This section looks at the particular challenges in cybersecurity education and compare to the approaches used in other computing disciplines.

One of the key challenges in cybersecurity education is addressing the skills gap. $(ISC)^2$ report (2016) suggest that there are 350,000 open / unfilled cybersecurity positions unfilled worldwide and that this number is growing. Oltsik (2017) suggests that the skills gap in cybersecurity is getting worse. Oltsik identifies a growing problem with organizations indicating more than a doubling of "problematic shortage" of cybersecurity staff, increasing from 23% in 2014 to 51% in 2018. This provides a real challenge for cybersecurity educators.

The objectives of the cybersecurity education will depend on the level of learning to be achieved, the previous experience and knowledge of the participants, the subjects and topics of interest to the participants and the desired learning outcomes from the education. There are many challenges in cybersecurity education, as we shall see later in this chapter. However, the range of people potentially interested in cybersecurity and the variability in the depth and breadth of cybersecurity knowledge that they have, and that they need, mean the cybersecurity educators can collaborate with a wide range of colleagues to share their experiences and provide a wide variety of educational experiences.

The National Cyber Security Centre (NCSC) have produced a cyber attack categorization framework (2018) designed to indicate the priority that should be given to investigating different cyber attacks. The new framework increases the number of classifications from three to six (category 1 'national cyber emergency' to category 6 'localized incident'. Whilst the framework is designed to improve consistency around response and provide a better outcome for victims, the framework also illustrates the complexity of the cybercrime environment. The complexity can also be seen in the need for cybersecurity education – ranging from a general awareness that cybersecurity is a potential threat, through to what the threats are to what can be done about cybersecurity at a personal level to in depth technical expertise in creating and implementing cybersecurity infrastructure.

It is not the intention in this chapter to provide a framework on which topics to cover at which level – suggestions have been recommended in the previous chapters in this book. Harris and Patten (2015) provide a very good discussion relating cybersecurity skills and knowledge to levels of learning, linking cybersecurity to Bloom's and Webb's taxonomies. The ACM/IEEE (2017) report suggests a series of expectations for the cybersecurity curriculum and recommends which cybersecurity topics to consider. A common theme from all those who examine and evaluate the cybersecurity curriculum is the progression from remembering and understanding the cybersecurity fundamental principles and theories, to applying the principles and theories to cybersecurity problems, to making judgements based on those principles (and on standards and legislation) to creating solutions and providing strategic direction for cybersecurity. As indicated earlier the spectrum of subjects covered in the cybersecurity curriculum range from mathematically based, through technical cybersecurity and practical skills development to almost social science type subjects looking at the impact of cybersecurity on society.

This has a direct bearing on the way cybersecurity is taught. In particular there is a need to consider different ways of teaching for different aspects of the curriculum and using appropriate approaches to contextualize the expected learning for students and learners.

A further challenge in cybersecurity teaching is the interdisciplinary / multi-disciplinary nature of cybersecurity. Whilst there are a range of diverse discipline including criminology, psychology, sociology, law and mathematics which inform a range of cybersecurity topics including policy, human factors, ethics, and risk management, cybersecurity remains fundamentally a computing-based discipline. The challenge in teaching cybersecurity is that cybersecurity is both informed by the interdisciplinary content and driven by the needs and perspectives of the computing disciplines that provide the underpinning fundamentals of cybersecurity.

The multi-disciplinary aspect of cybersecurity is not necessarily a benefit – it could be argued that the multi-disciplinary aspects potentially dilute the core of the subject. However, it is suggested in this chapter that drawing from other disciplines strengthens cybersecurity in terms of rigor and robustness and also strengthens the suggestion that cybersecurity can stand as a separate and distinct discipline in its own right.

In order to allow students to apply theory and develop cybersecurity skills there is a need to analyze appropriately complex case studies and problems. The challenge for teachers is to develop materials that allow problem solving, analysis and application of theory and at the same time provide an environment to practice and make mistakes without falling foul of regulations (for example JANet regulations in universities in the UK) and to protect students and learners from exposure to inappropriate cases.

In any cybersecurity problems in the real world there are many complex and inter-related variables to consider, a number of legal considerations to contend with, many technical issues to be aware of and many cybersecurity principles, theories and guidelines to apply. There is a challenge for cybersecurity educators to put over this complex environment in teaching the subject without overwhelming students.

WHAT TO TEACH?

The curricula aspects are covered in later chapters of this book. In addition, the material covered in the UK's National Cyber Security Strategy (2017) and the Cyber Security Body of Knowledge (CyBOK) project has been established to codify the foundational and generally recognized knowledge on cybersecurity. At the time of writing the first two Knowledge Areas – Cryptography and Software Security – are open for public consultation. They can be viewed at www.cybok.org. The ACM have provided a comprehensive document outlining the curriculum Guidelines for Post-Secondary Degree Programs in Cybersecurity (2017). Hallet et al (2018) indicate that there are a number of different cybersecurity curricula. The different bodies promoting cybersecurity curricula include the Institute of Information Security Professionals (IISP), Joint Task Force (JTF), National Initiative for Cybersecurity Education (NICE), and the National Cyber Security Centre (NCSC). All of these bodies have indicated what they consider to be important components of the cybersecurity curricula. All of the frameworks in the examples above cover some overlapping but also some significantly different aspects of cybersecurity which makes it difficult for educators to decide what to include in cybersecurity teaching.

In this chapter consideration is given about what to teach about cybersecurity depending on the audience of learners and the relationship to how to deliver cybersecurity education effectively. What to teach and how to teach it effectively will vary depending on the audience and the experience of those in the audience. There is a large spectrum of potentially interested learners ranging from school pupils (all pupils), through school pupils studying computing and computer science at GCSE and A – level to students at college and university (again with a split between cybersecurity specialists, to computer science students to students in other disciplines such as business and engineering) and on to practitioners and professionals requiring continued professional development (CPD).

As indicated earlier in the chapter cybersecurity practitioners will come across situations where they are required as professionals deal confidently with uncertainty and make judgments about complex situations. One of the ways to address the potential issues of judgement and confidence is to consider computer ethics in the context of cybersecurity.

There is a significant challenge in teaching ethical awareness and embedding ethical principles into the cybersecurity teaching. There is a need to make students aware of the potential for misuse of cybersecurity tools and techniques as well as the need to instill ethical and professional behavior into cybersecurity practices. The teaching of computer ethics is normally embedded throughout computer science programs in order to meet professional body (for example BCS) expectations and requirements. Teaching cybersecurity requires emphasis on ethical issues early in the curriculum in order to instill the importance of appropriate ethical behavior right at the beginning of the students' cybersecurity program so that they have the ethical tools and mind set to allow them to deal with complex and challenging ethical dilemmas faced in cybersecurity education.

The coverage of computer ethics focuses on the professional responsibilities of a cybersecurity practitioner, namely using the skills and techniques of cybersecurity professional to the benefit of society and not to use cybersecurity knowledge for criminal activity or personal gain. A further thread of ethical consideration is to deal with cases sensitively and professionally maintaining the confidentiality and anonymity of participants in case or problem being studied.

There is also a "gamekeepers and poachers" dilemma in teaching cybersecurity. In order to develop the skills and techniques required to become a cybersecurity practitioner, students need to develop understanding and knowledge of the tools and techniques applied by cyber criminals. As students realize the security vulnerabilities and weaknesses in procedures and systems the temptation to utilize this awareness may arise. The concern in the "gamekeeper poacher dilemma" is that universities could become complicit in creating cyber criminals of the future rather than developing practitioners who are motivated to work against cybercrime.

There is potentially a different type of ethical dilemma associated with the teaching of cybersecurity, namely cybersecurity has the potential to put forward an unbalanced view and perspective in tackling computer crime, cyber attacks and misuse of data. One way to redress this potential concern is to include topics such as civil liberties and the Human Rights Act (1998) in the ethical consideration of cybersecurity.

DELIVERING EDUCATION EFFECTIVELY

In this section a brief discussion on what we mean by delivering education effectively will be presented – looking at engagement of learners, how learners learn, getting the learning materials and concepts to learners and metrics how to evaluate effectiveness of learning. These topics will be explored in the cybersecurity context.

In order to provide effective teaching in cybersecurity there is an expectation that the lecturer has a level of expertise and understanding of the subject, knows how the students learn and understands the range of pedagogic approaches that can be utilized. Subject knowledge is required to enable the lecturer to determine the most appropriate way to put across the subject and to organize and structure the teaching activities (and the series of learning activities if appropriate) in such a way that enables students to learn. In order for teaching to be effective it is important that the lecturer understands the level that students are at in their learning and us such appreciate what it is students know. Understanding the audience of learners will help the lecturer to identify the most appropriate approach to ensure clear communication and to determine the best ways to stimulate, inspire and excite the students.

As well will see with all the methods discuss in the next section, effective teaching is not only dependent on good lecturers and good lecturing. There is a responsibility on students to engage with the learning opportunities afforded them. One way to male teaching more effective is to work with students so that they understand their role in learning.

It is important for providers of cybersecurity education to consider the effectiveness of the learning opportunities to enable students develop the wide range of skills needed to be a cybersecurity professional. As well as the theoretical knowledge and technical skills involved in cybersecurity as a subject there is the need for cybersecurity professionals to have expertise in team working, the ability to make judgments (often under pressure) and the capability to become lifelong learners.

It is all well and good looking to have effective education, but what is meant by effective education and how will it be known when cybersecurity education is effective? Effective education can be viewed from a number of perspectives and different stakeholders will have different views on effectiveness. Suffice to say is that there is a need to measure something – but what?

The focus of this chapter is what makes effective cybersecurity education from a student perspective, but first consideration will be given as to what might be a suitable metric to use in determining whether the cybersecurity education is effective.

It has long been acknowledged (Lundstedt, 1966) that it is difficult to quantify what is meant by effective teaching. Quantifying effective teaching remains problematic today – there is an acceptance that effectiveness relates to the communication between teacher and learner, but that there is also an understanding of the learner needs in making teaching effective. Recently there has been a move towards considering "value" and "value added" in considering effective teaching. Barnett (1992) suggests that "value added" is one of the metrics in measuring the success of Higher Education. Although, Schleicher (2015) argues that although valued added has been on the HE agenda for a number of years it remains notoriously difficult to quantify as a measure. That said, the concepts of "value" and "value added" are particularly relevant in considering effective teaching in cybersecurity.

There are of course a range of perspectives on what constitutes effective teaching. From a government perspective there is a desire to drive down the cost of teaching in Higher Education and at the same time improve quality assurance, which gives an interesting dilemma for providers of Higher Education. Linked to cost, effectiveness might be measured in terms of class size, or the amount of contact time – it will depend what is important for the education provider.

Since the introduction of the National Student Survey (NSS) in the UK there has been an increasing emphasis on measuring student satisfaction and using student satisfaction as a proxy for effective teaching. There has been a significant amount of debate as the veracity of student satisfaction as a measure of effective teaching (for example Williams and Cappuccini-Ansfield, 2007), but whether it is correct or not, the NSS remains a metric which is utilized by Higher Education managers, government and creators of league tables!

Other drivers as far as measuring effectiveness of teaching in HE focus on research, research outputs and research income. Putting an emphasis on research in cybersecurity might conflict with providing effective teaching. However, if the principles of the teaching research nexus (Jenkins and Healy, 2005) are embraced then embedding current research, developing students' skills as researchers, and applying research informed teaching there can benefit to the students' overall learning experience. This begs a question as to whether there are unique research skills for those studying cybersecurity. There are a number of specific subject areas that are unique to cybersecurity including the impact of cybersecurity breaches; technical developments in cybersecurity; cybersecurity futures as well as a series of applications that are cybersecurity specific. The Engineering and Physical Sciences Research Council (EPSRC) has identified Academic Centres of Excellence (ACE) in Cybersecurity – based on the quality of academic research and publication in cybersecurity, critical mass of researchers, and investment in cybersecurity facilities – and these certainly illustrate that there is a range of cybersecurity topics worthy of research. The research skills cybersecurity students need to be on undergraduate and postgraduate degrees have much in common with the research skills required for other computing disciplines but should be contextualized to the cybersecurity environment. Of course, care needs to be taken in creating physical resources to enable cybersecurity research – this is particularly important when experiments are to be undertaken as part of research. For example, if students are building cybersecurity defenses against potential breaches and the defenses need to be tested it may be prudent to take the whole experiment to an autonomous network – certainly one which is removed from the standard university network.

Looking at efficiency in cybersecurity teaching from a pedagogic perspective the purpose is not have passive, compliant, surface learners in cybersecurity but to have participants who are independent, active learners who will be equipped with higher level skills in cybersecurity. In structuring learning and teaching activities (discussed in the next section) it is important that think about how to develop higher skills and encourage learners to be independent and active. This links in to key questions on learning and teaching in cybersecurity:

- What do should the students to learn (linked to curriculum and syllabus – see related chapters in this book)?
- What are the students actually learning (and how to measure a level of understanding)? The measurement of actual learning will be returned to in the ways in which student understanding is assessed in cybersecurity, later in this chapter).

The points above suggests a process of constructive alignment, whereas Biggs (1996) suggests the "aspects of teaching and assessment are tuned to support high level learning, so that all students are encouraged to use higher-order learning processes".

As well as technical skills there is the need to develop the softer skills in cybersecurity and include the development of these skills in cybersecurity teaching. There are the common soft skills such as problem solving, group work and communication that can be applied in a cybersecurity context. However, there are soft skills, which are potentially unique to the cybersecurity learner – for example

- How to raise awareness about the threats of cybersecurity;
- How to provide information to senior colleagues about the impact of cybersecurity breaches in language that will be understandable to non-cybersecurity people;
- How to do both of the above in a professional manner;
- How to give cybersecurity advice and feedback in non-technical language without being patronizing.

If effective teaching and learning is examined from a student perspective (it is suggested in this chapter that this is the most important perspective) then other variables come in to play. According to

Cohen (1981) students want "systematic, stimulating and caring teaching that leads to success". In order to achieve this in cybersecurity is it suggested that learning providers try to ensure that:

- learning is transparent – i.e. it is clear to the learners what the learning objectives are and that the learners have the opportunity to put cybersecurity theory and principles into practice;
- teaching activities facilitate dialogue between teachers and learners and between learners; and
- there is the opportunity to develop communities of learners (based on Wegner (2000) and communities of practice.

The next section will examine tools and techniques for the delivery of cybersecurity teaching taking into account the aspiration and expectation that the teaching is effective.

APPROACHES TO LEARNING AND TEACHING CYBERSECURITY

In this section of the chapter a range of alternatives to enable learning in cybersecurity and encourage learner engagement, and effectiveness of the learning opportunity will be examined. Scheponik et al (2016) have argued that "despite the documented need to train and educate more cybersecurity professionals, we have little rigorous evidence to inform educators on effective ways to engage, educate, or retain cybersecurity students". Scheponik goes on to suggest that there is still a great deal of work to be undertaken in order to understand the most appropriate pedagogic approach in cybersecurity education. The different methods and approaches to teaching cybersecurity are not presented in any ranked order. The most appropriate method of delivery will depend on the subject matter and topic of cybersecurity, the level of cybersecurity experience of the learners and other variables such as group size and learning environment.

The benefits and issues associated with each approach will be presented. Each method will be discussed in the context of teaching cybersecurity and how they can enhance efficiency in the teaching of cybersecurity. Consideration will also be given as to where and how online learning and educational technology can be utilized to enhance the efficiency of the particular method.

Lectures

There is place for lecturing as a didactic learning method in cybersecurity, especially in situations where the audience is very new to cybersecurity or the speaker is particularly inspiring. Experienced cybersecurity practitioners are able to share real life examples or "war stories" which can be very beneficial in contextualizing cybersecurity theories, principles and issues for learners. Covill (2011) suggests that "students in a lecture-style class report learning a great deal, being involved in the learning process, and engaging in independent thinking and problem solving". Lectures continue to be a dominant form of teaching in Higher Education in the UK, despite the assertion lectures are not always the most effective way of engaging students. The learning that takes place as a result if a lecture depends on student engagement, the relevance of the subject matter and on the abilities and style of the lecturer.

Research carried out by Irons and Devlin (2012) on inspiring teaching identified (form a student perspective) what student considered to be important in lecture sessions and perhaps more importantly what they did not like in lecture sessions. The following list indicated what students didn't want from lectures or what they didn't like about lectures:

- Endless amounts of facts being dictated for long periods of time;
- Just reading from slides;
- Someone who is unprepared and uninspired by the subject they're teaching;
- Monotone, too many detailed slides, when the teacher is not interested in either the subject or the students' understanding;
- Boring;
- Teachers who talk down to you and treat you like you're back in secondary school;
- Too much information for 1 hour and we leave without complete understanding;
- When the teacher doesn't want to be there.

The detail provided by students on what the found to be uninspiring is a really useful list of things to avoid when lecturing on cybersecurity.

The following list suggests what make efficient lectures from a student perspective;

- Whenever someone gets up and is enthusiastic about what they're trying to teach you;
- When a teacher is comfortable enough about a subject to use examples of when they got it horribly wrong to help understanding;
- Yes – they're very knowledgeable and willing to help all of the time;
- They make jokes or use funny real-life situations;
- Use of stories or comparisons to help us learn;
- Their outlook and way of talking about things – friendly and approachable;
- Instead of just throwing information at you they got you involved in the subject;
- Passionate;
- They enjoy what they do;
- The way they delivered it – asked questions rather than giving answers;
- Their ability to make the subject relevant; and
- They broke down information into smaller more manageable sections.

The list of factors that appear to inspire students pertain to lecturing in cybersecurity. As well as the expectation of through subject knowledge it is important for those lecturing in cybersecurity to be enthusiastic, passionate and care about the subject matter. The subject matter and the relevance and currency of so many of the issues in cyber security and cybersecurity breaches can be drawn from current news stories. To this end, although it is a set of circumstances that should be avoided and prevented, the fact that there are so many news stories about cybersecurity, breaches of security, cyber attacks and cybercrime mean that it is possible to relate current affairs to the theories and principles that are conveyed in lectures.

Lectures can also be enhanced by use of technology – for example giving students access to lecture notes beforehand on virtual learning environments (VLEs) or by using lecture capture technology so that students can access materials outside the lecture session.

Flipped Classroom

The flipped classroom is an interesting way of changing the dynamic of lecture sessions. In a flipped learning session, the students have access to the planned material in advance, undertake learning before they come to the classroom and then use the class contact time to ask questions, discuss issues and explore the subject in more detail. Exponents of the flipped classroom (from example Alvarez, 2011, Johnston and Karafotias, 2016) suggest that this is an effective way to use student contact time for effective learning.

The author has used this approach in cybersecurity teaching and has had mixed results. When students engage in the process and come to the class prepared (having done the homework in advance of the class) then the teaching sessions can be very productive – in particular when students are willing to ask questions and to debate and discuss issues and principles the learning can be really exciting. From a teaching perspective it is important to a) be well prepared for a range of topics to be discussed (often not the ones that were expected) and b) to have a plan B when students haven't done the pre- work.

Webinars

Related to lectures in many ways, making use of technology, and much used in the cybersecurity subject area are webinars. Webinars enable those delivering sessions to deliver presentations to larger, geographically dispersed audiences. Webinars are live web-based video conference that use the internet to connect those hosting the webinar to the audience. The audience is not constrained by geography. Webinars are flexible in what is presented – audio, video, slideshows, demonstrations and can have multiple presenters from different locations. Some commentators, for example Joshi et al (2011) indicate that webinars are effective with "the most notable aspect of webinars was that it brought about the comparable gain in knowledge, skills and satisfaction".

Webinars and the technology supporting webinars enable a number of learning opportunities which contribute to their effectiveness. For example, webinars have the following features, including:

- **The Ability to Record the Webinar:** Which (like lecture capture) allows the material to be reviewed at a later date and re-used by the learner;
- **The Opportunity to Enable Chat Features:** Which allows students to type in questions and queries without disturbing the flow of the session. Chat questions can then be addressed later;
- **Application Sharing, Where Appropriate:** Allowing lecturers to share their desktops or applications, etc. to help the audience get a better understanding of the topic;
- **The Capacity to Conduct Opinion Polls:** By using this at strategic points in the webinar the lecturer can conduct polls and surveys for the audience, which helps in terms of getting a feel for audience understanding.

Practical Activities in Cybersecurity

In order to develop proficiency in cybersecurity there needs to be a balance between the theoretical and conceptual knowledge essential to understanding cybersecurity, and the practical skills that support the application of that knowledge. Weiss et al (2013) suggest that cybersecurity students learn best when they have hands-on experience. The challenge for lecturers and teachers is to ensure that the exercises enable student learning and push students to learn more about cybersecurity. As shall be illustrated later in this chapter when discussing case studies and problem-based learning it is difficult in cybersecurity to reflect the complexity of reality and at the same time design activities that can be successful at achieving in relatively short time periods. Practical activities can be standalone (not linked to other cybersecurity teaching) or more traditionally an opportunity to explore theoretical aspects of cybersecurity from lectures or research in a practical setting. The author has used practical activities in cybersecurity as short sharp learning opportunities, usually linked to a lecture session and as extended learning activities over a longer period of time. Longer activities start to move towards case studies and problem based / project-based learning approaches see below.

Case Studies and Scenarios

In order to address the challenge of realism a case study-based approach can be utilized. There are classic case studies already in cybersecurity such as the "Stuxnet", "Equifax" and "Wannacry" for example. Case studies and scenarios provide examples of people or organizations in real situations which allow learners the opportunity to examine and evaluate authentic problems, as well as apply potential solutions, that will provide clarity as opposed to trying to learn by the study of abstract theories or principles. Case studies attempt to mirror the type of situation that cybersecurity practitioners will encounter in the working environment by providing realistic learning opportunities. One of the interesting opportunities in teaching cybersecurity is the ever-growing number of instances that can be used to formulate case studies. It is almost the case that there is at least one significant breach every week that is worthy of study – ranging from attacks against individuals to attacks against organizations and even national states.

Use can be made of case studies in both teaching and practical sessions as well in the development of problem-solving approach and assessments. This approach provides the opportunity to illustrate the complexity of the cybersecurity environment and allows students to be guided through specific tasks in specific cases whilst at the same time developing their technical skill, their analytical skills and their problem-solving abilities. Scheponik et al (2016) have used scenarios in cybersecurity to develop students' skills in "adversarial thinking", a key skill in the analysis of cybersecurity situations and problems, helping students understand the issues from attack and defense positions but also from a legal perspective.

There is a difficulty in creating case studies from scratch both in terms of making them simple enough at one end of the scale to being complex enough at the other. At the same time the case studies need to be authentic and also motivate students. There are ethical considerations, which need to be taken into account when creating cases particularly around the use of live cases (albeit historical live cases) or simulations based on live cases. In order for case study creation to be efficient in the cybersecurity domain it would be very helpful for colleagues to work together to co-create and to share case studies. Recently (2016-17) there was an attempt by Higher Education Academy (now Advance HE) to establish collaborative projects leading to shared resources through a series of development grant funds.

The creation of case study material cases for analysis can potentially contravene the rights of those original involved in the cases (even when anonymity is used) issues. Case studies designed to provide students with appropriate experiences might actually infringe University regulations or even the law – for example when trying to simulate system breaches.

There is a further concern that using case studies based on reality might provide students with ideas for criminal activity that they didn't have prior to studying the case study. (see discussion on ethics in cybersecurity earlier in the chapter).

Problem-Based Learning

Problem-based learning (PBL) has been used to positive effect in a number of academic disciplines; Boud and Feletti (1997:1) advocate that PBL is the 'most significant innovation in education for the professions for many years. PBL has been used in many disciplines including computer science for a number of years to develop students' skills in solving authentic and realistic problems. Discussion of PBL examples from the computing science literature include: Nuutila, Törmä, and Malmi (2005), Fee and Holland-Minkley (2010) and van Merriënboer (2013). Kessler (2007:264) discusses the use of PBL in problem solving:

Ill-defined problems or scenarios can be a fun and interesting way for students to synthesize and/or expand their knowledge, making abstract concepts more real. In PBL problems and scenarios tend to be real, relevant, and tangible, students usually are more motivated to work hard on these projects, often making many real-world assumptions that are applicable to them, further helping to improve their problem-solving skills.

The author was part of a team that developed PBL materials for cybersecurity and one of the objectives of the project was to "improve the efficiency of cybersecurity education and to help students develop the wide range of skills needed to be a cybersecurity professional". In particular the project attempted to give students the opportunity to develop their cybersecurity understanding by reducing 'information overload' and stopping students from learning huge amounts of unnecessary theoretical detail. As part of the application of PBL students had the chance to improve their control over their learning by designing the PBL activities to allow students to self-direct, to locate what they need to know and give them possession of their learning.

One of the key aspects identified in the project is that although problem-based learning may appear to be the application of common sense (student perception) it is actually a difficult learning skill (set of learning skills) to master. Therefore, it is important when using PBL in cybersecurity teaching to include learning guides for tutors and learning guides for learners.

An example of a PBL task in Cybersecurity is given in Box 1.

This type of PBL learning in the context of cybersecurity, as the example illustrates, encourages students to examine the complexities associated with cybersecurity and work as a group to further their understanding of cybersecurity topics.

MOOCs

MOOCs are another example of where technology can be utilized in the teaching of cybersecurity. A number of institutions, for example Harvard, provide Massive Open Online Courses (MOOCs) for the public. The Harvard program (gs.harvardx.harvard.edu/cyber-security/online-course) provides learners

Box 1.

In this activity students are encouraged to reflect on the impact of Edward Snowden's disclosure of National Security Agency documentation. In particular consider the impact on the agencies in the UK, particularly GCHQ, MI5 and MI6.

Objectives

The objective of this activity is to analyze the impact of the actions of Edward Snowden in 2013 and the subsequent reaction of the public (impact on society), the security agencies in the UK, USA and around the globe, and an understanding of the legal issues that the scenario raises

Tasks

1. Undertake research into the timeline of the main points of the Edward Snowden case
2. Consider the legal, social and ethical issues that should be considered in light of the scenario
3. Identify the implications for the cybersecurity community
4. Relate to other similar scenarios – such as Bradley Manning

Outputs

At the end of this activity you should have developed

- Your own perspective on the correctness or otherwise of Snowden's actions

and have created

- A report on the legal issues associated with gathering data on the public;
- A diagram to illustrate the relationship between cybersecurity and surveillance / dataveillance;
- A set of questions from your PBL work on the Snowden example to discuss with your tutor and class.

with the opportunity to obtain a Harvard certificate. Advocates argue that MOOCs are the future of online education. There has been an exponential growth in the use of MOOCs including in cybersecurity. Although MOOCs do not normally provide the full coverage of a degree, they are very useful in prepping students for study and providing introductions to the cybersecurity subject area. There are two distinct types of MOOC: cMOOC and xMOOC. cMOOCs are collaborative MOOCs that provide learning space for students to collaborate. On the other hand, xMOOCs put existing courses into an online format and as such tend to adopt a more traditional format to courses.

There are a number of UK examples of cybersecurity MOOCs – for instance Newcastle University have teamed up with FutureLearn to produce a 3 week introductory MOOC on cybersecurity, https://www.futurelearn.com/courses/cyber-security. The course covers topics such as privacy, payment safety and online safety at home. The Open University's Centre for Policing Research and Learning has also created a MOOC introducing cybersecurity.

Bootcamps

Bootcamps appear to be growing in popularity and these tend to be shorter, focused courses often running for a week or 10 days. Bootcamps offer a different approach to education often being run by industry experts. At the author's institution we have put in place a series of weeklong bootcamps for final year undergraduate and masters students run by visiting professors in cybersecurity. The feedback from students has been very positive about this approach, particularly when it is blended in with a more traditional structure of delivery. The cybersecurity Bootcamps that have been used at the author's institution have the added advantage of providing a test at the end of the bootcamp and a certificate for those succeeding the assessment. The author has then used the bootcamp and the test completion as material for an evaluative assessment exercise (see section on assessment later in this chapter).

Peer Learning

Students have the opportunity to learn from each other in Higher Education – working in groups, participating in discussion, reviewing demonstrations and undertaking problem-based learning are all examples where peer learning can take place in cybersecurity. Boud (1988) suggests that peer learning moves from independent learning to interdependent learning. The concept of interdependent learning would seem to be appropriate for cybersecurity learning.

There is the potential in peer learning for students to enhance their knowledge of cybersecurity concepts by explaining their understanding to their colleagues and to other students. Peer discussions allow for collaborative working, giving and receiving feedback and potentially evaluating their own learning. Normally peer learning takes place between students in the same class / same level, but at the author's institution we have also introduced peer support between different levels through a peer mentoring project. The idea was to support learners at lower levels with peers who had been through those levels. Interestingly we found that it was peers at the higher level who benefited most and improved their understanding through the development of their skills in communication, organization and collaborative support.

Threat Sharing Platforms

Threat sharing platforms seek to protect against potential cyber attacks on organizations by providing the opportunity for sharing information on cyber threats via an online repository. The online repository provides a location to place intelligence on threats, attacks, vulnerabilities, and breaches in computer systems. A survey by Paloalto (2016) indicated that sharing increases resilience, "respondents believe that 39% of attacks can be prevented by shared intelligence". Whilst the majority of threat sharing platforms, such as the Cyber Security Information Sharing Partnership (CiSP) from the NCSC are closed member groups the concept of threat sharing platforms could be a useful educational tool in Higher Education, helping students understand the nature of cyber threats and appreciate the potential risk to business and industry.

ASSESSMENT AND LEARNING IN CYBERSECURITY

This part of the chapter examines the ways in which assessment can help learning in cybersecurity and what the assessment might indicate in terms of competence in cybersecurity. There are a variety of assessment instruments which can be used to help learning in cybersecurity including report writing, exams (written, multi-choice, oral), practical tests, portfolios, project work (including research projects, problem-based learning projects and work based learning projects) and reflective practice. The assessment strategy chosen will depend on the level and the amount of cybersecurity being taught (i.e. one module will be different to a whole specialist course).

Reviewing the literature suggests that assessment is one of the key motivators for students and is fundamental in determining what it is that students value in their education, and this can be applied to cybersecurity education. For example, Murphy (2006) suggests that it is assessment that indicates to students what really matters on a module or program of study and it is assessment that informs students about the goals of the module or program. As has been indicated earlier, the complexity of the cybersecurity environment can provide off-putting for students and assessment tasks may well help with their understanding. There is the potential for assessment to provide a mechanism for student learning and to act as a means of enabling student learning during assessment activities (Rowntree,1987). The concept of "assessment for learning" is proposed as a means to encourage student learning (Black et al, 2003; McDowell et al, 2005).

Brown et al (1997:7-8) put forward the argument that "assessment defines what students regard as important, how they spend their time and how they come to see themselves as individuals". Gibbs and Simpson (2004) support this perspective summarizing that assessment is seen to exert a profound influence on student learning; in areas such as: what students focus their attention on how much they study; the quality of engagement with learning tasks, and, through feedback, on their understanding and future learning. Hamdorf and Hall (2001) indicate that assessment is important because it has such a powerful influence on the learning behavior of students. Brown el al (1997:7) also identify one of the dilemmas in assessment in that "students take their cues from what is assessed rather than from what lecturers assert is important". So, in designing cybersecurity learning activities it is possible to consider utilizing assessment to help students focus on the important aspects.

The principles of assessment (Nicol and Macfarlane-Dick, 2004) require that assessment is reliable, valid, affordable and fit for purpose, i.e. usable. Reliability in assessment requires the assessment to be objective, accurate, repeatable and analytically sound, according to Knight (2001). In essence, reliability refers to the consistency of grades that are awarded and can be affected by marker consistency, inter-marker reliability and / or test / re-test reliability. Validity focuses on the extent to which an assessment measures what it intends to measure and as such contributes to assessing the things course specifications, course learning outcomes and module learning outcomes say are important and of value.

The author has employed a number of assessment instruments in cybersecurity to encourage students to use the assessment activities to enable student learning. The use of scenarios to encourage students to think both as attackers and defenders has been particularly helpful in enabling students to understand the cybersecurity environment. As an overall assessment strategy in cybersecurity attempts should be made to:

- get students to identify and critically evaluate threats – ranging from nuisance threats to "advanced persistent threats";
- design, develop and implement strategies to counter the threats;
- identify when breaches or attacks have taken place and critically evaluate the impact of those;
- design, develop and implement approaches to recover from attack;
- give students the opportunity to evaluate attacks and develop more robust cybersecurity defenses as a result.

The above can be done in the context of specific cybersecurity scenarios or case studies but can also be utilized to encourage students to think about and present policies and procedures for cybersecurity environments.

One particular assessment task that has been used by the author which helps pull together many of the cybersecurity threads and complexities is the use of "infographs". An extract from an assessment using infographs is given below.

The cybersecurity environment is a wide and complex one. For the first part of this assignment you are required to produce an infograph (1 page) outlining the typical threats that either a) individuals in society or b) organizations face from breaches of cybersecurity. The design of your infograph and the content of the infograph is left to you to decide but you should consider visual impact, key messages, data to support, examples and underpinning research. You will have the chance to present your infograph to your peers, academics and guests from industry. You should be able to discuss the points raised on your infograph, explaining the detail and answering any questions asked.

As well as allowing the student to analyze and evaluate a particular issue or concern the assessment enables the development and assessment of a series of professional competencies, including; communication, presentation skills, and the summarizing of complex cybersecurity issues.

One of the main functions of assessment is to provide a measurement of student understanding – and this can utilized in cybersecurity teaching to indicate to students where they are in the learning journey, but also to provide an indication to educators as to how well the students have grasped the cybersecurity concepts, [note – this can be an important aspect if assessment is to be used for certification, see discussion earlier in the chapter]. There is an argument put forward in Black (1999:118) who suggests summative assessment "serves to inform an overall judgement of achievement, which may be needed for reporting and review". Pelligrino et al (2001:42) support this position proposing that "assessment is a tool designed to observe students' behavior and produce data that can be used to draw reasonable inferences about what students know".

However, there has also been a level of concern regarding the appropriateness of this use of assessment for example, Biggs (1996) suggests that "testing has not always promoted good learning and indeed can have detrimental effects" and Black and Wiliam (1998), argue that summative assessment is not a particularly good means of finding out what it is that students know.

When students participate in assessment – both summative and formative – it provides an opportunity to give feedback to students. The provision of feedback is one of the primary functions of assessment and can enhance student learning. One of the key ways that assessment can be used to help with learning is through constructive feedback on assessment activities. When cybersecurity assessment activities are designed and when feedback is generated there is a need to make sure that students value the process and has time to engage in the process. Nicol and Macfarlane-Dick (2004:3) suggest that formative assessment and feedback should be "used to empower students as self-regulated learners and that more recognitions should be given to the role of feedback on learners' motivational beliefs and self-esteem". If the rationale of empowering and encouraging students in the direction of wanting to learn is used, then the value of assessment activities and the value of participating in those activities should become apparent.

Teachers in higher education put a great deal of time and effort into producing written, and indeed, oral feedback. It has already been shown that there is a huge amount of assessment and a growing number of students. Despite the changing environment of mass education students want the feedback process to be clear, explicit and fair (Holmes and Smith, 2003). If feedback is to contribute to student learning in cybersecurity and a great deal of effort is put into it by tutors – how can tutors be sure that it is having the desired effect on helping students?

Perhaps the simplest reason that students want feedback is that it will help them to learn. However, it is not quite as simple as that. The situation is also further complicated in that the types of feedback which are most effective will vary depending on the cybersecurity task being assessed. There is a need to make sure that the feedback that is provided will actually be useful and usable for students, and as such feedback should:

- **Be Understandable by Students:** There is the possibility that the feedback provided to students is often not understood by the students.
- **Be Valued by Students:** In order to be valued by students, feedback should be constructive and reflect the effort that they have put into any assessment activities but also be meaningful in the context of their future learning needs (feed-forward).
- **Allow Students to "Close the Gap" on Their Understanding:** If students know what to do to improve, they can "close the gap" between what they can do or know and what they need to do or know then there is the potential to make that learning opportunity effective.
- **Be of Appropriate Quality:** The quality of feedback given to learners has a significant impact on the quality of learning. The feedback should provide information that helps students trouble-shoot their own assessment performance and take action to close the gap between intent and effect.
- **Be Timely:** One of the key aspects in enhancing efficiency of learning is to ensure that feedback on assessment is timely. If students don't get the feedback soon enough then feedback is less likely to be perceived to be useful for their on-going studies.

Assessment tasks and the feedback associated with the assessment tasks provide an efficient and effective set of instruments to help students enhance their cybersecurity learning. It is important to think about the assessment design, the expectation of the assessment task and the resultant feedback (as well as the ways in which the student will be able to use the feedback).

Taking the above into account the author has used a phased approach in getting students to engage in assessment and to take into account the feedback provided on the assessment. Using this phased approach in cybersecurity enables the feedback on assessment to relate to the completeness of the assessment task but also to be specific to the cybersecurity environment. The following example illustrates the phased approach. This approach can be modified depending on whether the assessment is for one module or for a series of modules. The approach can also provide opportunities for the assessment(s) to be theoretical and / or practical in nature.

Phase 1: Identify and describe a series of cybersecurity threats (if practical is required, get students to design and potentially write a short program illustrating the algorithmic / logical nature of the threat).

Phase 2: Identify and describe defenses to the threats identified in phase 1 (again if practical get students to design and potentially write a short program illustrating the algorithmic / logical aspects of the defense – at this point only a very small portion of overall cybersecurity defense).

Phase 3: Discuss the implications and effect of cybersecurity threats as a series of attack vectors. At this point the concepts associated with impact can be introduced.

Phase 4: Get students to consider the risk (probability) and risk (business impact). Potentially also get students to think about continuity.

Phase 5: Depending on cybersecurity facilities available, simulate a real attack. This allows students to investigate the breach. The author has used this phase to develop digital forensics skills as well as introduce the consideration of how to improve cybersecurity as a result of what has happened in a breach.
Phase 6: Design and implement various levels of cybersecurity defense – depending on the students' level and the size of the assessment this can include programming the defenses.
Phase 7: Test and evaluate the defenses in phase 6.
Phase 8: If there is a need to take further then there is the opportunity to get students to think about policies and procedures required to improve cybersecurity.

There are various ways that the phases identified above can be utilized in assessment, either as a series of steps for an individual learner, or as a set of group activities. It is also possible to utilize the phases as an extended "capture the flag" type of activities.

Bootcamp assessment – as indicated earlier in this chapter Bootcamps can be a useful method for teaching cybersecurity. The author has used Bootcamp participation as an opportunity for students to undertake assessment. In this instance students are required to produce an evaluative and reflective report on what they have learned from the Bootcamp, how this can be applied to cybersecurity problems and how they have developed professionally as a result.

CONCLUSION

This chapter has drawn on current research and best practice on teaching and assessment in cybersecurity in higher education. Consideration has been given to the theoretical and pedagogical foundations for helping tutors make decisions about the methods and approaches to utilize in teaching and assessing the cybersecurity curriculum.

As has been discussed in this chapter there are many variables to take into account when considering effective teaching in cybersecurity. Irrespective of the variables or the objectives in the teaching it is important to focus on the learning needs of the participating student. The needs of the student will vary depending on the level of learning and the prior subject knowledge of the learner. The emphasis in this chapter has been to encourage providers to design cybersecurity teaching and learning opportunities that provide systematic and stimulating learning experiences that will give students the best chance to succeed in their learning. We have advocated that providers ensure that:

- learning is transparent;
- teaching activities facilitate dialogue between teachers and learners and between learners; and
- communities of learners are developed.

The principles and theories of cybersecurity and the associated application of those principles and theories exist in an ever-changing and rapidly developing environment. The environment is complex and complicated which provides further challenges for those seeking to teach cybersecurity effectively.

REFERENCES

ACM. (2017). *Cybersecurity Curricula 2017: Curriculum Guidelines for Post-Secondary Degree Programs in Cybersecurity. A Report in the Computing Curricula Series Joint Task Force on Cybersecurity Education*. Available at https://www.acm.org/binaries/content/assets/education/curricula-recommendations/csec2017.pdf

Alvarez, B. (2011). Flipping the classroom: Homework in class, lessons at home. Education Digest: Essential Readings Condensed For Quick Review, 77(8), 18 – 21.

Barnett, R. (1992). *Improving Higher Education: Total Quality Care*. Bristol, PA: OU Press.

Biggs, J. (1996). Assessment learning quality: Reconciling institutional, staff and educational demands. *Assessment & Evaluation in Higher Education*, *12*(1), 5–15. doi:10.1080/0260293960210101

Biggs, J. (1996). Enhancing teaching through constructive alignment. *Higher Education*, *33*(3), 347–364. doi:10.1007/BF00138871

Black, P. (1993). Formative and summative assessment by teachers. *Studies in Science Education*, *21*(1), 49–97. doi:10.1080/03057269308560014

Black, P., & Wiliam, D. (1998). Assessment and classroom learning. *Assessment in Education: Principles, Policy & Practice*, *5*(1), 7–74. doi:10.1080/0969595980050102

Black, P., & Wiliam, D. (1999). *Assessment for Learning: Beyond the Black Box. Cambridge*. Assessment Reform Group, University of Cambridge. Available at http://www.assessment-reform-group.org.uk/AssessInsides.pdf

Boud, D., Cohen, R., & Sampson, J. (1988). Peer Learning and Assessment. *Assessment & Evaluation in Higher Education*, *24*(4), 413–426. doi:10.1080/0260293990240405

Boud, D., & Feletti, G. (1997). *The challenges of problem based learning*. London: Kogan Page.

Brown, G., Bull, J., & Pendelbury, M. (1997). *Assessing Student Learning in Higher Education*. London: Routledge.

Cohen, P. A. (1981). Student ratings of institution and student achievement: A meta-analysis of multisection validity studies. *Review of Educational Research*, *51*(3), 281–309. doi:10.3102/00346543051003281

Covill, A. (2011). College students' perceptions of the traditional lecture method. *College Student Journal*, *45*(1), 92–101.

Disability Discrimination Act (1995) with Amendments. (2000). Available at http://www.legislation.hmso.gov.uk/acts/acts1995/Ukpga_19950050_en_1.htm

Fee, S. B., & Holland-Minkley, A. M. (2010). Teaching computer science through problems, not solutions. *Computer Science Education*, *20*(2), 129–144. doi:10.1080/08993408.2010.486271

Garet, M. S., Porter, A. C., Desimone, L., Birman, B. F., & Yoon, K. S. (2001). What Makes Professional Development Effective? Results from a National Sample of Teachers. *American Educational Research Journal*, *38*(4), 915–945. doi:10.3102/00028312038004915

Gibbs, G., & Simpson, C. (2004). Conditions under which assessment supports students' learning. *Learning and Teaching in Higher Education*, *1*(1), 3–31.

Hallet, J., Larson, J., & Rashid, A. (2018). Mirror Mirror on the Wall: What are we Teaching them at all? Characterising the Focus of Cybersecurity Curricular Frameworks. *ASE@USENIX Security Symposium 2018*. Available at https://www.usenix.org/sites/default/files/conference/protected-files/ase18_slides_hallett.pdf

Hamdorf, J., & Hall, J. C. (2001). The development of undergraduate curricula in surgery assessment. *The Australian and New Zealand Journal of Surgery*, *71*(3), 178–183. doi:10.1046/j.1440-1622.2001.02031.x PMID:11277149

Harris, M. A., & Patten, K. (2015). Using Bloom's and Web's Taxonomies to Integrate Emerging Cybersecurity Topics into a Computing Curriculum. *Journal of Information Systems Education*, *26*(3), 219 – 229.

HEFCE. (2002). *Successful Student Diversity*. Available at http://www.hefce.ac.uk/pubs/hefce/2002/02_48.htm

Higher Education Academy. (2006). *Embedding Success Enhancing the Learning Experience for Disabled Students*. York, UK: Higher Education Academy.

Holmes, L., & Smith, L. (2003, July). Student evaluation of faculty grading methods. *Journal of Education for Business*, 318 – 323.

Irons, A. D., & Devlin, S. (2012). *The Inspiring Teacher in Computing*. Paper presented at 1stAnnual Conference on Aiming for Excellence in STEM Learning and Teaching, London, UK.

Irons, A. D., Savage, N., Maple, C., & Davies, A. (2016, Summer). Embedding Cybersecurity in the Computer Science Curriculum. IT Now, 56 – 57.

Irons, A. D., & Thomas, P. (2016). Problem based learning in digital forensics. *Higher Education Pedagogies*, *1*(1), 95–105. doi:10.1080/23752696.2015.1134200

Jenkins, A., & Healy, M. (2005). *Institutional strategies to link teaching and research.* Higher Education Academy Publication.

Johnston, N., & Karafotias, T. (2016). Flipping the Classroom to Meet the Diverse Learning Needs of Library and Information Studies (LIS) Students. *Journal of Education for Library and Information Science*, *57*(3), 226–238. doi:10.3138/jelis.57.3.226

Joshi, P., Thukral, A., Joshi, M., Deorari, A. K., & Vatsa, M. (2011). Comparing the Effectiveness of Webinars and Participatory Learning on Essential Newborn Care (ENBC) in the Class Room in Terms of Acquisition of Knowledge and Skills of Student Nurses: A Randomized Controlled Trial. *In Indina J Pediatr*. Available at https://www.researchgate.net/profile/Anu_Thukral/publication/224914755

Kessler, G. C. (2007). Online education in computer and digital forensics: A case study. *IEEE Proceedings of the 40th Hawaii International Conference on System Sciences 2007*. 10.1109/HICSS.2007.407

Knight, P. (2001). *Formative and Summative, Criterion and Norm-Referenced Assessment*. LTSN Generic Centre, Assessment Series No. 7.

Lundstedt, S. (1966). Criteria for Effective Teaching. *Improving College and University Teaching*, *14*(1), 27–31. doi:10.1080/00193089.1966.10532492

McDowell, L., Sambell, K., Bazin, V., Penlington, R., Wakelin, D., Wickes, H., & Smailes, J. (2005). Assessment for Learning: Current Practice Exemplars from the Centre for Excellence. In Teaching and Learning. Northumbria University Red Guides, 11.

McGettreick, A. (2013). Toward effective cybersecurity education. *IEEE Security and Privacy*, *11*(6), 66–68. doi:10.1109/MSP.2013.155

Murphy, R. (2006). Evaluating new priorities for assessment in higher education. In Innovative Assessment in Higher Education. London: Routledge.

NCSC. (2018). *New Cyber Attack categorisation system to improve UK response to incidents*. Available at https://www.ncsc.gov.uk/news/new-cyber-attack-categorisation-system-improve-uk-response-incidents

Nicol, D., & Macfarlane-Dick, D. (2004). Rethinking formative assessment in HE. In C. Juwah, D. Mcfalane-Dick, B. Matthew, D. Nicol, D. Ross, & B. Smith (Eds.), *Enhancing Student Learning Through Effective Formative Feedback* (pp. 3–14). HE Academy.

Nuutila, E., Törmä, S., & Malmi, L. (2005). PBL and computer programming— The seven steps method with adaptations. *Computer Science Education*, *15*(2), 123–142. doi:10.1080/08993400500150788

Oltsik, J. (2017). *The Life and Times of Cybersecurity Professionals, ESG, ISSA Report*. Available at https://www.esg-global.com/hubfs/issa/ESG-ISSA-Research-Report-Life-of-Cybersecurity-Professionals-Nov-2017.pdf

Paloalto. (2016). *2016 Prediction #10: Cyberthreat Intelligence Sharing Goes Mainstream*. Available at https://researchcenter.paloaltonetworks.com/2015/12/2016-prediction-10-cyberthreat-intelligence-sharing-goes-mainstream/

Pelligrino, J. W., Chudowsky, N., & Glaser, R. (Eds.). (2001). *Knowing what Students Know – The Science and Design of Educational Assessment*. Washington, DC: National Academic Press.

Pfleeger, C. P., & Cooper, D. M. (1997). Security and Privacy: Promising Advances. *IEEE Software*, *14*(5), 27–32. doi:10.1109/52.605928

Rashid, A., Daneziz, G., Chivers, H., Lupu, E., Martin, A., Lewis, M., & Peersman, C. (2018). Scoping the Cyber Security Body of Knowledge. *IEEE Security and Privacy*, *16*(3), 96–102. doi:10.1109/MSP.2018.2701150

Rowntree, D. (1987). *Assessing Students: How Shall we Know Them* (2nd ed.). London: Kogan Page.

Scheponik, T., Sherman, A. T., DeLatte, D., Phatak, D., Olivia, L., Thompson, J., & Herman, G. L. (2016). How students reason about cybersecurity concepts. *2016 IEEE Frontiers in Education Conference*. Available at http://doi.ieeecomputersociety.org/10.1109/FIE.2016.7757363

Schleicher, A. (2015). Valued-added: How do you measure whether universities are delivering for their students? *Higher Education Policy Institute (HEPI) Annual Lecture 2015*. Available at https://www.hepi.ac.uk/wp-content/uploads/2016/01/Andreas-Schleicher-lecture.pdf

Wegner, E. (2000). *Communities of Practice: Learning, Meaning, And Identity (Learning in Doing: Social, Cognitive and Computational Perspectives)*. Cambridge, UK: Cambridge University Press.

Weiss, R., Mache, J., & Nilsen, E. (2013). Top 10 hands-on cybersecurity exercises. *Journal of Computing Sciences in Colleges*, *29*(1), 140–147.

Williams, J., & Cappuccini-Ansfield, G. (2007). Fitness for Purpose? National and Institutional Approaches to Publicising the Student Voice. *Quality in Higher Education*, *13*(2), 159–172. doi:10.1080/13538320701629186

Chapter 9
Cybersecurity Curricular Guidelines

Matt Bishop
University of California – Davis, USA

Diana Burley
The George Washington University, USA

Lynn A. Futcher
Nelson Mandela University, South Africa

ABSTRACT

The Cybersecurity Curricular Guidelines, a joint effort of the ACM, IEEE Computer Society, AIS SIGSAC, and IFIP WG 11.8, were created to provide developers of cybersecurity curricula with guidelines for material to include. The curricular guidelines have eight knowledge areas, broken down into knowledge units and topics. Underlying cross-cutting concepts provide linkages among the knowledge areas. Disciplinary lenses enable the developer to emphasize the knowledge units appropriate to the goals of the developed curricula. Each knowledge area also includes a list of essential concepts that all curricula should cover to an appropriate depth. The guidelines can be linked to workforce frameworks and certification criteria as well as academic curricula.

INTRODUCTION

The urgency of securing our information infrastructure is clear from the numerous compromises of personal data as well as from compromises of commercial and government information. A key part of this is securing the computing infrastructure, which consists of networks and computers in their various guises – the Internet, personal computers, laptops, servers, "smart" devices such as phones and sensors connected to the Internet — as well as the policies, procedures, and user and administrator interfaces controlling those components

Other chapters in this book cover the nature of threats, how the associated risks affect the proper handling of data and systems, and examples of notable compromises and their effects. The number and

DOI: 10.4018/978-1-5225-7847-5.ch009

Copyright © 2019, IGI Global. Copying or distributing in print or electronic forms without written permission of IGI Global is prohibited.

rate of compromises demonstrate that cybersecurity has not yet been fully integrated into the development, deployment, operation, and retirement of computing and network systems. Academic institutions are introducing courses and programs to teach students about cybersecurity. The topics covered, and the depth to which they are covered, vary greatly; thus, students who graduate from different cybersecurity programs may have very different skills and abilities. And as these programs are introduced, what to cover and to what depth it should be covered are among the primary considerations in the development of the curriculum.

There is no universally agreed upon cybersecurity curriculum, and indeed there cannot be. The security needs of a military organization, a commercial firm, a hospital, and an academic institution are often distinct. For example, a commercial firm may prize integrity above other security properties to ensure its products are not tampered with as they are developed and go to market. A military organization treats confidentiality and integrity as the most important properties, as it must protect plans and disposition of troops and ensure only authorized changes by authorized people occur. A hospital must protect both, because a failure in integrity could result in the death of a patient, and a violation of confidentiality could result in a large fine and multiple lawsuits. Thus, no one curriculum can encompass all cybersecurity needs. So rather than a standard curriculum, a set of guidelines will enable institutions introducing new cybersecurity programs to select those areas of cybersecurity most relevant to the needs of their constituents (such as typical employers of their students), and emphasize those while covering the other topics in less depth. Institutions with existing programs can also use guidelines to determine whether their curriculum covers the material appropriate for their needs, as different cybersecurity curricula will emphasize different aspects of security.

The effectiveness of guidelines has been shown by the impact of the Software Engineering Body of Knowledge's (Bourque & Fairley, 2014) effect on software engineering education (Ludi & Collofello, 2001; Fairley, Bourque, & Keppler, 2014; Alarifi, Zarour, Alomar, Alkshaikh, & Alsaleh, 2016). It has changed how software engineering programs are developed and evaluated.

In September 2015, the Association for Computing Machinery (ACM) Education Board, the IEEE Computer Society, the Association for Information Systems Special Interest Group on Information Security and Privacy, and the International Federation for Information Processing's Technical Committee on Information Security Education collaborated to launch the CSEC2017 Joint Task Force on Cybersecurity Education (JTF).

For 28 months, the JTF engaged with the cybersecurity community through presentations and discussions at U.S. and international conferences and workshops. Members of an Industrial Advisory Board ensured that the resulting work included input from industries; members of a Global Advisory Board provided input from educators and professionals from around the world. In all, more than 325 people from 35 countries and 6 continents contributed to the development of the cybersecurity guidelines.

The first version of the Cybersecurity Curricular Guidelines (CSEC2017) (Joint Task Force on Cybersecurity Education, 2017) was completed in December 2017. This chapter discusses those guidelines, their use, and their future.

BACKGROUND

Before 2000, cybersecurity was generally considered of little interest in most, but not all, academic institutions. During the first decade of the 21st century, interest in cybersecurity as an academic area of research and education picked up considerably as the lack of security in our systems and infrastructure resulted in successful large-scale attacks and effects. Funding increased, and research and technology grew. In 2013, the ACM included it in its computer science curricular guidelines (Joint Task Force on Computer Curricula, 2013). In 2014, the Cyber Education Project (CEP) began to develop curriculum guidelines for "cyber science" programs. A logical outgrowth of this was the idea of developing curricular guidelines for cybersecurity; this led to the establishment of the JTF, and the development of CSEC2017.

A variety of efforts have examined what students need to know in cybersecurity. For example, the U.S. National Initiative for Cybersecurity Education (NICE) has developed a Cybersecurity Workforce Framework (NCWF) (Newhouse, Keith, Scribner, & Witte, 2016) that presents the knowledge, skills, and abilities that enable workers to carry out specific tasks, and relates those tasks to work roles. The knowledge, skills, and abilities are general, such as "Knowledge of secure coding techniques" (K0140; Newhouse, Keith, Scribner, & Witte, 2016, p. 110), "Skill in conducting application vulnerability assessments (S0137; Newhouse, Keith, Scribner, & Witte, 2016, p. 80), and "Ability to apply cybersecurity and privacy principles to organizational requirements (relevant to confidentiality, integrity, availability, authentication, non-repudiation)" (A0123; Newhouse, Keith, Scribner, & Witte, 2016, p. 91). So the NIST NICE Framework would be good for people whose goal is to be able to satisfy the requirements of a specific cybersecurity work role, but they do not encompass the breadth that an academic program covers. Further, it does not provide guidance for those who are not working in the cybersecurity area, such as students of law, political science, medicine, and other disciplines. Curricular guidance for academic institutions must also provide guidance for curricula for these students. Thus, the NIST NICE Framework complements CSEC2017, and indeed some tasks may suggest specific exercises that may be incorporated as part of a cybersecurity curriculum. This is discussed in the section about workforce frameworks.

The ACM Computer Science Curricula 2013 provides curricular guidelines for undergraduate degree programs in computer science. Information assurance and security is one of 18 knowledge areas in the guidelines, and like CSEC2017 parts of it are distributed throughout the other knowledge areas. So it is much less detailed than CSEC2017, and it organizes KUs based on other computer science disciplines and not as intrinsic parts of cybersecurity. The ACM Information Technology Curricula 2017 (Task Group on Information Technology Curricula, 2017) includes Cybersecurity Principles as an essential IT domain, and Cybersecurity Emerging Challenges as a supplemental IT domain. The Cybersecurity Principles domain is essentially a cybersecurity core, with subdomains at a high level, and some of the subdomains augment other domains. The Cybersecurity Emerging Challenges domain speaks to topics that are rapidly changing, and so supplements the other domain. The two Curricula provided a basis for much of the CSEC2017 development in its early stages.

The US NSA/DHS Knowledge Units (KUs) for Centers of Academic Excellence in Cyber Defense (CAE-CD) provide a basis for determining whether a program meets the requirements for being designated a CAE-CD. These KUs focus on educating cybersecurity workers. It provides specific outcomes for each KU, and schools can map the outcomes of their classes to these to demonstrate they satisfy the requirements for that designation. CSEC2017 has different goals. It allows flexibility in the development of curricula for what is to be covered in different fields, and is not tied to any designation. Conklin and Bishop (2018) provide a detailed comparison.

Many curricula for cybersecurity are available to meet specific objectives. The (ISC)^2 Common Body of Knowledge (International Information Systems Security Certification Consortium, 2018) prepares students for the CISSP exam. The ISACA Online Courses on Cybersecurity also speaks to certifications

(ISACA, 2018). The IEEE Cyber Security Program's goals (IEEE, 2018) are to help businesses improve their practices. These are curricula, specific to their goals, and as such can provide insight and ideas for exercises to academic educators. As noted above, CSEC2017 has different goals. It is a set of guidelines rather than a prescriptive curriculum.

CYBERSECURITY

The term "cybersecurity professional" has many meanings. Cybersecurity professionals secure systems at corporations. They develop policies and plans to handle successful attacks, and to track unsuccessful ones. They work with legislators to write laws affecting the use and misuse of technology. Cybersecurity professionals can be found in almost all fields, performing a wide variety of jobs. As a result, people have different opinions of what a cybersecurity professional should know, and what skills and abilities they could have.

Given that the term "cybersecurity" has many different meanings, this is not surprising. Thus, a large number of educational programs and curricula fall under this term. Some organizations, such as NIST, have developed frameworks for the knowledge, skills, and abilities required for specific cybersecurity jobs. But these frameworks speak to specific jobs and not an education program in cybersecurity.

Cybersecurity is a discipline that touches many other disciplines, just as mathematics, which is found in the disciplines of physics, chemistry, and other physical sciences and social science disciplines. Any definition of cybersecurity should acknowledge these influences, and accept that it is "cross-disciplinary".

The Joint Task Force defined cybersecurity as:

A computing-based discipline involving technology, people, information, and processes to enable assured operations. It involves the creation, operation, analysis, and testing of secure computer systems. It is an interdisciplinary course of study, including aspects of law, policy, human factors, ethics, and risk management in the context of adversaries. (Joint Task Force on Cybersecurity Education, 2017, p. 10)

This formed the underpinning of the material in the guidelines.

THE CSEC2017 FRAMEWORK

The CSEC2017 framework begins with a model having three parts. The knowledge areas describe the subject matter relating to the discipline of cybersecurity. The cross-cutting concepts underlie multiple knowledge areas, providing interconnections among those areas. The disciplinary lenses show the content of the discipline of cybersecurity appropriate for that lens. These combine to produce a cohesive thought model that underlies the curricular guidelines. Figure 1 shows the model.

Basis for the Guidelines

The basis for the guidelines themselves drew on five bases.

First, a cybersecurity education program is based upon core knowledge and skills. These underlie all aspects of cybersecurity, and all ways in which cybersecurity manifests itself across other disciplines.

Figure 1. CSEC Thought Model
(Joint Task Force on Cybersecurity Education, 2017, p. 20)

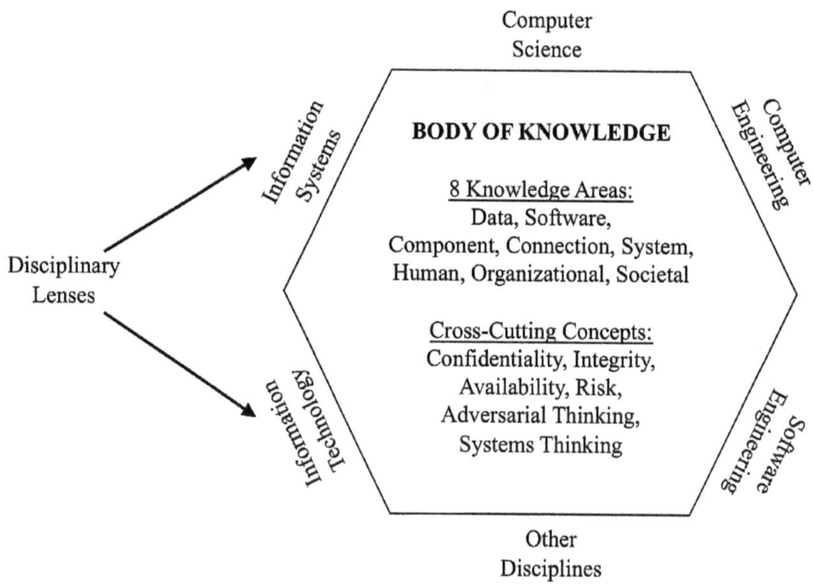

The particular understanding of cybersecurity may color the interpretation of the knowledge, and the use of skills. For example, confidentiality may encompass protecting data from being revealed to an adversary in one realm. In the guise of privacy, it may simply allow those to whom the information refers to control its distribution and use. But in both realms, a basic understanding of confidentiality is critical to the application of cybersecurity principles and mechanisms.

Next, cybersecurity has a computing-based foundation. This is an acknowledgement of the prefix "cyber". Computers and their infrastructure, including networks, are the focus of cybersecurity. The information to be protected is stored on those systems. The resources to be protected are controlled by those systems. For example, contact lists are stored on smartphones, and those must be protected against corruption and, usually, disclosure. Medical devices such as pacemakers must have their control programs be both assured and secured against unauthorized changes or interference. This assumption includes interactions between people, procedures, and computing systems. How computers are used affects how they are secured, and if policies and procedures provide inadequate or misguided security properties, then the computing system will be vulnerable.

Third, a good cybersecurity education program should enable students to undertake many different types of jobs in many different areas. The precise knowledge, skills, and abilities for each job will depend both on the nature of the job and the environment in which the employee works. As these differ among different employers and organizations, a graduate of a general cybersecurity program will need to learn the specific tasks expected, and how to work in the organization's political, legal, social, and human environment. The cybersecurity education program cannot teach these unless the program has as its specific goal the training of employees for that particular organization. But the program can teach the students so they are flexible and can quickly learn what specialized knowledge they need for a job in a given organization. Thus, the cybersecurity education program should teach concepts applicable to a broad range of cybersecurity expertise.

Conversely, cybersecurity education guidelines are flexible so programs can tailor their curriculum to specialized needs. For example, a legislator need not know the details of a cryptosystem, but she should know what cryptography is, how it works in a general sense, and – perhaps most important – what its limits are and how it can be compromised. A developer of medical systems need not know the details of cybersecurity theory, but must understand the need to provide mechanisms to enable process separation and protection of user data. If the goal of the program is to train a network analyst to use a Big System firewall, then the program should focus on those aspects of cybersecurity relevant to the configuration and use of that firewall and not, for example, stray into multilevel integrity policy enforcement by operating systems.

Finally, ethical issues are inherent in cybersecurity, and a cybersecurity education program should emphasize the ethical obligations and responsibilities that designing, implementing, and administering security measures entails. A good example is the adding of "back doors" to cryptographic mechanisms so trusted people can decipher any traffic using those mechanisms, or requiring that cryptographic keys be escrowed for that purpose. The former fails because of the difficulty in distinguishing legitimate requests from illegitimate ones, in light of the insider threat. The latter also may be unreasonable if the effect is the same as a "back door". But key escrow may be reasonable, for example if the mechanism is used for an organization's business data; should the user become unavailable, the organization needs a way to recover its data. Students and practitioners of cybersecurity need to apply ethics to their tasks to determine how best to do them, or indeed whether they should be done.

The Model

Knowledge areas (KAs) describe the subject matter of cybersecurity. They provide a tool for understanding or exploring cybersecurity ideas. Further, the material in the area can be learned in varying levels of detail and understanding.

The KAs are composed of knowledge units (KUs), which group multiple related topics. The topics are specific guidelines for the curricular content of the knowledge unit. The KAs are:

- Data Security;
- Software Security;
- Component Security;
- Connection Security;
- System Security;
- Human Security;
- Organizational Security; and
- Societal Security.

The KUs and topics may overlap different KAs. As an example, consider the design of a library that reads packets from a network and processes them. The library is privileged, and it must ensure that the contents of the packets are read properly and protected. Thus, this falls into the topics of using security features (restricting privileges) and encapsulating structures and modules in the implementation KU of the Software Security KA. It is also a composition of components, because the library interface ties the system and network together. Thus, that aspect of the design falls under the network traffic topic of the network defense KU of the Connection Security KA.

Learning outcomes would be tied into the topics in the KUs. With one exception, learning outcomes are not present in CSEC2017. The topics presented are simply examples of material the KU is to cover. Further the specific learning outcomes depend on the use to which the knowledge is to be put – that is, upon the disciplinary lens through which the topic is viewed, and upon the goals of the curriculum or program using the curricular guidelines. How best to incorporate them is a discussion for the future.

Cross-cutting concepts unify ideas underlying the KAs, and provide a framework for making connections among them. They span most, if not all, of the KAs, and are fundamental to students' understanding of core ideas, regardless of the discipline or program they are studying. This provides a coherent view of cybersecurity, and also reinforces the mindset of each of the knowledge units.

The KAs are common to all cybersecurity. However, the approach to teaching and learning the material in the KAs, and the depth to which they and the ancillary skills must be mastered, depends on how that knowledge will be used. A lawyer would be expected to understand much of the material in the Organizational, Societal, and Human Security KAs, and only a little from the other three KAs. Contrariwise, a software engineer would be expected to know much of the material in the Data, Component, Connection, System, and especially Software Security KAs, and only a minimal amount from the other three KAs. And a system designer would emphasize the Component, Connection and Systems Security KAs, while learning the basics about Organizational, Human, and Societal Security and more about Data and Software Security. Thus, the "view" of the KAs differs, depending on discipline.

CSEC2017 is designed to help with the development of a course, a curriculum, or a training program. As this development proceeds, the topics must be instantiated with specific material appropriate for that course. The content will undoubtedly change over the lifetime of the program as newer material becomes available. For example, the description of the topic "Logical data access controls" in the access control KU of the Data Security KA lists 9 example access controls such as access control lists, mandatory access control, role-based access control, and attribute-based access control. But a class on Android security will cover the Android access control mechanism in this topic, even though it is not explicitly listed in the description. As the Android phone does not provide many of the types of access control such as attribute-based access control, the course would not cover that even though it is listed explicitly in the description of that topic. Similarly, a course on cryptography would discuss the GCM mode as a mode of operation for block ciphers, which is in the symmetric (private key ciphers) topic of the cryptography KU in the Data Security KA, even though GCM is nowhere mentioned explicitly. These examples emphasize that the curricular guidance identifies topics that a cybersecurity curriculum might include. The curriculum developer must supply the specific contents for those topics because the developer knows the goals of the class, the needs of the students, and the resources available, and so can tailor how each topic is covered, and what is used to cover it.

Many topics also overlap a number of different KUs and KAs, because each KU and KA presents a different view of the topics. Take privacy as an example. In the Data Security KA, it appears in the Legal Issues KU because of the need to understand the conditions under which there is a right to privacy of data; the Secure Communication Protocols KU, in the guise of privacy-reserving protocols; and in the Data Privacy KU, which focuses on how the law views privacy in a variety of uses of data. In the Software Security KA, it is part of the learning outcomes of security requirements and an implicit part of the Design KU, because software developers must know how to use data anonymization techniques, and when not to record information, as part of the requirements analysis and software design. Privacy pervades the Human Security KA, being named explicitly in all but two KUs, and implicitly in those two. Privacy is part of the topic of identification and authentication (Identity Management KU) because identification information such as biometrics needs to be kept private. How users perceive risk to themselves includes a consideration of privacy, as does learning to identify phishing emails and unsafe web sites, and hence it is part of the Awareness and Understanding KU. It is explicitly named in the Social and Behavioral Privacy KU, the Personal Data Privacy and Security KU, and the Usable Security and Privacy KU. It is also a topic in the Security Governance and Policy KU of the Organizational Security KA because privacy is an element of those policies and governance procedures and requirements. In contrast to the technological orientiation of the topic in the Data Privacy KU in the Data Security KA, the non-technical view of privacy laws lies in the Cyber Law KU in the Societal Security KA. For obvious reasons, it is also its own KU in that KA.

Hardware security issues are another example of a topic that spans several KAs. Attacks such as Spectre and Meltdown (Kocher et al., 2018; Lipp et al., 2018), which deal with the interaction of software and hardware, fall into several KUs. The closest complete match would be component design security, a topic in the Component Design KU of the Component Security KA. Both take advantage of speculative execution in the chip. The best solutions are hardware-based, although some software-based mitigations have been proposed. Those software mitigations generally involve improving isolation, which falls under the topic of encapsulating structures and modules in the Implementation KU of the Software Security KA.

These examples show how CSEC2017 supports the view of the content presented for the same topic being different depending on the area being emphasized.

Knowledge Areas

The CSEC2017 task force assembled working groups to guide development of the KAs and their contents. Each working group developed the topics and KUs for a KA. The KAs, their KUs, topics, and essentials are shown in the Appendix. In order to provide a better understanding of the process followed for each KA, its related KUs, and topics, this section discusses the Software Security KA.

Example of Knowledge Areas Structure: The Software Security Knowledge Area

The Software Security KA focuses on the development and use of software that maintains the security of the information and systems it protects and is used on. Software is a key component of most systems currently in use. The security properties of the system, of the resources it protects, and of the information it holds rely on software to ensure those properties hold. As is well known, policies and procedures also determine the security of an entity, so how the software is designed, implemented, deployed, used, maintained and – at the end of life – decommissioned also bear on the security of both the software itself and what it protects. Directions for use must be clear and comprehensive, and the users must know what to do when something fails (even if they should simply call the vendor). Hence documentation also plays a role in software security. Ethical issues also abound; for example, when should vulnerabilities be announced, and to whom they should be reported. The purpose of the software may also raise ethical issues, and developers need to consider whether the software is to be used for malicious purposes (however those are defined). In light of this, ethical issues merit discussion in the context of software security.

The initial focus of the software security KA was the design principles. Several of the principles are from Saltzer's, Schroeder's, and Kaashoek's design principles (Saltzer & Schroeder, 1975; Saltzer & Kaashoek, 2009). The others come from principles of software engineering. The working group structured the resulting principles around three themes: simplicity, restriction, and methodology. These appeared in the final version, and are:

- KU: Fundamental Design Principles
  - Simplicity principles:
    - Economy of mechanism;
    - Minimize shared mechanisms; and
    - Least astonishment.
  - Restrictive principles:
    - Least privilege;
    - Fail-safe defaults;
    - Complete mediation;
    - Separation; and
    - Minimize trust.
  - Methodology principles:
    - Open design;
    - Layering;
    - Abstraction;
    - Modularity;
    - Complete linkage; and
    - Design for iteration.

Similar work led to six further KUs and their topics:

- KU: Design
  - Derivation of security requirements;
  - Specification of security requirements;
  - Software development lifecycle/security development lifecycle
  - Programming languages and type-safe languages.
- KU: Implementation
  - Validating input and checking its representation
  - Using APIs correctly;
  - Using security features;
  - Checking time and state relationships;
  - Handling exceptions and errors properly;
  - Programming robustly;
  - Encapsulating structures and modules; and
  - Taking environment into account.

- KU: Analysis and Testing
    - Static and dynamic analysis
    - Unit testing
    - Integration testing; and
    - Software testing.
- KU: Deployment and Maintenance
    - Configuring
    - Patching and the vulnerability lifecycle
    - Checking environment
    - DevOps
    - Decommissioning/retiring
- KU: Documentation
    - Installation documents
    - User guides and manuals
    - Assurance documentation; and
    - Security documentation.
- KU: Ethics
    - Ethical issues in software development
    - Social aspects of software development
    - Legal aspects of software development
    - Vulnerability disclosure
    - What, when, and why to test

These KUs cover the spectrum of software security, from conception (requirements analysis, specification) to deployment (decommissioning), and other critical aspects such as documentation and ethics. In the CSEC2017, each topic is augmented with curricular guidance. For example, the topic "Validating input and checking its representation," a topic in the KU Implementation, has as curricular guidance two items:

- Check bounds of buffers and values of integers to be sure they are in range, and
- Check inputs to make sure they are what is expected and will be processed/interpreted correctly.

The KUs in this knowledge area were validated by mapping the vulnerabilities of the OWASP Top 10 (OWASP, 2017), the MITRE/SANS Top 25 Programming Errors (Christey, 2011), and the design flaws identified in the IEEE Computer Society's Top 10 Security Design Flaws (Arce et al., 2015) against the KUs to ensure that all problems in those widely-used lists were covered. The Implementation KU topics are drawn from Tsipenyuk, Chess, and McGraw's taxonomy (2005). But the guidance does not identify any specific attacks that software developers should look for. Indeed, the topics, and their guidance, do not point out that cross-site scripting and injections fall into this group. Indeed, it does not present vulnerabilities from vulnerability lists, because those will change over time; indeed, cross-site scripting dropped from number 2 in the 2013 OWASP Top 10 list (OWASP, 2013) to number 7 in the 2017 OWASP Top 10 list (OWASP, 2017), and cross-site request forgery was dropped from the list. In a curriculum, these could be discussed to instantiate the topics. They make the subject matter come alive for the students. But for guidelines, the underlying problems creating those vulnerabilities is more important because the classes of vulnerabilities will continue to exist; only their instantiation, which those and other lists cover, will change.

Knowledge Areas as Curricular Guidance

The curricular guidance for topics sometimes presents specific protocols or instances as examples of what should be covered. Curricula that use other protocols or instances to teach the associated topics follow the guidelines, because the named protocols are simply intended as guidance. The topic "Application and transport layer protocols" in the KU Secure Communication Protocols of the Data Security KA identifies four protocols as examples (HTTP, HTTPS, SSH, and SSL/TLS). An instructor may choose not to discuss SSL, and add DNSSEC or SNMP to this list. This emphasizes the focus of the topics, and indeed of the CSEC2017: guidance, not prescription, for curricula.

Some of the KUs overlap KUs in other KAs. The Fundamental Design Principles KU of the Software Security KA overlaps a similar KU in the System Security KA, the Analysis and Testing KU overlaps with the Component Testing KU in the Component Security KA, and the Ethics KU overlaps with similar KUs in the Organizational Security KA and the Societal Security KA. But the emphasis on the material presented varies among the KAs. For example, Ethics in the Organizational Security KA focuses on laws, ethics, and compliance with regulatory and legal requirements, whereas in the Software Security KA, the emphasis is on the software itself and handling issues that arise from what the software is to do, how it does it, and how it is maintained and tested.

Essential Concepts

In addition to the KAs, KUs, and topics, each KA identifies a set of essential concepts and associated learning outcomes. These capture the content that every student of cybersecurity should know about that KA. The depth to which they should know these concepts and their application will vary among disciplines and programs, but every program should cover these essentials to some extent.

The Software Security KA identifies six essentials:

- Fundamental design principles including least privilege, open design, and abstraction;
- Security requirements and their role in design;
- Implementation issues;
- Static and dynamic testing;
- Configuring and patching; and
- Ethics, especially in development, testing and vulnerability disclosure.

In terms of Bloom's revised taxonomy (Committee for Computing Education in Community Colleges, 2000), the learning outcomes for each generally lie at the "understanding" and "applying" levels. Examples of these are:

- For the fundamental design principles, "discuss the implications of relying on open design or the secrecy of design for security";
- For security requirements, "explain why security requirements are important";

- For implementation issues, "explain why input validation and data sanitization are necessary";
- For static and dynamic testing, "discuss a problem that static testing cannot reveal";
- For configuring and patching, "discuss the need to update software to fix security vulnerabilities"; and
- For ethics, "discuss the ethical issues in disclosing vulnerabilities".

Each of these speak to the principles and concepts rather than specific instances. They can of course be tailored to specifics, but the goal of the essentials is to ensure that students learn key concepts at a high level, unless the discipline requires them to delve more deeply into that KA. Using the above as an example, a law student studying cyberlaw should be able to explain why "security through obscurity" is an inadequate defense by itself, but not necessarily how to combine it with other defenses – only that it should be. A software architect, of course, should know the latter as well as the former.

The learning outcomes are intended to apply across all disciplines. Hence they are oriented towards discussion and explanation rather than demonstration. For example, a law student studying cyberlaw should understand the limits of static testing, and hence be able to discuss a problem that static testing cannot reveal. However, for a software engineering student, this learning objective would be subsumed by another, specifically that the student be able to demonstrate the difference between static and dynamic testing (based on the topic static and dynamic testing, in the Analysis and Testing KU of the Software Security KA) by applying her knowledge to create a problem that static testing could not reveal.

Cross-Cutting Concepts

The cross-cutting concepts identify concepts underlying the KAs. The concepts are expressed in different ways in the different KAs, but they are present in most, if not all, of them.

The cross-cutting concepts are (Joint Task Force on Cybersecurity Education, 2017, p. 22):

- *Confidentiality*, or "rules that limit access to system data and information to authorized persons" (Joint Task Force on Cybersecurity Education, 2017, p. 22). Privacy is a form of confidentiality in which control of the data, and of the use of data, is emphasized.
- *Integrity*, or "assurance that the system, data, and information are accurate and trustworthy" (Joint Task Force on Cybersecurity Education, 2017, p. 22). This includes the level of assurance of the initial data as well as it being manipulated only by authorized users in authorized ways. It also includes the level of assurance that the hardware will work as expected.
- *Availability*, or "the data, information, and system are accessible" (Joint Task Force on Cybersecurity Education, 2017, p. 22). In practice, determining availability relies on quality of service requirements. Accessibility is not enough, as some uses may require specific levels of service rather than just being able to connect.
- *Risk*, or "the potential for gain or loss" (Joint Task Force on Cybersecurity Education, 2017, p. 22). Although often seen as undesirable, risk is an everyday phenomenon that businesses and organizations use to guide how they do their work.
- *Adversarial thinking*, a thought process "that considers the potential actions of the opposing force working against the desired result" (Joint Task Force on Cybersecurity Education, 2017, p. 22).

It requires understanding what threats could compromise the system, resources, or data, and how they could happen. It is sometimes called "playing the role of the attacker."

- *Systems thinking*, a thought process "that considers the interplay between social and technical constraints to enable assured operations" (Joint Task Force on Cybersecurity Education, 2017, p. 22).

As an example, consider confidentiality. This property is defined by rules controlling the spread of information. It is a cross-cutting concept. It is foundational to the Data Security, Systems Security, and Organizational Security KAs. In the guise of privacy, it is a component of human security. And Societal Security combines components of all these KAs but with a different emphasis, and confidentiality is one of the properties that carries over.

Disciplinary Lenses

Although the KAs cover the knowledge of cybersecurity, and the cross-cutting concepts show their interrelationships, an observation made earlier is that different disciplines require different levels of knowledge and expertise of cybersecurity. The depth, approach, and specific knowledge from the KA depends upon how that knowledge will be used in that discipline. This aspect of the model uses the ACM computing disciplines to provide examples of differing views. These are:

- Computer science;
- Computer engineering;
- Information systems;
- Information technology;
- Software engineering; and
- Mixed disciplines.

As an example, a student of software engineering would focus on the Software Security KA and possibly the Data Security KA. The depth to which the KUs and topics in the Societal Security KA are explored depends upon the nature of the software engineering program. One that focused on medical devices, for example, would need to emphasize privacy and the laws controlling access to medical data, so the students understood the risks and could develop countermeasures. One that focused on web development would also focus on Connection Security as well as Component Security.

The mixed disciplines includes disciplines that require some knowledge of cybersecurity. As mentioned earlier, lawyers specializing in cyberlaw, or dealing with computer-controlled assets such as driverless automobiles, will need to know enough about cybersecurity to understand the technology sufficiently to develop and present their cases. Doctors will need to know enough to understand why many medical records systems use multifactor authentication rather than a simple password, and why all accesses are logged and audited. Health informaticians will need to understand how to position medical systems to minimize the threat of compromise – for example, by ensuring they are not connected to the Internet, or if they are that the network security measures are sufficient.

Summary

The framework of knowledge areas, crosscutting concepts, and disciplinary lenses provide comprehensive guidelines for developing cybersecurity programs and curricula. Through the disciplinary lenses, developers of those curricula can determine what to include, and at what depth, and with what view, to meet the needs of the users of their curricula. Those who have developed curricula can compare them to the KAs, KUs, and topics to determine how comprehensive their curricula are, and can add material as needed.

APPLICATIONS

As the threats increase, and new methods of attack are uncovered, the need for cybersecurity professionals grows. Programs to increase the number of cybersecurity workers are training many, but the organization $(ISC)^2$ estimates that by 2022, there will be a shortage of almost 2 million cybersecurity jobs (International Information Systems Security Certification Consortium, 2017). Students graduating from technical programs have the breadth and depth of knowledge needed to succeed, but often lack the experience or specific skills that their job would require. Students graduating from non-technical programs often lack the depth of understanding of cybersecurity concepts to be able to apply them in their jobs. Linking the CSEC2017 guidelines to the workforce would help guide prospective employees to curricula that would support the jobs they they are interested in. This linking would also support employers because they can link their job requirements to specific guidelines and topics, and from that to specific academic curricula or workforce frameworks.

Cybersecurity practices, a critical component in cybersecurity education, refers to the knowledge, skills, and abilities required to perform the duties that a job, or set of jobs, require (Joint Task Force on Cybersecurity Education, 2017, p. 80). The guidelines must be linked to workforce frameworks and professional practice.

Application Areas

This is done through application areas. *Application areas* are an organizing framework for competency levels for each practice (Joint Task Force on Cybersecurity Education, 2017, p. 80). They bridge the thought model to specific workforce frameworks and practices. By defining them, the bodies of knowledge for workforce frameworks and job requirements can be codified by mapping the appropriate application area back to the CSEC2017 framework. Then the codifiers can extract both core knowledge and crosscutting concepts that are appropriate, and then view them through the appropriate disciplinary lens. The seven application areas mimic a system's life cycle, with supporting areas such as research added. The following descriptions give highlights of topics that people working in the application area need to know.

The *public policy* application area covers executive managers, members of boards of directors, legislators who write and pass laws about the development, deployment, and use of information systems, regulators who regulate those systems, and others who will develop public policy about those systems. They must understand how society and organizations use these systems, and how humans interact with them. This leads to an understanding of the advantages and drawbacks of rules and regulations governing the use of the systems. People working in this application area must also understand the basics of design because the design of the system affects how it is implemented, how it is used and how it can be used, and what it can and cannot do. Similarly, they must understand the risks that the public policy introduces. All this affects the cost of security in both financial and human terms, which are often the focus of people working in this application area.

People working in the *procurement* application area determine what is required to build a system, purchase the technology or have it designed and built, and hire the people who will work with it. They must understand how the systems and the people hired support the general goals of the organization as well as the specific purposes for which the information technology system was obtained and the people hired. This requires an understanding of risk management and business continuity, and from that what is required of people and infrastructure, and what policies, procedures, and processes will provide an appropriate level of security and assurance to ensure the specific and general goals are met.

Managers work in the *management* application area. They must understand business continuity issues, what laws, regulations, and policies must be complied with, and especially how to demonstrate that compliance. They need to know how changes to the system affect its use. They also will be the ones dealing with attacks and the consequences, and so must know how to handle incidents and how those incidents will affect the organization.

The *research* application area is composed of researchers who study cybersecurity. They need to know the foundations of cybersecurity, and beyond that understand topics in their area of research. A theoretician, for example, would need to know the details of formal models of access control. A researcher studying network security would need to know that such models exist, but would focus on how software-defined networking switches could be compromised.

This leads to the *software development* application area. Software must meet any operational requirements, including those determined by laws, regulations, plans, and environmental factors. Developers must design the software to do that, or recommend changes to the requirements. The implementation must satisfy the design and be robust (secure programming), so it must handle exceptions and errors including those arising from humans They must be able to gather assurance evidence to demonstrate assurance claims, and document the installation and use of the systems.

The *information technology security operations* application area deals with preserving the security of the system. The information security managers and personnel must understand how to translate the security requirements into procedures and configurations. They must ensure that identity and authorization management systems are installed, initialized, configured, and connected properly. They have to test the systems, infrastructure, and procedures, and analyze the results. Operations personnel must understand system maintenance under both normal conditions (patching and upgrading, for example) and abnormal conditions (incident handling and response, for example).

The *enterprise architecture* application area refers to the management of systems, operations, and information technology in the organization. This area spans the other six application areas, because policy drives the enterprise architecture; the architecture also drives procurement, management, and security operations. Software runs the infrastructure that supports the enterprise architecture, and research works out ways to improve the architecture or validate it. The enterprise architects must therefore understand elements of all these applications areas.

Workforce Frameworks

Many nations and groups have begun to develop frameworks describing the skills required to work successfully in the field of cybersecurity. As an example, the NIST NICE Cybersecurity Workforce Framework (NCWF) is intended to be comprehensive, providing a lexicon and taxonomy for cybersecurity work in all areas of employment. Other nations have similar efforts underway.

As an example of how academic institutions might link the curricular guidelines to the workforce framework, consider the NCWF. Figure 2 shows the general idea. Essentially, the list of topics in the workforce framework is linked to the list of KAs and KUs in CSEC2017 by topic and learning outcomes. As an example, in the NCWF, a software developer (work role ID SP-DEV-001) must know cybersecurity and privacy principles (K0004), which map into the Fundamental Design Principles KU in the software security KA. She must be able to analyze user needs and software requirements to assess the feasibility of the design (T0011), which maps into the design KU of the Software Security KA. She must be able to debug software (S0014), which covers elements of both the Implementation KU and the Analysis and Testing KU of the Software Security KA. Finally, they must be able to develop secure software using secure software development techniques (A0047),[1] which falls into a number of KUs, most especially the design KU (because it covers the security development life cycle) and the Deployment and Maintenance KU of the Software Security KA. The mapping of these to KUs in other KAs, and of the other knowledge, task, skill, and abilities requirements of the software developer job in the NCWF, is left as an exercise for the reader.

Figure 2. Linking the CSEC thought model and a workforce framework
(Adapted from Figure 4, Joint Task Force on Cybersecurity Education, 2017, p. 21)

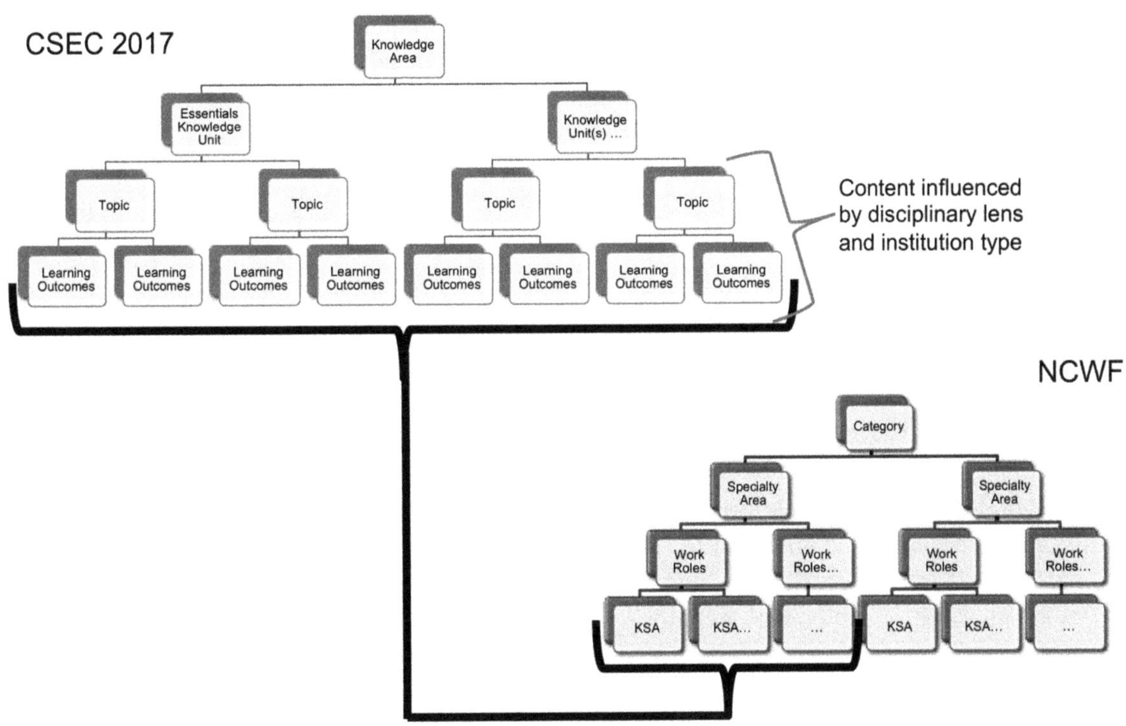

A similar approach is used for mapping courses and curricula to the CSEC2017 KAs and KUs. For example, an undergraduate course in computer security that presented the Fundamental Design Principles would map them to at least the Fundamental Design Principles KU in the Software Security KA, the Component Design KU of the Component Security KA, and the System Thinking KU of the System Security KA. Similarly, a course focusing on the application of the fundamental principles could look for the KUs that speak to those principles, and see whether the topics listed in those KUs are appropriate, or suggest others that are appropriate, for this course. This enables instructors to identify gaps. As an example, the cybersecurity program presented in the next chapter was developed with reference to the CSEC2017 guidelines.

Chapter 11 expands on workforce requirements, as certifications are intended to demonstrate competence of the holder. Thus, certifications and the CSEC2017 KUs and KAs can be mapped to one another, just as courses and the CSEC2017 KUs and KAs can.

To aid in this process, the CSEC2017 web site (Joint Task Force on Cybersecurity Education, 2017) has examples of these mappings, and templates with instructions on how to use the spread sheet provided on the web site to demonstrate the mapping. The JTF is encouraging people and groups to submit examples for their particular courses, curricula, and workforce framework. A subgroup of the task force will review them and assist the submitter in fixing any problems they find. The example will then be posted so others can work with it, or use it as a model for creating their own example.

As an example, CSEC2017 developers and industry partners such as Boeing and Intel are collaborating to map the curricular guidelines with specific professional requirements. The mapping process includes three phases. First, the industry partner identified a set of cybersecurity positions to map to the curricular guidance. For each position, the review team examined the detailed position descriptions for the knowledge, skills and abilities required to perform in the role; representative major tasks; typical education and experience requirements; and competencies. Next, the review team identified the CSEC2017 knowledge areas that included knowledge units and/or topics associated with the position requirements. Once the relevant content was identified, the position requirements were linked to CSEC2017 content through a series of mapping charts. These charts show the direct relationship between CSEC2017 recommended curricular content and specific professional requirements and provide a reference tool to facilitate communication between academic departments and their industry partners.

Each chart consists of a large box containing the job title and the key tasks for that job. In that box are sets of other boxes, one for each knowledge area relevant to the job. Within each box are the essential concepts and other KUs that are most relevant to the tasks the holder of the job will perform. The largest set, called the *primary* boxes, contains the KAs with most of the knowledge relevant to the job. The next set, called the *secondary* boxes, has KAs with a significant amount of knowledge for the job. The third set, called the *tertiary* boxes, represents KAs with more limited relevance. The third set may be omitted.

Burley and Lewis (2018) provide a detailed example of the mapping process and sample mapping charts for three positions in a major corporation. Consider the position of "incident response specialist," which in this organization performs the tasks of incident response activities, evidence collection, analysis, and determining the impact of the incident on resources; and incident reporting. The primary box contains the System Security KA, and all 8 essentials from that KA (holistic approach, security policy, authentication, access control, monitoring, recovery, testing, and documentation). The secondary box contains the Organizational Security KA, one essential (strategy and planning), and the Analytical

Tools KU and the Business Continuity, Disaster Recovery, and Incident Management KU in that KA. The corporation can then look to academic programs that follow the curricular recommendations tied to those KAs, and academic programs that want to prepare students for this type of job should follow those recommendations as well.

CONCLUSION

The goal of the CSEC2017 is to provide guidelines to aid developers of workforce frameworks and cybersecurity curricula in ensuring their work is as comprehensive as possible with respect to their goals. This recognizes that cybersecurity is not a monolithic discipline; it is a discipline made up of parts of many other disciplines, and its contents change over time, with focus shifting to meet the needs of the cybersecurity practitioners and those they support.

CSEC2017 is a beginning. As the field evolves, new topics, and perhaps new KUs, will be added; others will be dropped. Sooner than that will be the addition of new curricular and workforce mappings contributed by the community. The process for doing so is being tested, and several curricula and course syllabi are already available. CSEC2017 is also being matched to other efforts. As noted above, it has been compared to the NSA/DHS Centers of Academic Excellence KUs (Conklin & Bishop, 2018). The British SecTech effort (Furnell et al., 2018) is also mapping their certification framework into the CSEC2017, and CSEC2017 is being used as the basis for postgraduate cybersecurity education in South Africa (von Solms & Futcher, 2018).

CSEC2017 can expand in directions beyond the workforce and academic mappings. Its flexibility makes it suitable for curricular guidance in the cybersecurity area for other disciplines. The disciplinary lens "mixed disciplines" refers to these other disciplines. However, the cybersecurity component of a legal education would be different than the cybersecurity component of an education in physics, art, and sociology. So adding disciplinary lenses tailored to specific non-technical disciplines will enhance the utility of CSEC2017. This will require the collaboration of educators and others in those fields, and will probably begin when curricula for those disciplines are added to the ones for technical disciplines.

Thus, the focus of CSEC2017 is not on how to teach cybersecurity, or what specific material should be taught. Instead, it provides a framework for instructors or developers of curricula to determine what they should teach, and how to teach it. Any curriculum evolves over time; and the guidelines will also change. The Joint Task Force invites readers, and anyone else, to participate by contributing exemplars for industry jobs, for both training and academic programs, and for courses. By doing so, they will contribute to improving the state of cybersecurity education.

AVAILABILITY

This chapter presented an overview of CSEC2017. For more details, the interested reader is referred to the most current version of CSEC2017, available at https://cybered.acm.org.

ACKNOWLEDGMENT

This chapter reports on work done by many people. The authors are members of the Joint Task Force; the others are Scott Buck (Intel Labs), Joseph J. Ekstrom (Brigham Young University), David Gibson (U.S. Air Force Academy), Elizabeth K. Hawthorne (Union County College), Siddharth Kaza (Towson University), Yair Levy (Nova Southeastern University), Herbert Mattord (Kennesaw State University), and Allen Parrish (U.S. Naval Academy). Other contributors, too numerous to name here, are listed in the CSEC2017 Final Report; we thank them for their work and assistance.

We also gratefully acknowledge the financial support of the U.S. National Science Foundation under Award 1623104 and the U.S. National Security Agency under Grant H98230-17-10219. Any opinions, findings, and conclusions or recommendations expressed in this material are those of the author(s) and do not necessarily reflect the views of the U.S. National Science Foundation or the U.S. National Security Agency.

Additional financial support was provided by the Intel Corporation, the Association for Computing Machinery (ACM), the IEEE Computer Society (IEEE-CS), and the Association for Information Systems Special Interest Group on Information Security and Privacy (AIS SIGSAC). We thank them for this.

REFERENCES

Alarifi, A., Zarour, M., Alomar, N., Alkshaikh, Z., & Alsaleh, M. (2016). SECDEP: Software Engineering curricula development and evaluation process using SWEBOK. *Information and Software Technology*, *74*, 114–126. doi:10.1016/j.infsof.2016.01.013

Arce, I., Clark-Fisher, K., Daswani, N., DelGrosso, J., Dhillon, D., Kern, C., … West, J. (2015). *Avoiding the top 10 software security design flaws.* Retrieved from https://www.computer.org/cms/CYBSI/docs/Top-10-Flaws.pdf

Bourque, P., & Fairley, R. E. (2014). *Guide to the Software Engineering Body of Knowledge Version 3.0.* Piscataway, NJ: IEEE.

Burley, D. L., & Lewis, A. H. Jr. (2018). CSEC2017 and Boeing: Linking Curricular Guidance to Professional Practice. *IEEE Computer.* (Manuscript submitted for publication)

Christey, S. (2011). *2011 CWE/SANS top 25 most dangerous software errors.* Retrieved from http://cwe.mitre.org/top25/

Committee for Computing Education in Community Colleges. (2000). *Bloom's revised taxonomy.* Retrieved from http://ccecc.acm.org/assessment/blooms

Conklin, W. A., & Bishop, M. (2018). Contrasting the CSEC 2017 and the CAE designation requirements. In *Proceedings of the 51st Hawaii International Conference on System Sciences* (pp 1–7). Manoa, HI: ScholarSpace. Retrieved from https://scholarspace.manoa.hawaii.edu/handle/10125/50194

Fairley, R. E., Bourque, P., & Keppler, J. (2014). The impact of SWEBOK Version 3 on software engineering education and training. In *Proceedings of the IEEE 27th Conference on Software Engineering Education and Training* (pp. 192–200). Klagenfurt, Austria: IEEE. 10.1109/CSEET.2014.6816804

Furnell, S., K, M., Piper, F., &Ensor, C. (2018). A National Certification Programme for Academic Degrees in Cyber Security. In *Proceedings of the 11th IFIP WG 11.8 World Conference on Information Security Education* (pp. 133–146). Poznan, Poland: IFIP. 10.1007/978-3-319-99734-6_11

IEEE. (2018). *Cyber Security Tools for Today's Environment.* Retrieved from https://forms1.ieee.org/Cyber-Security-Program.html

International Information Systems Security Certification Consortium. (2017). *(ISC)² cybersecurity workforce shortage continues to grow worldwide, to 1.8 million in five years.* Retrieved from https://www.isc2.org/News-and-Events/Press-Room/Posts/2017/02/13/Cybersecurity-Workforce-Shortage-Continues-to-Grow-Worldwide

International Information Systems Security Certification Consortium. (2018). *The (ISC)² CBK.* Retrieved from https://www.isc2.org/Certifications/CBK

ISACA. (2018). *Cybersecurity Fundamentals Online Course.* Retrieved from https://www.isaca.org/Education/on-demand-learning/Pages/cybersecurity-fundamentals-online-course.aspx

Joint Task Force on Computing Curricula. (2013). *Computer Science Curricula 2013: Curriculum Guidelines for Undergraduate Degree Programs in Computer Science.* New York, NY: ACM. Retrieved from https://www.acm.org/binaries/content/assets/education/cs2013_web_final.pdf

Joint Task Force on Cybersecurity Education. (2017). *Cybersecurity Curricula 2017.* New York: ACM. Retrieved from https://cybered.acm.org

Kocher, P., Genkin, D., Gruss, D., Haas, W., Hamburg, M., Lipp, M., . . . Yaroim, Y. (2018). *Spectre Attacks: Exploiting Speculative Execution.* Retrieved from https://arxiv.org/abs/1801.01203

Lipp, M., Schwarz, M., Gruss, D., Prescher, T., Haas, W., Mangard, S., & Hamburg, M. (2018). *Meltdown.* Retrieved from https://arxiv.org/abs/1801.01207

Ludi, S., & Collofello, J. (2001). An analysis of the gap between the knowledge and skills learned in academic software engineering course projects and those required in real projects. In *Proceedings of the 31st Annual Frontiers in Education Conference* (pp. T2D-8–T2D-11). Reno, NV: Academic Press. 10.1109/FIE.2001.963881

Newhouse, W., Keith, S., Scribner, B., & Witte, G. (2017). *National initiative for cybersecurity education (NICE) cybersecurity workforce framework. NIST Special Publication 800-181.* Gaithersburg, MD: National Institute for Standards and Technology. doi:10.6028/NIST.SP.800-181

OWASP. (2013). *OWASP Top 10 – 2013: The ten most critical web application security risks.* Retrieved from https://www.owasp.org/images/f/f8/OWASP_Top_10_-_2013.pdf

OWASP. (2017). *OWASP Top 10 – 2017: The ten most critical web application security risks.* Retrieved from https://www.owasp.org/images/7/72/OWASP_Top_10-2017_%28en%29.pdf.pdf

Saltzer, J., & Kaashoek, M. (2009). *Principles of Computer System Design.* Burlington, VT: Morgan Kaufmann Publishers.

Saltzer, J., & Schroeder, M. (1975). The protection of information in computer systems. *Proceedings of the IEEE, 63*(9), 1278–1308. doi:10.1109/PROC.1975.9939

Task Group on Information Technology Curricula. (2017). *Information Technology Curricula 2017: Curriculum Guidelines for Baccalaureate Degree Programs in Information Technology.* New York: ACM. Retrieved from https://www.acm.org/binaries/content/assets/education/curricula-recommendations/it2017.pdf

Tsipenyuk, K., Chess, B., & McGraw, G. (2005). Seven pernicious kingdoms: A taxonomy of software security errors. *IEEE Security and Privacy, 3*(6), 81–84. doi:10.1109/MSP.2005.159

Von Solms, S., & Futcher, L. (2018). Identifying the Cybersecurity Body of Knowledge for a Postgraduate Module in Systems Engineering. In *Proceedings of the 11th IFIP WG 11.8 World Conference on Information Security Education* (pp. 121–132). Poznan, Poland: IFIP. 10.1007/978-3-319-99734-6_10

ADDITIONAL READING

Anderson, L. W., & Krathwohl, D. R. (2001). *A taxonomy for learning, teaching, and assessing: A revision of Bloom's taxonomy of educational objectives.* New York, NY: Longman.

Bicak, A., Liu, X., & Murphy, D. (2015). Cybersecurity curriculum development: Introducing specialties in a graduate program. *Information Systems Education Journal, 13*(3), 99–110.

Bishop, M., Burley, D., Buck, S., Ekstrom, J. J., Futcher, L., Gibson, D., ... Parrish, A. (2017). Cybersecurity curricular guidelines. In *Proceedings of the 2017 IFIP World Conference on Information Security Education: Information Security Education for a Global Digital Society* (pp. 3–13). doi: 10.1007/978-3-319-58553-6_1

Cooper, S., Nickell, C., Pérez, L., Oldfield, B., Brynielsson, J., Göcke, A. G., ... Wetzel, S. (2010). Towards information assurance (IA) curricular guidelines. In *Proceedings of the 15th Annual Conference on Innovation and Technology in Computer Science Education* (pp. 49–64). doi: 0.1145/1971681.1971686

Hoffman, L., Burley, D., & Toregas, C. (2012). Holistically building the cybersecurity workforce. *IEEE Security and Privacy, 10*(2), 33–39. doi:10.1109/MSP.2011.181

McDuffie, E. L., & Piotrowski, V. P. (2014). The future of cybersecurity education. *Computer, 47*(8), 67–69. doi:10.1109/MC.2014.224

KEY TERMS AND DEFINITIONS

Application Area: A structure linking academic curriculum to professional practice.

Cross-Cutting Concepts: Concepts that connect knowledge areas.

Cybersecurity: A computing-based discipline involving technology, people, information, and processes to enable assured operations. It involves the creation, operation, analysis, and testing of secure computer systems. It is an interdisciplinary course of study, including aspects of law, policy, human factors, ethics, and risk management in the context of adversaries.

Cybersecurity Practices: The combination of knowledge and skills required to perform in the field.

Disciplinary Lens: The view of a knowledge area, unit, or topic that focuses on those parts relevant to the discipline.

Discipline: A body of knowledge tied to a common theme.

Knowledge Area: A collection of critical knowledge forming a specialization within a discipline.

Knowledge Unit: A thematic grouping that encompasses multiple, related topics.

Workforce Framework: An organization of knowledge, skills, abilities, and competencies required to perform specific jobs or duties.

ENDNOTE

1 A0047 states "according to secure software deployment methodologies, tools, and practices" (Newhouse, Keith, Scribner, & Witte, 2016, p. 89). From the context, it is clear the word "deployment" should be "development".

APPENDIX

The Knowledge Areas

This appendix presents a description of each of the knowledge areas (except the Software Security KA, which is described in detail in the body of the paper).

- **Data Security KA:** The data security KA deals with the security of data when stored, when being processed, and when in transit.
- **Component Security KA:** The security of components making up a system have an effect on the security of a system. How that component is designed, fabricated, obtained, tested, integrated into the system, and maintained and disposed of when it reaches the end of its useful life affect the system's satisfying its desired security properties. This KA is concerned with all these aspects.
- **Connection Security KA:** Systems are made up of connected components, so the security of the connections affects the security of the system. The components interact through these connections. The connections can be short, as within a computer, or long, as in computer networks like the Internet. This KA focuses on the security of the connections between components, whether they be physical connections or logical connections.
- **System Security KA:** Understanding the security of a system requires more than understanding the security of its components and connections. It also requires understanding how these interact with one another, with the environment, and with users, policies, and procedures. Thus, the system must be viewed as a whole, and the system security KA does this.
- **Human Security KA:** Humans use and administer systems, and so need to ensure that the security properties of the systems, resources, and information they control hold. Thus, their actions are a critical component of computer and information security. The organizations and societies of which they are members impose both obligations and constraints within which they must act (or not act)
- **Organizational Security KA:** The extensive use of computer technology by organizations requires them to understand computer security. The aspects that are important vary with the goals of the organization, but certain generic attributes are common to all organizations. They are controlled by laws and regulations; they must manage people as well as equipment; and they handle sensitive data.
- **Societal Security KA:** Computer technology has had a profound impact on societies throughout the world. The Internet provides near-instantaneous communication among people and sites around the world. Previously private information about individuals can be derived by linking information in various databases. The law, policy, regulations, and ethics governing societies must take this information explosion, and the technology that supports it, into account.

Chapter 10
A Collaborative Cybersecurity Education Program

Teemu J. Tokola
University of Oulu, Finland

Thomas Schaberreiter
University of Vienna, Austria

Gerald Quirchmayr
University of Vienna, Austria

Ludwig Englbrecht
University of Regensburg, Germany

Günther Pernul
University of Regensburg, Germany

Sokratis K. Katsikas
Norwegian University of Science and Technology, Norway & Open University of Cyprus, Cyprus

Bart Preneel
Katholieke Universiteit Leuven, Belgium & imec, Belgium

Qiang Tang
Luxembourg Institute of Science and Technology, Luxembourg

ABSTRACT

This chapter presents an implementation of a cybersecurity education program. The program aims to address some issues identified in current cybersecurity teaching in higher education on a European level, like the fragmentation of cybersecurity expertise or resource shortage, resulting in few higher education institutions to offer full degree programs. As a result of the Erasmus+ strategic partnership project SecTech, the program tries to overcome those issues by introducing collaborative development to cybersecurity education. SecTech lays the foundations for a collaborative education program, like the definition of a clear content, module and delivery structure, and the appropriate tool support to facilitate collaboration and content reuse. Additional effort is required to achieve long-term success, including the creation of a community that drives the content creation and maintenance, as well as an independent governance structure to steer the project in the long-term. While the project focuses on European collaboration, a global community is envisioned.

DOI: 10.4018/978-1-5225-7847-5.ch010

Copyright © 2019, IGI Global. Copying or distributing in print or electronic forms without written permission of IGI Global is prohibited.

THE NEED FOR COLLABORATIVE CYBERSECURITY EDUCATION

Given the mounting cyber threat levels Europe is faced with, a coordinated cybersecurity education effort becomes more urgent than ever. The malware waves hitting Europe in May 2017 and recent Europol reports (European Union Agency for Law Enforcement Cooperation (Europol), 2017) give a clear warning of the dangers lying ahead, ranging from criminal activities to often state sponsored theft of intellectual property and a rising possibility of cyber sabotage. It is against this background that building on the EU cybersecurity strategy (European Commission and High Representative of the European Union for Foreign Affairs and Security Policy, 2013), new legislation aimed at strengthening privacy protection (THE COUNCIL OF THE EUROPEAN UNION, 2016) – the General Data Protection Regulation (GDPR) - and securing IT-dependent critical infrastructures (THE EUROPEAN PARLIAMENT AND THE COUNCIL OF THE EUROPEAN UNION, 2016) – the directive on security of network and information systems (NIS) - was introduced. Both GDPR and NIS have come into effect in 2018. The obligations introduced by this legislation at European level have also increased the demand for cybersecurity experts in an already overstretched market. It is obvious that an increased supply of talent becomes an absolute necessity if Europe as a whole aspires to meet the high aims set in the legislation and in European and national cybersecurity strategies. However, a joint and well-coordinated European approach to education in this field is still missing. Given the variety and diversity of topics that need to be covered, comprising such diverse areas as information and communications technology, management and organization, law, economics, sociology, criminology and psychological issues, it becomes painstakingly clear that a wide range of expertise needs to be accessed to create a thorough curriculum. That is one major reason for comprehensive academic programs on cybersecurity and privacy being a rare exception.

In line with those developments the Erasmus+ strategic partnership project SecTech was formed by seven European higher education institutions (KU Leuven, Luxembourg Institute of Science and Technology, Norwegian University of Science and Technology, University of Oulu, University of Plymouth, University of Regensburg, and University of Vienna) to collaboratively develop a European cybersecurity curriculum. The core motivation of the Erasmus+ SecTech project is to provide a seed curriculum including ready to use on-line teaching materials to give European academic institutions a much better starting point for implementing and delivering a cybersecurity education program, either on their own or in cooperation with other institutions. The primary contributions this project is aimed at supporting are the integration of knowledge that is currently available across Europe, but today is hardly combined and far from being integrated, the introduction of a curriculum template, the provision of seed on-line course material that can serve as a core and finally the establishment of an on-line repository and cooperation platform that can serve as basis for a Europe wide joint educational effort. As the free sharing of the developed course materials is expected to have an essential impact, established open standards and systems such as Moodle and SCORM will form the technological basis.

With information and cybersecurity experts becoming an increasingly scarce resource, the pooling and sharing of teaching materials at a European level is expected to have a significant impact on enabling in a first step the participating universities and in a following expansion phase other tertiary level institutions to much easier offer credible cybersecurity degree programs and to incorporate modules or parts of modules in existing computer science and information systems programs. While in the course of the project we have not given specific focus on determining the advantages of such a curriculum for learners, one of the most obvious advantages is a more complete learning experience due to more extensive material and teaching expertise that would not be available at partner institutions without a collaborative curriculum.

The Erasmus+ SecTech project is therefore aimed at helping to provide a practicable way of countering the current shortage of teaching expertise in a field that is becoming strategic for the European economy and society through a Europe wide collaborative development and delivery approach. Given the current lack of experts, lecturers and the high cost of maintaining teaching resources, the integrative approach demonstrated by this project can serve as a basis for more effectively and efficiently developing the cybersecurity skills so urgently needed in the European economy. Having an on-line shareable, resource-backed European cybersecurity curriculum can consequently offer a way to finally change the situation in favor of substantially raising the levels of cybersecurity and privacy that can be offered, thereby making a significant contribution to reaching the goals laid out by the recent European legislation. In the long-term, and taking into account the global nature of cyberspace, the project partners see the work on a collaborative cybersecurity curriculum as a global challenge that should be driven by a global community.

CYBERSECURITY EDUCATION AS A MULTI-DISCIPLINARY CHALLENGE

Cybersecurity is an extremely complex problem that requires domain knowledge from many disciplines to allow cybersecurity experts and professionals to fully understand the dangers of cyberspace and to be able to develop and implement protection strategies for several use cases, for example, to provide cybersecurity in the personal, organizational or critical infrastructure context. With the dynamic and quickly evolving cybersecurity threat landscape as well as the multitude of application domains in mind, the challenge for cybersecurity education is to allow learners to develop sophisticated cybersecurity skills based on a multi-disciplinary understanding of the problem domain that is also able to keep up with ever-changing cybersecurity developments. The European Cyber Security Organisation (ECSO) highlights this issue and identifies in a recent position paper (European Cyber Security Organisation (ECSO), 2018) that the lack of sufficiently trained IT security specialists is a European-wide problem and highlights the need for a strong multi-disciplinary approach towards cybersecurity.

Besides the multi-disciplinary angle, a second requirement relating to curriculum development that specifically relates to the collaborative aspect of the SecTech project is that a curriculum does not only need to be multi-disciplinary by design, but also needs to be able to accommodate the different focus areas of education institutions and degree programs at those institutions, since the developed content should be reusable. While the areas that need to be covered may be similar, the focus on specific topics may shift depending if the degree program is, for example, technically or organizationally focused.

The goal of the SecTech curriculum is to rely on existing templates and guidelines used for the development of cybersecurity education programs that would fulfil the requirements identified above. To achieve this, various industry related standards and other cybersecurity curricula have been examined. At the first stage *CS2013*, the Computer Science Curricula 2013: Curriculum Guidelines for Undergraduate Degree Programs in Computer Science (Association for Computing Machinery (ACM) and IEEE Computer Society, 2013) and *IT2017*, the Information Technology Curricula 2017: Curriculum Guidelines for Baccalaureate Degree Programs in Information Technology (Association for Computing Machinery (ACM) and IEEE Computer Society, 2017) have been reviewed. In *CS2013* a curriculum guideline for undergraduate degree programs in computer science is presented. Within these guidelines the Body of Knowledge is organized by 18 Knowledge Areas. Especially the Knowledge Area "Information Assurance and Security (IAS)" covers the field computer and network security and has been added due the high demand in this area. It is noteworthy that a relatively broad oriented curriculum for Computer Science already includes cybersecurity as an important part of the curriculum. The *IT2017* curriculum guidelines presents a framework which groups competencies in essential and supplemental IT domains. Thereby a specific cybersecurity domain is included as an essential IT domain and reaffirms the importance of cybersecurity in undergraduate degree programs.

Also the U.S. National Initiative for Cybersecurity Education (NICE) Cybersecurity Workforce Framework (Santos, 2016), the Guide to the Systems Engineering Body of Knowledge (Guide to the Systems Engineering Body of Knowledge (SEBok) v.1.9, 2018) and various national courses and degree programs focusing on IT and cybersecurity have been examined. While the above-mentioned standards and guidelines provide excellent recommendations for the contexts they were designed for, none of them provided adequate solutions to the requirements the project has identified for SecTech. The curriculum guidelines that have been selected as the template for the SecTech collaborative cybersecurity curriculum are the 2017 cybersecurity curricular guidelines (CSEC2017) (ACM, IEEE, AIS, IFIP, 2017), jointly developed by ACM, IEEE, the Association for Information Systems Special Interest Group on Security (AIS SIGSEC) and the International Federation for Information Processing Technical Committee on Information Security Education (IFIP).

As detailed in the previous chapter, the structure of CSEC2017 supports to a large extend the ideas of a multi-disciplinary and collaborative cybersecurity education program. The curriculum is grouped around a variety of knowledge areas and allows to look at those knowledge areas with both an institutional lens as well as a disciplinary lens in order to identify the concrete topics that are relevant for the degree program in a specific institution or profession and relate and integrate to the specific degree program covered at this institution. Specifically, this property was recognized as a key factor for the creation of a cybersecurity curriculum within the SecTech project. The CSEC2017 was developed to support academic institutions in creating their own cybersecurity curricula. The guideline represents a flexible model for designing a curriculum, and this flexibility enables users to develop a cybersecurity program tailored to their institution type. Different knowledge backgrounds of learners will be considered. For example, the thought model of CSEC2017 offers the possibility to look at the learning content from different perspectives and thereby to look at it in a different granular depth. Another aim of the CSEC2017 is to provide a guideline that allows IT security personnel to be as broadly and diversely specialized as possible.

For the intended development of a multi-disciplinary and flexible cybersecurity curriculum through the SecTech project, these knowledge areas could be used for the practical implementation of a curriculum for higher education. The knowledge areas specified in CSEC2017 are explained in Table 1. These knowledge areas were designed with a high flexibility in their adoption in mind. Depending on the institutional lens, disciplinary lens and topics, these knowledge areas allow to define the content of a curriculum in such a way that security programs can be created for different purposes. These could be programs designed for, amongst others, university degrees, polytechnic degrees, professional certifications. This feature was used for the development of the SecTech cybersecurity curriculum. For this purpose, the cybersecurity body of knowledge was determined by applying a mixed-disciplinary lens. The CSEC knowledge units (within the 8 knowledge areas) were evaluated by all SecTech project

Table 1. The CSEC2017 knowledge areas

Knowledge Area	Description
Data Security	The knowledge area Data Security focuses on the protection of information processed and stored within information systems. In order to impart sufficient skills in this area, it is important that the application of mathematical and analytical algorithms is taught.
Software Security	Software Security is aimed at the development and the application of secure software. An essential focus is the protection of the information to be processed by an IT system. Fundamental aspects of secure software development are taught to the students. The different phases of software development (design, implementation, test, deployment and maintenance) with regard to security measures are considered.
Component Security	Not only the security of the software in use, but also the used hardware, is an important aspect for the development of a secure system. The knowledge area component security looks at the phases design, procurement, testing, analysis and maintenance within the life cycle of hardware components that are used in larger systems. The security-relevant preconditions and precautions of the supply chain are thereby considered.
Connection Security	Another important area of cybersecurity knowledge is connection security. The transmission of data via physical and logical connections needs to be studied. The intention of this area is to provide a profound basic knowledge in network technology and in communication between IT systems in order to manage risks along the transmission path.
System Security	The combination of individual components to build a larger system involves various IT security risks. The knowledge area system security provides a holistic view of the connected components and subsystems. Students are required to understand interactions and dependencies between the system components to identify security issues and to provide adequate countermeasures.
Human Security	The protection of an individual's personal data, both in private and professional environments, is covered by the knowledge area human security. This also includes the behavior of people in situations that are relevant to IT security, like for example security awareness or social engineering.
Organizational Security	Both public and private organizations can be a preferred target for cyber criminals. This may not only cause economic loss, it may also affect government functions. The knowledge area organizational security aims to impart competencies in the management of risks and to ensure their functionality.
Societal Security	The continuous integration of information systems into our daily lives inevitably involves the consideration of IT security aspects. Existing and absent protective mechanisms can have an influence on our society. The knowledge area societal security considers cybercrime, legislation, ethics, policy and privacy.

partners. The focus was on the development of a flexible and decentralized cybersecurity curriculum in which each partner can contribute its core competencies. However, just providing knowledge is not enough to equip students for real-life situations. It is an essential part of the ability to understand and adequately communicate information about cyber attacks and their defense within an organization. This is important to properly inform decision makers in the organization and to confirm the relevance for further initiatives in cybersecurity. This aspect of competence transfer was also taken into account in the development of the SecTech curriculum and has already been implemented through workshops organized by the project together with national partner organizations. The content developed within the project has been disseminated in lecture and workshop sessions to interested participants, ranging from university students to education professionals as well as industry and government representatives. The feedback from those workshops has in turn been used to further refine and develop the ideas of the SecTech curriculum and has strengthened the belief of the project partners that multi-disciplinarity is one of the core features of a modern cybersecurity curriculum.

The development of teaching programs in the field of cybersecurity has also found to be of great relevance by partner organizations on a national and international level. The goal is not only to combat the lack of trained employees in cybersecurity, but also to take up the fight against cybercrime with well-educated students in cybersecurity. For this purpose, the SecTech project aims to bundle the competences of seven European partner universities and research centers in a multi-disciplinary cybersecurity curriculum. The analysis of best practices presented here have led to a close alignment of the SecTech curriculum with the CSEC2017 guidelines. The knowledge areas Data Security, Software Security, Component Security, Connection Security, System Security, Human Security, Organizational Security and Societal Security have been identified and adopted as relevant topics. In addition to that the institutional lenses and the disciplinary lenses from the CSEC2017 guidelines provide a decisive advantage for the development of a curriculum that creates a multi-disciplinary understanding of cybersecurity.

DELIVERY STRATEGY

The need for and the benefit of high-quality European and international curricula is clear. The success of individual efforts, however, is not guaranteed. The quality of the material produced is certainly one measure of success, but the impact of the produced material and curriculum has definite measures: the amount of time saved in individual organizations thanks to the high-quality material, the improvement of teaching material quality and width of the topics covered, and most importantly the reach of the material across countries, institutions, students and time.

This impact is realized by the success of the curriculum delivery effort: the adoption of the curriculum and materials in different institutions, the engagement of the target audience, the future participation of current and new contributors of material and all similar measures of success in an international curriculum project are consequences of well-executed delivery activities.

An international collaboration on developing teaching materials on any subject matter that is evolving at a rapid pace poses a number of important challenges and risks. The risk scenarios themselves are quite clear: at the time of delivery, the material developed could lack depth or relevance, it might not reach the target audiences or it could fail to integrate into teaching organizations' curricula, and further, the risk exists that the material is not sufficiently maintained and loses relevance too quickly over the years, it is abandoned more than adopted and the invested effort ultimately is not worth the impact produced. Accounting for these risks in the content delivery is a key part of a curriculum process. If these are the risks, then what are the key areas in which to succeed and to counteract these risks? The key delivery activities are:

- Promoting adoption
- Retaining internal interest
- Retaining external interest

For promoting adoption of curricula and their modules, the curriculum process needs to have definitive answers to the question of why institutions should adopt the curriculum, provide effortless way of incorporating parts of the curriculum into the institutions own teaching activities and to make it effortless and enticing for teachers to use the materials and tools provided. Quality of the material and tools produced, credibility of the contributing community, compatibility with local curriculum features and international reference curricula all contribute to this.

While it can be said that development consortia in itself represent a group of stakeholders in the success of curriculum projects, both the initial contributing partners and future participants are asked for two key resources, time and effort, and expending these requires commitment to the success of the curriculum process. After all, once materials and curriculum details have been created, they need to be regularly maintained to retain the relevance and the interest in the material. Consequently, the contributing community needs to have the answers for the following questions: why should individual contributors keep their materials or the curriculum as a whole updated and why should new contributors join the community? In short, there needs to be benefits to the time and effort spent: the direct benefit of having the materials from other contributors available, the pull of the large external audience that have adopted the material and of course the societal impact of a successful campaign.

Similarly, retaining the interest of external organizations that have adopted the curriculum or parts thereof is a challenge with a definite set of questions to be answered. Why should organizations continue to use the material or adopt new parts? Why should new institutions start using the material provided? Does the curriculum cover enough topics to be relevant and interesting? Institutions tend to adopt new curricula, new course and module structures, new technological tools and implement new study programs - will the material and curriculum be a hindrance or even a benefit at that point? Will it easily live through these different types of changes?

In many ways the internal and external interest work in tandem: an external interest in the material will create the audience and consequently the demand for internal activities and keep the internal community motivated to contribute, and similarly a strong internal community of motivated, active domain experts and a good coverage of the curriculum will promote external interest and adoption of the material.

Consequently, a strong curriculum project will have a clear plan for promoting both adoption, internal and external interest, and a good understanding on the internal and external status of the project. Internally, the project needs to measure the dedication and activity of contributors, recruit new ones and keep existing ones active, and externally, the project needs to be able to measure the reach of the curriculum, and improve this reach to become relevant in the eyes of both contributors, funding organizations and students.

The SecTech project has a strong starting point for this work: the consortium represents a strong collection of excellent contributors with the areas of expertise and provided modules covering a wide area of reference curricula. The project is also working on creating a suitable representation between the course contents and the ACM reference curriculum: Figure 1 shows a draft version of how mapping between courses and curriculum topics are collected into an overview of how well different knowledge units of the reference curriculum are covered by the courses. Once the project concludes with all the planned modules ready, with the support of the dedicated consortium, the SecTech curriculum has a good chance of attracting a large external interest and consequently create a beneficial, upward spiral of both internal and external interest and dedication to the project.

COLLABORATIVE DEVELOPMENT: TAPPING INTO EXISTING EXPERTISE DISTRIBUTED ACROSS EUROPE

As pointed out in the ECSO position paper on the gaps in European cyber education and training (European Cyber Security Organisation (ECSO), 2018), cybersecurity education needs to be interdisciplinary covering a broad range of aspects well beyond purely technical ones. If one starts from the academic von Humboldt model of education based on research, one concludes that cybersecurity education should be

Figure 1. Mapping of course contents to reference curriculum topics (upper table) and the derived overview of how well the knowledge units of the reference curriculum are covered by the developed courses (lower table).

Knowledge area	Knowledge unit	Topic	FOCUS							Leuven	Leuven	Leuven	Leuven
			S	5	4	3	2	1	Introduction to cy	Introduction to C	Cryptography	Introduction to P	Privacy
									2	1	2	1	2
Data Security	Secure Communication Protocols	Data link layer	0.00	0	0	0	0	0					
Data Security	Cryptanalysis	Classical attacks	0.25	0	0	1	0	0					
Data Security	Cryptanalysis	Side-channel attacks	0.50	0	0	2	0	0					
Data Security	Cryptanalysis	Attacks against private- key ciphers	0.00	0	0	0	0	0					
Data Security	Cryptanalysis	Attacks against public- key ciphers	0.00	0	0	0	0	0					
Data Security	Cryptanalysis	Algorithms for solving the Discrete Log Problem	0.00	0	0	0	0	0					
Data Security	Cryptanalysis	Attacks on RSA	0.00	0	0	0	0	0					
Data Security	Data Privacy	Overview	1.00	0	0	4	0	0					
Data Security	Information Storage Security	Disk and file encryption	0.25	0	0	1	0	0					
Data Security	Information Storage Security	Data erasure	0.00	0	0	0	0	0					
Data Security	Information Storage Security	Data masking	0.00	0	0	0	0	0					
Data Security	Information Storage Security	Database security											
Data Security	Information Storage Security	Data security law											
Software Security	Fundamental Principles	Least privilege											
Software Security	Fundamental Principles	Fail-safe defaults											
Software Security	Fundamental Principles	Complete mediation											
Software Security	Fundamental Principles	Separation											
Software Security	Fundamental Principles	Minimize trust											
Software Security	Fundamental Principles	Economy of mechanism											
Software Security	Fundamental Principles	Minimize common mechanism											

Knowledge area	Knowledge unit	# of topics	Coverage
Cyber Security Basics	Introduction to Cyber Security	1	25%
Data Security	Cryptography	6	2%
Data Security	Digital Forensics	10	13%
Data Security	Digital Forensics	10	13%
Data Security	Data Integrity and Authentication	4	9%
Data Security	Access Control	4	13%
Data Security	Secure Communication Protocols	5	15%
Data Security	Cryptanalysis	6	13%
Data Security	Data Privacy	1	100%
Software Security	Fundamental Principles	14	0%
Software Security	Design	4	6%
Software Security	Implementation	8	19%
Software Security	Analysis and testing	4	50%
Software Security	Deployment and maintenance	5	10%
Software Security	Documentation	4	0%
Software Security	Ethics	5	28%
Component security	Component Design	6	3%
Component security	Component Procurement	3	17%
Component security	Component Testing	2	50%
Component security	Component Reverse Engineering	3	29%
Connection security	Physical Media	4	0%
Connection security	Physical Interfaces and Connectors	3	8%

based on large interdisciplinary research groups that cover all relevant aspects of cybersecurity. In very few universities such research teams are available. Even if one considers only the technical dimensions, there are currently a handful universities in Europe that cover all aspects of cybersecurity technology research. If one considers topics beyond core technical expertise such as usability of security, cybersecurity economics or organizational aspects of cybersecurity, the number of research groups in Europe is rather small.

A second aspect is that collaboration with industry is essential to develop strong cybersecurity education programs, as there are clearly strong benefits in bringing together an academic approach with practical experience from industry. For several topics such as designing and operating Security Operating Centers (SOCs), configuring complex identity management systems, Common Criteria certification or large-scale malware filtering, expertise is concentrated in industry; this means that industry input in the cybersecurity education, for example by inviting guest lecturers, is essential for any state-of-the art cybersecurity program. The same holds mutatis mutandis for governance related expertise, and in particular national cybersecurity policies.

A third dimension are cultural differences among EU member states, which are reflected in the education programs in Europe. Even if the Bologna process has resulted in more integration in terms of names of degrees and credit systems, the fundamental vision on academic education is still very different across Europe. As an example, France and Belgium still believe in a broad basis for the engineering Bachelor education based on mathematics and science, followed by specialization during the Master's degree, while in The Netherlands and Germany engineering students can select their specialty (in a few universities even cybersecurity or information security) from the first Bachelor year onwards. Even if the education system would be the same, there are still cultural differences between EU member states. These differences are translated in their approach to cybersecurity, such as how to manage risks or how to define privacy and identity. As an example, some European countries have mandatory identity cards, while others have optional identity cards or none at all; similarly, some countries have central registers collecting information on their citizens, while others believe in distributed databases with various level of interlinking. In spite of having a common regulation governing the protection of personal data (the GDPR), the way the governments collect information about citizens is very different, and this is also reflected on how industry processes data. Of course, these cultural differences affect the level of maturity of the EU member states in terms of cybersecurity awareness. This can be deduced from the gaps between the publication dates of the national cybersecurity strategies across the EU or in the budgets of government agencies concerned with cybersecurity.

All these aspects clearly point towards the need for academic collaboration at a European level, or even collaboration at an international level beyond Europe. First, collaboration between universities is the only way that the required multi-disciplinary expertise can be entered into the cybersecurity education programs: this is essential to cover the seven knowledge areas discussed in Table 1 at a sufficient level of depth. Second, for industry input to cybersecurity education collaboration at European level is also essential: some of the expertise is only present at a few large industry players; in particular for smaller countries, the required expertise may not be present in the national industry. While the cultural diversity in Europe presents challenges, it is also opening opportunities: tackling a multi-dimensional and complex problem such as cybersecurity can greatly benefit from experts with various educational background, viewpoints and approaches. Ideally, this cultural diversity is already presented during the education programs so that the cybersecurity experts are aware of the challenges and opportunities brought by this diversity.

There are of course other reasons why education in cybersecurity can strongly benefit from European collaborations. Cybersecurity is by definition a problem that does not stop at the border: it is a global challenge that can only be addressed based on strong international collaboration. Moreover, in view of the scarcity of expertise in cybersecurity, there are strong benefits from developing a cybersecurity workforce at European level that is trained both with an understanding of cultural differences and with a view that surpasses national borders. The clear path towards creating such a workforce is to start from close collaboration between the Universities with expertise in cybersecurity. By bringing together their research and education expertise, their industry networks, and their understanding of cultural issues, they can together develop a more global and integrated approach to cybersecurity education that they could never create on their own and build the basis for the community able to develop and maintain a collaborative cybersecurity education program in the long-term.

CONTENT MODEL AND MODULE STRUCTURE

Delivering content in a varied environment creates challenges on their own. Despite the ECTS and Bologna processes, the reality remains that individual countries, institutions, faculties and even departments inside faculties can have drastically different practices and cultures with regards to courses and teaching.

There is significant room for variation: the amount of ECTS credits that individual courses should have, the real amount of work one ECTS should incur on the student, individuality of the students' effort, the type and difficulty of that work, the situation of individual subject matters on the 3-year bachelor studies, 1 or 2-year master studies or post-graduate studies, the grading of student activities, the distribution of time between lectures, exercises and individual work etc.

Eradication of these differences and standardization of teaching activities across nations might be a worthwhile goal or perhaps not, but certainly it is not the prerequisite for a curriculum project whose main aim is to improve the quality and impact of teaching materials of a specific discipline. As a result, curriculum projects need to take these differences into account in order to improve the adaptability of the curriculum. In order to be applicable to various environments, the project outcome needs to provide ready answers to the issue of what difficulties may arise, and how local teachers can easily adapt the material and justify the adaptation to themselves and to administration. As discussed before, external interest is key to the impact of the project and also for retaining the interest of internal contributors, and as adaptability is a key factor in increasing adaptation, the details related to adaptability should be thoroughly thought out. The project has identified following curricula properties that cater adaptability and content reusability:

- small granularity of modules
- separation of practical and theoretical work
- adjustability of grading activities
- strong connection with reference curricula
- applicability to different disciplines (multi-disciplinarity)

The ECTS credit system provides the opportunity of creating courses of many different sizes, with ideally same amount of workload, with one ECTS credit corresponding to 25 to 30 hours of work. How much students should be able to cover during that time, and how much prior knowledge is required in order to manage in that time, however, is obviously left up to the course organizers. Individual institutions and countries might have different practices regarding the course sizes: some might opt to have 3 ECTS courses as the standard, with 5 ECTS left for advanced courses and 7 or 8 ECTS for project courses, some others might have smaller, and some even offer larger courses of 10 ECTS. To make the curriculum adaptable, the curriculum should have a small granularity and separation of theory and practice in order to fit into different schemes: from sufficiently small modules, individual institutions can build cybersecurity courses of desired ECTS workload and with desired distribution of practical and theoretical content. On the contrary, if the curriculum project tries to essentially lock an answer by having bigger units and a set distribution of theory and practice, individual institutions might find it impossible to fit the courses into their structures and practices. Whereas one could argue that such rigidity should not belong to contemporary teaching, from the perspective of international curricula there is no need to force that argument.

Similarly, module content should not lock the grading activities: when adapting modules to local environments, institutions should have the benefit of using a similar basis for assessment, while retaining control over how individual assessments affect the final grade from any learning activities. With different priorities with regards to content and on the scale from theory to practice, the modules should permit giving different weights to different activities for the purpose of grading.

For planning local adaptation, another issue is matching module contents with the plans of local curriculum planners: while module descriptions obviously are important in helping local institutions to choose appropriate content to complement their local teaching activities, defining the relationship of the modules and courses with regards to reference curricula such as the ACM curriculum is a key activity in module planning. Adapting organizations need to be able to clearly understand the content relationships to any reference curricula that they are working with.

Working with an international body of possible adopters of curriculum contents and individual modules, and with cybersecurity being increasingly a concern in a growing number of fields, planning of an international curriculum and designing content modules can no longer be done from just, for example, the engineering point of view. Being able to use the multi-disciplinary lenses, essentially asking the question of how this content should look like to representatives of a certain discipline, and whether the module can somehow serve that perspective, is a key part of making the modules adaptable to different institutions and disciplines.

The SecTech project participants represent a wide range of different expertise areas, institutions and academic traditions, and consequently the consortium has a good view on what should and could be provided in terms of module contents and arrangements. The consortium has settled on providing modules of 0.5, 1 or 2 ECTS credits to allow external organizations adapt modules of suitable size as either complete courses of any desired ECTS size or as parts of existing courses. Also, theory and practice has been divided into different modules to permit multi-disciplinarians to either include or exclude practical parts (for example programming) in disciplines where they are unnecessary. As an example, the modules on practical security testing provided by University of Oulu, Finland, provides a theoretical introduction of 1 ECTS and additionally practical 2 ECTS modules including programming exercises.

In order to facilitate the creation of individual modules, template module structures have been created for the SecTech project, with 0,5 and 1 ECTS theory modules and 1.5 and 2.0 ECTS modules with both practice and theory and 2.0 ECTS modules with project-oriented practical work, as shown in Figure 2 With these modules further subdivided to theoretical and practical parts and thus making it possible to adapt modules to interdisciplinary requirements, the module structure should be well-defined enough to create a feeling of common structure but at the same time flexible enough to be adaptable to local traditions and practices.

Figure 2. Overview of the teaching module templates employed by the SecTech project

LECTURE PACKAGE 1 ECTS	
Component	**ECTS**
Introduction	0,5
Lectures, preparatory work	
Deepen the knowledge	0,5
Lectures and associated work	
no practical exercise	0
Optional quizzes	
10 - 15 multiple choice questions for self-study.	0
Total	1

LECTURES AND EXERCISES 1,5 ECTS	
Component	**ECTS**
Introduction	0,5
Lectures, preparatory work	
Deepen the knowledge	0,5
Lectures and associated work	
Practical exercise	
2-3 hour exercise and related preparatory and reporting work	0,5
Optional quizzes	
10 - 15 multiple choice questions for self-study.	0
Total	1,5

LECTURES AND EXERCISES 2 ECTS	
Component	**ECTS**
Introduction	0,5
Lectures, preparatory work	
Deepen the knowledge	0,5
Lectures and associated work	
Workshop sessions and assignment	
A half-day workshop, preparatory work and exercise such as an essay	1
Optional quizzes	
10 - 15 multiple choice questions for self-study.	0
Total	2

PROJECT PACKAGE 2 ECTS	
Component	**ECTS**
Introduction	0,5
Introduction to project, preparatory work	
Practical project	1,5
40 hour practical project	
Total	2

SUITABLE DELIVERY PLATFORMS

Recent years have seen a rapid change in the learning environment and the possibilities offered to learners by new education concepts enabled through technological advance. A prominent example for such an environment are MOOCs (Massive Open Online Courses) that provide on-line courses available to anyone who is interested in a topic, often free of charge. MOOC providers usually offer, besides the course material, interactive community support through on-line communication channels. MOOCs are enabled by technological advances that allow a completely virtual learning environment. In contrast, most higher education institutions still predominantly rely on traditional classroom education. This is a proven concept that still has many advantages over pure on-line courses, for example the development of social skills like team building, communication or interpersonal skills; and the possibility of a teacher to adjust to the individual needs of a learner (European Cyber Security Organisation (ECSO), 2018). Our implementation of a cybersecurity curriculum does not try to replace traditional classroom education, since the project partners are convinced that in the current form classroom education as it is realized nowadays in the majority of higher education institutions has advantages for a positive learning outcome in students that cannot be substituted by pure on-line education. Our intention is to supplement traditional education approaches in a meaningful way, in order to simplify processes that are complex or time consuming in traditional learning environments. Such processes may relate to course management and administration, which is traditionally a manual and labor-intensive task, but can be largely automated when integrated in the on-line learning environment. Furthermore, interactive learning environments help to improve the communication to other students, teachers and teaching assistants without the need to schedule specific and time-consuming appointments. A third advantage that is specifically interesting to our approach of a collaborative cybersecurity curriculum is the ability to develop and manage content and courses in a distributed and collaborative fashion. Collaborative authoring as well as the ability to share always up to date content are seen as a precondition for a European cybersecurity program that is developed by several independent higher education institutions.

At the core of each learning environment setup is the content that enables students to learn. In traditional classroom education, this content is usually a static set of slides presented to the learners by the teacher. Virtual environments allow for a different way of interaction by the students with the content, therefore providing opportunities to engage students in a dynamic way by embedding interactive elements, like for example quizzes, directly into the content. For a teacher, new possibilities for tracking the learning progress of students (completion, time, scores) is available. In order for this to work, the Advanced Distributed Learning Initiative (ADL) (The Advanced Distributed Learning Initiative, 2018) has proposed a standard that allows content to interact with learning management systems. The Shareable Content Object Reference Model (SCORM) or, in a recent evolution to overcome limitations of SCORM, the ExperienceAPI was developed. Those standards form the basis for most current virtual learning environment set-ups in their interaction with content, since they allow rich and dynamic content to be presented and integrated in the learning environment. Learning tool interoperability (LTI) by the IMS global learning consortium (IMS Global Learning Consortium, 2018) is another important standard in this context that allows content from an LTI provider (e.g. an authoring tool) to be integrated directly with one or more LTI consumers (e.g. a learning management system), including all the interactive features SCORM provides. One of the core advantages of LTI is that if the content is modified at provider side, the changes are immediately reflected at consumer side.

The project has identified that a basic virtual learning environment to support traditional classroom education, as well as the collaborative development and lecturing of content/courses in a European context, requires following basic tool set: An authoring tool that allows to create interactive and dynamic content according to, for example, the SCORM standard; a learning management system (LMS) that can host the content and provides a virtual environment for course management and administration, as well as a virtual classroom environment that can be used in addition to traditional classrooms. A virtual learning environment set-up should be as easy to use as possible. Ideally, all above described functionalities should be integrated in one single tool, however due to the different requirements posed such a tool may not exist. Alternatively, the set-up should aim for close integration of individual tools and ease of use for both students and teachers. A set-up that requires local install of software components should be avoided, and a web service based set-up should be favored. Access and rights management should be kept as simple as possible, one account that allows access to all services in the tool set should be aspired. In many cases tools are, even if developed by different organizations, tightly integrated with the central LMS system and may be configured to rely on the authentication credentials of the LMS. Our analysis has shown that there are many commercial as well as free and open source tools available that provide the functionalities of such a virtual learning environment. Our analysis has focused on setting up a completely free and open source learning environment and our experiences have shown that this goal can be achieved, and that large and active communities are driving the development of the chosen tool set.

The central role of a virtual learning environment is the LMS system. The concrete feature set varies between the implementations of different providers, but the basic feature of an LMS is to present activities (e.g. content) relating to a course and allow access to those activities according to the roles of the participants (e.g. teachers and students). LMS systems usually allow to facilitate communication among the course participants via mechanisms such as course specific forums, group chats or personal messages. A calendar functionality will allow to plan course activities and remind of upcoming deadlines. Regarding course administration, LMS systems usually allow to track the progress of students within course activities and allow teachers to derive grades based on those measures. The project has found Moodle (The Moodle project, 2018) to be the favored choice to fulfil our requirements for a collaborative cybersecurity curriculum. The deciding factor has been that Moodle has a long and active development history, the wide-spread use in learning institutions, and a very dynamic community that drives and supports the project.

Authoring tools are used to create learning content. The most widespread form of authoring tools is software able to create presentation slides. More recent authoring tools include the ability to create dynamic content, for example according to the SCORM/ExperienceAPI standards. Such authoring tools usually create content in HTML format, in order to integrate better with web based LMS tools, since no special software other than a web browser is required to display the content. While tools exist to convert traditional presentation slides to SCORM and HTML format, the project has identified Xerte online toolkits (XOT) (Xerte Online Toolkits, 2018) as a suitable authoring tool for our collaborative cybersecurity curriculum. Xerte is deployed as an on-line service, and allows integration and authentication using Moodle user accounts. Xerte allows to collaborate on content creation and allows to create content in SCORM compatible HTML5. Furthermore, configuration as an LTI provider is possible to allow direct integration with LMS systems.

The third class of virtual learning environment tool the project considers essential is a virtual classroom environment. While this functionality is not absolute necessary in an approach that tries to supplement and not replace traditional classroom education, a virtual classroom environment can be a convenient alternative to overcome for example scheduling issues or room shortage. A virtual classroom environment is a conferencing solution that allows similar activities than in a traditional classroom. A teacher is able to check student attendance, is able to present according to a slide set, and is able to visualize content via a blackboard/whiteboard. Teachers and students can communicate via various methods like audio, video or real-time chat. Most conferencing systems specifically developed for distance learning have other classroom specific features like for example the ability to group students in separate virtual rooms for group work. The project has identified BigBlueButton (BigBlueButton, 2018), a free and open source virtual classroom solution, to fulfil the requirements for a collaborative cybersecurity curriculum. BigBlueButton was chosen because of its large and active development community, as well as its ability to embed with LMS systems and authenticate participants according to their LMS credentials.

This Section provided an overview of the current state-of-the-art for virtual learning environments and have given examples of a set-up suited to the needs of a cybersecurity curriculum that is collaborative developed by several European higher education institutions, supporting traditional classroom education. This constitutes a basic set-up that does not take into account tool support for field specific activities (e.g. a code repository for programming exercises) but covers all the basic use cases of authoring and delivering content to students, managing courses and tracking results. The project partners have had positive experiences regarding the ease of use of those tools as well as the mostly seamless integration of tools developed by different communities. Especially initiatives like LTI support the concept of collaborative content development, since it allows seamless integration of content in LMS system of choice of the participating education institutions.

THE CONTENT AND MODULE STRUCTURE IN PRACTICE

To demonstrate how the SecTech content and module structure works in practice, an example of a SecTech module on Critical Infrastructure Security and Resilience is illustrated in this Section.

Various definitions exist for critical infrastructures and different methods for identifying critical infrastructures are being used by nations, reflecting different views on what constitutes a critical infrastructure. According to the Council Directive 2008/114/EC of 8 December 2008 on the identification and designation of European critical infrastructures and the assessment of the need to improve their protection, "Critical infrastructure means an asset, system or part thereof located in member states which is essential for the maintenance of vital societal functions, health, safety, security, economic or social well-being of people, and the disruption or destruction of which would have a significant impact in a member state as a result of the failure to maintain those functions" (THE EUROPEAN PARLIAMENT AND THE COUNCIL OF THE EUROPEAN UNION, 2008). Electric Power, electronic communications, water supply and sewage, transport, oil and gas, and banking are examples of industry sectors characterized as being critical infrastructures.

The subject of critical infrastructure security and resilience is interdisciplinary by nature and entails strategic, political, legal and technical aspects. Accordingly, this module aims to provide a holistic understanding of various approaches to critical infrastructure security and resilience, applicable to different sectors. It provides an introduction to the theoretical foundations; and of the techniques and methods used in critical infrastructure cybersecurity and resilience. It describes the concepts relevant to critical infrastructures and their cybersecurity; the elements of risk; models of critical infrastructures and ways of modelling interdependencies among them. It then focuses on particular aspects of critical infrastructures, namely cyber-physical systems; and industrial control systems and discusses issues, challenges, methods and techniques for their cybersecurity. The application of the methods and techniques discussed in the module to a number of critical infrastructures is demonstrated by means of case studies. The module is designed to promote subject-matter understanding, critical analysis of issues, and insight into the theory and application of cybersecurity methods and techniques.

The introductory part of the module (0.5 ECTS) consists of 1 - 1.5 h lecture units which give students an overview of the subject area. In general, no previous knowledge is required. Specifically, topics covered in this part are definitions of critical infrastructures and discussion of similarities and differences among them; examples of cybersecurity incidents that have involved and affected critical infrastructures, including some technical detail on how the relevant attacks were launched; statistics on the distribution of incidents per industry sector and per attack vector; the impact of cyber incidents; and the top vulnerabilities that have made these incidents possible. This discussion leads to making the point that the cybersecurity of critical infrastructures is primarily a human rather than a technology issue and should therefore be viewed in a structured and holistic manner that considers people, processes and technology. Such an approach is best implemented by means of national cybersecurity strategies and follows all phases of the NIST Framework for Improving Critical Infrastructure Cybersecurity (National Institute of Standards and Technology, 2018). This component also contains administrative information on the module.

A number of 2 - 3 h lecture units, each of 0.5 ECTS, which go deeper into the content of the introduction, each addressing one of the following topics or combinations thereof have been designed:

1. Threat actors and agents in critical infrastructures
2. Infrastructure modelling, robustness and dependencies
3. Cyber-physical systems and their security
4. Open research challenges in critical infrastructure security and resilience
5. Legislative impact of GDPR and NIS on critical infrastructure security

The unit on threat actors and agents in critical infrastructures discusses and analyses

- Assets, vulnerabilities, advanced persistent threats and threat agents in critical infrastructures
- Threat analysis, vulnerability assessment, likelihood estimation, impact assessment in critical infrastructures
- Risk aggregation and analysis in critical infrastructures
- Strategies and approaches for risk management in critical infrastructures.

The unit on infrastructure modelling, robustness and dependencies

- Introduces concepts of dependencies, interdependencies, and robustness in networks
- Discusses modelling approaches for critical (information) infrastructures at different levels of granularity and predictive power
- Presents model-based understanding of faults, robustness, and vulnerability to cascading faults in (infrastructure) networks
- Provides understanding into the network structure and dynamics in the design and construction of attacks

The unit on cyber-physical systems and their security

- Introduces cyber-physical systems and their distinctive characteristics
- Discusses attacks on cyber-physical systems and hybrid attacks
- Discusses and analyze security and privacy issues in the Internet of Things
- Discusses and analyses security and privacy issues in embedded systems
- Introduces and analyses moving target defense mechanisms for cyber-physical systems
- Reviews Intrusion Detection, Prevention, and Response Systems for cyber-physical systems

The unit on open research challenges in critical infrastructure security and resilience

- Reviews existing research agendas as they relate to critical infrastructure security and resilience
- Leverages the NIST cybersecurity framework (National Institute of Standards and Technology, 2018) to organize research challenges
- Extensively discusses and analyses open research challenges in these areas

The unit on legislative impact of GDPR and NIS on critical infrastructure security

- Reviews the General Data Protection Regulation and the Network and Information Security Directive
- Highlights provisions of the GDPR relevant to critical infrastructure security
- Leverages the Lloyd's emerging risks report 2017 (Lloyd's of London and Cyence, 2017) to identify and discuss the impact of the GDPR on areas where trouble can arise

A set of multiple-choice questions completes each 1.0 ECTS module. An example set of such questions for advanced persistent threats has been developed. Four possible answers are provided to the student, and more than one answers are sometimes correct. The system provides feedback to each student response stating whether the answer was correct or not. In the latter case, additional feedback including sources to consult is given.

For the 1.5 ECTS module, the learning content is further deepened through practical exercises. For this purpose, the students will receive clearly defined tasks. The working time of the students should be about 2 to 3 hours. It should be noted that the lecturer must find time for preparation, execution and wrap-up. The practical exercise requires the students to get prepared through reading list provided by the course lecturer. An example of such a practical exercise is the study of the 2015-2016 attacks against the Ukrainian power grid. The students will be expected to go through the provided reading list and analyze the incidents by mapping them to the ICS cyber kill chain (Assante & Lee, 2015). Another example is the US CERT Alert (TA18-074A) on "Russian Government Cyber Activity Targeting Energy and Other Critical Infrastructure Sectors" (US-CERT - United States Computer Emergency Readiness Team, 2018), which the students are invited to study and then answer questions on how the GDPR and the NIS would apply for taking preparatory measures to prevent the incidents and for notifying affected parties.

In the case of the 2.0 ECTS module, the above practical exercise is substituted by a half-day workshop conducted with the students. Ideally, this workshop is based on previously learned knowledge. The workshop session itself requires the students to get prepared through reading list provided by the course lecturer. After the course students will have to carry out an assignment on the selected topic, usually in the form of an essay. In our example, this can be implemented by means of a number of case studies on the applicability of the GDPR in various scenarios, such as the following:

- Personal data from EU used locally
- Personal data from EU used outside of the EU
- Personal data saved in a cloud based in the EU
- Personal data saved in a cloud based in the USA
- Personal data saved in a cloud based outside the OECD

CONCLUSION

Cybersecurity is becoming an increasingly important topic in the digital world. Through different types of attacks, cyber criminals are threatening our society and economy, for example by influencing the democratic process or by causing substantial economic losses. Such attacks can be driven by a variety of motivations, including financial, political or social aspects. The prevention and mitigation of cyber attacks and their effects have become an urgent and worldwide topic. From the history of the Internet and its associated technologies, it can be observed that security is often not an issue that is given the highest priority on a social level by the general population, or even at an organizational level in both the day to day operation of established or emerging businesses, and when bringing new technologies to the market. This makes it ultimately difficult to address security issues at a later stage. The SecTech project has observed that the education of cybersecurity professionals cannot keep up with the rapid change in the cybersecurity landscape and the education system is also not able to educate enough skilled graduates to cater to the current demand. In the European Union, the challenge also comes from the large number of member states and their imbalanced educational developments. While some higher education institutions are able to provide a high-quality five-year degree programs in cybersecurity, most higher education institutions do not have the resources or educational focus to provide dedicated cybersecurity degree programs - usually cybersecurity would be an add-on or specialization to existing degree programs in e.g. computer science or engineering, with a maximum of 2-year degree programs focused on cybersecurity. Driven by the digital single market strategy of the European Union, there is a great incentive to have a universal cybersecurity curriculum so that member states can have a common framework for cybersecurity education. With a common curriculum, it will become easier to cross-validate the academic degrees in different countries and facilitate the movement of talents in the job market. It also makes it easier for the employers to evaluate the job candidates regardless of where they have been educated in the EU.

In the Erasmus+ strategic partnership project SecTech, referring to the CSEC2017 cybersecurity curriculum guidelines, the project partners have collaboratively developed a distributed cybersecurity curriculum and associated seed lecture material that can be freely used by higher education institutions. It is our hope that the clear curriculum guideline and a focused content and module structure that was developed in SecTech helps to facilitate the development of a community of cybersecurity educators and professionals to provide, maintain and reuse content in the long-term, and to be able to fulfil all content requirements for a full cybersecurity program as laid out by CSEC2017 - even when looking through different institutional and disciplinary lenses. The tool support selected by SecTech, based on free and open source solutions, facilitates and supports collaborative content development and maintenance, and helps to deliver the content in a way that supports traditional classroom education, the most widely used form of teaching at higher education institutions. The SecTech content is designed to be freely available to project partners and collaborators. The possibilities of collaboration can range from simply using the provided lecture material, to utilizing recorded lectures or invited talks either locally or via virtual classrooms. This may be particularly useful if a participating higher education institution lacks the teaching expertise in specific areas. For example, in Luxembourg, there is no expertise in software security and digital forensics, while strong expertise in those areas is available in Finland and Germany respectively. Furthermore, the joint effort will allow to develop content in new and emerging security topics more quickly and achieve a wide-spread availability of high-quality content in such areas at the same time.

While the project has been able to gain a good understanding of what is required to achieve a comprehensive cybersecurity education program for higher education, and how to best develop and deliver it in a collaborative way, there are some points that have not been addressed during the project that are important to ensure long-term sustainability. In the long-term it needs to be ensured that such a program can achieve freedom in terms of institutional governance and financing, and that it can build a community that is large enough to develop and maintain content in all the topics covered by the curriculum. Furthermore, a shift from European centric development to a global community needs to be achieved. The free and open-source software movement is an excellence example of how a free and open cybersecurity education program could be organized: Larger open source projects usually are divided in a foundation that is focused on the strategic planning as well as the fund raising for the project, while the project itself will lead the community-based development and maintenance efforts according to an appropriate management structure. A similar structure could be adopted for the SecTech curriculum development, for example by assigning dedicated maintainers to each of the identified knowledge areas or even knowledge units. A second aspect that was not covered by the SecTech project is multi-language support for lecture material. Many lecturers at higher education institutions, especially in the field of technology where many terms are only available in English language, already use a hybrid approach to teaching where the lecture material is English, and the presentations will be in the native language. However, depending on the cultural context or institutional policies, lecture material in native language may be required. In the long-term it is expected that SecTech will include multi-lingual support for lecture material. Furthermore, the SecTech project has only looked at the requirements for higher education. It is expected however that the knowledge that is to be disseminated to learners in different contexts like school education or professional education is the same or very similar to the knowledge relevant to higher education, but the requirements to content and module structure as well as the delivery strategy may be significantly different. In future, SecTech would like to look into ways to utilize the existing knowledge base to also address learners outside of higher education, for example by expanding on the concepts of institutional and disciplinary lenses to a much broader context.

Through the experiences gained in the SecTech project the partners are confident that a collaboratively developed cybersecurity program is a huge step forward in overcoming the current limitations in cybersecurity education. It was observed that due to advances in technological support there are nowadays few limitations regarding content creation and delivery in a collaborative set-up, and to increase reusability of content. However, more steps need to be taken to allow such a program to become self-sustainable, and to be able to produce and maintain high quality content in the long-term and on a global scale, which the project partners hope to achieve through the establishment of a community-based governance and management structure.

ACKNOWLEDGMENT

The SecTech project is funded by the European Union's Erasmus+ program as a strategic partnership in higher education with the grant number 2016-1-LU01-KA203-013834.

REFERENCES

ACM, IEEE, AIS, IFIP. (2017). Curriculum Guidelines for Post-Secondary Degree Programs in Cybersecurity. ACM.

Assante, M. J., & Lee, R. M. (2015). *The Industrial Control System Cyber Kill Chain*. Retrieved from SANS Institute InfoSec Reading Room: https://www.sans.org/reading-room/whitepapers/ICS/industrial-control-system-cyber-kill-chain-36297

Association for Computing Machinery (ACM) and IEEE Computer Society. (2013). *Computer Science Curricula 2013: Curriculum Guidelines for Undergraduate Degree Programs in Computer Science*. New York: ACM.

Association for Computing Machinery (ACM) and IEEE Computer Society. (2017). *Information Technology Curricula 2017: Curriculum Guidelines for Baccalaureate Degree Programs in Information Technology*. New York: ACM.

BigBlueButton. (2018, June). Retrieved from https://bigbluebutton.org/

European Commission and High Representative of the European Union for Foreign Affairs and Security Policy. (2013). *Cybersecurity Strategy of the European Union: An Open, Safe and Secure Cyberspace*. JOIN(2013) 1 final.

European Cyber Security Organisation (ECSO). (2018). *Position Paper: Gaps in European Cyber Education and Professional Training*. ECSO.

European Union Agency for Law Enforcement Cooperation (Europol). (2017). *Internet organised crime threat assessment (IOCTA) 2017*. Retrieved from https://www.europol.europa.eu/activities-services/main-reports

Guide to the Systems Engineering Body of Knowledge (SEBok) v.1.9. (2018, June). Retrieved from http://sebokwiki.org/wiki/Guide_to_the_Systems_Engineering_Body_of_Knowledge_(SEBOK)

IMS Global Learning Consortium. (2018, June). Retrieved from http://www.imsglobal.org/

Lloyd's of London and Cyence. (2017). *Emerging Risks Report 2017: Counting the cost - Cyber exposure decoded.* Retrieved from https://www.lloyds.com/~/media/files/news-and-insight/risk-insight/2017/cyence/emerging-risk-report-2017---counting-the-cost.pdf

National Institute of Standards and Technology. (2018, April). *Framework for Improving Critical Infrastructure Cybersecurity - Version 1.1.* Retrieved from https://www.nist.gov/publications/framework-improving-critical-infrastructure-cybersecurity-version-11

Santos, D. (2016). *National Initiative for Cybersecurity Education.* NICE.

The Advanced Distributed Learning Initiative. (2018, June). Retrieved from http://www.adlnet.gov/

The Council of the European Union. (2016). Regulation (EU) 2016/679 of the European Parliament And of the Council of 27 April 2016 on the protection of natural persons with regard to the processing of personal data and on the free movement of such data, and repealing Directive 95/46/EC. *Official Journal of the European Union, L, 119*(1).

The European Parliament and the Council of the European Union. (2008). Council Directive 2008/114/EC of 8 December 2008 on the identification and designation of European critical infrastructures and the assessment of the need to improve their protection. *Official Journal of the European Union, L, 345*(75).

The European Parliament and the Council of the European Union. (2016). Directive (EU) 2016/1148 of the European Parliament and of the Council of 6 July 2016 concerning measures for a high common level of security of network and information systems across the Union. *Official Journal of the European Union, L, 194*(1).

The Moodle project. (2018, June). Retrieved from https://moodle.org/

US-CERT - United States Computer Emergency Readiness Team. (2018). *Alert (TA18-074A) - Russian Government Cyber Activity Targeting Energy and Other Critical Infrastructure Sectors.* Retrieved from https://www.us-cert.gov/ncas/alerts/TA18-074A

Xerte Online Toolkits. (2018, June). Retrieved from https://www.xerte.org.uk

Section 4
Addressing the Profession

Chapter 11
A Cybersecurity Skills Framework

Peter James Fischer
Institute of Information Security Professionals, UK

ABSTRACT

This chapter traces the evolution of cybersecurity skills requirements and development over the past 40 years, from the early days of computer security (Compusec) to the present day. The development of cybersecurity skills is traced from an initial focus upon national security and confidentiality through to the current recognition as business driver. The main part of the chapter concentrates on the development of a specific skills framework from the Institute of Information Security Professionals. Originally conceived in 2006 and initially used for purposes of membership accreditation, the IISP Skills Framework has since been used extensively by commerce, industry, government and academia in the UK and more widely. Version 2 of the framework was published in 2016, and the chapter discussion outlines both the original structure and the notable changes in the later release. These developments collectively illustrate the ongoing recognition of cybersecurity skills, as well as the evolution of the skills themselves.

INTRODUCTION

The content of this chapter is based on the evolving requirement for identifiable, specific and measurable skills in cybersecurity disciplines to enable organizations to identify the range and blend of skill sets they require to secure their business and to gain assurance that the individuals employed to deliver the required cybersecurity services are competent to the required level. As a corollary to this, individual cybersecurity professionals need to be able to measure themselves against an appropriate subset of cybersecurity skills in order to deliver effective cybersecurity services to their employer or customer.

The Institute of Information Security Professionals (IISP) Skills Framework was developed to identify the range of cybersecurity skills needed in the modern business world and provide some criteria against which practitioners could measure the level of their skill. It is used as the main focus for describing cybersecurity skills and knowledge. However, it should be recognized that other frameworks

DOI: 10.4018/978-1-5225-7847-5.ch011

Copyright © 2019, IGI Global. Copying or distributing in print or electronic forms without written permission of IGI Global is prohibited.

have been developed and are in common use, most notably those developed by ISC² and ISACA. In terms of knowledge, the Cyber Security Body of Knowledge (CyBOK) Project sponsored by the UK National Cyber Security Centre (NCSC) will enhance further the knowledge standards and criteria for cybersecurity professionals.

However, it was felt that it would be useful to provide some historical perspective on the development of, and the need for, cybersecurity skills over the past 40 years or so. In doing so, the modern term 'cybersecurity' has been used throughout, although different terms were used at the time, including Computer Security (Compusec), Data Security, Information Security (Infosec) and Information Assurance (IA). There is a strong UK focus in the text, but reference is made to seminal work in the USA and also within Europe which has influenced and contributed to the UK positions.

BACKGROUND

In this section, we cover cybersecurity perspectives from the 1970s to the early 2000s, showing the changes in skill requirements.

The Early Days: Confidentiality Is King

Research by David Bell and Leonard LaPadula in the 1970s, building on work by Ware (1967), resulted in the Bell–LaPadula Security Model (Bell and LaPadula, 1973; Bell and LaPadula, 1976). This was used as a basis for the US Trusted Computer Security Evaluation Criteria (TCSEC), commonly referred to as 'The Orange Book'. TCSEC was issued by the US National Computer Security Center (NCSC) in 1983 and published as a Department of Defense Standard in 1985. Its focus was unashamedly the protection of confidentiality, based on national security classifications and labels and, as such, became the benchmark for government security in both the UK and US during the late 1980s.

TCSEC utilized four categories of security functionality and assurance (DoD 1985):

D: Minimal protection, reserved for products which had failed evaluation at a higher level
C: Discretionary Protection (C1 and C2)
B: Mandatory Protection (B1, B2 and B3)
A: Verified Protection (A1)

The rigor of the development and evaluation processes were linked to the functionality levels, i.e. C1 systems possessed relatively limited security functionality and assurance, whereas A1 systems possessed finely-defined security functionality combined with rigorous standards for development and evaluation, including formal methods.

A range of supporting standards and guides were published by the US National Computer Security Center (NCSC) during the period 1988-1995. These were published with covers in different colors and were known as the 'Rainbow Series'. Arguably, the most notable of these were the Trusted Network Interpretation (TNI) and the Trusted Database Interpretation (TDI) published with red and purple covers respectively, although the color purple was also used for guides on the procurement of trusted systems.

Under the regime of TCSEC and the Rainbow Series, the need for cybersecurity skills, as defined in the IISP Skills Framework, was restricted more or less to Security Architecture, Secure Development and Security Evaluation plus, on the user side, Security Policy and Standards. There was little scope for either risk assessment or risk management and government security authorities tended to mandate compliance, with little regard for business requirements.

Around the same time there were integrity models such as Biba (1975), Clark-Wilson (1987) and Brewer-Nash (1989), but these tended to be the inverse of the Bell-LaPadula model and had little influence on development and implementation, given the confidentiality focus of government organizations. Consequently, they had little influence on the need for cybersecurity skills.

By the late 1980s, security practitioners, in Europe at least, were finding TCSEC constraining. Efforts to extend the criteria to cover networking and related areas were not entirely satisfactory, and the close linkage between functionality and assurance did not meet many business models, for example the need for C2 functionality and B1 assurance or vice-versa. Also, TCSEC evaluations were funded by the US Government and therefore not available to non-US developers. As a result, the European Commission, recognizing that national evaluation criteria had been developed and were being used in the UK, and evaluation criteria were being developed by France, Germany and the Netherlands, brought the contributors together to develop a single, European set of security evaluation criteria, the Information Technology Security Evaluation Criteria (ITSEC), published in 1990.

The success of ITSEC caused a degree of consternation in the US as it meant that they had lost their pre-eminent position in cybersecurity as recognized at that time. After a brief flirtation with a draft Federal Criteria, the US authorities met with the European Commission and an agreement was made to join forces on developing a Common Criteria. Canada had also developed its own Canadian Trusted Computer Product Evaluation Criteria (CTCPEC), but also joined the Common Criteria initiative. Common Criteria was underpinned by the Common Criteria Recognition Arrangement (CCRA) under which nations recognized evaluations certified by other nations. Common Criteria was incorporated as an ISO standard (ISO15408) in 1999.

However, the focus remained on confidentiality and the flawed view that cybersecurity could be delivered primarily through the use of evaluated products and systems. Moreover, the credibility of the scheme was undermined by the insistence that products and systems should be re-evaluated following every change, i.e. patches should not be applied to products until they had been re-evaluated – a time-consuming and costly process which did not recognize the timescales of technical refresh.

In terms of cybersecurity skills, the focus during this period focused strongly on Security Architecture, Secure Software Development, Security Evaluation, Policy and Standards. Threat and risk assessment and analysis, which has formed the foundation for cybersecurity in the UK over the past 20 years, was the preserve of the few in the 1980s and early 1990s. Given the strong government focus, threat intelligence and assessment were the preserve of the Intelligence Agencies, and risk assessment was often simplistically based on the security classification of the data and the security clearances of the users. Computer security audit was in its infancy and not highly valued. Penetration testing as a specialism was non-existent, although the evaluators in the two UK Evaluation Facilities (EFs) at Logica and Admiral conducted some effective penetration testing work in the late 1980s, outside the constraints of TCSEC. Integrity and Availability were viewed by senior management as IT project and management issues, not cybersecurity.

It should be recognized that some excellent research into the wider aspects of cybersecurity was being undertaken in academia, especially in the USA, throughout this period, but this was not cascading into the organizational profile of cybersecurity.

Intervention by Business and Commerce

In the mid-1990s business and commerce began to recognize the importance of cybersecurity in terms of the protection of their business interests. This was driven to a large extent by the development of the Internet as a global communications mechanism and exacerbated by the fact that it was designed with no reference to security. The continuous growth of the Internet as a global communications mechanism has continued to fuel the evolution of threats.

This intervention from business brought a much broader perspective to the subject of cybersecurity. No longer was it tightly focused on the confidentiality of classified government information, but included a host of supporting controls and functions, including governance, policies, compliance with legal and regulatory requirements, risk assessment and management, and ongoing security management. This broader approach was re-enforced by high profile corporate financial governance issues such as those uncovered by the Enron scandal in 2001, which led to the bankruptcy of the Enron Corporation, the effective dissolution of Arthur Andersen as an audit and accountancy partnership and the Sarbanes-Oxley Act of 2002, commonly referred to as SOX. As a consequence, the cybersecurity skills requirements profile became much richer and broader.

The Institute of Information Security Professionals (IISP)

It was against this background that a few luminaries in the field of cybersecurity recognized that the subject was becoming too important to continue as a marginal interest group under the umbrella of other professional bodies but needed to become a profession in its own right. Hence, in 2006 the Institute of Information Security Professionals (IISP) was born.

From the outset it was decided that professional membership of the Institute must be based on a combination of knowledge and practical, real-world experience. Whilst other professional bodies were prepared to accept candidates for Associate Membership based solely on academic qualifications, the IISP believed that practical experience in applying the knowledge and understanding was critical to the recognition of professional status. The problem with this approach was how individuals applying for professional membership of the Institute could express their skills and capabilities, and how the Institute could assess and validate those claims. Thus, the need for a Skills Framework was identified.

AN OVERVIEW OF THE IISP SKILLS FRAMEWORK

The IISP Skills Framework[1] was originally developed by a group led by Bob Coles of Royal Bank of Scotland and Chris Ensor of CESG[2]. The main purpose of this was to define the cybersecurity skills extant at the time in order to support the assessment of each individual's knowledge, understanding and competence profile for assessment for professional membership on the Institute.

The Framework is structured as a series of Security Disciplines, representing broad areas of security provision in which skills may be needed, each of which is then broken down into a number of Skills Groups, representing more focused areas of particular activity in which individuals may then develop knowledge and experience. Recognizing that these may be needed and developed to differing degrees in different contexts, the framework also defines a number of Skill Levels at which each skill can exist.

Security Disciplines and Skills Groups

Skills Group definitions were deliberately kept at a high level in recognition of the fact that cybersecurity disciples and skills were evolving at a significant pace, and maintenance of a Skills Framework containing highly-specific definitions would be onerous to maintain and would become outdated quickly.

Version 1 of the Skills Framework defined 35 Skills across 11 Security Disciplines. Of these Security Disciplines, 9 (A-I) were categorized as "technical skills" and the remaining two (J-K) as "soft skills". In version 2, these were reduced to 33 Skills in 10 Security Disciplines, as summarized in Table 1 (noting that Discipline G, which was present in version 1 of the framework, is no longer used).

Skill Levels

There were four Skills Levels defined in version 1 of the IISP Skills Framework, these Awareness, Basic Application, Skillful Application and Expert. However, over several years of using these in practice, it was considered by many that four levels did not meet either the real-world scenarios of job roles or personal development within corporate organizations. Some had introduced Level 3- and Level 3+ to address is issue. There were also concerns regarding a single Skill Level (1) covering the wide waterfront of awareness, knowledge and understanding.

To address these concerns, six Skill Levels were introduced in version 2.0. Initially, all six level descriptors were mapped against the National Occupational Standards (NOS) for Cyber Security, developed by e-Skills UK. However, practical use of version 2.0, especially in developing the IISP Knowledge Framework, indicated that the NOS descriptions at Levels 1 and 2 did not reflect the usage of these levels. Consequently, these descriptors were revised to reflect Bloom's taxonomy in versions 2.1 onward, and the specifics of each level are presented in Table 2.

Use of these levels in practice both within the IISP (for assessment for membership) and a range of corporates (for job definitions, personal development, etc.) indicates that these levels better reflect the real world of cybersecurity professionalism.

To aid understanding of how the levels come together for specific Security Disciplines and Skills Groups, Table 3 illustrates the application in the context of the Threat Intelligence, Assessment and Threat Modelling skill group within the discipline of Threat Assessment and Information Risk Management.

EVOLUTION OF SECURITY DISCIPLINES AND SKILLS

Although originally developed for use in assessing applications for membership of the Institute, the Skills Framework was used by commerce and industry, in the form of IISP Corporate Members, for internal staff management and development purposes. It was used to:

- Define the skills requirements for specific roles and job families;
- Performance assessment;
- Staff personal development; and
- Corporate cybersecurity training and education strategies.

Table 1. Breakdown of security disciplines showing subordinate skill groups

Security Discipline	Skills Groups
A - Information Security Governance and Management Capable of determining, establishing and maintaining appropriate governance of (including processes, roles, awareness strategies, legal environment and responsibilities), delivery of (including polices, standards and guidelines), and cost-effective solutions (including impact of third parties) for information security within a given organization).	A1 – Governance A2 – Policy and Standards A3 – Information Security Strategy A4 – Innovation and Business Improvement A5 – Behavioural Change A6 – Legal & Regulatory Environment and Compliance A7 – Third Party Management
B - Threat Assessment and Information Risk Management Capable of articulating the different forms of threat to, and vulnerabilities of, information systems and assets. Comprehending and managing the risks relating to information systems and assets.	B1 – Threat Intelligence, Assessment and Threat Modelling B2 – Risk Assessment B3 – Information Risk Management
C - Implementing Secure Systems Comprehends the common technical security controls available to prevent, detect and recover from security incidents and to mitigate risk. Capable of articulating security architectures relating to business needs and commercial product development that can be realized using available tools, products, standards and protocols, delivering systems assured to have met their security profile using accepted methods	C1 – Enterprise Security Architecture C2 – Technical Security Architecture C3 – Secure Development
D - Assurance: Audit, Compliance and Testing Develops and applies standards and strategies for verifying that measures taken mitigate identified risks. Capable of defining and implementing the processes and techniques used in verifying compliance against security policies, standards, legal and regulatory requirements.	D1 – Internal and Statutory Audit D2 – Compliance Monitoring and Controls Testing D3 – Security Evaluation and Functionality Testing D4 – Penetration Testing
E - Operational Security Management Capable of managing all aspects of a security program, including reacting to new threats and vulnerabilities, secure operational and service delivery consistent with security polices, standards and procedures, and handling security incidents of all types according to common principles and practices, consistent with legal constraints and obligations.	E1 – Secure Operations Management E2 – Secure Operations and Service Delivery
F - Incident Management, Investigation and Digital Forensics Capable of managing or investigating an information security incident at all levels, including the use of digital forensic techniques.	F1 – Intrusion Detection and Analysis F2 – Incident Management, Incident Investigation and Response F3 – Forensics
H - Business Resilience Capable of defining the need for, and of implementing processes for establishing business continuity.	H1 – Business Continuity and Disaster Recovery Planning H2 – Business Continuity and Disaster Recovery Management H3 – Cyber Resilience
I - Information Security Research Original investigation in order to gain knowledge and understanding relating to information security, including the invention and generation of ideas, performances and artefacts where these lead to new or substantially improved insights; and the use of existing knowledge in experimental development to produce new or substantially improved devices, products and processes.	I1 – Research I2 – Applied Research
J - Management, Leadership, Business and Communications Recognizes the importance of wider communication and interpersonal skills in order to enable the effective communication and integration of cybersecurity within an organizational context.	J1 – Management, Leadership and Influence J2 – Business Skills J3 – Communication and Knowledge Sharing
K - Contributions to the Information Security Profession and Professional Development Recognizes the need for ongoing development of cybersecurity practitioners, and their potential to contribute to the wider community and profession.	K1 – Contributions to the Community K2 – Contributions to the IS Profession K3 – Professional Development

Table 2. The skill level definitions in version 2.2 of the IISP skills framework

Level	Title	Description	
		Knowledge	**Practice**
1	Knowledge	Has acquired and can demonstrate basic knowledge associated with the skill, e.g. through training or self-tuition.	N/A
2	Knowledge and Understanding	Has acquired and can demonstrate the basic knowledge associated with the skill, for example has attended a training course or completed an academic module in the skill. Understands how the skill should be applied.	Can explain the principles of the skill and how it should be applied. This might include experience of applying the skill to basic tasks in a training or academic environment, for example through participation in syndicate exercises, undertaking practical exercises in using the skill, and/or passing a test or examination. Should be aware of recent developments in the skill.
3	Practitioner (Apply)	Has acquired a good understanding of the knowledge associated with the skill and understands how the skill should be applied.	Has experience of applying the skill to a variety of basic tasks. Can work as an effective member of a team. Contributes ideas in the application of the skill. Demonstrates awareness of recent developments in the skill. Has experience of training potential and actual IS practitioners in the basics of the skill. Demonstrates awareness of recent developments in the skill.
4	Senior Practitioner (Enable)	Has acquired a deep understanding of the knowledge associated with the skill. Understands how the skill should be applied.	Has experience of applying the skill to a variety of tasks, including some complex tasks under supervision. Contributes ideas in the application of the skill. Demonstrates awareness of recent developments in the skill. Contributes ideas for technical development and new areas for application of the skill. Has experience of training IS professionals in the skill above an introductory level. Demonstrates awareness of recent developments in the skill. Contributes ideas for technical development and new areas for application of the skill.
5	Principal Practitioner (Advise)	Has acquired a deep understanding of the knowledge associated with the skill. Understands how the skill should be applied across a number of projects in different client environments and/or within a large corporate organization.	Has experience of applying the skill to a variety of complex tasks. Demonstrates significant personal responsibility or autonomy, with little need for escalation. Contributes ideas in the application of the skill. Demonstrates awareness of recent developments in the skill. Contributes ideas for technical development and new areas for application of the skill and contributes to public discussion/debate on the skill. Has effective leadership and management skills. Has experience of training IS professionals in the skill at an advanced level or as a university lecturer. Demonstrates awareness of recent developments in the skill. Contributes ideas for technical development and new areas for application of the skill.
6	Expert/Lead Practitioner (Initiate, Enable, Ensure)	As for Level 5.	Has oversight responsibility for overall application of the skill across a range of customers or within a large corporate organization, often reporting at Board level. Recognized as a Subject Matter Expert within a large organization. Has experience of applying the skill in circumstances without precedence. Proposes, conducts, and/or leads innovative work to enhance the skill. Is approached to provide keynote presentations or papers on the skill. Develops and leads programs of advanced training in the skill. A Professor or Senior Lecturer contributing sessions on the skill at MSc level.

Table 3. An example of a skills group definition and the skills at different levels

Skills Group	Principles	Example Skills
B1 – Threat Intelligence, Assessment and Threat Modelling	Assesses and validates information on current and potential Cyber and Information Security threats to the business, analyzing trends and highlighting information security issues relevant to the organization, including Security Analytics for Big Data. Processes, collates and exploits data, taking into account its relevance and reliability to develop and maintain 'situational awareness'. Predicts and prioritizes threats to an organization and their methods of attack. Analyses the significance and implication of processed intelligence to identify significant trends, potential threat agents and their capabilities. Predicts and prioritizes threats to an organization and their methods of attack. Uses human factor analysis in the assessment of threats. Uses threat intelligence to develop attack trees. Prepares and disseminates intelligence reports providing threat indicators and warnings.	**Level 1:** Can describe the concepts and principles of threat intelligence, modelling and assessment. **Level 2:** Can explain the principles of threat intelligence, modelling and assessment. This might include experience of applying threat intelligence, modelling and assessment principles in a training or academic environment, for example through participation in syndicate exercises, undertaking practical exercises, and/or passing a test or examination. **Level 3:** Undertakes/assesses routine threat intelligence/modelling tasks or threat assessments under supervision. **Level 4:** Undertakes/assesses routine threat intelligence/modelling tasks or threat assessments without close supervision. Undertakes complex threat intelligence tasks or threat assessments under supervision. **Level 5:** Undertakes/assesses complex threat intelligence/ modelling tasks or threat assessments without supervision. Manages threat intelligence/assessment teams. **Level 6:** Leads corporate threat intelligence processes, reporting to the Board.

There were also various examples of wider adoption. For instance, the Framework was adopted by CESG, the UK National Technical Authority for Information Assurance, as the basis for the CESG Certified IA Professional (CCP) Scheme and also for developing the criteria for approved cybersecurity degree programs. Meanwhile, it was also used by e-Skills UK to produce the standards for cybersecurity apprenticeships. As can be deduced from this, the Skills Framework has proven to have had a valid role in the definition of cybersecurity skills requirements for job roles and families in the workplace, and in training and education.

However, whilst version 1 of the Skills Framework (with a few minor changes) remained the *de facto* standard for cybersecurity skills definition for 10 years, over this period specific issues were reported back to the IISP. While the high-level definitions enabled users to 'shoe-horn' evolving skills into the Framework, this was becoming increasingly difficult. Also, as previously mentioned, the constraints of the four Skill Levels were becoming increasingly problematic. As such, in 2015, the IISP Board commissioned a study to assess whether there was a requirement for a fundamental review of the Skills Framework, The conclusion from that study was that, whilst the Framework remained largely fit for purpose, it would benefit from a full review to assess and address the issues reported by users and issues identified by the Board, specifically the desire to attract more members from academia and the need to re-focus the membership application process better to reflect and serve the cybersecurity profession.

The review of the Skills Framework involved in-depth consultation with business (conducted with the IISP Corporate Members), internally within the IISP (e.g. with IISP Assessors and Interviewers), CREST (a not-for profit organization representing the technical information security industry), and with CESG as the (then) National Technical Authority for Information Assurance. Consideration was given to the Skills Framework for the Information Age (SFIA – see www.sfia-online.org) – a framework developed and maintained by the SFIA Foundation to match the skills of the workforce to the needs of the business - but it was felt that the two frameworks were complementary rather than identical in that SFIA focuses on levels of responsibility and authority, whereas the Skills Framework focuses on technical knowledge, understanding and experience. Many IISP Corporate Members use both, but in different contexts.

This section examines the notable changes that were made to the Skills Framework, in terms of the top-level Security Disciplines and (more particularly) the underlying Skills Groups in the years since the 2006. In doing so, it serves to illustrate the evolving recognition of cybersecurity skills and how they integrate together.

Security Discipline A: Information Security Governance

In 2006, as today, effective cybersecurity within an organization depended on commitment from the top, demonstrated by an effective governance and management regime, involving definition (and acceptance) of ownership, clear lines of delegated authority, and with cybersecurity policies, standards and practices supporting the business and ensuring compliance with legal and regulatory requirements. Consequently, Security Discipline A – Information Security Management came first.

The changes were subtle. First of all, the Security Discipline title was changed to *Information Security Governance and Management* to re-enforce the point that management supports and is driven by governance (the original wording was felt to imply that somehow governance was subordinate to management).

The title of Skill A5 was changed to *Behavioural Change* and the criteria amended to reflect the increased awareness within organizations that training courses and awareness campaigns were not enough in themselves but need to be supported by mechanisms to measure changes in security attitudes and culture. Several organizations have introduced mechanisms to assess the security culture within the organization, e.g. by running exercises to assess the response to false malicious emails and assessing the results.

The title of Skill A6 was changed to add *Compliance* to reflect the increasing requirement on organizations to monitor and maintain records of compliance with legal and regulatory instruments.

A number of observations can be made based upon the experience of using these Skills Groups in practice:

- **A1 - Governance:** In practice, the IISP has found that most cybersecurity professionals operate at project/program level with respect to governance, i.e. Skill Level 3-4. A few, mainly CISOs and Principal Consultants operating at Board level have the involvement at corporate level required for Skill Level 5-6.
- **A2 - Policy and Standards:** Early assessment against this Skill Group found that much of the evidence concentrated on Her Majesty's Government (HMG) standards published by the Cabinet Office, e.g. the Security Policy Framework and constituent documents such as the CESG Infosec Standards. However, as cybersecurity in the private sector became more mature, the focus switched to ISO/IEC 27001 and compliance checks against the controls specified in the Statement of Applicability. Experience in assessing applicants for membership of the IISP indicates that initial gap analyses against ISO/IEC 27001 uncover the absence of essential policies covering issues such as acceptable use, use of removable media and associated disciplinary policies.

- **A3 - Information Security Strategy:** The main foci of this Skill Group are: the balancing of cost against security risk for the business; and balancing technical and non-technical controls to achieve a cost-effective solution. Here again, there is a tension between cybersecurity professionals working in the public sector, where security rules tend to be more prescriptive, and in the private sector where there is usually more flexibility to take into account business drivers. However, this gap has lessened over time, especially outside the HMG 'High Threat Club', i.e. those Government Departments processing large volumes of highly-classified information marked SECRET and TOP SECRET.
- **A4 - Innovation and Business Improvement:** This Skill Group concentrates on 'security as an enabler', i.e. how security could improve the business. An example would be hardening a web service so that it can support online services rather than just brochure-ware. In practice, this Skill Group has tended to focus on resolving conflicts between the business and security in order that business benefits can be delivered securely. An example of this would be the resolution of a situation whereby the CIO wishes to authorize the use of BYOD without considering the cybersecurity risks involved and the options for addressing at least some of the security concerns. This Skill Group also addresses the use of cybersecurity products, the analysis of their efficacy and management overheads, and making recommendations based on cost/benefit analysis principles.
- **A5 – Behavioural Change:** This Skill Group originally focused on the identification of cybersecurity training needs within an organization, gaining management commitment to training and the development and delivery of training programs. Initially, practitioners in this Skill Group concentrated on the development and delivery of formal training to individuals with cybersecurity responsibilities, progressing to cover user training involving other methods such as CBT. In response to feedback from IISP Corporate members on common practice, the criteria were extended to cover behavioral analysis, security culture management programs, with the application of analysis of human factors.
- **A6 - Legal & Regulatory Environment and Compliance:** This is a very broad Skill Group addressing a wide range of legal and regulatory instruments. In recent years, the focus of expertise has been the Data Protection Act 1998, with the General Data Protection Regulation (GDPR) taking center stage more recently. Experience of assessing applicants for membership of the IISP has shown that many cybersecurity professionals need knowledge and understanding of legislation in other countries when working for multi-national organizations, and of specific regulatory requirements such as those applying to the nuclear and oil and gas industries, and in the financial sector.
- **A7 - Third Party Management:** The importance of this Skill Group has increased over the years, with more and more organizations outsourcing functions not deemed to be core business and working more closely with partners. In practice, within this Skill Group, cybersecurity professionals tend to work with corporate legal and contractual authorities to ensure that security risk management is adequately covered in contracts and partnership agreements, in conducting compliance checks against those requirements, and assisting the third-party organizations in resolving any issues identified.

Security Discipline B: Threat Assessment and Information Risk Management

Moving on from governance and management, the next Security Discipline is Information Risk Management, as this should underpin the whole ethos of cybersecurity within an organization. Cybersecurity policies, strategies and controls need to be firmly grounded on a foundation of risk management, taking into account the business drivers and constraints.

Risk assessment and management are often considered to be core disciplines in the cybersecurity profession. Not only are these core skills in their own right – e.g. the majority of cybersecurity consultants consider them to be their main business – but risk assessment and management knowledge and expertise are crucial components for a range of cybersecurity job families including security architects, penetration testers, system security managers, Security Operations Center (SOC) staff and incident managers.

Security Discipline B originally contained two Skill Groups: Risk Assessment and Risk Management. However, several IISP Corporate Members suggested that this did not adequately reflect the growing importance of Threat Intelligence in their risk management processes. Consequently, the Discipline was expanded to 3 Skill Groups: Threat Intelligence, Assessment and Threat Modelling; Risk Assessment; and Risk Management.

The associated observations from practical use in these cases are as follows:

- **B1 - Threat Intelligence, Assessment and Threat Modelling**: Reflects the increasing importance of Threat Intelligence and associated disciplines, especially within large corporate organizations. It covers activities such as:
    - Assessing and validating information from several sources on current and potential Cyber and Information Security threats to the business.
    - Analyzing trends and highlighting Information Security issues relevant to the
    - organization, including Security Analytics for Big Data.
    - Processing data, taking into account its relevance and reliability to develop and maintain 'situational awareness'.
    - Predicting and prioritizing threats to an organization and their methods of attack.
    - Analyzing intelligence to identify significant trends, potential threat agents and their capabilities.
    - Predicting and prioritizing threats to an organization and their methods of attack.
    - Using human factor analysis in the assessment of threats.
    - Using threat intelligence to develop attack trees.
    - Preparing and disseminating intelligence reports providing threat indicators and warnings.
    - Providing input to the development of scenarios for Red Team testing.
- **B2 - Risk Assessment:** Common practice within this Skill Group tended to concentrate on HMG Infosec Standard 1&2 (IS1&2) in the public sector, and ISO/IEC 27005, ISO/IEC 31000 and risk assessment methodologies such as the Information Security Forum IRAM2 in the private sector. Since IS1&2 was withdrawn as an HMG Standard, there has been much convergence of practice within the cybersecurity community towards bespoke risk assessment approaches based on ISO/IEC 27005 and modifications to one of the standard risk assessment methodologies, including IS1&2. The IISP continues to find that a few Government Departments, most notably the Ministry of Defence, continue to use IS1&2.
- **B3 - Risk Management:** Practice in this Skills Group typically includes the development of risk registers and risk treatment plans. Risk management needs to take into account the risk appetite of the organization, the organization's risk tolerance for a particular activity – which might be different from the risk appetite, and an understanding of how risk management could support the taking

of opportunities by the business. Examples of opportunities during the life of version 1 of the IISP Skills Framework included several examples of moving into online sales and services.

Security Discipline C: Implementing Secure Systems

The focus here is defining effective security architectures for systems and networks and developing secure products which can then be incorporated into systems and networks. The Discipline originally contained two Skill Groups: Security Architecture and Secure Development. This was based on the view in 2006, which was heavily influenced by the culture of previous years, i.e. secure systems and networks are built from secure products. In consultation with practicing security architects, the definitions were changed to moderate the focus on secure products and to separate Security Architecture into two Skills Groups – Enterprise Security Architecture and Technical Security Architecture. Although it was recognized that there was significant overlap between the two, it was felt that some architects tended to concentrate on enterprise level aspects and others on the technical detail closer to design and development.

- **C1 - Enterprise Secure Architecture:** Although there can be a significant skill overlap between Enterprise and Technical security architects, it was felt important to separate the two, if only to stress the corporate business and risk drivers for security architecture at the enterprise level. The skills profile of the Enterprise Security Architect therefore focuses on using organizational security requirements in the development of Enterprise Information Security Architectures, interpreting security policies and threat/risk profiles to develop secure architectural solutions that mitigate the risks, conform to legislation and regulations, and relate to business needs.
- **C2 - Technical Secure Architecture:** Whilst many of the skill definitions for the Technical Security Architect replicate those of the Enterprise Architect, the skills focus is more on:
  - The development of Computer, Network and Storage Security Architectures, incorporating hosting, infrastructure applications and cloud-based solutions.
  - Applying security architecture principles to networks, IT systems, Control Systems (e.g. SCADA, ICS), infrastructures and products.
  - Devising standard solutions that address requirements delivering specific security functionality.
  - Maintaining awareness of the security advantages and vulnerabilities of common products and technologies.
- **C3 - Secure Development:** This focuses on the design, development and implementation of secure systems and products using appropriate standards and practices, including verifying that the security criteria are met. Whilst in 2006 this Skill Group was targeted largely at the development of secure products, this has changed over the years and was expanded to cover secure systems development. Nevertheless, concerns remain over the quality and robustness of all software, not just security software, and the IISP is working with the Trustworthy Software Foundation and the Information Assurance Advisory Council (IAAC) to raise awareness of this issue.

Security Discipline D: Assurance: Audit, Compliance, and Testing

This is the Security Discipline where the most significant changes between versions 1 and 2 of the Framework have occurred. In 2006, this Security Discipline was entitled *Information Assurance Meth-*

odologies and Testing and contained two Skills Groups, Information Assurance Methodologies and Security Testing. Largely as a result of representations from IISP Corporate Members, this was changed radically in version 2. The arguments were:

- Security Methodologies were no longer viewed as a skill in themselves, but needed to be recognized as an important factor in each of the skills, e.g. risk assessment methodologies should be addressed under Skill Group B2, Secure Architecture methodologies under C1/C2, etc.
- Organizations, especially at Board level viewed skills like audit, compliance and testing as essentially part of the corporate security assurance process, so it was felt that these should be incorporated in the same Security Discipline.
- As a result of the increase in compliance monitoring and testing since 2006, it was felt that this should be recognized by separating these functions from traditional audit as the practices, training and qualifications were significantly different. Both were covered by a single Skill Group in version 1 which, it was felt, led to confusion and conflict.
- The testing of security functionality should be separated from penetration testing, as the knowledge and skills requirements were significantly different.

As a result, Security Discipline D was renamed as *Assurance: Audit, Compliance and Testing*, and divided into four Skill Groups: Internal and Statutory Audit; Compliance Monitoring and Controls Testing; Security Evaluation and Functionality Testing; and Penetration Testing. The related observations from experience here are as follows:

- **D1 - Internal and Statutory Audit:** During the life of version 1 of the framework, compliance monitoring became an increasingly important tool in the corporate security armory. Whilst there had been a tendency to 'shoe-horn' these skills under the Security Audit Skill Group, this resulted in some confusion and a degree of conflict between professional auditors and compliance monitors. As a result, it was decided to split these into two separate Skill Groups.
- **D2 - Compliance Monitoring and Controls Testing:** As indicated above, this Skill Group covers compliance monitoring against recognized standards such as ISO/IEC27001, the Payment Card Industry Data Security Standard, the HMG Information Assurance Maturity Model (IAMM), and also against legal and regulatory instruments.
- **D3 - Security Evaluation and Functionality Testing:** In version 1, security evaluation, security functionality testing and penetration testing (but not vulnerability assessment) were covered by a single Skill Group. In recognition of the different knowledge and skill requirements between these two Skill Groups, it was decided to move security evaluation and functionality testing to a separate Skill Group in version 2. In practice, the IISP has found that security evaluation skills are applied mainly against secure products. Since the demise of the CESG (formerly CSIA) Claims Tested Mark (CCTM) scheme and the marginalization of Common Criteria (ISO/IEC 15408), security functionality testing has concentrated on systems. The scope of such testing tends to be equally split between confidentiality and availability requirements.
- **D4 - Penetration Testing:** For purposes of consistency, and to reflect common practice, the technical vulnerability assessment skill has been transferred from Operational Security Management in version 1 to become part of the D4 Skill Group in version 2.

Security Discipline E: Operational Security Management

It has been argued that this particular Security Discipline is covered by the Information Technology Infrastructure Library (ITIL). Whilst this is largely true, it is important to recognize the importance of cybersecurity professionalism in this area. Consequently, those elements of operational IT management which are directly relevant to security were included in version 1 of the Skills Framework and have been retained in version 2.

There were three Skill Groups in version 1, but these were reduced to two. The Group removed was *Vulnerability Assessment*, with the majority of the skill definitions being transferred to Skill Group F1, e.g. monitoring, reviewing and filtering external vulnerability reports and analyzing internal problem reports. The removal of this Skill Group also removed a source of confusion regarding technical vulnerability assessment, which is more properly included in Skill Group D4 as it is closely related to penetration testing.

Security Discipline F: Intrusion and Incident Management, Investigation and Forensics

In version 1 of the Skills Framework this Security Discipline was entitled *Incident Management* and contained three Skill Groups – Incident Management, Investigation and Forensics. In version 2 it was renamed as *Intrusion and Incident Management, Investigation and Forensics.* It still contains three Skill Groups, but the first 2 have been changed significantly:

- **F1 - Intrusion Detection and Analysis:** This Skill Group was introduced to reflect the increase in Security Operations Center and Security Incident and Event Management (SIEM) systems since 2006. It recognizes the skill sets needed to identify potential intrusion or other anomalous behavior, the use of security analytics to monitor and filter external vulnerability reports, and the production of targeted warning material.
- **F2 - Incident Management, Incident Investigation and Response**: In version 1, Incident Management and Incident Investigation were listed as separate Skill Groups. This caused some confusion as the skills sets and activities were inextricably linked. Under version 2 this Skill Group covers managing and investigating incidents as well as responding, which is of equal importance. This reflects common practice in the real world.

Security Discipline G

The only Skill Group (Audit and Review) in this Security Discipline was relocated to Security Discipline D. It is retained it as a blank discipline in order to ensure comparability and avoid confusion amongst parties referring across both versions of the framework.

Security Discipline H: Business Resilience

As with Security Discipline E, there are arguments that this is a separate set of professional skills covered by other organizations. However, the same counter-arguments apply. In version 1 of the Skills Framework the Discipline was named *Business Continuity Management* with 2 Skill Groups – *Business*

Continuity Planning (H1) and *Business Continuity Management.* It was renamed in Version 2 as *Business Resilience* and a third Skill Group was added following representations from stakeholders to cover the need to address cybersecurity resilience in implementation and operations:

- **H3 - Cyber Resilience:** Whilst this largely replicated in other Security Disciplines (especially B, C, E and F), it was felt important to bring cybersecurity resilience issues into the corporate business continuity and disaster recovery processes.

There is also an additional element in this Skill Group and that is putting in place mechanisms to manage the fallout from serious security breaches. It is not just about recovering processing capability, but also about managing the interaction with individuals (customers and/or staff members) whose personal information has been compromised. Activities include: engagement with the Information Commissioner's Office (ICO); deciding what follow-up action would be appropriate (e.g. legal assistance with identity theft); setting up and briefing a help desk to deal with enquiries from individuals affected by the breach. The issue of obtaining and managing cybersecurity insurance to cover such circumstances is also covered in this Skill Group.

Security Discipline I

This Security Discipline was named *Information Systems Research* in version 1, but changed to correctly reflect its focus in version 2. It originally contained three Skill Groups – *Research, Academic Research, and Applied Research* – but these were reduced to two to reflect the confusion by many stakeholders between the, admittedly rather vague, definitions.

- **I1 - Research:** This Skill Group covers, for example:
    - Conducting original investigation to gain knowledge and understanding relating to cybersecurity.
    - Defining research goals.
    - Writing/presenting papers on the results of research.
    - Contributing to the development of an organization's Information Security research policy.
    - Developing new or improved cybersecurity models or theories including new cryptographic algorithms.
    - In cybersecurity, using existing knowledge to produce new or improved devices, products and processes or to improve understanding of behavioral response to security controls.
- **I2 - Applied Research:** By contrast, this group covers aspects such as:
    - Vulnerability Research and Discovery, leading to the development of exploits, reverse engineering and researching mitigation bypasses.
    - Cryptographic research leading to the assessment of existing algorithms.

Security Discipline J: Management, Leadership, Business, and Communications

There was an argument in favor of removing the J Security discipline from the Skills Framework on the basis that these skills should be covered under each of the individual skills in the Framework. However, stakeholders argued strongly in favor of retaining a subset of the original seven Skill Groups as they were considered important to the effective use of the Framework. Indeed, this is an area of increasing importance. There have been cases where senior managers have stated that it is easier to teach cybersecurity skills to business experts than teach business knowledge and understanding to cybersecurity specialists. Whilst one can understand the dilemma, it really is not that easy, and cybersecurity professionals need to recognize business drivers and not just follow the security mantras. There have been several examples whereby individuals with long experience and a strong reputation in the standards and policy areas have moved into the "real world", often the financial sector and had a rude awakening by realizing that implementation of standard policies, principles and practices was not as easy as they thought.

- **J1 - Management, Leadership and Influence:** This Skill Group concentrates on working with and managing teams, exercising leadership in promoting cybersecurity and interfacing effectively with management.
- **J2 - Business Skills:** To a great extent, this Skill Group replicates the content of A3 and A4 (Information Security Strategy and Innovation & Business Improvement). Corporate stakeholders felt strongly that it should be included specifically as a soft skill to reinforce the point that cybersecurity needs to recognize and take account of business opportunities and drivers.
- **J3 - Communication and Knowledge Sharing:** Recognizes the importance of good communications skills, written and verbal, for a cybersecurity professional, and also the need for cybersecurity professionals to share knowledge, mentor and educate those that they work with.

Security Discipline K: Contributions to the Information Security Community and Professional Development

This final Discipline covers Contributions to the Community, Contributions to the Profession, and Professional Development. The focus of these Skill Groups is self-explanatory, the change in version 2 separated contributions to the community from those to the profession.

CONTINUING DEVELOPMENT AND MOVING FORWARD

Whilst the IISP skills framework remained stable and relevant for 10 years, there is no doubt that cybersecurity challenges and the need for new or more refined skills were expanding at an increasing pace. This was largely due to the rise of cybercrime (such as ransomware), fraudulent activity, the impact of breaches involving personal information and, possibly to a lesser extent, concerns over national state activity in the cyber arena. Cybersecurity issues are now taken seriously at corporate Board level, and this resulted in two further significant changes to the IISP Skills Framework as it moved towards version 2.3:

- **D4 – Penetration Testing:** Penetration testing has proved to be a growth industry over the past 10+ years and continues to provide an important assurance. However, it is recognized that, in the current hostile cyber environment, penetration testing, i.e. testing against known public domain vulnerabilities, is not enough. In the past year or so a requirement for extensive testing and attack exercises using scenarios based on threat intelligence has evolved. These activities are commonly categorized as red, blue, purple and white teaming:

- Red Teaming exercises mimic an attack against an organization using scenarios developed from (often independently provided) threat intelligence to evaluate the effectiveness of its security defenses, including people and processes.
- Blue Teaming describes the operation of an organization's internal security team to detect and respond to Red Team activities.
- Purple Teaming describes an arrangement whereby experience Red Teamers are embedded into the Blue Team to assist and mentor.
- White Teaming describes a non-intrusive method of assessing the ability of an organization to resist attack, although the IISP has found no evidence from applicants for membership of this approach being used in anger.

The knowledge and skill requirements involved in these activities will be more extensive that those traditionally assigned to penetration testers, or Security Operations Center (SOC) staff for that matter.

- **H3 - Cyber Resilience:** The whole issue of managing cybersecurity breaches has escalated and is now, rightly, considered seriously at Board level. The cost, impact on the business, and resource overheads of managing and recovering from an incident are a serious concern, and issues which most companies and corporations are ill-equipped to cope with. The UK Data Protection Act 2018, which embodies the standards published in the EU General Data Protection Regulation, has raised the bar regarding breaches involving personal information, and it is only a matter of time before the Information Commissioner's Office serves heavy fines for breaches. The issue of cyber breach insurance has also moved on, with many major insurance companies and large consultancy firms now offering security breach management services.

The IISP Skills Framework has proven itself to be a valuable tool in assessing cybersecurity skills for a range of purposes including personal development, the definition skill requirements of job roles, job families and professional membership. It has also been used effectively in the definition of cybersecurity skills requirements for academic qualifications and apprenticeship schemes.

Many of the specific uses of version 1 of the Framework are described earlier in this chapter. Version 2 has been used by Qufaro (see qufaro.uk) to underpin its Extended Project Qualification coursework and qualification, an AS-level qualification aimed at bridging the gap between school curricula at GCSE level and degree programs. The IISP will be working with Qufaro to assist in the development of Level 3 apprenticeship criteria (as opposed to the Level 4 and higher apprenticeship criteria currently in place). It also hopes to work with the London Institute of Banking and Finance who are seeking to introduce an apprenticeship scheme with a specific focus on cybersecurity in banking and finance.

Even so, the Skills Framework cannot stand still. Issues such as red/blue/purple and white teaming (Skill D4) and security breach management (Skill H3) mentioned earlier in this chapter are not adequately addressed in Version 2.2 of the IISP Skills Framework. Action is in hand to address these issues in version 2.3. There are also the evolving security issues surrounding the Internet of Things (IoT) which will no doubt have an impact of the IISP Skills Framework, as well as the IISP Knowledge Framework and Common Body of Knowledge work mentioned below.

Also, it must be recognized that the strength of the IISP Skills Framework is also its weakness. The skills definitions within the Framework are deliberately set at a high level to minimize the need for constant change, although changes will still be required to reflect new technologies and specialisms, perhaps more so than in the past as the pace of change seems to be increasing. As with all high-level definitions, their interpretation is subjective and can result in inconsistency. It is also true that knowledge, understanding and expertise in a specific skill can be relevant to several Skill Groups. An example is Cryptography, which falls to a greater or lesser extent under all the Skill Groups in Security Disciplines A, C, D and F, and in Skill Groups B3, E2 and H3.

All of this points to the need for a Common Body of Knowledge (CBK) for the cybersecurity profession, and in the UK context this was recognized by both the IISP and NCSC in 2016, albeit with different requirements and priorities.

The IISP sees the priority and a baseline set of knowledge and understanding which represents the baseline for anyone wishing to call themselves a cybersecurity professional. This recognizes the issue that a number of self-professed cybersecurity professionals have a deep and expert knowledge in certain skill areas, bit little or no broad knowledge across the cybersecurity skill spectrum. From the IISP perspective, this is a little like a neurological consultant having no knowledge of physiology. Consequently, the priority for the IISP, driven by its Corporate members, was to develop a body of knowledge covering Level 1, and edging into Level 2, across Security Disciplines A through H.

Meanwhile, the NCSC, given its position as the UK National Technical Authority for cybersecurity, felt that a comprehensive body of knowledge was needed, covering not just the baseline criteria, but also the specialist technical areas against which Subject Matter Experts could be trained and assessed. Whilst the IISP continued to work with the NCSC on the resulting CyBOK project (www.cybok.org), it took the initiative in developing a Knowledge Framework to meet its own priorities, primarily the development of a baseline framework of knowledge and understanding across the whole cyber skills waterfront. Version 1 of the Knowledge Framework was published in 2017, but (as with CyBOK) the level of detail means that changes in technology, threats and attack vectors will require a constant review and update process in order to ensure that currency is maintained in later years.

CONCLUSION

Cybersecurity, then called Computer Security, first came to prominence as a study and career specialism in the 1980s. For many years the skills requirements remained limited for a number of reasons including: limited threats; limited networking capability; and the focus on the confidentiality of classified information.

This changed in the late 1990s when industry and commerce began to take a real interest; a factor in this being the evolution of the Internet as a global communications medium. This led to the development of commercial standards, and the cybersecurity skill sets expanded significantly to address the whole range of confidentiality, integrity and availability issues. This trend accelerated in the new millennium, with the growth of cybercrime, fraud and much-publicized corporate financial governance failures. This was reflected, amongst other things, in the growth of the penetration testing industry, SIEM technology and the development of Security Operations Centers (SOCs) and, later, the evolution of Threat Intelligence as a major plank in corporate cybersecurity strategies.

By 2018, the increasing frequency and sophistication of attacks by cyber criminals, and the financial and reputational damage caused by compromises of personal information have raised the profile of cybersecurity to Board level. This is reflected by penetration testing being complemented by, and in some cases replaced by teaming exercises simulating attacks based on scenarios developed from threat intelligence. The growing concerns of the security of control systems, the Internet of Things (IoT) and the evolving disciplines in Artificial Intelligence (AI) – which could be a force for good and bad – are issues that the profession will need to get to grips with.

Whilst the IISP Skills Framework has maintained its position as the basis of cyber skills definition and categorization, it has been recognized that these high-level definitions, although important, are not sufficient in themselves. As a result, the IISP has developed a Knowledge Framework to complement the Skills Framework by providing baseline definitions of knowledge and understanding of cybersecurity skills sufficient for an entry level to the profession. At the same time, the NCSC has let a contract to academia to develop a comprehensive Cyber Security Body of Knowledge covering the whole range of Skill Levels, not just Levels 1 and 2.

The challenge facing the profession, and the bodies with professional responsibilities, is to maintain and expand the frameworks and bodies of knowledge to reflect adequately the skills requirements to meet and manage threats, which are evolving at an ever-increasing rate.

REFERENCES

Bell, D. E., & LaPadula, L. J. (1973). Secure Computer Systems: Mathematical Foundations. In Secure Computer Systems: Mathematical Foundations (MTR–2547, Vol. 1). The MITRE Corporation. (ESD–TR–73–278–I)

Bell, D. E., & LaPadula, L. J. (1976). Secure Computer System: Unified Exposition and Multics Interpretation. MTR–2997. The MITRE Corporation. (ESD–TR–75–306). doi:10.21236/ADA023588

Biba, K. J. (1975). *Integrity Considerations for Secure Computer Systems.* The MITRE Corporation.

Brewer, D. F. C., & Nash, M. J. (1989) The Chinese Wall Security Policy. *Proceedings of IEEE Symposium on Security and Privacy.*

Clark, D. D., & Wilson, D. R. (1987). A comparison of Commercial and Military Computer Security Policies. *Proceedings of the 1987 IEEE Symposium on Research in Security and Privacy,* 184-193. 10.1109/SP.1987.10001

DoD. (1985). *DoD Trusted Computer Security Evaluation Criteria (DoD 5200.28-STD).* US Department of Defense Computer Security Center.

Ware, W. H. (Ed.). (1967). *Security Controls for Computer Systems: Report of Defense Science Board Task Force of Computer Security.* RAND Corporation for the Office of the Secretary of Defense.

KEY TERMS AND DEFINITIONS

Cyber Resilience: The ability of an organization to deliver continuously the intended outcome despite adverse cyber events, including the ability to respond holistically to adverse cyber events and to restore regular delivery mechanisms.

Penetration Testing: The assessment of an IT system, infrastructure, or application to identify public domain vulnerabilities and assess the risk of these being exploited.

Security Discipline: A collection of skill groups with a common high-level focus (e.g., governance, assurance, etc.).

Security Evaluation: The assessment and testing of an IT product or system against specified security claims using an established methodology such as Common Criteria (ISO15408).

Skill (Skill Group): The definition of a skill of group of skills against which a cyber security practitioner can be assessed.

Skill Level: A scale of six (formerly four) levels defining the level of knowledge, understanding, and practical competence in a cyber security skill.

Skills Framework: A framework of cyber security skills developed and maintained by the Institute of Information Security Professionals.

Threat Intelligence: The collection of intelligence related to cyber security threats to an organization. Sources include open source intelligence, social media intelligence, and the dark web.

Vulnerability Assessment: The assessment of an IT system, infrastructure, or application to identify potential public domain vulnerabilities. Vulnerability assessment differs from penetration testing in that no attempt is made to exploit the identified vulnerabilities.

ENDNOTES

1. A copy of the current version of the Skills Framework can be required via the IISP's website at www.iisp.org.
2. CESG, formerly the Communications-Electronics Security Group, is the UK government's National Technical Authority for Information Assurance and is part of the National Cyber Security Centre.

Chapter 12
The Role of Cybersecurity Certifications

Adrian Davis
ObjectTech Group, UK

ABSTRACT

The chapter looks at the burgeoning field of certification for individuals in the field of information security or cybersecurity. Individual information security certifications cover a wide range of topics from the deeply technical to the managerial. These certifications are used as a visible indication of an individual's status and knowledge, used to define experience and status, used in job descriptions and screening, and may define expectations placed on the individual. This chapter examines how these certifications are produced, the subjects they cover, and how they integrate and the various audiences to which the certifications are aimed. The role, the perceived and real value, and benefits of certification within the field of information security both from an individual and an organizational perspective are discussed. Finally, some conclusions on certification are presented.

INTRODUCTION

Information security[1] certifications now form a significant part of the wider information security industry, with a powerful influence on individuals and organizations within that industry. Certifications are often a prerequisite for senior jobs, working in government or for employment in specific roles; they are also widespread across the industry. The major certification bodies – (ISC)², ISACA, EC Council and SANS – claim to have trained or have as members well over 500,000 individuals in total. Certification is also a big business, with annual reports from two of the major players in the field ((ISC)², 2017 and ISACA, 2017a) both indicating revenue for each of over US$50 million from education, examinations, membership and publications.

Before embarking on a review of these certifications, the definition of certification as used in this chapter should be provided. This chapter uses the term certification with the following meaning: "the

DOI: 10.4018/978-1-5225-7847-5.ch012

Copyright © 2019, IGI Global. Copying or distributing in print or electronic forms without written permission of IGI Global is prohibited.

act of certifying or state of being certified" (Collins, 2018) here we use the last part of the definition to indicate that an individual is in the state of being certified, i.e. they hold a certificate, which is an official document received when a course of study or training is completed.

The chapter is structured as follows. A very brief background is given to explain the rise of information security certifications. This is followed by a review of certification bodies and their characteristics, then an in-depth review of information security certifications at the time of publication. The discussion continues by examining the role of certifications from a personal and organizational perspective, the perceived value and benefit and then the misuse and abuse to which certifications can be put. Finally, some future trends in the field of information security certification are highlighted.

A BRIEF HISTORY OF INFORMATION SECURITY CERTIFICATIONS

Information security – originally computer security – came from an IT background. It was considered to be an IT specialism for a number of years and so didn't really require much in the way of oversight, a single unified voice, certification or qualifications. Typically, certifications were created by one or more groups of willing, interested and altruistic individuals either responding to a perceived need or trying to set a standard that could be readily understood. By setting standards, these groups hoped to both define what made an individual competent and knowledgeable in the field of information security and provide a mechanism to identify those who were perhaps less than capable. There was not the need to submit to scrutiny or oversight as the numbers involved were small, the individuals knew each other and the roles many of the individuals worked in required some form of government vetting and clearance – and most, if not all of the groups were based in the United States. From these beginnings rose the information security certification industry we see today.

Today, there is no one "global body" that can truly claim to represent information security and the individuals in the field. Whilst there are a number of organizations who have global membership and reach, they do not capture everyone who works in the field, nor does everyone in the field want to hold the certifications they offer. Thanks to its multi-disciplinary nature, information/cyber security is a "big tent" and covers more than just technical roles. Thirty-five roles (CyberSN, 2018) related to security have been identified, ranging from the highly technical security analyst to CEO. These example roles – and all 35 – will have widely differing requirements for skills, knowledge and experience; yet all will require some knowledge of information/cyber security. However, for many non-technical roles, possession of certain certifications will not be possible, as they will not possess the relevant skills and experience – and they might never gain them. Examples of these individuals could include those people working in marketing, PR and finance for information security organizations.

From an academic perspective, information security is a new discipline that has been recognized as such for about thirty years or so. It is multi-disciplinary in nature, covering both technical and non-technical subjects, including programming, hardware design and function, networking, economics, law and business as well as security-related topics such as cryptography and risk management. As a result, it has been difficult to create educational pathways for students that meet both academic standards and industry needs.

Typically, universities have also found difficulties in establishing undergraduate degree courses in the subject, as it has been difficult to understand the needs of industry, establish demand for such degrees and create information security courses with enough differentiation from those degrees, such as computing, already offered. Additionally, many of the topics are covered in computer science or related degrees, with security has been offered as an optional module near the end of the course. However, the last few years, cybersecurity undergraduate degrees have started to be developed and offered to prospective students, some in response to the government cybersecurity guidelines and some in response to industry needs.

The first information security degrees were postgraduate, and this trend has continued, with a significant number of universities offering this option to students. One advantage of this approach is that the student will have experience and/or subject knowledge, meaning that the course can focus on the security aspects rather than the fundamentals of IT and networking.

So, the multi-disciplinary nature of information security has both created opportunity for multiple certifications and differing educational approaches. But information security defies easy categorization: is it a technical discipline, where knowledge of the inner workings of IT and cryptography are a must, or is it a hybrid discipline, where knowledge of people, process and technology are a must? Whilst this author is of the latter opinion, the sheer diversity of the field and the roles in it means that probably both are valid perspectives: and therein lies the problem. What are the fundamentals that matter? What are the fundamentals that everyone should know? How should individuals prove their knowledge and skill?

Contributing to this issue is that the certification bodies have been created from and possess different philosophies and perspectives. For example, ISACA, given its audit background, typically defines tasks that certification holders should be able to perform and then tests against those tasks; ISACA also has its own standard (COBIT, ISACA 2012) against which performance can be measured. These different starting points and perspectives mean that the certification bodies prioritize different domains of knowledge, different experience and different approaches (such as technically-oriented or management-oriented).

Additionally, although standards bodies such as BSI, NIST and ISO have published numerous information security standards, many of those focus on the technical and managerial, not the individual, perspective. It can be argued that ISO 27021:2017 Competence requirements for information security management systems professionals (ISO 2017) does state the competences (meaning the combination of knowledge and skills, CEN (2014)) required or expected of professionals managing an ISMS; however, it does not specify a personal certification or qualification scheme.

As information security has evolved, this lack of a unifying voice for the profession, coupled with dissatisfaction about certifications and low barriers of entry has meant that numerous bodies have stepped into the vacuum and created education, training, certifications and qualifications they believe will be of use. Each certification body has its own views on what is important, what is required and what individuals should know and be able to do to gain the certification and declare themselves to be capable of working in information security. Alongside this, professional and certification bodies in other industries are offering information security education, training and certifications to their membership.

The preceding paragraphs should not be taken as criticism of the institutions or individuals involved: rather, they indicate the evolving and changing natures of this topic, of information security careers and of the knowledge and skill requirements, characteristic of an emerging profession. With such uncertainty and fluidity, it can be very difficult for academic institutions and certification bodies to create pathways, qualifications, certifications and frameworks whilst having the confidence that these developments will have long-term viability and recognition. Allied to this is the rapid technological change and developments in technology which are challenging to keep abreast of, integrate into formal education and to estimate their impact and relevance.

Undoubtedly, the power of the market has also played a part in creating the range and number of information security certifications currently available. Creating a certification can result in significant revenue opportunities associated with the sale of associated education, training, memberships and publications. Additionally, at the time of writing, all things "cyber" are in vogue, so many organizations are seeking to capitalize on this trend by offering "cyber" courses and the like.

Having briefly discussed the history of information security certifications, we now turn our attention to the certification bodies that administer the certifications currently available and their core activities.

CERTIFICATION BODIES

Behind the certifications are organizations, termed certification bodies, that produce, administer, market and sell certifications. They may also offer and administer membership, membership benefits and continuing education opportunities. This section focuses upon three key activities the certification bodies deliver, namely certification; membership; and certification maintenance and update.

Certification

The major certification bodies all follow a similar process. An individual wanting to gain a certification must know, learn or refresh a body of knowledge. The bodies offer various pathways to learn the body of knowledge, ranging from self-study to online courses to face-to-face training. There is also typically a range of published (both physical and electronic) books, study guides, presentations and practice tests. Training is carried by authorized instructors or authorized training partners (collectively termed authorized providers), who are supplied with the most current education materials. The individual is then examined by a written examination and, in some cases, a practical hands-on examination as well. Once the individual passes the examination(s), a certificate detailing what the individual has obtained is produced.

Membership

Many certification bodies offer membership as a result of a successful examination result. Membership is usually conditional on meeting eligibility criteria and signing up to a code of ethics. However, unlike many professional bodies, the certification bodies typically only have two levels of membership: the first is full membership, where an individual has the requisite years of experience and holds a certification; the second where an individual holds the certification but hasn't obtained the experience required to be a full member (sometimes termed "Associate"). The certification bodies do not necessarily offer the path of progression offered by true professional bodies; once the certification is obtained, there is no further progression – once a member, always a member – although other certifications can be obtained.

These bodies typically require that an individual maintains their membership. This is usually achieved by paying an annual fee and, in many cases, obtaining a certain number of hours of continuing professional education (CPE) or similar. The guidelines for what actually qualifies as a CPE can be complex (see for example CompTIA no date, GIAC 2018 and ISACA 2018a) but the intention is to drive individuals to undertake education and activities outside the normal performance of their role, so that the individuals develop and grow throughout their membership.

Typically, an individual will either have an annual target of continuing professional education to attain or will have to reach a target over a three-year cycle, with yearly minima and maxima. The minima and maxima are set to stop individuals doing nothing for two years and then collecting all their CPE in one go. Individuals are responsible for maintaining their record of CPE obtained and many organizations randomly audit a percentage of their members annually to check if CPE are being recorded in accordance with published guidelines.

To aid members in obtaining CPE credits, all the bodies offer a range of webcasts, podcasts, events and quizzes, many of which are free to members; they also offer CPE credits for volunteering and mentoring. Other organizations can offer CPE opportunities, such as conference, training and education providers.

Codes of ethics are prevalent across the industry. Undoubtedly, due to the knowledge and access possessed by individuals working in information security, those individuals could cause significant harm to people, IT systems, organizations and even governments. Such codes of ethics are designed to set out and reinforce a set of behaviors an individual is expected to demonstrate and usually have sanctions (or disciplinary measures) for breaching the code. Usually the sanction is expulsion from the membership and loss of the certification. Disciplinary action is usually organized and overseen by the certification body acting on complaints or reports of violations of the code of ethics. Sample codes of ethics are shown in Table 1.

The table above highlights three interesting points. First, that the code of ethics may be publicly available, so that anyone can read it; second, there is an altruistic imperative to serve clients/stakeholders, protect the wider community and advance the profession as viewed by the certification body. Third, they are not focused solely on the protection or use of technology; the codes are focused on the human side of information security.

Efforts have been made to harmonize these codes of ethics (see Cybersecurity Credentials Collaborative, 2015a) but they have not yet reached fruition. The harmonized code binds the individual certification bodies' code of ethics together and provides a code of ethics which is applicable industry-wide. The harmonized code covers four main areas: integrity, objectivity, confidentiality and professional competence.

Certification Maintenance and Update

The certification bodies discussed in this chapter invest significant resources in updating and enhancing their certification and associated materials. Using $(ISC)^2$ as an example, all of their certifications are on a two or three-year update cycle. For an individual certification, there is a methodical process, which concentrates on the examination and ensures it tests the tasks that are performed by security professionals who are engaged in the profession. The tasks are defined by workshops comprised of members, non-members and experts which produce Job Task Analyses (JTA). The JTA are then used to develop the examination and its associated questions. Once the examination is updated, a separate team will be given the outputs of the JTA (the knowledge required) to produce educational material covering the

Table 1. Codes of ethics published by selected certification bodies (note ISACA present their code as a numeric list)

(ISC)²	GIAC	ISACA
• Protect society, the common good, necessary public trust and confidence, and the infrastructure. • Act honorably, honestly, justly, responsibly, and legally. • Provide diligent and competent service to principles. • Advance and protect the profession.	Respect for the Public • I will accept responsibility in making decisions with consideration for the security and welfare of the community. • I will not engage in or be a party to unethical or unlawful acts that negatively affect the community, my professional reputation, or the information security discipline. Respect for the Certification • I will not share, disseminate, or otherwise distribute confidential or proprietary information pertaining to the GIAC certification process. • I will not use my certification, or objects or information associated with my certification (such as certificates or logos) to represent any individual or entity other than myself as being certified by GIAC. Respect for my Employer • I will deliver capable service that is consistent with the expectations of my certification and position. • I will protect confidential and proprietary information with which I come into contact. • I will minimize risks to the confidentiality, integrity, or availability of an information technology solution, consistent with risk management practice. Respect for Myself • I will avoid conflicts of interest. • I will not misuse any information or privileges I am afforded as part of my responsibilities. • I will not misrepresent my abilities or my work to the community, my employer, or my peers.	1. Support the implementation of, and encourage compliance with, appropriate standards and procedures for the effective governance and management of enterprise information systems and technology, including: audit, control, security and risk management. 2. Perform their duties with objectivity, due diligence and professional care, in accordance with professional standards. 3. Serve in the interest of stakeholders in a lawful manner, while maintaining high standards of conduct and character, and not discrediting their profession or the Association. 4. Maintain the privacy and confidentiality of information obtained in the course of their activities unless disclosure is required by legal authority. Such information shall not be used for personal benefit or released to inappropriate parties. 5. Maintain competency in their respective fields and agree to undertake only those activities they can reasonably expect to complete with the necessary skills, knowledge and competence. 6. Inform appropriate parties of the results of work performed including the disclosure of all significant facts known to them that, if not disclosed, may distort the reporting of the results. 7. Support the professional education of stakeholders in enhancing their understanding of the governance and management of enterprise information systems and technology, including: audit, control, security and risk management.

knowledge required. Considerable effort is expended in the running the JTA, producing the examination and the educational material and in keeping the examination and education teams apart. Of interest is the fact that the examination is developed first – then the education.

Certification bodies administer certifications and we now turn our attention to reviewing those certifications.

INFORMATION SECURITY CERTIFICATIONS

As of writing, one survey (Wikipedia 2018) has identified 102 recognized information security-related certifications; there are also other professional certifications, awarded by bodies such as the BCS, The Chartered Institute for IT, the Security Institute and the IEEE, which also award certifications and/or membership to individuals who work in this field.

Not all these recognized information security certifications are as well-known or recognized by the industry as others. Rather than survey the entire one hundred certifications, this section focuses on the better known and most popular (in terms of certification holders) information security certifications, which are shown in Table 2.

The rest of this chapter discusses these certifications, and highlight points of interest, similarity and divergence. To aid the reader, the following sections provide an overview of the certifications available, divided into three categories: technical, managerial and specialist. These categories are based on the predominant content of the certification, so the divisions are somewhat arbitrary in that many certifications contain elements of all three categories. However, this approach provides a useful framework to comprehend the scale and breadth of information security certifications and the related industry.

Alongside the certification bodies are a number of professional bodies that offer membership and certification in information security for individuals working in information security, along with professional bodies for IT and other professions; these are also covered to provide as full a picture as possible.

Note that the following paragraphs focus only on those certifications which are considered to be relevant to information security; thus many IT certifications, which may have some information security component, will be ignored. Vendor certifications will also not be covered.

TECHNICAL CERTIFICATIONS

Technical certifications are those which focus on particular technologies, hardware and software associated with information security. These certifications are typically very focused, covering a particular technology or software package; they may also require the student to display practical knowledge and skills by conducting tasks in a controlled environment (such as an online laboratory).

Table 2. Well known information security certifications (in alphabetical order of awarding body)

Certification	Certification Body	Experience Requirements	Exam	Code of Ethics	Maintenance Requirements
CISSP	$(ISC)^2$	Five years or more	Yes	Yes	Yes
SSCP	$(ISC)^2$	One year	Yes	Yes	Yes
CCSP	$(ISC)^2$	Five years or more	Yes	Yes	Yes
CISMP	BCS	None	Yes		
Security+	CompTIA	None (but recommended)	Yes	Yes	Yes
CEH	EC Council	Two years or more	Yes	Yes	Yes
GIAC Certifications	GIAC	Varies	Yes	Yes	Yes
GSE	GIAC	Must hold GIAC certifications	Yes	Yes	Yes
CISM	ISACA	5 years or more	Yes	Yes	Yes
CISA	ISACA	5 years or more	Yes	Yes	Yes
CSXP	ISACA	Not stated	Yes	Yes	Yes

The SANS Institute probably offers the widest variety of information security courses, numbering over 55 (SANS 2018), covering everything from information security fundamentals to security awareness to securing code in Java/EE. SANS began by offering hands-on technical training and has expanded to cover the non-technical to meet demand and to reflect the changes in the information security industry. SANS major strength is in delivering very intensive five- or six-day face-to-face training courses, led by an instructor, although many of the courses are now available online. SANS uses a small group of rigorously selected instructors (about 100) to deliver their courses; the instructors perform their teaching in addition to their day jobs, meaning that the instructors are current and have deep experience in the topics they teach.

SANS courses are aligned to and can be used to obtain certifications from Global Information Assurance Certification (GIAC). GIAC offers 28 certifications (GIAC 2016), covering five domains: cyber defense, application security, penetration testing, digital forensics and management, legal and audit. For each certification gained, an individual can submit a research paper on the subject of the certification; if accepted, the individual gains a GIAC Gold certification. Additionally, once an individual has completed a set of prerequisites, including GIAC Gold, they may sit both an exam and a hands-on practical to become a GIAC Security Expert (GSE). GIAC certifications require either maintenance by CPE accumulation or by retaking the examination; the GSE can only be renewed by examination.

Whereas SANS has a deserved reputation for advanced technical training, CompTIA has aimed its cybersecurity certification at the entry-level and thus filled an important area. CompTIA offer a range of IT and information security certifications and their entry-level offering in information security is the Security+. This certification covers network security; compliance and operational security; threats and vulnerabilities; application, data and host security; access control and identity management; and cryptography (CompTIA 2016). Security+ has a set of maintenance requirements, including an annual maintenance fee and a three-year continuing education cycle; there is also an option to resit the examination. This certificate is also part of a certification pathway for an individual aspiring to have a career in IT or information security (CompTIA 2018).

ISACA offer their CSXP (CybersecurityNexus Practitioner, ISACA 2015), which is designed to evaluate an individual's ability to perform cybersecurity tasks, through hands-on testing. CSXP is unique in that no formal training is offered by ISACA; instead, individuals are told what they should be able to achieve and the tools and techniques they will need to apply. This approach is designed to overcome the limitations of written examinations and provide both individuals and organizations with a robust assessment of what an individual can achieve in a practical sense. CSXP uses a three-year cycle for certificate maintenance, with all holders required to resit the examination at the end of the cycle. ISACA do not state the experience required to sit the exam; however, the list of tasks and tools is extensive and indicates to your author that at least two years' experience is needed.

MANAGERIAL CERTIFICATIONS

Moving on from the technical certifications, the second category of certifications are the managerial. These typically take a broader view of information security, and are focused on processes, standards, business context and the management of information security in an organization. Technical knowledge is assumed or is provided at a higher level than provided for in the technical certifications.

There are two certifications that dominate this category: the Certified Information Systems Security Professional (CISSP) from $(ISC)^2$ and the Certified Information Security Manager (CISM) from ISACA. Both are aimed at individuals with five or more years' experience and both require an individual to know (and recall) a Common Body of Knowledge. Both are gained by examination, proof of experience, and for the CISSP, endorsement by an $(ISC)^2$ member. This last condition, which is unique to $(ISC)^2$ as far as the author knows, means the individual seeking a certification from $(ISC)^2$ must have their application countersigned by an existing $(ISC)^2$ member. This has three important implications: first, should an individual falsify the proof of experience, then the endorser may lose their certification, so the endorser should know the individual or check the veracity of the individual; second, it encourages individuals to build networks and engage with $(ISC)^2$ members before they gain their certification; and third, it creates a tight-knit community where groups of certificate holders know and trust each other.

There is much debate about which of these certifications is better, or what they cover. Table 3 highlights the knowledge domains for each certification.

CISSP was launched in 1994 ($(ISC)^2$ 2018) and has a deserved reputation within the industry for setting the standard for individuals working at intermediate and senior roles in information security. The CISSP requires individuals to know both the technical aspects of information security, with detailed sections on networking protocols, cryptography and access control, and the non-technical aspects, such as risk management, auditing and legal aspects. These are all presented in the Common Body of Knowledge (CBK), which all individuals aspiring to the CISSP should know. The CISSP has been accused of being "a mile wide and an inch deep", but there is no doubt it attempts to be comprehensive and authoritative.

CISM on the other hand is built around tasks an individual is expected to be able to achieve and the associated knowledge an individual should possess to achieve the task. This, it can be argued, provides more structure to the learning and also reflects better the tasks and activities an information security manager may be asked to accomplish.

In addition to possessing the knowledge related to the topics covered by the domains listed above, individuals wishing to gain the certification must be able to show relevant experience in at least two of the domains. CISSP and CISM both require a minimum of five years' experience in the domains, although individuals can pass the examination and then gain the experience.

Both CISSP and CISM offer several study methods, including self-study, online learning and face-to-face teaching. The latter, with the use of intensive "boot camp" training has garnered some criticism

Table 3. The CISSP and CISM knowledge domains

CISSP Domains ($(ISC)^2$ 2018)	CISM Domains (ISACA 2017b)
Security and Risk Management	Information Security Governance
Asset Security	Information Risk Management
Security Engineering	Information Security Program Development and Management
Communication and Network Security	Information Security Incident Management
Identity and Access Management	
Security Assessment and Testing	
Security Operations	
Software Development Security	

in that an individual can spend four or five days cramming and then sit the exam – and emerge at the end of a (very) intensive week with the certification. The boot camp model is very popular with time-poor individuals working in information security, as it provides a quick method of gaining the desired certification. However, as in all training, the process can be gamed by an individual who intensively studies for the week, and then regurgitates the facts to pass the exam, yet may have little hands-on or real-world experience, or ability to apply the knowledge insightfully.

Alongside the CISSP and CISM, there are newer certifications aimed at individuals working at more senior levels of the industry, or those individuals aspiring to reach such levels. Typical of these is the EISM (Information Security Manager) and CCISO (Certified Chief Information Security Officer, offered by the EC-Council. The EISM uses the same courseware and training as the CCISO certification, but goes onto less depth, as does the corresponding exam. Both the EISM and CCISO are built around five domains (EC Council 2018a), as shown in Table 4.

At this point, it is worth stating that all three certifications cover similar ground but are differently organized and take different perspectives. For example, all three certifications cover well-known standards such as ISO/IEC 27001, ISO/IEC 27005 and NIST; all three cover incident management; all three cover similar technologies such as access control; and all three require five years' experience.

SPECIALIST CERTIFICATIONS

The third category, specialist certifications, differs from the previous two in that they are not technology-focused, nor do they take a broad view of information security. These specialist certifications may cover particular activities, such as auditing or hacking, or cover particular technologies from technical, information security and business contexts.

There are number of specialist certifications of particular relevance to individuals working in information security, namely CISA, CCSK, CCSP, CEH (and related certifications) and OCSP.

Table 4. The CISSP, CISM and CCISO knowledge domains

CISSP Domains ((ISC)^2 2018)	CISM Domains (ISACA 2017b)	EISM/CCISO Domains (EC Council 2018a)
Security and Risk Management	Information Security Governance	Governance (Policy, Legal, and Compliance)
Asset Security	Information Risk Management	IS Management Controls and Audit Management
Security Engineering	Information Security Program Development and Management	Management of Projects, Technology, and Operations
Communication and Network Security	Information Security Incident Management	Information Security Core Concepts
Identity and Access Management		Strategic Planning and Finance
Security Assessment and Testing		
Security Operations		
Software Development Security		

The first and the longest serving is the CISA (Certified Information Systems Auditor) launched by ISACA in 1978 (ISACA 2018b). This certification is almost an industry prerequisite for individuals wanting to develop and further a career in IT and information security auditing. CISA, in a manner similar to CISM, has five knowledge domains:

- The Process of Auditing Information Systems
- Governance and Management of IT
- Information Systems Acquisition, Development and Implementation
- Information Systems Operations, Maintenance and Service Management
- Protection of Information Assets.

With the move to cloud computing and the introduction of the "as a Service" model, certifications covering cloud security were an obvious opportunity for the certification bodies. The first true cloud security certification was the CCSK, offered by the Cloud Security Alliance (Cloud Security Alliance 2011), and now updated to version 4. CCSK has a body of knowledge based on the CSA Cloud Security Guidance v4 (Cloud Security Alliance 2017a), the CSA Cloud Control Matrix (Cloud Security Alliance 2017b) and the ENISA Cloud Computing Risk Assessment report (ENISA 2009). The Cloud Security Guidance covers 14 domains, listed below:

1. Cloud Computing Concepts and Architectures
2. Governance and Enterprise Risk Management
3. Legal Issues, Contracts and Electronic Discovery
4. Compliance and Audit Management
5. Information Governance
6. Management Plane and Business Continuity
7. Infrastructure Security
8. Virtualization and Containers
9. Incident Response
10. Application Security
11. Data Security and Encryption
12. Identity, Entitlement and Access Management
13. Security as a Service
14. Related Technologies

Domain 14, Related technologies, covers topics such as Big Data, Internet of Things and serverless computing. The CCSK does not require any maintenance, but holders of the certification are encouraged to retake the latest version, to keep their knowledge up to date.

Following on from the CCSK, the Cloud Security Alliance collaborated with $(ISC)^2$ to create the Certified Cloud Security Professional (CCSP). The CCSP has much in common with the CSSK and the CISSP but takes a more strategic view than the CCSK and includes privacy and traditional security approaches. The CCSP (like the CISSP) has a CBK which covers six domains, namely Architectural Concepts & Design Requirements; Cloud Data Security; Cloud Platform and Infrastructure Security;

Cloud Application Security; Operations; and Legal & Compliance ((ISC)^2 2015). The certification is gained by examination and has maintenance requirements similar to the CISSP, with a three-year cycle requiring 90 CPE.

Next in this overview of technical certifications is the Certified Ethical Hacker (CEH), awarded by the EC Council. CEH was launched in 2002 (EC Council 2017) and the latest version, version 10, covers the following domains (EC Council 2018b):

1. Background
2. Analysis/Assessment
3. Security
4. Tools/Systems/Programs
5. Procedures/Methodology
6. Regulation/Policy
7. Ethics.

Gaining the CEH is through a written exam; certificate holders can also take the CEH (Practical), launched in 2018. The CEH (Practical) is a hands-on examination where the individual has to perform various hacking techniques such as packet sniffing, SQL Injection and cryptographic attacks. CEH and CEH (Practical) provide a route to move to the EC Security Analyst and EC Security Analyst (Practical) and then the expert-level Licensed Penetration Tester (Master). Of interest is the emphasis on hands-on practical examination as an adjunct to the written tests. EC Council also have a code of ethics and typically require a certificate holder has to maintain the credential over a two or three-year cycle, in which varying numbers of CPE must be earned.

The technical certification section is rounded off by OSCP (Offensive Security Certified Professional), offered by Offensive Security (Offensive Security, 2018a). OSCP requires an individual to conduct a full penetration test of an unknown system, using Kali Linux. The individual is given 24 hours to complete the test and create a penetration test report, with in-depth notes and screenshots detailing their findings. Points are awarded for each compromised host, based on their difficulty and level of access obtained. OSCP (and other certifications offered by Offensive Security) do not have a maintenance requirement; once passed they never expire.

The prerequisite course for OSCP, entitled Penetration Testing with Kali Linux, has the following syllabus: (Offensive Security 2018b):

1. Getting Comfortable with Kali Linux
2. The Essential Tools
3. Passive Information Gathering
4. Active Information Gathering
5. Vulnerability Scanning
6. Buffer Overflows
7. Win32 Buffer Overflow Exploitation
8. Linux Buffer Overflow Exploitation
9. Working with Exploits
10. File Transfers

11. Privilege Escalation
12. Client Side Attacks
13. Web Application Attacks
14. Password Attacks
15. Port Redirection and Tunnelling
16. The Metasploit Framework
17. Bypassing Antivirus Software
18. Assembling the Pieces: Penetration Test Breakdown.

The prerequisite syllabus is very detailed and focused on the technical aspects of conducting a penetration test.

PROFESSIONAL MEMBERSHIP

Professional bodies cover a significant number of human activities and typically follow a common path, in that an individual will progress from a junior to a senior level of membership. This progression may be marked by gaining experience, by the gaining of knowledge or skill and by the passing of exams. Using a UK body (BCS, The Chartered Institute for IT) as an example, membership of a professional body typically follows the route shown in Figure 1.

So, as Figure 1 illustrates for an individual, joining a professional body provides a clear path for progression, with way points and criteria for advancement clearly defined. In some professions, medicine and accountancy being two examples, professional qualifications and certifications are required to practice, so the professional body also provides the "licence to practice".

Figure 1. Typical professional pathway
(after BCS, 2014)

	Student	Associate	Member	Chartered Member	Fellow/ Chartered Fellow
Qualifications		Degree in unrelated subject OR Non-degree OR undergraduate degree	Undergraduate degree		
Experience/ years	0	0 – 10	3 – 5	5+	10+
Career level	Foundational	Operational	Operational	Tactical	Strategic
Typical titles			Team Leader Manager Lecturer	Team Leader Deputy Head of... Senior Manager Senior Lecturer Reader	Head of... Professor Director Partner

The key to moving upwards through the membership is experience and passing the requisite criteria. For some professions, that may mean passing exams to join and move upwards or passing interviews to gain the next level of membership. As a result, progression is often seen as a milestone for an individual.

Within information security, there are two well-known professional bodies. The first is CREST which provides technical certifications for individuals working in penetration testing, threat intelligence, incident response and security architecture. CREST (CREST 2016) offers individuals a pathway from Practitioner (entry-level) through Registered (competent to work independently without supervision) to Certified (technically competent to run major projects and teams). At each level, examinations have to be passed and each level requires documented evidence of experience – Practitioner requiring 2,500 hours, Registered requiring at least 6,000 hours and Certified requiring at least 10,000 hours of relevant experience (CREST 2017). CREST examinations can include both written and practical components. CREST also provides accreditation for organizations working in particular segments of the information security industry and standards for topics such as penetration testing.

The second professional body is the IISP, Institute of Information Security Professionals. Like CREST, the IISP was formed in the UK and offers individual and corporate membership. The individual membership pathway has four levels (IISP 2018a) from Student to Fellow. Supporting the membership pathway is the Skills Framework, which can be used to guide individuals as they develop. The Skills Framework can also indicate to individuals when they can progress through the membership; it is also used to assess individuals to ensure they hold the correct membership.

As discussed in the previous chapter, the IISP Skills Framework is composed of 10 skills areas and disciplines, as follows (IISP 2018b):

1. Information security governance and management
2. Threat assessment and information risk management
3. Implementing secure systems
4. Assurance, audit, compliance and testing
5. Operational security management
6. Incident management, investigation and digital forensics
7. Security discipline (not used)
8. Business resilience
9. Information security research
10. Management, leadership, business and communications
11. Contributions to the information security profession and professional development.

Each of these skills areas and disciplines are broken down into skills groups. For each skill group, a descriptor indicates what an individual should know and be able to accomplish, using levels from 1 (basic knowledge) to 6 (expert/lead practitioner).

Within IT and engineering, professional bodies such as BCS, the Chartered Institute for IT (BCS), the Institution for Engineering Technology (IET) and the Institute of Electrical and Electronics Engineers (IEEE) count information security individuals within their membership and also provide information security education and training for their members. The BCS, The Chartered Institute for IT, also offers an entry-level information security certificate, the Certificate in Information Security Management Principles (CISMP). This certificate is aimed at IT professionals either wishing to expand their knowledge or individuals who wish to move into the information security field. The knowledge is divided into nine modules (BCS, 2017):

1. Information Security Management Principles
2. Information Risk
3. Information Security Framework
4. Procedural/People Security Controls
5. Technical Security Controls
6. Software Development and Lifecycle
7. Physical and Environmental Security Controls
8. Disaster Recovery and Business Continuity Management
9. Other Technical Aspects.

The knowledge is tested by examination; once passed there are no further requirements on the individual. CISMP is a stepping stone into practitioner-level qualifications (which examine particular aspects of information security in more detail) and ultimately the UK Government Certified Professional scheme (originally CESG Certified Professional, now Certified Professional; NCSC 2016).

AN ALTERNATIVE VIEW OF CERTIFICATIONS

Besides grouping the certifications by their content, they can also be grouped by the level of experience and knowledge the individual is expected to possess. Certification bodies typically use three categories – entry-level, intermediate and senior – and Table 5 illustrates both typical definitions and where popular (and previously discussed certifications) are placed.

The table serves an important purpose, in that it dispels a common myth that there are no entry-level certifications for information security. Thanks to their status, certifications such as CISSP and CISA dominate discussions and job descriptions (see the section entitled Misuse and Abuse), so new entrants

Table 5. Information security certifications grouped by level of experience required (in alphabetical order of certification body)

Entry-Level	Intermediate	Senior
No previous experience required	Typically require two or more years' experience	Typically require five or more years' experience
$(ISC)^2$ SSCP BCS CISMP CSA CCSK CompTIA Security+ ISACA CSX Cybersecurity Fundamentals certificate GIAC Information Security Fundamentals	CompTIA Cybersecurity Analyst+ EC Council Certified Ethical Hacker GIAC Security Essentials ISACA CXSP (assumed)	$(ISC)^2$ CISSP (and concentrations) $(ISC)^2$ CCSP ISACA CISM ISACA CISA EC Council CCISO EC Council LPT(M) GIAC Security Expert

and career changers believe that an individual must have a CISSP or similar to work in information security. This misconception does deter individuals from joining the information security workforce.

It also highlights that a pathway exists for individuals who wish to develop their skills and knowledge by taking and passing relevant certifications through their career. An individual can use certifications to define certain points in a career, because the stated experience requirements and successful completion of the examination(s) can be used to highlight increasing knowledge and skill.

The table provides an insight into how certifications can be combined to produce a roadmap for an individual. Many certifications are stand-alone, so it can be difficult for an individual to choose the certification that provides the greatest benefit and to create a pathway to move from entry-level to senior certifications. Figure 2 illustrates how the certifications discussed in this chapter can be combined to produce such a pathway.

Figure 2 above again confirms the complexity and multiplicity of certifications and highlights how an individual, who can meet the relevant criteria, can demonstrate their progress and development. It also indicates how an individual can plan their development; for example, if an individual comes from a technical role and aspires to a leadership role, then they examine the prerequisites for a management certification and plan to gain the relevant experience and knowledge, through education and practice.

Having examined certifications in detail, we now turn to the role of certification to an individual and their career and to an organization and its information security.

ROLE OF CERTIFICATION: INDIVIDUAL

For an individual, certification typically comes after university-level education, and may occur quite a few years after the conclusion of formal education, as Figure 3 shows.

Figure 2. Example certification pathways from entry to senior level

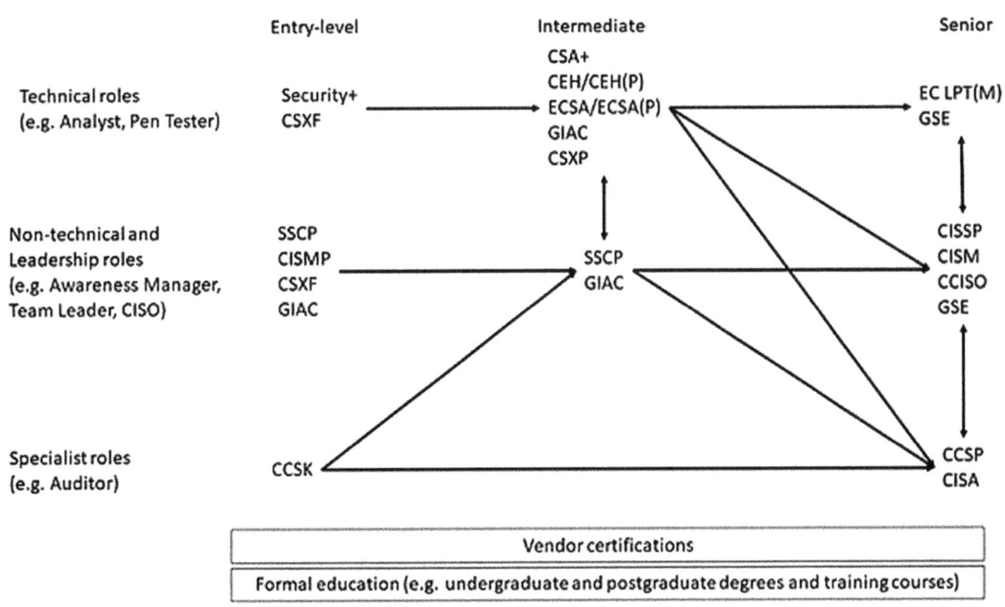

Figure 3. Relationship of education and certification
(after Davis, 2017)

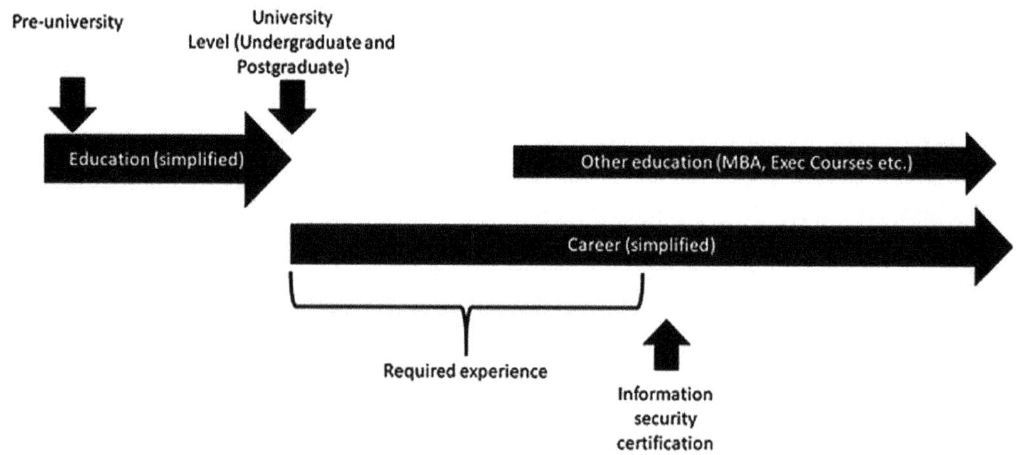

The figure highlights that for many individuals, certification comes after formal education and occurs during their career. Note that certifications may be taken in addition to other education qualifications and that, multiple certifications may be taken by an individual during their career. Individuals typically view certifications as a mechanism to achieve one or more of the following:

1. Develop a career
2. Get a new job
3. Get my bosses' job
4. Get a pay rise
5. Get a promotion
6. Keep the individual's current job
7. Prove professional knowledge and experience
8. Keep up with peers
9. Move into a new career
10. Earn CPE.

Note the list above is neither is in priority order nor will stay the same throughout an individual's career. However, the decision to obtain a certification will often be driven by one or more of the above; as will the reasoning behind the decision.

Certifications are often seen as a mechanism to advance an individual's career. The acquisition of a defined set of information security knowledge, coupled with an independent assessment of that knowledge is seen as a passport to success. In some cases, particular roles or jobs require the possession of a particular certification (for example Government roles), so gaining a certification allows the individual to enter that particular field. This places a heavy burden on the individual from two directions: concerns over actually obtaining the certification and concerns that failure may impair the individual's immediate and future prospects. It is worth noting that many individuals who decide to sit (or write) a certification examination may have not studied for a number of years, and so have to relearn the tools and techniques of effective studying and revision, as well as the actual education material related to the certification.

Certifications are also viewed as a mechanism to enter the information security industry. Due to the wide currency afforded certain certifications, many new entrants believe they must obtain the senior certification before they start in any information security role; they also do not realize that there are entry-level certifications, or courses of education that would be of more relevance.

ROLE OF CERTIFICATION: ORGANIZATIONAL

From an organizational perspective, a certification can indicate a number of things about an individual or an employee. First, possession indicates that an individual can pass an exam or a set of entry criteria, as discussed above. Second, it shows that an individual is prepared to spend time and effort, and in some cases, considerable sums of money, to gain knowledge and skills and develop themselves in their chosen field. Third, the possession of a certification may indicate a desire to either be seen as an expert in a field, or a desire to become such an expert; the certification is a spring-board to achieve that. Fourth, the individual possesses a set of knowledge as defined by the certification body and has ready access to that knowledge. Fifth, the certification possessed will indicate (to some extent) the level of knowledge and experience of the individual from entry-level to expert. Finally, the certification may also indicate the behavior the individual should demonstrate, and the organization can expect.

As well as these positive indicators, there are negative ones. Possession of a certification cannot tell an organization whether the individual is the right fit for the role, the organization and the team; the specific, detailed experience an individual has in the field; their delivery successes and failures; and whether the individual which actually listen to their new bosses and peers.

For organizations, certifications provide a useful standard or benchmark to evaluate candidates for roles, produce job descriptions and set levels of seniority. Thanks to the criteria for obtaining certifications, which are widely known and available, a certification can be used very quickly to determine both a candidate's experience and suitability for a post (but see "misuse and abuse below"); the possession (or not) can also be used as a sifting mechanism to select suitable candidates for interview and beyond.

Offering routes to certification can also be a powerful tool to retain and motivate staff. Many of the certifications require an investment in time and money to obtain and maintain, so having the financial and/or resource support of an employer is often welcomed. Tying promotion opportunities, pay rises and other recognition to gaining certifications or promoting individuals who gain a certification are typical approaches.

For an organization, employing certified individuals can be used to indicate that information security is a management concern and that the organization has committed to invest in expertise.

Professionalization and Certification

There is a debate within information security as to whether it is a profession and whether individuals who work in the field and who have gained certifications can call themselves "information security professionals". Certification bodies, with their entry requirements, membership obligations and codes of ethics believe they have an important role to play in professionalizing the industry and are, in fact, doing so.

To examine the debate on professionalization closely, a starting point is to reflect upon what makes a profession:

A profession is a disciplined group of individuals who adhere to ethical standards and who hold themselves out as, and are accepted by the public as possessing special knowledge and skills in a widely recognised body of learning derived from research, education and training at a high level, and who are prepared to apply this knowledge and exercise these skills in the interest of others. It is inherent in the definition of a profession that a code of ethics governs the activities of each profession. Such codes require behaviour and practice beyond the personal moral obligations of an individual. They define and demand high standards of behaviour in respect to the services provided to the public and in dealing with professional colleagues. Further, these codes are enforced by the profession and are acknowledged and accepted by the community. (Professions Australia, 2018)

And, from a similar source, what makes a professional:

A professional is a member of a profession. Professionals are governed by codes of ethics, and profess commitment to competence, integrity and morality, altruism, and the promotion of the public good within their expert domain. Professionals are accountable to those served and to society. (Professional Standards Councils, 2018)

These quotes, albeit lengthy, capture the overall requirements of a profession and a professional. In essence, we can reduce these quotes to the following characteristics, shown in Table 6.

Using these characteristics and reviewing the activities of the certification bodies discussed in this chapter, many (if not all) of the bodies, have met, or are striving to meet, all of those characteristics. Following on from this, because of the emphasis on codes of ethics and indeed, the expectations of both individuals within the information security industry and the people they work for, a very high percentage of individuals within the information security industry hold themselves to the characteristics listed in Table 6 as well.

However, despite meeting many of the characteristics mentioned above, many information security certifications are not regulated by formal education bodies or regulators. This results in the certifica-

Table 6. Characteristics of a profession and a professional

Profession	Professional
Specialized knowledge	Honest
Formal qualifications	Integrious
Best practice materials	Accountable
Research	Self-regulating
Accreditation	Credible
Supervision	Ethical
Code of ethics	Confidential

tions having no academic standing, as they are not mapped to national academic frameworks, such as England's Regulated Qualifications Framework (OfQual, 2015 and 2016) or regional frameworks, such as the European Qualifications Framework (EQF; CEDEFOP, 2008), nor can they be compared to recognized academic qualifications, such as undergraduate and postgraduate degrees. In the information security industry, the lack of inclusion in these educational frameworks does not limit the effectiveness and importance of information security certifications but this lack of inclusion does hinder widespread understanding outside of the industry and hinders acceptance of the certification bodies as representing a profession and certificate holders as professionals.

VALUE AND BENEFIT OF CERTIFICATION

As can be seen from the above, most (if not all) certifications require an individual (or their employer) to expend time, money and effort to both gain the certification and to then maintain it. Individuals wishing to obtain certifications can spend considerable sums, with costs of about GBP5,000 for face-to-face training, examination fees and supporting material not uncommon. Individuals also have to make time to study, prepare and then sit the examination, usually while carrying out their day job.

So, why make the investment? Individual professional certifications provide an indication of an individual's knowledge and/or skills measured by some form of independent assessment. They provide a method by which an individual can assess and demonstrate their progress, their level of knowledge and their level of skill – or, in other words, their competence, or a demonstrated ability to apply knowledge, skills and attitudes for achieving observable results (CEN 2014).

The benefit of holding a certification is both tangible and intangible. Tangible benefits include:

- **Better Remuneration:** For example, the Global Information Security Workforce Study (Frost and Sullivan, 2015) states that the holder of a CISSP can expect to receive a salary premium of 35% compared to non-CISSP holders for the same role
- **Better Opportunities:** Holders of certifications are more likely to be considered for roles at all levels and at the more senior levels, a certification is a prerequisite for selection. They may also be offered unadvertised roles as well, or the certification may allow them to pursue particular roles or careers
- **Better Networking:** Many of the organizations involved are membership organizations, so gaining the certification allows an individual to widen their circle of knowledgeable and helpful individuals
- **Better Access to Education:** Most (if not all) of the organizations mentioned in the chapter provide a range of member benefits, including continuing education, webcasts, tutorials, resources and events.

The intangible benefits include:

- **Greater Industry Recognition:** A number of the certifications discussed here are well known and respected globally and hence don't require explanation or justification

- **Greater Impact:** Possession of a certification places the individual above someone who doesn't possess a certification as there is an assumption of greater insight, knowledge, expertise and experience ("you know what you are doing") of the certified individual
- **Higher Prestige:** Because many of the certifications are perceived to be difficult to obtain (and many are in reality), possession of one or more certifications marks an individual out amongst peers
- **Greater Respect:** The individual gains a measure of respect because people know how difficult it is to get the certification; they respect the effort and determination of the individual
- **Better Moral Compass:** Because certifications usually require the individual to agree to code of ethics, the individual may be seen as more trustworthy, more altruistic and to have an ethical approach to the work they do.

The Cybersecurity Credentials Collaborative has published a presentation outlining the value of certification (Cybersecurity Credentials Collaborative, 2015b). This insider view lists the following value propositions for certification:

1. confidence in competency and quality of work
2. tool for hiring managers
3. contribute to career success
4. establishment of ethical bonds.

From an organizational viewpoint, the same source list these value propositions from an organizational perspective:

- Certification preparation leads to confidence. Well-trained IT professionals are more confident that the skills they possess are appropriate and useful for their responsibilities.
- Validation reliably attests to the level of knowledge. Certified employees can be relied on to perform at a higher level and have more domain knowledge than untrained employees.
- Execution is the performance of important business activities. Certified employees can be expected to perform assigned tasks more consistently, increasing reliability and overall organizational execution.

Despite the value of certification, many individuals find it difficult to decide which certification is best for them. Each of the certification bodies (naturally) touts the advantages and benefits associated with their certification(s); many magazines, training organizations and blogs have frequently updated "best/top/best-paying five/ten cybersecurity certifications/qualifications" articles; and if the individual has peers or friends in the industry, then their advice will often be tempered by the experience they have and the certifications they hold. Often, the best advice for an individual is to research the certifications thoroughly, take time to understand what they offer to the individual (at that time) and then, using all the facts gathered, decide.

MISUSE AND ABUSE

Certifications, because of the value and benefit they bring, along with professional recognition and even prestige, are highly prized. It doesn't take much thought to realize that the certifications can be misused and abused.

Obvious methods are to simply lie about the possession of certifications – adding particular certifications to an individual's CV for example – to gain an advantage in a job selection or increase the daily rate that can be charged. All the bodies are alert to this and expend considerable effort to stop such practices.

More subtle is to add terms such as "Master" or "Lead" to the title of the certification, implying greater knowledge, more experience or even a high passing grade. The terms are then used to justify higher fees, differentiate education opportunities and even offer examination guarantees. As discussed above, a number of these certifications only have one level and so these designations are both meaningless and misleading. However, for new entrants looking for education and guidance, these terms are taken at face value and may lead the new entrants to spend more time and money that is necessary to gain the education they want.

The use of digital badging for example can assist in reducing both types of misrepresentation, as can legal action. However, legal action can be slow and expensive and often means that these misrepresentations can continue until the legal process is exhausted. It should be stressed that these occurrences are few and far between, but they do exist, and individuals and organizations should be aware of these and the actions that are taken.

Perhaps the greatest misuse of certifications is what your author calls "shorthand". Shorthand encompasses the use of certifications to screen candidates and/or where a certification is added to a job description, regardless of the suitability of the certification to the job described. The former, screening candidates, makes the possession of one or more certifications the minimum requirement. Thus, regardless of expertise, experience, attitude or aptitude, suitable candidates may be rejected out of hand or stopped from applying for a particular role. This can reduce the pool of candidates dramatically and may actually not be beneficial to the hiring organization. Well known examples of the latter are where a certification requiring five or more years' experience is required for an entry-level or junior post requiring between none and two years' experience. The use of the certification drives away individuals who do not possess the certification (typically the right candidates) and also more experienced candidates who see the role as unsuitable (a step back perhaps) and who also infer that the hiring organization does not understand what it wants or what it is trying to accomplish. Unfortunately, many HR functions and recruitment consultancies are guilty of both of these types of shorthand, often because the individuals in those functions or consultancies do not understand the certifications in detail.

There is also the "groupthink" factor to address. If a security team is made up of individuals who all possess the same qualifications and/or certifications, then there is a possibility that the group will look at issues, problems, challenges and information security operations from one particular perspective. Whilst this may promote consistency and stability of approach, it may mean that certain approaches, creative thinking and activities are missed or downplayed, which may lower the overall security status of an organization and make it more vulnerable to an event or incident.

Finally, certification training is an attractive revenue opportunity. The certification bodies cannot necessarily meet the demand for courses (even moving online), so a "grey market" of unauthorized instructors and training organizations exist. These typically offer certification education at a discount compared to authorized providers, may use previous versions of education material and typically do not use authorized instructors. Grey market providers split the certification industry: one on hand, they are competition and offer a less than premium product and experience, perhaps tarnishing the certification's brand; on the other, they are often found in areas where no authorized providers exist, expend time and resource to advertise and attract individuals and provide a route to membership for individuals who cannot afford the authorized providers.

FUTURE TRENDS

In the near future, certification will continue to play a major role in the industry. With demand for individuals to work in information security and a documented global skills shortage (Center for Cyber Safety and Education 2017), certifications may actually become more important. The certification bodies will play an important role in the professionalization of information security, as they provide an objective measure of knowledge, sometimes skill, and a code of ethics and behavior to hold individuals to account.

Certification bodies are regularly enjoined to create new certifications in the field and examples being proposed certifications in fields such as the Internet of Things and Artificial Intelligence, alongside updating their current certifications. It is likely that new certifications will emerge, or current certifications will expand their coverage of these new technologies.

The rise of university education in cybersecurity at all levels can be seen as a challenge to certification, as more individuals enter the industry with formal qualifications. Entry-level certificates may lose their value and hence market share, whilst intermediate and senior level certifications will hold or increase their value, benefit and market share. Certification bodies will work hard to increase the value and benefits their certifications offer.

CONCLUSION

Certification and certification bodies have had and continue to have a significant impact on both individuals working in information security and on the information security industry itself. Certifications fulfil a number of roles for individuals and within the industry, and their importance shows no sign of diminishing in the near future.

Despite their differing genesis, philosophies and perspectives, information security certifications possess marked similarities, in terms of knowledge domains, experience and maintenance. Whilst the multiplicity and variety of information security certifications may be confusing to the uninitiated or outside observer, it reflects an industry that is growing and developing in real time. This multiplicity of certifications also reflects the range of roles, knowledge, skills and importance of information security in today's world and the varied approaches to protecting information.

Interestingly, given the scale and impact of these certifications, your author has seen very little academic research carried out into the various aspects of certification discussed here. As a final conclusion, your author would draw the readers' attention to this fact and encourage research into this topic.

REFERENCES

Australia, P. (2018). *What is a Profession?* Retrieved from http://www.professions.com.au/defineprofession.html

BCS. (2014). *Membership can make the difference.* Retrieved from https://www.bcs.org/upload/pdf/membership-difference.pdf

BCS. (2017). *BCS Foundation Certificate in Information Security Management Principles Syllabus Version 8.2 March 2017.* Retrieved from https://certifications.bcs.org/upload/pdf/infosec-ismp-syllabus.pdf

CEDEFOP. (2008). *European qualifications framework (EQF).* Retrieved from http://www.cedefop.europa.eu/en/events-and-projects/projects/european-qualifications-framework-eqf

CEN. (2014). *European e-Competence Framework 3.0, A common European Framework for ICT Professionals in all industry sectors.* CWA 16234:2014 Part 1.

Center for Cyber Safety and Education. (2017). *Global Information Security Workforce Study.* Retrieved from https://iamcybersafe.org/GISWS/

Cloud Security Alliance. (2011). *Certificate of Cloud Security Knowledge.* Retrieved from https://cloudsecurityalliance.org/education/ccsk/#_overview

Cloud Security Alliance. (2017a). *Security Guidance for Critical Areas of Focus in Cloud Computing v4.0.* Retrieved from https://cloudsecurityalliance.org/download/security-guidance-v4/

Cloud Security Alliance. (2017b). *Cloud Controls Matrix v3.0.1 (9-1-17 Update).* Retrieved from https://cloudsecurityalliance.org/download/cloud-controls-matrix-v3-0-1/

Collins. (2018). *Free Online Dictionary.* Retrieved from https://www.collinsdictionary.com/dictionary/english/certification

CompTIA. (2016). *CompTIA Security+ Certification Exam Objectives EXAM NUMBER: SY0-401.* Retrieved from https://certification.comptia.org/docs/default-source/exam-objectives/comptia-security-sy0-401.pdf

CompTIA. (2018). *IT Certification Roadmap.* Retrieved from https://certification.comptia.org/docs/default-source/downloadablefiles/it-certification-roadmap.pdf

CompTIA. (n.d.). *Continuing Education (CE) Activities Chart.* Retrieved from https://certification.comptia.org/docs/default-source/downloadablefiles/comptia-continuing-education-activity-chart.pdf

Council, E. C. (2017). *CEH Candidate Handbook v2.2.* Retrieved from https://cert.eccouncil.org/images/doc/CEH-Handbook-v2.2.pdf

Council, E. C. (2018a). *What are the five CCISO Domains?* Retrieved https://ciso.eccouncil.org/cciso-certification/ciso-faq/#four

Council, E. C. (2018b). *CEH Exam Blueprint v2.0*. Retrieved from https://cert.eccouncil.org/images/doc/CEH-Exam-Blueprint-v2.0.pdf

CREST. (2016). *Professional Qualifications*. Retrieved from http://www.crest-approved.org/examinations/index.html

CREST. (2017). *CREST Examinations*. Retrieved from https://www.crest-approved.org/wp-content/uploads/Exams-Overview.pdf

Cyber, S. N. (2018). *35 Cybersecurity Jobs*. Retrieved from https://www.cybersn.com/products/35-job-categories.html

Cybersecurity Credentials Collaborative. (2015a). *A Unified Principles of Professional Ethics in Cyber Security*. Retrieved from http://www.cybersecuritycc.org/

Cybersecurity Credentials Collaborative. (2015b). *Why certification* matters. Retrieved from http://www.cybersecuritycc.org/C3_Value_of_IT_Certification_2015.pdf

Davis, Adrian (2017). Presentation given to University of Manchester students

ENISA. (2009). *Cloud Computing Risk Assessment*. Retrieved from https://www.enisa.europa.eu/publications/cloud-computing-risk-assessment

Frost and Sullivan. (2015). *The 2015 (ISC)² Global Information Security Workforce Study*. Retrieved from https://iamcybersafe.org/wp-content/uploads/2017/01/FrostSullivan-ISC%C2%B2-Global-Information-Security-Workforce-Study-2015.pdf

GIAC. (2016). *GIAC certificate brochure*. Retrieved from https://www.giac.org/media/about/cert-brochure.pdf

GIAC. (2018). *GIAC Certification Renewal: Guidelines and Requirements*. Retrieved from https://www.giac.org/certifications/renewal

IISP (Institute of Information Security Professionals). (2018a). *Membership Levels*. Retrieved from https://www.iisp.org/iisp/Membership/Individuals/Membership_Levels/iispv2/Membership/Membership_Levels2.aspx

IISP (Institute of Information Security Professionals) (2018b). *Skills framework, version 2.2, IISP, March 2018*. IISP.

Infosec Institute. (2018). *CIA Triad*. Retrieved from https://resources.infosecinstitute.com/cia-triad/#gref

ISACA. (2012). *COBIT 5*. Retrieved from http://www.isaca.org/cobit/pages/default.aspx

ISACA. (2015). *CSX Practitioner Certification*. Retrieved from https://cybersecurity.isaca.org/csx-certifications/csx-practitioner-certification#0-about-this-certification

ISACA. (2017). *Job Practice Areas 2017* Retrieved from http://www.isaca.org/Certification/CISM-Certified-Information-Security-Manager/Job-Practice-Areas/Pages/default.aspx

ISACA. (2017). *ISACA Annual report*. Retrieved from http://www.isaca.org/About-ISACA/annual-report/Pages/default.aspx

ISACA. (2018a). *How to Report and Earn CPE*. Retrieved from http://www.isaca.org/Certification/Additional-Resources/Pages/How-to-Earn-CPE.aspx

ISACA. (2018b). *The CISA Certification*. Retrieved from http://www.isaca.org/Certification/CISA-Certified-Information-Systems-Auditor/Documents/ISACA_CISA_40th_Anniversary_Infographic_0618.pdf

(ISC)². (2015). *CCSP Certification Exam Outline, effective date April 2015*. Retrieved from https://www.isc2.org/-/media/ISC2/Certifications/Exam-Outlines/CCSP-Exam-Outline.ashx

(ISC)². (2017). *2017 Annual report*. Retrieved from https://www.isc2.org/-/media/ISC2/Data-Privacy-and-Security-Briefings/2018/2017AnnualReport.ashx

(ISC)². (2018). *CISSP Certification Exam Outline, effective date April 2018*. Retrieved from https://www.isc2.org/-/media/ISC2/Certifications/CISSP/CISSP-Exam-Outline-121417--Final.ashx

(ISC)². (2018). *History of (ISC)²*. Retrieved from https://www.isc2.org/About

ISO. (2017). *ISO/IEC 27021:2017 Information technology -- Security techniques -- Competence requirements for information security management systems professionals*. Retrieved from https://www.iso.org/standard/61003.html

NCSC. (2016). *About the certified professional scheme*. Retrieved from https://www.ncsc.gov.uk/articles/about-certified-professional-scheme

Ofqual (2015). *Regulated Qualifications Framework: a postcard*. Retrieved from https://www.gov.uk/government/publications/regulated-qualifications-framework-a-postcard

Ofqual (2016). *Awarding organisations: understanding our regulatory requirements*. Retrieved from https://www.gov.uk/guidance/awarding-organisations-understanding-our-regulatory-requirements

Parker, D. B. (1998). *Fighting Computer Crime*. New York, NY: John Wiley & Sons.

Professional Standards Councils. (2018). *What is a Profession?* Retrieved from https://www.psc.gov.au/what-is-a-profession

SANS. (2018). *Information Security Training Winter/Spring 2018 Course Catalogue*. Retrieved from https://www.sans.org/media/security-training/course-catalog-2018.pdf

Security, O. (2018a). *Offensive Security Certified Professional*. Retrieved from https://www.offensive-security.com/information-security-certifications/oscp-offensive-security-certified-professional/

Security, O. (2018b). *Penetration Testing with Kali Linux*. Retrieved from https://www.offensive-security.com/documentation/penetration-testing-with-kali.pdf

Wikipedia. (2018). *List of computer security certifications*. Retrieved from https://en.wikipedia.org/wiki/List_of_computer_security_certifications

ENDNOTE

1 The term "information security" is used throughout the text, rather than "cybersecurity", as many certifications in this space are referred to as "information security certifications".

Compilation of References

$(ISC)^2$. (2015). *CCSP Certification Exam Outline, effective date April 2015*. Retrieved from https://www.isc2.org/-/media/ISC2/Certifications/Exam-Outlines/CCSP-Exam-Outline.ashx

$(ISC)^2$. (2017). *2017 Annual report*. Retrieved from https://www.isc2.org/-/media/ISC2/Data-Privacy-and-Security-Briefings/2018/2017AnnualReport.ashx

$(ISC)^2$. (2018). *CISSP Certification Exam Outline, effective date April 2018*. Retrieved from https://www.isc2.org/-/media/ISC2/Certifications/CISSP/CISSP-Exam-Outline-121417--Final.ashx

$(ISC)^2$. (2018). *History of* $(ISC)^2$. Retrieved from https://www.isc2.org/About

Abawajy, J. (2014). User preference of cyber security awareness delivery methods. *Behaviour & Information Technology*, *33*(3), 237–248. doi:10.1080/0144929X.2012.708787

ACM, IEEE, AIS, IFIP. (2017). Curriculum Guidelines for Post-Secondary Degree Programs in Cybersecurity. ACM.

ACM. (2017). *Cybersecurity Curricula 2017: Curriculum Guidelines for Post-Secondary Degree Programs in Cybersecurity. A Report in the Computing Curricula Series Joint Task Force on Cybersecurity Education*. Available at https://www.acm.org/binaries/content/assets/education/curricula-recommendations/csec2017.pdf

Alarifi, A., Zarour, M., Alomar, N., Alkshaikh, Z., & Alsaleh, M. (2016). SECDEP: Software Engineering curricula development and evaluation process using SWEBOK. *Information and Software Technology*, *74*, 114–126. doi:10.1016/j.infsof.2016.01.013

AlHogail, A. (2015). Cultivating and Assessing an Organizational Information Security Culture: An Empirical Study. *International Journal of Security and Its Applications*, *9*(7), 163–178. doi:10.14257/ijsia.2015.9.7.15

AlHogail, A. (2015). Design and validation of information security culture framework. *Computers in Human Behavior*, *49*, 567–575. doi:10.1016/j.chb.2015.03.054

Alkhurayyif, Y. &. (2017). Evaluating Readability as a Factor in Information Security Policies. *International Journal of Trend in Research and Development*, 54-64.

All European Academics (ALLEA). (2017). *The European Code of Conduct for Research Integrity.* Retrieved from https://ec.europa.eu/research/participants/data/ref/h2020/other/hi/h2020-ethics_code-of-conduct_en.pdf

Alnatheer, M. (2012). Understanding and Measuring Information Security Culture in Developing Countries: Case of Saudi Arabia. In *Proceedings of the Pacific Asia Conference on Information Systems (PACIS)*. Ho Chi Minh City, Vietnam: Association of Information Systems.

Alvarez, B. (2011). Flipping the classroom: Homework in class, lessons at home. Education Digest: Essential Readings Condensed For Quick Review, 77(8), 18 – 21.

Anderson, L. W. (2002). *Revising Bloom's taxonomy.* Ohio State University.

Anderson, R. H. (1999). *Research and Development Initiatives Focused on Preventing, Detecting, and Responding to Insider Misuse of Critical Defense Information Systems (No. RAND-CF-151-OSD).* Rand Corp.

Arce, I., Clark-Fisher, K., Daswani, N., DelGrosso, J., Dhillon, D., Kern, C., … West, J. (2015). *Avoiding the top 10 software security design flaws.* Retrieved from https://www.computer.org/cms/CYBSI/docs/Top-10-Flaws.pdf

Ashenden, D., & Sasse, A. (2013). CISOs and organizational culture: Their own worst enemy? *Computers & Security*, *39*, 396–405. doi:10.1016/j.cose.2013.09.004

Assante, M. J., & Lee, R. M. (2015). *The Industrial Control System Cyber Kill Chain*. Retrieved from SANS Institute InfoSec Reading Room: https://www.sans.org/reading-room/whitepapers/ICS/industrial-control-system-cyber-kill-chain-36297

Association for Computing Machinery (ACM) and IEEE Computer Society. (2013). *Computer Science Curricula 2013: Curriculum Guidelines for Undergraduate Degree Programs in Computer Science.* New York: ACM.

Association for Computing Machinery (ACM) and IEEE Computer Society. (2017). *Information Technology Curricula 2017: Curriculum Guidelines for Baccalaureate Degree Programs in Information Technology*. New York: ACM.

Association for Computing Machinery (ACM). (n.d.). *ACM code of ethics and professional conduct.* Retrieved from www.acm.org/about/code-of-ethics

Audit Commission. (2001). yourbusiness@risk – An Update on IT Abuse 2001. Audit Commission Publications.

Aurigemma, S., & Panko, R. (2012). January. A composite framework for behavioral compliance with information security policies. In *45th Hawaii International Conference on System Science (HICSS)* (pp. 3248-3257). IEEE.

Australia, P. (2018). *What is a Profession?* Retrieved from http://www.professions.com.au/defineprofession.html

Azaria, A., Richardson, A., Kraus, S., & Subrahmanian, V. S. (2014). Behavioral analysis of insider threat: A survey and bootstrapped prediction in imbalanced data. *IEEE Transactions on Computational Social Systems*, *1*(2), 135–155. doi:10.1109/TCSS.2014.2377811

Babie, E. (2004). *The practice of social research* (10th ed.). Belmont, CA: Thomson Wadsworth.

Backhouse, J., & Dhillon, G. (1996). Structures of responsibility and security of information systems. *European Journal of Information Systems*, *5*(1), 2–9. doi:10.1057/ejis.1996.7

Baracaldo, N., & Joshi, J. (2012). A trust-and-risk aware RBAC framework: tackling insider threat. In *Proceedings of the 17th ACM symposium on Access Control Models and Technologies* (pp. 167-176). ACM. 10.1145/2295136.2295168

Barnett, R. (1992). *Improving Higher Education: Total Quality Care*. Bristol, PA: OU Press.

Barth, S., & Jong, M. D. (2017). The privacy paradox – Investigating discrepancies between expressed privacy concerns and actual online behavior – A systematic literature review. *Telematics and Informatics*, *34*(7), 1038–1058. doi:10.1016/j.tele.2017.04.013

BCS. (2014). *Membership can make the difference*. Retrieved from https://www.bcs.org/upload/pdf/membership-difference.pdf

BCS. (2017). *BCS Foundation Certificate in Information Security Management Principles Syllabus Version 8.2 March 2017*. Retrieved from https://certifications.bcs.org/upload/pdf/infosec-ismp-syllabus.pdf

Bell, D. E., & LaPadula, L. J. (1973). Secure Computer Systems: Mathematical Foundations. In Secure Computer Systems: Mathematical Foundations (MTR–2547, Vol. 1). The MITRE Corporation. (ESD–TR–73–278–I)

Bell, D. E., & LaPadula, L. J. (1976). Secure Computer System: Unified Exposition and Multics Interpretation. MTR–2997. The MITRE Corporation. (ESD–TR–75–306). doi:10.21236/ADA023588

Beris, O., Beautement, A., & Sasse, M. A. (2015). Employee rule breakers, excuse makers and security champions: Mapping the risk perceptions and emotions that drive security behaviors. *NSPW '15: Proceedings of the 2015 New Security Paradigms Workshop*, 73-84.

Berry, M. L., & Houston, J. P. (1993). *Psychology at work*. Brown and Benchmark Publishers.

Biba, K. J. (1975). *Integrity Considerations for Secure Computer Systems*. The MITRE Corporation.

BigBlueButton. (2018, June). Retrieved from https://bigbluebutton.org/

Biggs, J. (1996). Assessment learning quality: Reconciling institutional, staff and educational demands. *Assessment & Evaluation in Higher Education*, *12*(1), 5–15. doi:10.1080/0260293960210101

Biggs, J. (1996). Enhancing teaching through constructive alignment. *Higher Education*, *33*(3), 347–364. doi:10.1007/BF00138871

Bishop, M., & Gates, C. (2008). Defining the insider threat. In *Proceedings of the 4th annual workshop on Cyber security and information intelligence research: developing strategies to meet the cyber security and information intelligence challenges ahead* (p. 15). ACM.

Black, P., & Wiliam, D. (1999). *Assessment for Learning: Beyond the Black Box. Cambridge.* Assessment Reform Group, University of Cambridge. Available at http://www.assessment-reform-group.org.uk/AssessInsides.pdf

Black, P. (1993). Formative and summative assessment by teachers. *Studies in Science Education, 21*(1), 49–97. doi:10.1080/03057269308560014

Black, P., & Wiliam, D. (1998). Assessment and classroom learning. *Assessment in Education: Principles, Policy & Practice*, *5*(1), 7–74. doi:10.1080/0969595980050102

Blackwell, C. (2009). A security architecture to protect against the insider threat from damage, fraud and theft. In *Proceedings of the 5th Annual Workshop on Cyber Security and Information Intelligence Research: Cyber Security and Information Intelligence Challenges and Strategies* (p. 45). ACM. 10.1145/1558607.1558659

Bloom, B. S. (1956). *Taxonomy of educational objectives*. New York: Longmans, Green.

Borg, I., & Mastrangelo, P. M. (2008). *Employee surveys, tools and practical applications. Employee surveys in management: theories, tools and practical applications*. Cambridge, MA: Hogrefe.

Boud, D., Cohen, R., & Sampson, J. (1988). Peer Learning and Assessment. *Assessment & Evaluation in Higher Education*, *24*(4), 413–426. doi:10.1080/0260293990240405

Boud, D., & Feletti, G. (1997). *The challenges of problem based learning*. London: Kogan Page.

Boud, D., & Middleton, H. (2003). Learning from others at work: Communities of practice and informal learning. *Journal of Workplace Learning*, *15*(5), 194–202. doi:10.1108/13665620310483895

Bourque, P., & Fairley, R. E. (2014). *Guide to the Software Engineering Body of Knowledge Version 3.0*. Piscataway, NJ: IEEE.

Bowen, P., Hash, J., & Wilson, M. (2006). *NIST Special Publication 800-100: Information Security Handbook: A Guide for Managers*. Retrieved July 9, 2018 from https://nvlpubs.nist.gov/nistpubs/Legacy/SP/nistspecialpublication800-100.pdf

Brewer, D. F. C., & Nash, M. J. (1989) The Chinese Wall Security Policy. *Proceedings of IEEE Symposium on Security and Privacy.*

Brown, G., Bull, J., & Pendelbury, M. (1997). *Assessing Student Learning in Higher Education*. London: Routledge.

Burley, D. L., & Lewis, A. H. Jr. (2018). CSEC2017 and Boeing: Linking Curricular Guidance to Professional Practice. *IEEE Computer*. (Manuscript submitted for publication)

Bursztein, E., Benko, B., Margolis, D., Pietraszek, T., Archer, A., Aquino, A., ... Savage, S. (2014). Handcrafted Fraud and Extortion: Manual Account Hijacking in the Wild. *Proceedings of the 2014 Conference on Internet Measurement Conference (IMC'14)*, 347-358. 10.1145/2663716.2663749

Byars, L. L., & Rue, L. W. (1997). *Human resource management* (5th ed.). Boston: McGraw-Hill.

Cappelli, D., Moore, A., Trzeciak, R., & Shimeall, T. J. (2009). *Common sense guide to prevention and detection of insider threats 3rd edition–version 3.1*. Published by CERT, Software Engineering Institute, Carnegie Mellon University. Retrieved from http://www. cert. org

CEDEFOP. (2008). *European qualifications framework (EQF)*. Retrieved from http://www.cedefop.europa.eu/en/events-and-projects/projects/european-qualifications-framework-eqf

CEN. (2014). *European e-Competence Framework 3.0, A common European Framework for ICT Professionals in all industry sectors*. CWA 16234:2014 Part 1.

Center for Cyber Safety and Education. (2017). *Global Information Security Workforce Study*. Retrieved from https://iamcybersafe.org/GISWS/

Chapman, S., & MacKenzie, R. (2010). The global research neglect of unassisted smoking cessation: Causes and consequences. *PLoS Medicine*, *7*(2), e1000216.

Cheng, L., Li, Y., Li, W., Holm, E., & Zhai, Q. (2013). Understanding the violation of is security policy in organization: An integrated model based on social control and deterrence theory. *Computers & Security*, *39*, 447–459. doi:10.1016/j.cose.2013.09.009

Chen, X., Wu, D., Chen, L., & Teng, J. (2018). Sanction severity and employees' information security policy compliance: Investigating mediating, moderating, and control variables. *Information & Management*, *55*(8), 1049–1060. doi:10.1016/j.im.2018.05.011

Chen, Y., Ramamurthy, K., & Wen, K. (2013). Organizations' information security policy compliance: Stick or carrot approach? *Journal of Management Information Systems*, *29*(3), 157–188. doi:10.2753/MIS0742-1222290305

Chen, Y., Ramamurthy, K., & Wen, K. (2015). Impacts of comprehensive information security programs on information security culture. *Journal of Computer Information Systems*, *55*(3), 11–19. doi:10.1080/08874417.2015.11645767

Chinchani, R., Iyer, A., Ngo, H. Q., & Upadhyaya, S. (2005). Towards a theory of insider threat assessment. In *Proceedings. International Conference on Dependable Systems and Networks, 2005 (DSN 2005)* (pp. 108-117). IEEE. 10.1109/DSN.2005.94

Choo, K. K. R. (2011). *Cyber threat landscape faced by financial and insurance industry. Trends & issues in crime and criminal justice No. 408*. Canberra: Australian Institute of Criminology.

Christey, S. (2011). *2011 CWE/SANS top 25 most dangerous software errors*. Retrieved from http://cwe.mitre.org/top25/

CIS. (n.d.). *CIS controls frequently asked questions (FAQ)*. Retrieved from https://www.cisecurity.org/controls/cis-controls-faq/

Clark, D. D., & Wilson, D. R. (1987). A comparison of Commercial and Military Computer Security Policies. *Proceedings of the 1987 IEEE Symposium on Research in Security and Privacy,* 184-193. 10.1109/SP.1987.10001

Claycomb, W. R., & Nicoll, A. (2012). Insider threats to cloud computing: Directions for new research challenges. In *IEEE 36th Annual Computer Software and Applications Conference (COMPSAC)* (pp. 387-394). IEEE.

Cloud Security Alliance. (2011). *Certificate of Cloud Security Knowledge*. Retrieved from https://cloudsecurityalliance.org/education/ccsk/#_overview

Cloud Security Alliance. (2017a). *Security Guidance for Critical Areas of Focus in Cloud Computing v4.0*. Retrieved from https://cloudsecurityalliance.org/download/security-guidance-v4/

Cloud Security Alliance. (2017b). *Cloud Controls Matrix v3.0.1 (9-1-17 Update)*. Retrieved from https://cloudsecurityalliance.org/download/cloud-controls-matrix-v3-0-1/

Cohen, P. A. (1981). Student ratings of institution and student achievement: A meta-analysis of multisection validity studies. *Review of Educational Research, 51*(3), 281–309. doi:10.3102/00346543051003281

Cole, E. (2015). *Insider threats and the need for fast and directed response*. SANS Institute InfoSec Reading Room, Tech. Rep.

Collins. (2018). *Free Online Dictionary*. Retrieved from https://www.collinsdictionary.com/dictionary/english/certification

Colwill, C. (2009). Human factors in information security: The insider threat–Who can you trust these days? *Information Security Technical Report, 14*(4), 186–196. doi:10.1016/j.istr.2010.04.004

Committee for Computing Education in Community Colleges. (2000). *Bloom's revised taxonomy*. Retrieved from http://ccecc.acm.org/assessment/blooms

CompTIA. (2016). *CompTIA Security+ Certification Exam Objectives EXAM NUMBER: SY0-401*. Retrieved from https://certification.comptia.org/docs/default-source/exam-objectives/comptia-security-sy0-401.pdf

CompTIA. (2018). *IT Certification Roadmap*. Retrieved from https://certification.comptia.org/docs/default-source/downloadablefiles/it-certification-roadmap.pdf

CompTIA. (n.d.). *Continuing Education (CE) Activities Chart*. Retrieved from https://certification.comptia.org/docs/default-source/downloadablefiles/comptia-continuing-education-activity-chart.pdf

Cone, B.D., Irvine, C.E., Thompson, M.F., & Nguyen, T.D. (2007). A video game for cyber security training and awareness. *Computers & Security, 26*(1), 63-72.

Conklin, W. A., & Bishop, M. (2018). Contrasting the CSEC 2017 and the CAE designation requirements. In *Proceedings of the 51st Hawaii International Conference on System Sciences* (pp 1–7). Manoa, HI: ScholarSpace. Retrieved from https://scholarspace.manoa.hawaii.edu/handle/10125/50194

Correa, D. (2016). 82% of global IT pros admit to a shortage of cyber-security skills. *SC Magazine*. Retrieved from http://www.scmagazineuk.com/82-of-global-it-pros-admit-to-a-shortage-of-cyber-security-skills/article/512830

Council, E. C. (2017). *CEH Candidate Handbook v2.2*. Retrieved from https://cert.eccouncil.org/images/doc/CEH-Handbook-v2.2.pdf

Council, E. C. (2018a). *What are the five CCISO Domains?* Retrieved https://ciso.eccouncil.org/cciso-certification/ciso-faq/#four

Council, E. C. (2018b). *CEH Exam Blueprint v2.0*. Retrieved from https://cert.eccouncil.org/images/doc/CEH-Exam-Blueprint-v2.0.pdf

Covill, A. (2011). College students' perceptions of the traditional lecture method. *College Student Journal*, *45*(1), 92–101.

Cresswell, J. W. (2014). *Research design – Qualitative, quantitative, and mixed methods approaches* (4th ed.). Los Angeles, CA: SAGE Publications.

CREST. (2016). *Professional Qualifications*. Retrieved from http://www.crest-approved.org/examinations/index.html

CREST. (2017). *CREST Examinations*. Retrieved from https://www.crest-approved.org/wp-content/uploads/Exams-Overview.pdf

Cyber, S. N. (2018). *35 Cybersecurity Jobs*. Retrieved from https://www.cybersn.com/products/35-job-categories.html

Cybersecurity Credentials Collaborative. (2015a). *A Unified Principles of Professional Ethics in Cyber Security*. Retrieved from http://www.cybersecuritycc.org/

Cybersecurity Credentials Collaborative. (2015b). *Why certification* matters. Retrieved from http://www.cybersecuritycc.org/C3_Value_of_IT_Certification_2015.pdf

D'Arcy, J., Hovav, A., & Galletta, D. (2009). User awareness of security countermeasures and its impact on information systems misuse: A Deterrence Approach. *Information Systems Research*, *20*(1), 79–98. doi:10.1287/isre.1070.0160

Da Veiga, A. (2016b). A cybersecurity culture research philosophy and approach to develop a valid and reliable measuring instrument. In *Proceedings of 2016 Science and Information Computing Conference* (SAI2016) (pp. 1006-1115), London: IEEE. 10.1109/SAI.2016.7556102

Da Veiga, A. (2016a). Comparing the information security culture of employees who had read the information security policy and those who had not: Illustrated through an empirical study *Information &. Computers & Security*, *22*(24), 139–155. doi:10.1108/ICS-12-2015-0048

Da Veiga, A. (2017). Ethical and privacy considerations for research. In N. Martins, E. Martins, & R. Viljoen (Eds.), *Organizational Diagnosis: A guide for practitioners* (pp. 273–298). Randburg, South Africa: Knowledge Resources.

Da Veiga, A., & Eloff, J. H. P. (2010). A framework and assessment instrument for information security culture. *Computers & Security*, *29*(2), 196–207. doi:10.1016/j.cose.2009.09.002

Da Veiga, A., & Martins, N. (2015a). Improving the information security culture through monitoring and implementation actions illustrated through a case study. *Computers & Security*, *49*, 162–176. doi:10.1016/j.cose.2014.12.006

Da Veiga, A., & Martins, N. (2015b). Information security culture and information protection culture: A validated assessment instrument. *Computer Law & Security Review*, *31*(2), 243–256. doi:10.1016/j.clsr.2015.01.005

Da Veiga, A., & Martins, N. (2017). Defining and identifying dominant information security cultures and subcultures. *Computers & Security*, *70*, 72–94. doi:10.1016/j.cose.2017.05.002

Davis, Adrian (2017). Presentation given to University of Manchester students

Day, J. (2017). *$2.5 Million Settlement Reached as HIPAA Crackdown Continues on Unsecured Portable Devices*. Retrieved from www.jdsupra.com/legalnews/2-5-million-settlement-reached-as-hipaa-64406/

DCMS. (2018). Cyber Security Breaches Survey 2018. Main report. Department for Digital, Culture, Media & Sport.

Dhillon, G. (2008). Organizational competence for harnessing IT: A case study. *Information & Management*, *45*(5), 297–303. doi:10.1016/j.im.2008.01.008

Dhillon, G., & Backhouse, J. (2000). Technical opinion: Information system security management in the new millennium. *Communications of the ACM*, *43*(7), 125–128. doi:10.1145/341852.341877

Dhillon, G., & Backhouse, J. (2001). Current directions in IS security research: Towards socio-organizational perspectives. *Information Systems Journal*, *11*(2), 127–153. doi:10.1046/j.1365-2575.2001.00099.x

Dhillon, G., & Kolkowska, E. (2011). Can a cloud be really secure? A Socratic dialogue. In *Computers, privacy and data protection: an element of choice* (pp. 345–360). Dordrecht: Springer. doi:10.1007/978-94-007-0641-5_16

Disability Discrimination Act (1995) with Amendments. (2000). Available at http://www.legislation.hmso.gov.uk/acts/acts1995/Ukpga_19950050_en_1.htm

DLA PIPER. (2018). *Data protection laws of the world*. Retrieved from https://www.dlapiperdataprotection.com/index.html

DoD. (1985). *DoD Trusted Computer Security Evaluation Criteria (DoD 5200.28-STD)*. US Department of Defense Computer Security Center.

Dojkovski, S., Lichtenstein, S., & Watten, M. J. (2010). Enabling information security culture: Influences and challenges for Australian SMEs. *Proceedings of the Australasian Conference on Information Systems, (ACIS).*

DTI. (2006). *Information security breaches survey – technical report.* London, UK: Department of Trade and Industry.

Eggenschwiler, J., Agrafiotis, I., & Nurse, J. R. (2016). Insider threat response and recovery strategies in financial services firms. *Computer Fraud & Security*, *2016*(11), 12–19. doi:10.1016/S1361-3723(16)30091-4

ENISA. (2009). *Cloud Computing Risk Assessment.* Retrieved from https://www.enisa.europa.eu/publications/cloud-computing-risk-assessment

ENISA. (2018). *Cyber Security Culture In Organisations.* Retrieved from ENISA: https://www.enisa.europa.eu/publications/cyber-security-culture-in-organisations/at_download/fullReport

EU. (n.d.a). *European Commission: 2018 reform of EU data protection rules.* Retrieved from https://ec.europa.eu/commission/priorities/justice-and-fundamental-rights/data-protection/2018-reform-eu-data-protection-rules_en, Accessed July 11, 2018.

EU. (n.d.b). *European Commission: A new era for data protection in the EU: What changes after May 2018?* Retrieved from https://ec.europa.eu/commission/sites/beta-political/files/data-protection-factsheet-changes_en.pdf

European Commission and High Representative of the European Union for Foreign Affairs and Security Policy. (2013). *Cybersecurity Strategy of the European Union: An Open, Safe and Secure Cyberspace.* JOIN(2013) 1 final.

European Cyber Security Organisation (ECSO). (2018). *Position Paper: Gaps in European Cyber Education and Professional Training.* ECSO.

European Union Agency for Law Enforcement Cooperation (Europol). (2017). *Internet organised crime threat assessment (IOCTA) 2017.* Retrieved from https://www.europol.europa.eu/activities-services/main-reports

European Union Agency for Network and Information Security (ENISA). (2017). *Cyber security culture in organizations.* Retrieved from doi:10.2824/10543

Evans, T. (2014). $1.44M HIPAA award upheld after Walgreen pharmacist shared patient data. *Indianapolis Star.* Retrieved from www.indystar.com/story/news/2014/11/14/m-award-upheld-walgreen-pharmacist-shared-patient-data/19035783/

EY. (2017). *Cybersecurity regained: preparing to face cyber attacks. 20th Global Information Security Survey 2017–18. EYG no. 06574-173Gbl.* EYGM Limited.

EY. (2018). *Is cybersecurity about more than protection? EY Global Information Security Survey 2018-19. EYG no. 011483-18Gbl.* EYGM Limited.

Fairley, R. E., Bourque, P., & Keppler, J. (2014). The impact of SWEBOK Version 3 on software engineering education and training. In *Proceedings of the IEEE 27th Conference on Software Engineering Education and Training* (pp. 192–200). Klagenfurt, Austria: IEEE. 10.1109/CSEET.2014.6816804

FCC. (2017). *Children's Internet Protection Act: CIPA*. Retrieved from https://www.fcc.gov/consumers/guides/childrens-internet-protection-act

Fee, S. B., & Holland-Minkley, A. M. (2010). Teaching computer science through problems, not solutions. *Computer Science Education*, *20*(2), 129–144. doi:10.1080/08993408.2010.486271

FISMA. (2018). Retrieved from https://csrc.nist.gov/Projects/Risk-Management/Detailed-Overview

Fleming, N. D. (2006). *Teaching and learning styles: VARK strategies* (2nd ed.). Christchurch, New Zealand: Neil D Fleming.

Flowerday, S., & Von Solms, R. (2006). Trust an element of information security. In *Proceedings of Security and Privacy in Dynamic Environments (IFIP/SEC2005)* (pp. 87–98). Boston: Kluwer Academic Publishers. doi:10.1007/0-387-33406-8_8

Flynn, L., Huth, C., Trzeciak, R., Buttles, P., & Nations, A. (2013). *Best Practices Against Insider Threats in All Nations. Technical Note CMU/SEI-2013-TN-023*. Software Engineering Institute.

Franqueira, V. N., van Cleeff, A., van Eck, P., & Wieringa, R. (2010). External insider threat: A real security challenge in enterprise value webs. In *International Conference on Availability, Reliability, and Security 2010 (ARES'10)* (pp. 446-453). IEEE. 10.1109/ARES.2010.40

Frost & Sullivan. (2015). *The 2015 (ISC)² Global Information Security Workforce Study*. Retrieved from https://iamcybersafe.org/wp-content/uploads/2017/01/FrostSullivan-ISC²-Global-Information-Security-Workforce-Study-2015.pdf

Frost and Sullivan. (2015). *The 2015 (ISC)² Global Information Security Workforce Study*. Retrieved from https://iamcybersafe.org/wp-content/uploads/2017/01/FrostSullivan-ISC%C2%B2-Global-Information-Security-Workforce-Study-2015.pdf

FTC. (2018a). *Financial institutions and customer information: Complying with the safeguards rule*. Retrieved from https://www.ftc.gov/tips-advice/business-center/guidance/financial-institutions-customer-information-complying

FTC. (2018b). *Federal Trade Commission: children's online privacy protection rule: a six-step compliance plan for your business*. Retrieved from https://www.ftc.gov/tips-advice/business-center/guidance/childrens-online-privacy-protection-rule-six-step-compliance

Furnell, S., K, M., Piper, F., &Ensor, C. (2018). A National Certification Programme for Academic Degrees in Cyber Security. In *Proceedings of the 11th IFIP WG 11.8 World Conference on Information Security Education* (pp. 133–146). Poznan, Poland: IFIP. 10.1007/978-3-319-99734-6_11

Furnell, S., & Clarke, N. (2005). Organisational security culture: Embedding security awareness, education and training. *Proceedings of the 4th World Conference on Information Security Education*, 67-74.

Furnell, S., & Moore, L. (2014). Security literacy: The missing link in today's online society? *Computer Fraud & Security*, *2014*(May), 12–18. doi:10.1016/S1361-3723(14)70491-9

Furnell, S., & Thomson, K. (2009). From culture to disobedience: Recognising the varying user acceptance of IT security. *Computer Fraud & Security*, *2009*(February), 5–10. doi:10.1016/S1361-3723(09)70019-3

Gabriel, T., & Furnell, S. (2011). Selecting Security Champions. *Computer Fraud & Security*, *2011*(August), 8–12. doi:10.1016/S1361-3723(11)70082-3

Garet, M. S., Porter, A. C., Desimone, L., Birman, B. F., & Yoon, K. S. (2001). What Makes Professional Development Effective? Results from a National Sample of Teachers. *American Educational Research Journal*, *38*(4), 915–945. doi:10.3102/00028312038004915

Gcaza, N., & Von Solms, R. (2017). A strategy for a cybersecurity culture: A South African perspective. *The Electronic Journal on Information Systems in Developing Countries*, *80*(1), 1–17. doi:10.1002/j.1681-4835.2017.tb00590.x

Geeling, S., Brown, I., & Weimann, P. (2016). Information systems and culture – a systematic hermeneutic literature review. In *Proceedings of the International Conference on Information Resource Management (CONF-IRM)* (paper 40). South Africa, Cape Town: Association for Information Systems.

GIAC. (2016). *GIAC certificate brochure*. Retrieved from https://www.giac.org/media/about/cert-brochure.pdf

GIAC. (2018). *GIAC Certification Renewal: Guidelines and Requirements*. Retrieved from https://www.giac.org/certifications/renewal

Gibbs, G., & Simpson, C. (2004). Conditions under which assessment supports students' learning. *Learning and Teaching in Higher Education*, *1*(1), 3–31.

Glaspie, H. W., & Karwowski, W. (2018). Human Factors in Information Security Culture : A Literature Review Human Factors in Information Security Culture : A Literature Review. In *Proceedings of Advances in Intelligent Systems and Computing* (pp. 269–280). Springer.

Glasser, J., & Lindauer, B. (2013). Bridging the gap: A pragmatic approach to generating insider threat data. In IEEE Security and Privacy Workshops (SPW), 2013 (pp. 98-104). IEEE. doi:10.1109/SPW.2013.37

Government, H. M. (2018). *Cyber Security Skills: A guide for business*. Retrieved from HM Government: https://assets.publishing.service.gov.uk/government/uploads/system/uploads/attachment_data/file/386248/bis-14-1276-cyber-security-skills-a-guide-for-business.pdf

Grasmick, H., & Bursik, R. (1990). Conscience, significant others, and rational choice: Extending the deterrence model. *Law & Society Review*, *24*(3), 837–861. doi:10.2307/3053861

Greitzer, F. L., & Frincke, D. A. (2010). Combining traditional cyber security audit data with psychosocial data: towards predictive modeling for insider threat mitigation. In *Insider threats in cyber security* (pp. 85–113). Boston, MA: Springer. doi:10.1007/978-1-4419-7133-3_5

Greitzer, F. L., Moore, A. P., Cappelli, D. M., Andrews, D. H., Carroll, L. A., & Hull, T. D. (2008). Combating the insider cyber threat. *IEEE Security and Privacy*, *6*(1), 61–64. doi:10.1109/MSP.2008.8

Guide to the Systems Engineering Body of Knowledge (SEBok) v.1.9. (2018, June). Retrieved from http://sebokwiki.org/wiki/Guide_to_the_Systems_Engineering_Body_of_Knowledge_(SEBOK)

Hadlington, L. (2017). Human factors in cybersecurity; examining the link between Internet addiction, impulsivity, attitudes towards cybersecurity, and risky cyber security behaviours. *Heliyon (London)*, 00346.

Hallet, J., Larson, J., & Rashid, A. (2018). Mirror Mirror on the Wall: What are we Teaching them at all? Characterising the Focus of Cybersecurity Curricular Frameworks. *ASE@USENIX Security Symposium 2018*. Available at https://www.usenix.org/sites/default/files/conference/protected-files/ase18_slides_hallett.pdf

Hamdorf, J., & Hall, J. C. (2001). The development of undergraduate curricula in surgery assessment. *The Australian and New Zealand Journal of Surgery*, *71*(3), 178–183. doi:10.1046/j.1440-1622.2001.02031.x PMID:11277149

Handley, S. M. (2012). The perilous effects of capability loss on outsourcing management and performance. *Journal of Operations Management*, *30*(1), 152–165. doi:10.1016/j.jom.2011.10.003

Han, J., Kim, Y., & Kim, H. (2017). An integrative model of information security policy compliance with psychological contract: Examining a bilateral perspective. *Computers & Security*, *66*, 52–65. doi:10.1016/j.cose.2016.12.016

Harris, M. A., & Patten, K. (2015). Using Bloom's and Web's Taxonomies to Integrate Emerging Cybersecurity Topics into a Computing Curriculum. *Journal of Information Systems Education*, *26*(3), 219 – 229.

Harris, M. A. (2012). Shaming as a technique for information security policy and training adherence. *Proceedings of the Southern Association for Information Systems Conference*, 92-97.

Harris, M., & Furnell, S. (2012). Routes to security compliance: Be good or be shamed? *Computer Fraud & Security*, *2012*(12), 12–20. doi:10.1016/S1361-3723(12)70122-7

Hayden, M. (1999). *The Insider Threat to U.S. Government Information Systems* (NSTISSAM-INFOSEC/1-99). National Security Agency.

Haydon, L. (2016). *People centric security – Transforming your enterprise security culture*. McGraw-Hill Education.

Health Professions Council of South Africa (HPCSA). (2008). *General Ethical Guidelines for the Health Professions Council of South Africa, Annexure 12*. Retrieved from http://www.hpcsa.co.za/conduct/Ethics

HEFCE. (2002). *Successful Student Diversity*. Available at http://www.hefce.ac.uk/pubs/hefce/2002/02_48.htm

Hellriegel, D., Slocum, J. W. Jr, & Woodman, R. W. (1998). *Organizational behavior* (8th ed.). Cincinnati, OH: South-Western College.

Herath, T., & Rao, H. (2009). Encouraging information security behaviors in organizations: role of penalties, pressures and perceived effectiveness. *Decision Support Systems, 47*, 154-165.

Herold, R. (2011). *Managing an information security and privacy awareness and training program* (2nd ed.). Boca Raton, FL: Taylor and Francis Group.

He, W. (2012). A review of social media security risks and mitigation techniques. *Journal of Systems and Information Technology*, *14*(2), 171–180. doi:10.1108/13287261211232180

HHS. (2013). *HIPAA administrative simplification, u.s. department of health and human services office for civil rights*. Retrieved from https://www.hhs.gov/sites/default/files/ocr/privacy/hipaa/administrative/combined/hipaa-simplification-201303.pdf?language=es

Hiatt, J. M. (2006). *ADKAR: A Model for Change in Business, Government and our Community*. Loveland, CO: Library of Congress.

Higher Education Academy. (2006). *Embedding Success Enhancing the Learning Experience for Disabled Students*. York, UK: Higher Education Academy.

Hirschi, T. (1969). *Causes of delinquency*. Berkeley, CA: University of California Press.

Hlavac, G., & Easterly, E. (2015). *Ferpa primer: The basics and beyond*. Retrieved March 3, 2019 from https://www.naceweb.org/public-policy-and-legal/legal-issues/ferpa-primer-the-basics-and-beyond/

Hofstede, G., Hofstede, G. J., & Minkov, M. (2010). *Cultures and Organizations: Software of the mind* (3rd ed.). The McGraw-Hill Companies.

Holmes, A. (2007). *Your guide to good-enough compliance*. Retrieved from https://www.cio.com/article/2439324/risk-management/your-guide-to-good-enough-compliance.html

Holmes, L., & Smith, L. (2003, July). Student evaluation of faculty grading methods. *Journal of Education for Business*, 318 – 323.

Home Office. (2018). *A Call to Action: The Cyber Aware Perception Gap*. Retrieved from https://www.gov.uk/government/publications/cyber-aware-perception-gap-report

Human Sciences Research Council (HSRC). (2018). *Code of Research Ethics*. Retrieved from http://www.hsrc.ac.za/en/about/research-ethics/code-of-research-ethics

Humphreys, E. (2008). Information security management standards: Compliance, governance and risk management. *Information Security Technical Report*, *13*(4), 247–255. doi:10.1016/j.istr.2008.10.010

Hunker, J., & Probst, C. W. (2011). Insiders and Insider Threats-An Overview of Definitions and Mitigation Techniques. *Journal of Wireless Mobile Networks, Ubiquitous Computing and Dependable Applications*, *2*(1), 4–27.

IBM Analytics. (2018). *IBM SPSS Statistics*. Retrieved from https://www.ibm.com/analytics/data-science/predictive-analytics/spss-statistical-software

IEEE. (2018). *Cyber Security Tools for Today's Environment*. Retrieved from https://forms1.ieee.org/Cyber-Security-Program.html

IISP (Institute of Information Security Professionals) (2018b). *Skills framework, version 2.2, IISP, March 2018*. IISP.

IISP (Institute of Information Security Professionals). (2018a). *Membership Levels*. Retrieved from https://www.iisp.org/iisp/Membership/Individuals/Membership_Levels/iispv2/Membership/Membership_Levels2.aspx

IMS Global Learning Consortium. (2018, June). Retrieved from http://www.imsglobal.org/

Information Systems Audit and Control Association (ISACA). (2017). *Cybersecurity Fundamentals Study Guide* (2nd ed.). ISACA.

Information Systems Audit and Control Association (ISACA). (2018). *Code of Professional Ethics*. Retrieved from http://www.isaca.org/certification/code-of-professional-ethics/pages/default.aspx

Infosec Institute. (2018). *CIA Triad*. Retrieved from https://resources.infosecinstitute.com/cia-triad/#gref

International Information Systems Security Certification Consortium. (2017). *(ISC)² cybersecurity workforce shortage continues to grow worldwide, to 1.8 million in five years*. Retrieved from https://www.isc2.org/News-and-Events/Press-Room/Posts/2017/02/13/Cybersecurity-Workforce-Shortage-Continues-to-Grow-Worldwide

International Information Systems Security Certification Consortium. (2018). *The (ISC)² CBK*. Retrieved from https://www.isc2.org/Certifications/CBK

Irons, A. D., & Devlin, S. (2012). *The Inspiring Teacher in Computing*. Paper presented at 1stAnnual Conference on Aiming for Excellence in STEM Learning and Teaching, London, UK.

Irons, A. D., Savage, N., Maple, C., & Davies, A. (2016, Summer). Embedding Cybersecurity in the Computer Science Curriculum. IT Now, 56 – 57.

Irons, A. D., & Thomas, P. (2016). Problem based learning in digital forensics. *Higher Education Pedagogies*, *1*(1), 95–105. doi:10.1080/23752696.2015.1134200

ISACA. (2012). *COBIT 5*. Retrieved from http://www.isaca.org/cobit/pages/default.aspx

ISACA. (2015). *CSX Practitioner Certification*. Retrieved from https://cybersecurity.isaca.org/csx-certifications/csx-practitioner-certification#0-about-this-certification

ISACA. (2017). *ISACA Annual report*. Retrieved from http://www.isaca.org/About-ISACA/annual-report/Pages/default.aspx

ISACA. (2017). *Job Practice Areas 2017* Retrieved from http://www.isaca.org/Certification/CISM-Certified-Information-Security-Manager/Job-Practice-Areas/Pages/default.aspx

ISACA. (2018). *Cybersecurity Fundamentals Online Course.* Retrieved from https://www.isaca.org/Education/on-demand-learning/Pages/cybersecurity-fundamentals-online-course.aspx

ISACA. (2018a). *How to Report and Earn CPE.* Retrieved from http://www.isaca.org/Certification/Additional-Resources/Pages/How-to-Earn-CPE.aspx

ISACA. (2018b). *The CISA Certification.* Retrieved from http://www.isaca.org/Certification/CISA-Certified-Information-Systems-Auditor/Documents/ISACA_CISA_40th_Anniversary_Infographic_0618.pdf

ISACA. (n.d.). Retrieved July 7, 2018 from https://www.isaca.org/about-isaca/Pages/default.aspx

ISACA. (n.d.a). Retrieved from https://www.isaca.org/Pages/Glossary.aspx

ISACA. (n.d.b). Retrieved from https://cobitonline.isaca.org/about

ISF. (2014). *From Promoting Awareness to Embedding Behaviours - Secure by choice, not by chance.* Information Security Forum. Retrieved from https://www.securityforum.org/uploads/2015/03/From-Promoting-Awareness-ES-2014_Marketing.pdf

ISO. (2013). *International Organization for Standardization, ISO/IEC 27001: 2013, information technology, security techniques, information security management systems, Requirements.* Retrieved from https://www.iso.org/obp/ui/#iso:std:iso-iec:27001:ed-2:v1:en

ISO. (2017). *ISO/IEC 27021:2017 Information technology -- Security techniques -- Competence requirements for information security management systems professionals.* Retrieved from https://www.iso.org/standard/61003.html

ISO. (n.d.). *ISO/IEC 27000 family - information security management systems.* Retrieved from https://www.iso.org/isoiec-27001-information-security.html

ISO/IEC. (2013). *ISO/IEC 27002: Information technology – security techniques – code of practice for information security management.* BSI.

Jenkins, A., & Healy, M. (2005). *Institutional strategies to link teaching and research.* Higher Education Academy Publication.

Johnston, N., & Karafotias, T. (2016). Flipping the Classroom to Meet the Diverse Learning Needs of Library and Information Studies (LIS) Students. *Journal of Education for Library and Information Science, 57*(3), 226–238. doi:10.3138/jelis.57.3.226

Joint Task Force on Computing Curricula. (2013). *Computer Science Curricula 2013: Curriculum Guidelines for Undergraduate Degree Programs in Computer Science.* New York, NY: ACM. Retrieved from https://www.acm.org/binaries/content/assets/education/cs2013_web_final.pdf

Joint Task Force on Cybersecurity Education. (2017). *Cybersecurity Curricula 2017.* New York: ACM. Retrieved from https://cybered.acm.org

Jones, A., & Colwill, C. (2008). Dealing with the malicious insider. *Australian Information Security Management Conference*, 52.

Joshi, P., Thukral, A., Joshi, M., Deorari, A. K., & Vatsa, M. (2011). Comparing the Effectiveness of Webinars and Participatory Learning on Essential Newborn Care (ENBC) in the Class Room in Terms of Acquisition of Knowledge and Skills of Student Nurses: A Randomized Controlled Trial. *In Indina J Pediatr*. Available at https://www.researchgate.net/profile/Anu_Thukral/publication/224914755

Kaspersky. (2016). *Lack of Security Talent: An Unexpected Threat to Corporate Cybersafety*. IT Security Risks Special Report Series 2016, Kaspersky Lab. Retrieved from https://www.kaspersky.com/blog/security_risks_report_lack_of_security_talent/

Kazmi, S. A., & Naarananoja, M. (2014). Collection of change management models – an opportunity to make the best choice from the various organizational transformational techniques. *GSTG International Journal on Business Management*, *3*(3), 71–79.

Kessler, G. C. (2007). Online education in computer and digital forensics: A case study. *IEEE Proceedings of the 40th Hawaii International Conference on System Sciences 2007*. 10.1109/HICSS.2007.407

Kiani, A., & Shah, M. H. (2014). An application of ADKAR change model for the change management competencies of school heads in Pakistan. *Journal of Managerial Sciences*, *VIII*(1), 77–95.

Kleck, G., Sever, B., Li, S., & Gertz, M. (2005). The missing link in general deterrence research. *Criminology*, *43*(3), 623–660. doi:10.1111/j.0011-1348.2005.00019.x

Knight, P. (2001). *Formative and Summative, Criterion and Norm-Referenced Assessment*. LTSN Generic Centre, Assessment Series No. 7.

Kocher, P., Genkin, D., Gruss, D., Haas, W., Hamburg, M., Lipp, M., . . . Yaroim, Y. (2018). *Spectre Attacks: Exploiting Speculative Execution*. Retrieved from https://arxiv.org/abs/1801.01203

KPMG. (1998). *Information Security Survey 1998*. London, UK: KPMG Information Risk Management.

Kraemer, S., & Carayon, P. (2005). Computer and Information Security Culture: Findings from two Studies. In *Proceedings of the Human Factors and Ergonomics Society Annual Meeting* (pp. 1483-1487). Orlando, FL: Human Factors and Ergonomic Society. 10.1177/154193120504901605

Krejcie, R. V., & Morgan, D. W. (1970). Determining Sample Size for Research Activities. *Educational and Psychological Measurement*, *30*(3), 607–610. doi:10.1177/001316447003000308

Kyobe, M. (2005). Addressing e-crime and computer security issues in homes and small organizations in South Africa. *European management and technology conference on the integration of management and technology*, 1-13.

Lado, A. A., & Wilson, M. C. (1994). Human resource system and sustainable competitive advantage: A competency-based perspective. *Academy of Management Review*, *19*(4), 699–727. doi:10.5465/amr.1994.9412190216

Ledimo, O. (2017). Preparing and involving all stakeholders. In N. Martins, E. Martins, & R. Viljoen (Eds.), *Organizational Diagnosis: A guide for practitioners* (pp. 25–38). Randburg, South Africa: Knowledge Resources.

Lee, S., Lee, S.-G., & Yoo, S. (2004). An intergrative model of computer abuse based on social control and general deterrence theories. *Information & Management, 41*(6), 707–718. doi:10.1016/j.im.2003.08.008

Li, H., Zhang, J., & Sarathy, R. (2010). Understanding compliance with internet use policy from the perspective of rational choice theory. *Decision Support Systems, 48*(4), 635–645. doi:10.1016/j.dss.2009.12.005

LippM.SchwarzM.GrussD.PrescherT.HaasW.MangardS.HamburgM. (2018). *Meltdown*. Retrieved from https://arxiv.org/abs/1801.01207

Liu, D., Wang, X., & Camp, J. (2008). Game-theoretic modeling and analysis of insider threats. *International Journal of Critical Infrastructure Protection, 1*, 75–80. doi:10.1016/j.ijcip.2008.08.001

Lloyd's of London and Cyence. (2017). *Emerging Risks Report 2017: Counting the cost - Cyber exposure decoded*. Retrieved from https://www.lloyds.com/~/media/files/news-and-insight/risk-insight/2017/cyence/emerging-risk-report-2017---counting-the-cost.pdf

Ludi, S., & Collofello, J. (2001). An analysis of the gap between the knowledge and skills learned in academic software engineering course projects and those required in real projects. In *Proceedings of the 31st Annual Frontiers in Education Conference* (pp. T2D-8–T2D-11). Reno, NV: Academic Press. 10.1109/FIE.2001.963881

Luiijf, E., Besseling, K., & De Graaf, P. (2013). Nineteen national cyber security strategies. *International Journal of Critical Infrastructures, 9*(1/2), 2–31. doi:10.1504/IJCIS.2013.051608

Lundstedt, S. (1966). Criteria for Effective Teaching. *Improving College and University Teaching, 14*(1), 27–31. doi:10.1080/00193089.1966.10532492

Magklaras, G. B., & Furnell, S. M. (2005). A preliminary model of end user sophistication for insider threat prediction in IT systems. *Computers & Security, 24*(5), 371–380. doi:10.1016/j.cose.2004.10.003

Mahfuth, A., Yussof, S., Baker, A. A., & Ali, N. (2017). A systematic literature review: Information security culture. In *Proceedings of the International Conference on Research and Innovation in Information Systems* (ICRIIS) (pp. 456-463). Langkawi, Kedah, Malaysia: IEEE. 10.1109/ICRIIS.2017.8002442

Martinez-Moyano, I. J., Rich, E., Conrad, S., Andersen, D. F., & Stewart, T. R. (2008). A behavioral theory of insider-threat risks: A system dynamics approach. *ACM Transactions on Modeling and Computer Simulation, 18*(2), 7. doi:10.1145/1346325.1346328

Martins, E. C. (2017). Planning and coordinating an organizational diagnosis. In N. Martins, E. Martins, & R. Viljoen (Eds.), *Organizational Diagnosis: A guide for practitioners* (pp. 1–23). Randburg, South Africa: Knowledge Resources.

Martins, E. C., & Ledimo, O. (2017). Developing and sourcing assessment instruments. In N. Martins, E. Martins, & R. Viljoen (Eds.), *Organizational Diagnosis: A guide for practitioners* (pp. 39–83). Randburg, South Africa: Knowledge Resources.

Martins, E. C., & Ledimo, O. (2017b). Survey administration process. In N. Martins, E. Martins, & R. Viljoen (Eds.), *Organizational Diagnosis: A guide for practitioners* (pp. 85–112). Randburg, South Africa: Knowledge Resources.

Martins, E. C., & Martins, N. (2016). Organizational culture. In S. P. Robbins, A. Odendaal, & G. Roodt (Eds.), *Organizational Behaviour* (3rd ed.; pp. 606–641). Cape Town, South Africa: Pearson Education.

Matthews, S. K., & Agnew, R. (2008). Extending deterrence theory: Do delinquent peers condition the relationship between perceptions of getting caught and offending? *Journal of Research in Crime and Delinquency*, *45*(2), 91–118. doi:10.1177/0022427807313702

McBride, M., Carter, L., & Warkentin, M. (2012). *Exploring the role of individual employee characteristics and personality on employee compliance with cybersecurity policies*. RTI International-Institute for Homeland Security Solutions.

McConnell, M. (2002). Information assurance in the twenty-first century. *Computer*, *35*(4), supl16-supl19.

McCormac, A., Parsons, K., & Butavicius, M. (2012). *Preventing and profiling malicious insider attacks (No. DSTO-TR-2697). Defence Science and Technology Organisation Edinburgh*. Command Control Communications And Intelligence Div.

McDowell, L., Sambell, K., Bazin, V., Penlington, R., Wakelin, D., Wickes, H., & Smailes, J. (2005). Assessment for Learning: Current Practice Exemplars from the Centre for Excellence. In Teaching and Learning. Northumbria University Red Guides, 11.

McGettreick, A. (2013). Toward effective cybersecurity education. *IEEE Security and Privacy*, *11*(6), 66–68. doi:10.1109/MSP.2013.155

McGrath, R. G., MacMillan, I. C., & Venkataraman, S. (1995). Defining and developing competence: A strategic process paradigm. *Strategic Management Journal*, *16*(4), 251–275. doi:10.1002mj.4250160402

Miller, R. L., & Brewerton, J. D. (2003). *The A-Z of Social Research*. London: Sage Publications. doi:10.4135/9780857020024

Miller, R., & Maxim, M. (2015). *I Have to Trust Someone.... Don't I?* CA Technologies.

Mitchell, M. L., & Jolley, J. M. (2007). *Research design explained* (6th ed.). London: Thomson Wadsworth.

Mohelska, H., & Sokolova, M. (2015). Organizational culture and leadership – joint vessels? *Procedia: Social and Behavioral Sciences*, *171*, 1011–1016. doi:10.1016/j.sbspro.2015.01.223

Molok, N. N. A., Ahmad, A., & Chang, S. (2011). Information leakage through online social networking: Opening the doorway for advanced persistence threats. *Journal of the Australian Institute of Professional Intelligence Officers*, *19*(2), 38.

Muncaster, P. (2017). Cisco: Complacency and Ignorance Make Staff Major Security Threat. *Infosecurity Magazine*. Retrieved from https://www.infosecurity-magazine.com/news/complacency-and-low-awareness/

Murphy, R. (2006). Evaluating new priorities for assessment in higher education. In Innovative Assessment in Higher Education. London: Routledge.

Nagin, D., & Pogarsky, G. (2001). Integrating celerity, impulsivity, and extralegal sanction threats into a model of general deterrence: Theory and evidence. *Criminology*, *39*(4), 865–888. doi:10.1111/j.1745-9125.2001.tb00943.x

NAO. (2013). *The UK cyber security strategy: Landscape review*. National Audit Office. Retrieved from https://www.nao.org.uk/report/the-uk-cyber-security-strategy-landscape-review

National Institute of Standards and Technology. (2018, April). *Framework for Improving Critical Infrastructure Cybersecurity - Version 1.1*. Retrieved from https://www.nist.gov/publications/framework-improving-critical-infrastructure-cybersecurity-version-11

NCSC. (2015). *10 Steps: User Education and Awareness*. National Cyber Security Centre. Retrieved from https://www.ncsc.gov.uk/guidance/10-steps-user-education-and-awareness

NCSC. (2016). *About the certified professional scheme*. Retrieved from https://www.ncsc.gov.uk/articles/about-certified-professional-scheme

NCSC. (2018). *New Cyber Attack categorisation system to improve UK response to incidents*. Available at https://www.ncsc.gov.uk/news/new-cyber-attack-categorisation-system-improve-uk-response-incidents

Neumann, P. G. (2010). Combatting insider threats. In *Insider Threats in Cyber Security* (pp. 17–44). Boston, MA: Springer. doi:10.1007/978-1-4419-7133-3_2

Newhouse, W., Keith, S., Scribner, B., & Witte, G. (2017). *National initiative for cybersecurity education (NICE) cybersecurity workforce framework. NIST Special Publication 800-181*. Gaithersburg, MD: National Institute for Standards and Technology. doi:10.6028/NIST.SP.800-181

Nguyen, N., Reiher, P., & Kuenning, G. H. (2003). Detecting insider threats by monitoring system call activity. In *Information Assurance Workshop*, 2003. *IEEE Systems, Man and Cybernetics Society* (pp. 45-52). IEEE. 10.1109/SMCSIA.2003.1232400

Nicol, D., & Macfarlane-Dick, D. (2004). Rethinking formative assessment in HE. In C. Juwah, D. Mcfalane-Dick, B. Matthew, D. Nicol, D. Ross, & B. Smith (Eds.), *Enhancing Student Learning Through Effective Formative Feedback* (pp. 3–14). HE Academy.

Nieles, M., Dempsey, K., & Pillitteri, V. (2017). *NIST Special Publication 800-12 Revision 1: An introduction to information security*. Retrieved from https://nvlpubs.nist.gov/nistpubs/SpecialPublications/NIST.SP.800-12r1.pdf

NIST. (2017). *Digital Identity Guidelines - Authentication and Lifecycle Management*. NIST Special Publication 800-63B. June 2017. doi:10.6028/NIST.SP.800-63b

NIST. (2017). *Draft special publication 800-53, r5. Security and privacy controls for information systems and organizations*. Retrieved from https://csrc.nist.gov/CSRC/media//Publications/sp/800-53/rev-5/draft/documents/sp800-53r5-draft.pdf

NIST. (n.d.). *NIST: national vulnerability database*. Retrieved from https://nvd.nist.gov/ncp/repository

Northcutt, S., Shenk, J., Shackleford, D., Rosenberg, T., Siles, R., & Mancini, S. (2006). *SANS Institute, penetration testing: assessing your overall security before attackers do.* Retrieved from https://www.sans.org/reading-room/whitepapers/analyst/penetration-testing-assessing-security-attackers-34635

Nurse, J. R., Legg, P. A., Buckley, O., Agrafiotis, I., Wright, G., Whitty, M., ... Creese, S. (2014). A critical reflection on the threat from human insiders–its nature, industry perceptions, and detection approaches. In *International Conference on Human Aspects of Information Security, Privacy, and Trust* (pp. 270-281). Springer. 10.1007/978-3-319-07620-1_24

Nuutila, E., Törmä, S., & Malmi, L. (2005). PBL and computer programming— The seven steps method with adaptations. *Computer Science Education, 15*(2), 123–142. doi:10.1080/08993400500150788

Oates, B. J. (2012). *Researching Information Systems and Computing*. London: SAGE Publications, Inc.

Ofqual (2015). *Regulated Qualifications Framework: a postcard.* Retrieved from https://www.gov.uk/government/publications/regulated-qualifications-framework-a-postcard

Ofqual (2016). *Awarding organisations: understanding our regulatory requirements.* Retrieved from https://www.gov.uk/guidance/awarding-organisations-understanding-our-regulatory-requirements

Okere, I., Van Niekerk, J., & Carroll, M. (2012). Assessing Information Security Culture: A Critical Analysis of Current Approaches. In *Proceedings of the Information Security for South Africa Conference (ISSA)* (pp. 136-143). IEEE. 10.1109/ISSA.2012.6320442

Oltsik, J. (2017). T*he Life and Times of Cybersecurity Professionals, ESG, ISSA Report.* Available at https://www.esg-global.com/hubfs/issa/ESG-ISSA-Research-Report-Life-of-Cybersecurity-Professionals-Nov-2017.pdf

Organization for Economic Co-Operation and Development (OECD). (2002). *Guidelines for the security of information systems and networks. Towards a culture of security.* Retrieved from http://www.oecd.org/internet/ieconomy/15582260.pdf

Orton, J. D., & Weick, K. E. (1990). Loosely coupled systems: A reconceptualization. *Academy of Management Review, 15*(2), 203–223. doi:10.5465/amr.1990.4308154

OWASP. (2013). *OWASP Top 10 – 2013: The ten most critical web application security risks.* Retrieved from https://www.owasp.org/images/f/f8/OWASP_Top_10_-_2013.pdf

OWASP. (2017). *OWASP Top 10 – 2017: The ten most critical web application security risks.* Retrieved from https://www.owasp.org/images/7/72/OWASP_Top_10-2017_%28en%29.pdf.pdf

Padayachee, K. (2012). Taxonomy of compliant information security behavior. *Computers & Security, 31*(5), 673–680. doi:10.1016/j.cose.2012.04.004

Paloalto. (2016). *2016 Prediction #10: Cyberthreat Intelligence Sharing Goes Mainstream.* Available at https://researchcenter.paloaltonetworks.com/2015/12/2016-prediction-10-cyberthreat-intelligence-sharing-goes-mainstream/

Parker, D. B. (1998). *Fighting Computer Crime*. New York, NY: John Wiley & Sons.

Park, J. S., & Ho, S. M. (2004). Composite role-based monitoring (CRBM) for countering insider threats. In *International Conference on Intelligence and Security Informatics* (pp. 201-213). Springer. 10.1007/978-3-540-25952-7_15

Pattinson, M., & Anderson, G. (2005). Risk Communication, Risk Perception and Information Security. *Security Management, Integrity and Internal Control in Information Systems, Proceedings of IFIP TC-11 WG11.1 & WG11.5 Joint Working Conference*, 175-184.

PCI. (2010). *PCI security standards council, PCI DSS quick reference guide*. Retrieved from https://www.pcisecuritystandards.org/documents/PCI%20SSC%20Quick%20Reference%20Guide.pdf

PCI. (2010). *PCI security standards council, PCI DSS quick reference guide*. Retrieved July 13, 2018 from https://www.pcisecuritystandards.org/documents/PCI%20SSC%20Quick%20Reference%20Guide.pdf

Pelligrino, J. W., Chudowsky, N., & Glaser, R. (Eds.). (2001). *Knowing what Students Know – The Science and Design of Educational Assessment*. Washington, DC: National Academic Press.

Pfleeger, C. P., & Cooper, D. M. (1997). Security and Privacy: Promising Advances. *IEEE Software*, *14*(5), 27–32. doi:10.1109/52.605928

Pfleeger, C. P., Pfleeger, S. L., & Margulies, J. (2015). *Security in Computing* (5th ed.). Upper Saddle River, NJ: Prentice Hall.

Pogarsky, G., Piquero, A., & Paternoster, R. (2004). Modeling change in perceptions about sanction threats: The neglected linkage in deterrence theory. *Journal of Quantitative Criminology*, *20*(4), 343–369. doi:10.100710940-004-5868-z

Ponemon Institute. (2017). *The true cost of compliance with data projection regulations*. Retrieved from https://www.globalscape.com/resources/whitepapers/data-protection-regulations-study

Powers, C. (2018). *Are hackers targeting your industry? Find out in the 2015 Cybersecurity Intelligence Index*. Retrieved from IBM: https://www.ibm.com/developerworks/community/blogs/81c130c7-4408-4e01-adf5-658ae0ef5f0c/entry/Are_hackers_targeting_your_industry_Find_out_in_the_2015_Cyber_Security_Intelligence_Index?lang=en

Probst, C. W., Hunker, J., Gollmann, D., & Bishop, M. (2010). Aspects of insider threats. In *Insider Threats in Cyber Security* (pp. 1–15). Boston, MA: Springer. doi:10.1007/978-1-4419-7133-3_1

Professional Standards Councils. (2018). *What is a Profession?* Retrieved from https://www.psc.gov.au/what-is-a-profession

Puleo, A. J. (2006). *Mitigating insider threat using human behavior influence models (No. AFIT/GCE/ENG/06-04)*. Air Force Inst Of Tech Wright-Patterson Afb Oh School of Engineering And Management.

Qualtrics. (2018). *Qualtrics Research Core*. Retrieved from https://www.qualtrics.com/research-core/

Randazzo, M.R., Keeney, M., Kowalski, E., Cappelli, D.M., & Moore, A.P. (2005). *Insider threat study: Illicit cyber activity in the banking and finance sector*. Academic Press.

Rashid, A., Daneziz, G., Chivers, H., Lupu, E., Martin, A., Lewis, M., & Peersman, C. (2018). Scoping the Cyber Security Body of Knowledge. *IEEE Security and Privacy*, *16*(3), 96–102. doi:10.1109/MSP.2018.2701150

Robbins, S. P. (1997). *Essentials of Organizational behavior* (5th ed.). Upper Saddle River, NJ: Prentice Hall.

Robbins, S. P. (2001). *Organizational behaviour* (9th ed.). Prentice Hall.

Robbins, S. P., Odendaal, A., & Roodt, G. (2003). *Organizational behaviour – Global and Southern African perspectives*. Cape Town, South Africa: Pearson Education.

Rossouw, D., & Van Vuuren, L. (2013). *Business ethics* (5th ed.). Oxford University Press.

Rousseau, D. (1995). *Psychological contracts in organizations: Understanding written and unwritten agreements*. Sage Publications.

Rowntree, D. (1987). *Assessing Students: How Shall we Know Them* (2nd ed.). London: Kogan Page.

Ruighaver, A. B., Maynard, S. B., & Chang, S. (2007). Organizational security culture: Extending the end-user perspective. *Computers & Security*, *26*(1), 56–62. doi:10.1016/j.cose.2006.10.008

Safa, N., Von Solms, R., & Furnell, S. (2016). Information security policy compliance model in organizations. *Computers & Security*, *56*, 70–82. doi:10.1016/j.cose.2015.10.006

Saltzer, J., & Kaashoek, M. (2009). *Principles of Computer System Design*. Burlington, VT: Morgan Kaufmann Publishers.

Saltzer, J., & Schroeder, M. (1975). The protection of information in computer systems. *Proceedings of the IEEE*, *63*(9), 1278–1308. doi:10.1109/PROC.1975.9939

SANS. (2018). *Information Security Training Winter/Spring 2018 Course Catalogue*. Retrieved from https://www.sans.org/media/security-training/course-catalog-2018.pdf

SANS. (n.d.a). *CIS critical security controls*. Retrieved from https://www.sans.org/critical-security-controls

SANS. (n.d.b). *SANS Institute, information security policy templates*. Retrieved from https://www.sans.org/security-resources/policies

Santos, D. (2016). *National Initiative for Cybersecurity Education*. NICE.

Sarkar, K. R. (2010). Assessing insider threats to information security using technical, behavioural and organisational measures. *Information Security Technical Report*, *15*(3), 112–133. doi:10.1016/j.istr.2010.11.002

Saunders, M., Lewis, P., & Thornhill, A. (2016). *Research methods for business students* (7th ed.). Pearson Education Limited.

Scantron. (2018). *SurveyTracker*. Retrieved from http://www.scantron.com/software/survey/surveytracker-plus/overview

Scarfone, Benigni, & Grance (n.d.). *Cyber Security Standards, NIST.* Retrieved March 4, 2019 from https://ws680.nist.gov/publication/get_pdf.cfm?pub_id=152153

Schein, E. H. (1985). *Organizational culture and leadership*. San Francisco: Jossey-Bass Publishers.

Scheponik, T., Sherman, A. T., DeLatte, D., Phatak, D., Olivia, L., Thompson, J., & Herman, G. L. (2016). How students reason about cybersecurity concepts. *2016 IEEE Frontiers in Education Conference*. Available at http://doi.ieeecomputersociety.org/10.1109/FIE.2016.7757363

Schleicher, A. (2015). Valued-added: How do you measure whether universities are delivering for their students? *Higher Education Policy Institute (HEPI) Annual Lecture 2015*. Available at https://www.hepi.ac.uk/wp-content/uploads/2016/01/Andreas-Schleicher-lecture.pdf

Schlienger, T., & Teufel, S. (2003). Analyzing information security culture: Increased trust by an appropriate information security culture. In *Proceedings of the International Workshop on Trust and Privacy in Digital Business (TrustBus 2003) in conjunction with the 14th International Conference on Database and Expert Systems Applications (DEXA 2003)*. Prague: IEEE. 10.1109/DEXA.2003.1232055

Schlienger, T., & Teufel, S. (2005). Tool supported management of information security culture. In *Proceedings of IFIP 20th International Information Security Conference proceedings* (pp.65-77). Springer. 10.1007/0-387-25660-1_5

Schneider, A. L., & Ervin, L. (1990). Specific deterrence, rational choice, and decision heuristics: Applications in juvenile justice. *Social Science Quarterly*, *71*(3), 585–601.

Schneiderman, R. (2016). *Cyber Skills in High Demand Well Into The Future*. newswise. Retrieved from http://www.newswise.com/articles/view/660345/

Schneier, B. (2013). *On Security Awareness Training*. DARKReading. Retrieved from https://www.darkreading.com/risk/on-security-awareness-training/d/d-id/1139381

SEC. (2016). *SEC: Morgan Stanley failed to safeguard customer data*. Retrieved from https://www.sec.gov/news/pressrelease/2016-112.html

Security, O. (2018a). *Offensive Security Certified Professional*. Retrieved from https://www.offensive-security.com/information-security-certifications/oscp-offensive-security-certified-professional/

Security, O. (2018b). *Penetration Testing with Kali Linux*. Retrieved from https://www.offensive-security.com/documentation/penetration-testing-with-kali.pdf

Sheperd, M. L., Harris, M. L., Chung, H., & Himes, E. M. (2014). Using the Awareness, Desire, Knowledge, Ability, Reinforcement Model to build a shared governance culture. *Journal of Nursing Education and Practice*, *6*(4), 90–104.

Siponen, M., Pahnila, S., & Mahmood, A. (2010). *Compliance with information security policies: an empirical investigation.* IEEE Computer Society.

Siponen, M., Pahnila, S., & Mahmood, A. M. (2006). A new model for understanding users' is security compliance. PACIS 2006 Proceedings, 48.

Siponen, M. T. (2000). A conceptual foundation for organizational information security awareness. *Information Management & Computer Security*, *8*(1), 31–41. doi:10.1108/09685220010371394

Smith, S., Smith, S., Bailey, N., & Cahill, P. (2017). Why 'WannaCry' Malware Caused Chaos for National Health Service in U.K. *NBC News*. Retrieved from https://www.nbcnews.com/news/world/why-wannacry-malware-caused-chaos-national-health-service-u-k-n760126

Stafford, M. C., & Warr, M. (1993). A reconceptualization of general and specific deterrence. *Journal of Research in Crime and Delinquency*, *30*(2), 123–135. doi:10.1177/0022427893030002001

Stavrou, V., Kandias, M., Karoulas, G., & Gritzalis, D. (2014). Business Process Modeling for Insider threat monitoring and handling. In *International Conference on Trust, Privacy and Security in Digital Business* (pp. 119-131). Springer. 10.1007/978-3-319-09770-1_11

SurveyMonkey. (2018). Retrieved from http://www.surveymonkey.com

Tang, M., Li, M., & Zhang, T. (2015). The impacts of organizational culture on information security culture: A case study. *Information Technology Management*, *17*(2), 1–8.

Task Group on Information Technology Curricula. (2017). *Information Technology Curricula 2017: Curriculum Guidelines for Baccalaureate Degree Programs in Information Technology*. New York: ACM. Retrieved from https://www.acm.org/binaries/content/assets/education/curricula-recommendations/it2017.pdf

The Advanced Distributed Learning Initiative. (2018, June). Retrieved from http://www.adlnet.gov/

The Council of the European Union. (2016). Regulation (EU) 2016/679 of the European Parliament And of the Council of 27 April 2016 on the protection of natural persons with regard to the processing of personal data and on the free movement of such data, and repealing Directive 95/46/EC. *Official Journal of the European Union, L, 119*(1).

The European Parliament and the Council of the European Union. (2008). Council Directive 2008/114/EC of 8 December 2008 on the identification and designation of European critical infrastructures and the assessment of the need to improve their protection. *Official Journal of the European Union, L, 345*(75).

The European Parliament and the Council of the European Union. (2016). Directive (EU) 2016/1148 of the European Parliament and of the Council of 6 July 2016 concerning measures for a high common level of security of network and information systems across the Union. *Official Journal of the European Union, L, 194*(1).

The European Parliament. (2016). *The European Council. General Data Protection Regulation (GDPR), Regulation (EU) 2016/679.* Official Journal of the European Union.

The Information Systems Security Association (ISSA). (2018). *ISSA code of ethics*. Retrieved from www.issa.org/?page=codeofethics

The Moodle project. (2018, June). Retrieved from https://moodle.org/

The Singapore Statement on Research Integrity. (2010). Retrieved from www.singaporestatement.org

Theoharidou, M., Kokolakis, S., Karyda, M., & Kiountouzis, E. (2005). The insider threat to information systems and the effectiveness of ISO17799. *Computers & Security*, *24*(6), 472–484. doi:10.1016/j.cose.2005.05.002

Tittel, E., Lemons, M., & Kyle, M. (2017). *Information security certifications: Introductory level*. TechTarget. Retrieved from http://searchsecurity.techtarget.com/tip/SearchSecuritycom-guide-to-information-security-certifications

Tomlinson, K. (2016). An examination of deterrence theory: Where do we stand? *Federal Review*, *80*, 3.

Tree Solution. (2018). *Sicherheitskultur*. Retrieved from http://www.treesolution.ch/10-0-Smart-Tools-fuer-mehr-Sicherheit.html

Tsipenyuk, K., Chess, B., & McGraw, G. (2005). Seven pernicious kingdoms: A taxonomy of software security errors. *IEEE Security and Privacy*, *3*(6), 81–84. doi:10.1109/MSP.2005.159

Ula, M., & Fuadi, W. (2017). A Method for Evaluating Information Security Governance (ISG) Components in Banking Environment. *Journal of Physics: Conference Series*, *812*(1), 012031. doi:10.1088/1742-6596/812/1/012031

US-CERT - United States Computer Emergency Readiness Team. (2018). *Alert (TA18-074A) - Russian Government Cyber Activity Targeting Energy and Other Critical Infrastructure Sectors*. Retrieved from https://www.us-cert.gov/ncas/alerts/TA18-074A

USDE. (2018). *U.S. Department of Education: Family Educational Rights and Privacy Act (FERPA)*. Retrieved from https://www2.ed.gov/policy/gen/guid/fpco/ferpa/index.html

Van Niekerk, J. F., & Von Solms, R. (2010). Information security culture: A management perspective. *Computers & Security*, *29*(4), 476–486. doi:10.1016/j.cose.2009.10.005

Vance, A., Lowry, P., & Eggett, D. (2013). Using accountability to reduce access policy violations in information systems. *Journal of Management Information Systems*, *29*(4), 263–289. doi:10.2753/MIS0742-1222290410

Vance, A., Lowry, P., & Eggett, D. (2015). Increasing accountability through user-interface design artifacts: A new approach to addressing the problem of access-policy violations. *Management Information Systems Quarterly*, *39*(2), 345–366. doi:10.25300/MISQ/2015/39.2.04

Vasileiou, I., & Furnell, S. (2019). Personalising Security Education - Factors influencing individual awareness and compliance. In P. Mori, S. Furnell, & O. Camp (Eds.), *Information Systems Security and Privacy, Fourth International Conference, ICISSP 2018, Madeira, Portugal, Jaruary 22-24, 2018, Revised Selected Papers*. Communications in Computer and Information Science, Springer.

Verizon. (2017). *Data breach investigations report* (10th ed.). Retrieved from http://www.verizonenterprise.com/verizon-insights-lab/dbir/2017/

Verizon. (2018). *2018 Data Breach Investigations Report* (11th ed.). Research Report. https://enterprise.verizon.com/resources/reports/DBIR_2018_Report.pdf

Von Solms, B., & Von Solms, R. (2018). Cybersecurity and information security – what goes where? *Information and Computer Security*, *26*(1), 2–9. doi:10.1108/ICS-04-2017-0025

Von Solms, R., & Van Niekerk, J. (2013). From information security to cyber security. *Computers & Security*, *38*, 97–102. doi:10.1016/j.cose.2013.04.004

Von Solms, S., & Futcher, L. (2018). Identifying the Cybersecurity Body of Knowledge for a Postgraduate Module in Systems Engineering. In *Proceedings of the 11th IFIP WG 11.8 World Conference on Information Security Education* (pp. 121–132). Poznan, Poland: IFIP. 10.1007/978-3-319-99734-6_10

Ware, W. H. (Ed.). (1967). *Security Controls for Computer Systems: Report of Defense Science Board Task Force of Computer Security*. RAND Corporation for the Office of the Secretary of Defense.

Warkentin, M., & Willison, R. (2009). Behavioral and policy issues in information systems security: The insider threat. *European Journal of Information Systems*, *18*(2), 101–105. doi:10.1057/ejis.2009.12

Web Accessibility Initiative. (2018). *Web Content Accessibility Guidelines (WCAG) Overview*. Retrieved from Web Accessibility Initiative: https://www.w3.org/WAI/standards-guidelines/wcag/

Wegner, E. (2000). *Communities of Practice: Learning, Meaning, And Identity (Learning in Doing: Social, Cognitive and Computational Perspectives)*. Cambridge, UK: Cambridge University Press.

Weick, K. E. (1979). *The social psychology of organizing* (2nd ed.). Reading, MA: Addison-Wesley.

Weick, K. E. (1995). *Sensemaking in organizations*. Beverly Hills, CA: Sage Publications.

Weick, K. E., & Roberts, K. H. (1993). Collective mind in organizations: Heedful interrelating on flight decks. *Administrative Science Quarterly*, *38*(3), 357–381. doi:10.2307/2393372

Weiss, R., Mache, J., & Nilsen, E. (2013). Top 10 hands-on cybersecurity exercises. *Journal of Computing Sciences in Colleges*, *29*(1), 140–147.

White, S. (2017). *What is COBIT? A framework for alignment and governance*. Retrieved from https://www.cio.com/article/3243684/methodology-frameworks/what-is-cobit-a-framework-for-alignment-and-governance.html

Whitman, M. E. (2003). Enemy at the gate: Threats to information security. *Communications of the ACM*, *46*(8), 91–95. doi:10.1145/859670.859675

Whitman, M. E., & Mattord, H. J. (2012). *Principles of information security* (4th ed.). Course Technology Cengage Learning.

Whitman, M. E., & Mattord, H. J. (2017). *Management of information security* (5th ed.). Course Technology Cengage Learning.

Wikipedia. (2018). *List of computer security certifications*. Retrieved from https://en.wikipedia.org/wiki/List_of_computer_security_certifications

Wild, J. (2018). *Five most common security frameworks explained, origin security*. Retrieved from https://originit.co.nz/the-strongroom/five-most-common-security-frameworks-explained/

Williams, J., & Cappuccini-Ansfield, G. (2007). Fitness for Purpose? National and Institutional Approaches to Publicising the Student Voice. *Quality in Higher Education*, *13*(2), 159–172. doi:10.1080/13538320701629186

Wilson, M., de Zafra, D. E., Pitcher, S. I., Tressler, J. D., & Ippolito, J. B. (1998). *Information Technology Security Training Requirements: A Role- and Performance-Based Model. NIST Special Publication 800-16*. Technology Administration, National Institute of Standards and Technology. doi:10.6028/NIST.SP.800-16

Xerte Online Toolkits. (2018, June). Retrieved from https://www.xerte.org.uk

Yayla, A. A. (2011). Controlling insider threats with information security policies. *European Conference on Information Systems*, 242.

Related References

To continue our tradition of advancing information science and technology research, we have compiled a list of recommended IGI Global readings. These references will provide additional information and guidance to further enrich your knowledge and assist you with your own research and future publications.

Abbas, R., Michael, K., & Michael, M. G. (2017). What Can People Do with Your Spatial Data?: Socio-Ethical Scenarios. In A. Marrington, D. Kerr, & J. Gammack (Eds.), *Managing Security Issues and the Hidden Dangers of Wearable Technologies* (pp. 206–237). Hershey, PA: IGI Global. doi:10.4018/978-1-5225-1016-1.ch009

Abulaish, M., & Haldar, N. A. (2018). Advances in Digital Forensics Frameworks and Tools: A Comparative Insight and Ranking. *International Journal of Digital Crime and Forensics*, *10*(2), 95–119. doi:10.4018/IJDCF.2018040106

Ahmad, F. A., Kumar, P., Shrivastava, G., & Bouhlel, M. S. (2018). Bitcoin: Digital Decentralized Cryptocurrency. In G. Shrivastava, P. Kumar, B. Gupta, S. Bala, & N. Dey (Eds.), *Handbook of Research on Network Forensics and Analysis Techniques* (pp. 395–415). Hershey, PA: IGI Global. doi:10.4018/978-1-5225-4100-4.ch021

Ahmed, A. A. (2017). Investigation Approach for Network Attack Intention Recognition. *International Journal of Digital Crime and Forensics*, *9*(1), 17–38. doi:10.4018/IJDCF.2017010102

Akhtar, Z. (2017). Biometric Spoofing and Anti-Spoofing. In M. Dawson, D. Kisku, P. Gupta, J. Sing, & W. Li (Eds.), Developing Next-Generation Countermeasures for Homeland Security Threat Prevention (pp. 121-139). Hershey, PA: IGI Global. doi:10.4018/978-1-5225-0703-1.ch007

Akowuah, F. E., Land, J., Yuan, X., Yang, L., Xu, J., & Wang, H. (2018). Standards and Guides for Implementing Security and Privacy for Health Information Technology. In Y. Maleh (Ed.), *Security and Privacy Management, Techniques, and Protocols* (pp. 214–236). Hershey, PA: IGI Global. doi:10.4018/978-1-5225-5583-4.ch008

Akremi, A., Sallay, H., & Rouached, M. (2018). Intrusion Detection Systems Alerts Reduction: New Approach for Forensics Readiness. In Y. Maleh (Ed.), *Security and Privacy Management, Techniques, and Protocols* (pp. 255–275). Hershey, PA: IGI Global. doi:10.4018/978-1-5225-5583-4.ch010

Aldwairi, M., Hasan, M., & Balbahaith, Z. (2017). Detection of Drive-by Download Attacks Using Machine Learning Approach. *International Journal of Information Security and Privacy*, *11*(4), 16–28. doi:10.4018/IJISP.2017100102

Alohali, B. (2017). Detection Protocol of Possible Crime Scenes Using Internet of Things (IoT). In M. Moore (Ed.), *Cybersecurity Breaches and Issues Surrounding Online Threat Protection* (pp. 175–196). Hershey, PA: IGI Global. doi:10.4018/978-1-5225-1941-6.ch008

AlShahrani, A. M., Al-Abadi, M. A., Al-Malki, A. S., Ashour, A. S., & Dey, N. (2017). Automated System for Crops Recognition and Classification. In N. Dey, A. Ashour, & S. Acharjee (Eds.), *Applied Video Processing in Surveillance and Monitoring Systems* (pp. 54–69). Hershey, PA: IGI Global. doi:10.4018/978-1-5225-1022-2.ch003

Anand, R., Shrivastava, G., Gupta, S., Peng, S., & Sindhwani, N. (2018). Audio Watermarking With Reduced Number of Random Samples. In G. Shrivastava, P. Kumar, B. Gupta, S. Bala, & N. Dey (Eds.), *Handbook of Research on Network Forensics and Analysis Techniques* (pp. 372–394). Hershey, PA: IGI Global. doi:10.4018/978-1-5225-4100-4.ch020

Anand, R., Sinha, A., Bhardwaj, A., & Sreeraj, A. (2018). Flawed Security of Social Network of Things. In G. Shrivastava, P. Kumar, B. Gupta, S. Bala, & N. Dey (Eds.), *Handbook of Research on Network Forensics and Analysis Techniques* (pp. 65–86). Hershey, PA: IGI Global. doi:10.4018/978-1-5225-4100-4.ch005

Aneja, M. J., Bhatia, T., Sharma, G., & Shrivastava, G. (2018). Artificial Intelligence Based Intrusion Detection System to Detect Flooding Attack in VANETs. In G. Shrivastava, P. Kumar, B. Gupta, S. Bala, & N. Dey (Eds.), *Handbook of Research on Network Forensics and Analysis Techniques* (pp. 87–100). Hershey, PA: IGI Global. doi:10.4018/978-1-5225-4100-4.ch006

Antunes, F., Freire, M., & Costa, J. P. (2018). From Motivation and Self-Structure to a Decision-Support Framework for Online Social Networks. In V. Ahuja & S. Rathore (Eds.), *Multidisciplinary Perspectives on Human Capital and Information Technology Professionals* (pp. 116–136). Hershey, PA: IGI Global. doi:10.4018/978-1-5225-5297-0.ch007

Atli, D. (2017). Cybercrimes via Virtual Currencies in International Business. In M. Moore (Ed.), *Cybersecurity Breaches and Issues Surrounding Online Threat Protection* (pp. 121–143). Hershey, PA: IGI Global. doi:10.4018/978-1-5225-1941-6.ch006

Baazeem, R. M. (2018). The Role of Religiosity in Technology Acceptance: The Case of Privacy in Saudi Arabia. In J. McAlaney, L. Frumkin, & V. Benson (Eds.), *Psychological and Behavioral Examinations in Cyber Security* (pp. 172–193). Hershey, PA: IGI Global. doi:10.4018/978-1-5225-4053-3.ch010

Bailey, W. J. (2017). Protection of Critical Homeland Assets: Using a Proactive, Adaptive Security Management Driven Process. In M. Dawson, D. Kisku, P. Gupta, J. Sing, & W. Li (Eds.), Developing Next-Generation Countermeasures for Homeland Security Threat Prevention (pp. 17-50). Hershey, PA: IGI Global. doi:10.4018/978-1-5225-0703-1.ch002

Bajaj, S. (2018). Current Drift in Energy Efficiency Cloud Computing: New Provocations, Workload Prediction, Consolidation, and Resource Over Commitment. In S. Aljawarneh & M. Malhotra (Eds.), *Critical Research on Scalability and Security Issues in Virtual Cloud Environments* (pp. 283–303). Hershey, PA: IGI Global. doi:10.4018/978-1-5225-3029-9.ch014

Balasubramanian, K. (2018). Hash Functions and Their Applications. In K. Balasubramanian & M. Rajakani (Eds.), *Algorithmic Strategies for Solving Complex Problems in Cryptography* (pp. 66–77). Hershey, PA: IGI Global. doi:10.4018/978-1-5225-2915-6.ch005

Balasubramanian, K. (2018). Recent Developments in Cryptography: A Survey. In K. Balasubramanian & M. Rajakani (Eds.), *Algorithmic Strategies for Solving Complex Problems in Cryptography* (pp. 1–22). Hershey, PA: IGI Global. doi:10.4018/978-1-5225-2915-6.ch001

Balasubramanian, K. (2018). Secure Two Party Computation. In K. Balasubramanian & M. Rajakani (Eds.), *Algorithmic Strategies for Solving Complex Problems in Cryptography* (pp. 145–153). Hershey, PA: IGI Global. doi:10.4018/978-1-5225-2915-6.ch012

Balasubramanian, K. (2018). Securing Public Key Encryption Against Adaptive Chosen Ciphertext Attacks. In K. Balasubramanian & M. Rajakani (Eds.), *Algorithmic Strategies for Solving Complex Problems in Cryptography* (pp. 134–144). Hershey, PA: IGI Global. doi:10.4018/978-1-5225-2915-6.ch011

Balasubramanian, K. (2018). Variants of the Diffie-Hellman Problem. In K. Balasubramanian & M. Rajakani (Eds.), *Algorithmic Strategies for Solving Complex Problems in Cryptography* (pp. 40–54). Hershey, PA: IGI Global. doi:10.4018/978-1-5225-2915-6.ch003

Balasubramanian, K., & K., M. (2018). Secure Group Key Agreement Protocols. In K. Balasubramanian, & M. Rajakani (Eds.), *Algorithmic Strategies for Solving Complex Problems in Cryptography* (pp. 55-65). Hershey, PA: IGI Global. doi:10.4018/978-1-5225-2915-6.ch004

Balasubramanian, K., & M., R. (2018). Problems in Cryptography and Cryptanalysis. In K. Balasubramanian, & M. Rajakani (Eds.), *Algorithmic Strategies for Solving Complex Problems in Cryptography* (pp. 23-39). Hershey, PA: IGI Global. doi:10.4018/978-1-5225-2915-6.ch002

Balasubramanian, K., & Abbas, A. M. (2018). Integer Factoring Algorithms. In K. Balasubramanian & M. Rajakani (Eds.), *Algorithmic Strategies for Solving Complex Problems in Cryptography* (pp. 228–240). Hershey, PA: IGI Global. doi:10.4018/978-1-5225-2915-6.ch017

Balasubramanian, K., & Abbas, A. M. (2018). Secure Bootstrapping Using the Trusted Platform Module. In K. Balasubramanian & M. Rajakani (Eds.), *Algorithmic Strategies for Solving Complex Problems in Cryptography* (pp. 167–185). Hershey, PA: IGI Global. doi:10.4018/978-1-5225-2915-6.ch014

Balasubramanian, K., & Mathanan, J. (2018). Cryptographic Voting Protocols. In K. Balasubramanian & M. Rajakani (Eds.), *Algorithmic Strategies for Solving Complex Problems in Cryptography* (pp. 124–133). Hershey, PA: IGI Global. doi:10.4018/978-1-5225-2915-6.ch010

Balasubramanian, K., & Rajakani, M. (2018). Secure Multiparty Computation. In K. Balasubramanian & M. Rajakani (Eds.), *Algorithmic Strategies for Solving Complex Problems in Cryptography* (pp. 154–166). Hershey, PA: IGI Global. doi:10.4018/978-1-5225-2915-6.ch013

Balasubramanian, K., & Rajakani, M. (2018). The Quadratic Sieve Algorithm for Integer Factoring. In K. Balasubramanian & M. Rajakani (Eds.), *Algorithmic Strategies for Solving Complex Problems in Cryptography* (pp. 241–252). Hershey, PA: IGI Global. doi:10.4018/978-1-5225-2915-6.ch018

Barone, P. A. (2017). Defining and Understanding the Development of Juvenile Delinquency from an Environmental, Sociological, and Theoretical Perspective. In S. Egharevba (Ed.), *Police Brutality, Racial Profiling, and Discrimination in the Criminal Justice System* (pp. 215–238). Hershey, PA: IGI Global. doi:10.4018/978-1-5225-1088-8.ch010

Beauchere, J. F. (2018). Encouraging Digital Civility: What Companies and Others Can Do. In R. Luppicini (Ed.), *The Changing Scope of Technoethics in Contemporary Society* (pp. 262–274). Hershey, PA: IGI Global. doi:10.4018/978-1-5225-5094-5.ch014

Behera, C. K., & Bhaskari, D. L. (2017). Malware Methodologies and Its Future: A Survey. *International Journal of Information Security and Privacy, 11*(4), 47–64. doi:10.4018/IJISP.2017100104

Benson, V., McAlaney, J., & Frumkin, L. A. (2018). Emerging Threats for the Human Element and Countermeasures in Current Cyber Security Landscape. In J. McAlaney, L. Frumkin, & V. Benson (Eds.), *Psychological and Behavioral Examinations in Cyber Security* (pp. 266–271). Hershey, PA: IGI Global. doi:10.4018/978-1-5225-4053-3.ch016

Berbecaru, D. (2018). On Creating Digital Evidence in IP Networks With NetTrack. In G. Shrivastava, P. Kumar, B. Gupta, S. Bala, & N. Dey (Eds.), *Handbook of Research on Network Forensics and Analysis Techniques* (pp. 225–245). Hershey, PA: IGI Global. doi:10.4018/978-1-5225-4100-4.ch012

Berki, E., Valtanen, J., Chaudhary, S., & Li, L. (2018). The Need for Multi-Disciplinary Approaches and Multi-Level Knowledge for Cybersecurity Professionals. In V. Ahuja & S. Rathore (Eds.), *Multidisciplinary Perspectives on Human Capital and Information Technology Professionals* (pp. 72–94). Hershey, PA: IGI Global. doi:10.4018/978-1-5225-5297-0.ch005

Bhardwaj, A. (2017). Ransomware: A Rising Threat of new age Digital Extortion. In S. Aljawarneh (Ed.), *Online Banking Security Measures and Data Protection* (pp. 189–221). Hershey, PA: IGI Global. doi:10.4018/978-1-5225-0864-9.ch012

Bhattacharjee, J., Sengupta, A., Barik, M. S., & Mazumdar, C. (2018). An Analytical Study of Methodologies and Tools for Enterprise Information Security Risk Management. In M. Gupta, R. Sharman, J. Walp, & P. Mulgund (Eds.), *Information Technology Risk Management and Compliance in Modern Organizations* (pp. 1–20). Hershey, PA: IGI Global. doi:10.4018/978-1-5225-2604-9.ch001

Bruno, G. (2018). Handling the Dataflow in Business Process Models. In V. Ahuja & S. Rathore (Eds.), *Multidisciplinary Perspectives on Human Capital and Information Technology Professionals* (pp. 137–151). Hershey, PA: IGI Global. doi:10.4018/978-1-5225-5297-0.ch008

Carneiro, A. D. (2017). Defending Information Networks in Cyberspace: Some Notes on Security Needs. In M. Dawson, D. Kisku, P. Gupta, J. Sing, & W. Li (Eds.), Developing Next-Generation Countermeasures for Homeland Security Threat Prevention (pp. 354-375). Hershey, PA: IGI Global. doi:10.4018/978-1-5225-0703-1.ch016

Chakraborty, S., Patra, P. K., Maji, P., Ashour, A. S., & Dey, N. (2017). Image Registration Techniques and Frameworks: A Review. In N. Dey, A. Ashour, & S. Acharjee (Eds.), *Applied Video Processing in Surveillance and Monitoring Systems* (pp. 102–114). Hershey, PA: IGI Global. doi:10.4018/978-1-5225-1022-2.ch005

Chaudhari, G., & Mulgund, P. (2018). Strengthening IT Governance With COBIT 5. In M. Gupta, R. Sharman, J. Walp, & P. Mulgund (Eds.), *Information Technology Risk Management and Compliance in Modern Organizations* (pp. 48–69). Hershey, PA: IGI Global. doi:10.4018/978-1-5225-2604-9.ch003

Cheikh, M., Hacini, S., & Boufaida, Z. (2018). Visualization Technique for Intrusion Detection. In Y. Maleh (Ed.), *Security and Privacy Management, Techniques, and Protocols* (pp. 276–290). Hershey, PA: IGI Global. doi:10.4018/978-1-5225-5583-4.ch011

Chen, G., Ding, L., Du, J., Zhou, G., Qin, P., Chen, G., & Liu, Q. (2018). Trust Evaluation Strategy for Single Sign-on Solution in Cloud. *International Journal of Digital Crime and Forensics*, *10*(1), 1–11. doi:10.4018/IJDCF.2018010101

Chen, J., & Peng, F. (2018). A Perceptual Encryption Scheme for HEVC Video with Lossless Compression. *International Journal of Digital Crime and Forensics*, *10*(1), 67–78. doi:10.4018/IJDCF.2018010106

Chen, K., & Xu, D. (2018). An Efficient Reversible Data Hiding Scheme for Encrypted Images. *International Journal of Digital Crime and Forensics*, *10*(2), 1–22. doi:10.4018/IJDCF.2018040101

Chen, Z., Lu, J., Yang, P., & Luo, X. (2017). Recognizing Substitution Steganography of Spatial Domain Based on the Characteristics of Pixels Correlation. *International Journal of Digital Crime and Forensics*, *9*(4), 48–61. doi:10.4018/IJDCF.2017100105

Cherkaoui, R., Zbakh, M., Braeken, A., & Touhafi, A. (2018). Anomaly Detection in Cloud Computing and Internet of Things Environments: Latest Technologies. In K. Munir (Ed.), *Cloud Computing Technologies for Green Enterprises* (pp. 251–265). Hershey, PA: IGI Global. doi:10.4018/978-1-5225-3038-1.ch010

Chowdhury, A., Karmakar, G., & Kamruzzaman, J. (2017). Survey of Recent Cyber Security Attacks on Robotic Systems and Their Mitigation Approaches. In R. Kumar, P. Pattnaik, & P. Pandey (Eds.), *Detecting and Mitigating Robotic Cyber Security Risks* (pp. 284–299). Hershey, PA: IGI Global. doi:10.4018/978-1-5225-2154-9.ch019

Cortese, F. A. (2018). The Techoethical Ethos of Technic Self-Determination: Technological Determinism as the Ontic Fundament of Freewill. In R. Luppicini (Ed.), *The Changing Scope of Technoethics in Contemporary Society* (pp. 74–104). Hershey, PA: IGI Global. doi:10.4018/978-1-5225-5094-5.ch005

Crosston, M. D. (2017). The Fight for Cyber Thoreau: Distinguishing Virtual Disobedience from Digital Destruction. In M. Korstanje (Ed.), *Threat Mitigation and Detection of Cyber Warfare and Terrorism Activities* (pp. 198–219). Hershey, PA: IGI Global. doi:10.4018/978-1-5225-1938-6.ch009

da Costa, F., & de Sá-Soares, F. (2017). Authenticity Challenges of Wearable Technologies. In A. Marrington, D. Kerr, & J. Gammack (Eds.), *Managing Security Issues and the Hidden Dangers of Wearable Technologies* (pp. 98–130). Hershey, PA: IGI Global. doi:10.4018/978-1-5225-1016-1.ch005

Dafflon, B., Guériau, M., & Gechter, F. (2017). Using Physics Inspired Wave Agents in a Virtual Environment: Longitudinal Distance Control in Robots Platoon. *International Journal of Monitoring and Surveillance Technologies Research*, *5*(2), 15–28. doi:10.4018/IJMSTR.2017040102

Dash, S. R., Sheeraz, A. S., & Samantaray, A. (2018). Filtration and Classification of ECG Signals. In C. Pradhan, H. Das, B. Naik, & N. Dey (Eds.), *Handbook of Research on Information Security in Biomedical Signal Processing* (pp. 72–94). Hershey, PA: IGI Global. doi:10.4018/978-1-5225-5152-2.ch005

Dhavale, S. V. (2018). Insider Attack Analysis in Building Effective Cyber Security for an Organization. In J. McAlaney, L. Frumkin, & V. Benson (Eds.), *Psychological and Behavioral Examinations in Cyber Security* (pp. 222–238). Hershey, PA: IGI Global. doi:10.4018/978-1-5225-4053-3.ch013

Dixit, P. (2018). Security Issues in Web Services. In G. Shrivastava, P. Kumar, B. Gupta, S. Bala, & N. Dey (Eds.), *Handbook of Research on Network Forensics and Analysis Techniques* (pp. 57–64). Hershey, PA: IGI Global. doi:10.4018/978-1-5225-4100-4.ch004

Doraikannan, S. (2018). Efficient Implementation of Digital Signature Algorithms. In K. Balasubramanian & M. Rajakani (Eds.), *Algorithmic Strategies for Solving Complex Problems in Cryptography* (pp. 78–86). Hershey, PA: IGI Global. doi:10.4018/978-1-5225-2915-6.ch006

E., J. V., Mohan, J., & K., A. (2018). Automatic Detection of Tumor and Bleed in Magnetic Resonance Brain Images. In C. Pradhan, H. Das, B. Naik, & N. Dey (Eds.), *Handbook of Research on Information Security in Biomedical Signal Processing* (pp. 291-303). Hershey, PA: IGI Global. doi:10.4018/978-1-5225-5152-2.ch015

Escamilla, I., Ruíz, M. T., Ibarra, M. M., Soto, V. L., Quintero, R., & Guzmán, G. (2018). Geocoding Tweets Based on Semantic Web and Ontologies. In M. Lytras, N. Aljohani, E. Damiani, & K. Chui (Eds.), *Innovations, Developments, and Applications of Semantic Web and Information Systems* (pp. 372–392). Hershey, PA: IGI Global. doi:10.4018/978-1-5225-5042-6.ch014

Farhadi, M., Haddad, H. M., & Shahriar, H. (2018). Compliance of Electronic Health Record Applications With HIPAA Security and Privacy Requirements. In Y. Maleh (Ed.), *Security and Privacy Management, Techniques, and Protocols* (pp. 199–213). Hershey, PA: IGI Global. doi:10.4018/978-1-5225-5583-4.ch007

Fatma, S. (2018). Use and Misuse of Technology in Marketing: Cases from India. *International Journal of Technoethics*, *9*(1), 27–36. doi:10.4018/IJT.2018010103

Fazlali, M., & Khodamoradi, P. (2018). Metamorphic Malware Detection Using Minimal Opcode Statistical Patterns. In Y. Maleh (Ed.), *Security and Privacy Management, Techniques, and Protocols* (pp. 337–359). Hershey, PA: IGI Global. doi:10.4018/978-1-5225-5583-4.ch014

Filiol, É., & Gallais, C. (2017). Optimization of Operational Large-Scale (Cyber) Attacks by a Combinational Approach. *International Journal of Cyber Warfare & Terrorism*, *7*(3), 29–43. doi:10.4018/IJCWT.2017070103

Forge, J. (2018). The Case Against Weapons Research. In R. Luppicini (Ed.), *The Changing Scope of Technoethics in Contemporary Society* (pp. 124–134). Hershey, PA: IGI Global. doi:10.4018/978-1-5225-5094-5.ch007

G., S., & Durai, M. S. (2018). Big Data Analytics: An Expedition Through Rapidly Budding Data Exhaustive Era. In D. Lopez, & M. Durai (Eds.), *HCI Challenges and Privacy Preservation in Big Data Security* (pp. 124-138). Hershey, PA: IGI Global. doi:10.4018/978-1-5225-2863-0.ch006

Gammack, J., & Marrington, A. (2017). The Promise and Perils of Wearable Technologies. In A. Marrington, D. Kerr, & J. Gammack (Eds.), *Managing Security Issues and the Hidden Dangers of Wearable Technologies* (pp. 1–17). Hershey, PA: IGI Global. doi:10.4018/978-1-5225-1016-1.ch001

Gamoura, S. C. (2018). A Cloud-Based Approach for Cross-Management of Disaster Plans: Managing Risk in Networked Enterprises. In S. Aljawarneh & M. Malhotra (Eds.), *Critical Research on Scalability and Security Issues in Virtual Cloud Environments* (pp. 240–268). Hershey, PA: IGI Global. doi:10.4018/978-1-5225-3029-9.ch012

Gao, L., Gao, T., Zhao, J., & Liu, Y. (2018). Reversible Watermarking in Digital Image Using PVO and RDWT. *International Journal of Digital Crime and Forensics*, *10*(2), 40–55. doi:10.4018/IJDCF.2018040103

Geetha, S., & Sindhu, S. S. (2016). Audio Stego Intrusion Detection System through Hybrid Neural Tree Model. In B. Gupta, D. Agrawal, & S. Yamaguchi (Eds.), *Handbook of Research on Modern Cryptographic Solutions for Computer and Cyber Security* (pp. 126–144). Hershey, PA: IGI Global. doi:10.4018/978-1-5225-0105-3.ch006

Geethanjali, P. (2018). Bio-Inspired Techniques in Human-Computer Interface for Control of Assistive Devices: Bio-Inspired Techniques in Assistive Devices. In D. Lopez & M. Durai (Eds.), *HCI Challenges and Privacy Preservation in Big Data Security* (pp. 23–46). Hershey, PA: IGI Global. doi:10.4018/978-1-5225-2863-0.ch002

Ghany, K. K., & Zawbaa, H. M. (2017). Hybrid Biometrics and Watermarking Authentication. In S. Zoughbi (Ed.), *Securing Government Information and Data in Developing Countries* (pp. 37–61). Hershey, PA: IGI Global. doi:10.4018/978-1-5225-1703-0.ch003

Hacini, S., Guessoum, Z., & Cheikh, M. (2018). False Alarm Reduction: A Profiling Mechanism and New Research Directions. In Y. Maleh (Ed.), *Security and Privacy Management, Techniques, and Protocols* (pp. 291–320). Hershey, PA: IGI Global. doi:10.4018/978-1-5225-5583-4.ch012

Hadlington, L. (2018). The "Human Factor" in Cybersecurity: Exploring the Accidental Insider. In J. McAlaney, L. Frumkin, & V. Benson (Eds.), Psychological and Behavioral Examinations in Cyber Security (pp. 46-63). Hershey, PA: IGI Global. doi:10.4018/978-1-5225-4053-3.ch003

Haldorai, A., & Ramu, A. (2018). The Impact of Big Data Analytics and Challenges to Cyber Security. In G. Shrivastava, P. Kumar, B. Gupta, S. Bala, & N. Dey (Eds.), *Handbook of Research on Network Forensics and Analysis Techniques* (pp. 300–314). Hershey, PA: IGI Global. doi:10.4018/978-1-5225-4100-4.ch016

Hariharan, S., Prasanth, V. S., & Saravanan, P. (2018). Role of Bibliographical Databases in Measuring Information: A Conceptual View. In J. Jeyasekar & P. Saravanan (Eds.), *Innovations in Measuring and Evaluating Scientific Information* (pp. 61–71). Hershey, PA: IGI Global. doi:10.4018/978-1-5225-3457-0.ch005

Hore, S., Chatterjee, S., Chakraborty, S., & Shaw, R. K. (2017). Analysis of Different Feature Description Algorithm in object Recognition. In N. Dey, A. Ashour, & P. Patra (Eds.), *Feature Detectors and Motion Detection in Video Processing* (pp. 66–99). Hershey, PA: IGI Global. doi:10.4018/978-1-5225-1025-3.ch004

Hurley, J. S. (2017). Cyberspace: The New Battlefield - An Approach via the Analytics Hierarchy Process. *International Journal of Cyber Warfare & Terrorism*, *7*(3), 1–15. doi:10.4018/IJCWT.2017070101

Hussain, M., & Kaliya, N. (2018). An Improvised Framework for Privacy Preservation in IoT. *International Journal of Information Security and Privacy*, *12*(2), 46–63. doi:10.4018/IJISP.2018040104

Ilahi-Amri, M., Cheniti-Belcadhi, L., & Braham, R. (2018). Competence E-Assessment Based on Semantic Web: From Modeling to Validation. In V. Ahuja & S. Rathore (Eds.), *Multidisciplinary Perspectives on Human Capital and Information Technology Professionals* (pp. 246–267). Hershey, PA: IGI Global. doi:10.4018/978-1-5225-5297-0.ch013

Jambhekar, N., & Dhawale, C. A. (2018). Cryptography in Big Data Security. In D. Lopez & M. Durai (Eds.), *HCI Challenges and Privacy Preservation in Big Data Security* (pp. 71–94). Hershey, PA: IGI Global. doi:10.4018/978-1-5225-2863-0.ch004

Jansen van Vuuren, J., Leenen, L., Plint, G., Zaaiman, J., & Phahlamohlaka, J. (2017). Formulating the Building Blocks for National Cyberpower. *International Journal of Cyber Warfare & Terrorism*, *7*(3), 16–28. doi:10.4018/IJCWT.2017070102

Jaswal, S., & Malhotra, M. (2018). Identification of Various Privacy and Trust Issues in Cloud Computing Environment. In S. Aljawarneh & M. Malhotra (Eds.), *Critical Research on Scalability and Security Issues in Virtual Cloud Environments* (pp. 95–121). Hershey, PA: IGI Global. doi:10.4018/978-1-5225-3029-9.ch005

Jaswal, S., & Singh, G. (2018). A Comprehensive Survey on Trust Issue and Its Deployed Models in Computing Environment. In S. Aljawarneh & M. Malhotra (Eds.), *Critical Research on Scalability and Security Issues in Virtual Cloud Environments* (pp. 150–166). Hershey, PA: IGI Global. doi:10.4018/978-1-5225-3029-9.ch007

Javid, T. (2018). Secure Access to Biomedical Images. In C. Pradhan, H. Das, B. Naik, & N. Dey (Eds.), *Handbook of Research on Information Security in Biomedical Signal Processing* (pp. 38–53). Hershey, PA: IGI Global. doi:10.4018/978-1-5225-5152-2.ch003

Jeyakumar, B., Durai, M. S., & Lopez, D. (2018). Case Studies in Amalgamation of Deep Learning and Big Data. In D. Lopez & M. Durai (Eds.), *HCI Challenges and Privacy Preservation in Big Data Security* (pp. 159–174). Hershey, PA: IGI Global. doi:10.4018/978-1-5225-2863-0.ch008

Jeyaprakash, H. M. K., K., & S., G. (2018). A Comparative Review of Various Machine Learning Approaches for Improving the Performance of Stego Anomaly Detection. In G. Shrivastava, P. Kumar, B. Gupta, S. Bala, & N. Dey (Eds.), Handbook of Research on Network Forensics and Analysis Techniques (pp. 351-371). Hershey, PA: IGI Global. doi:10.4018/978-1-5225-4100-4.ch019

Jeyasekar, J. J. (2018). Dynamics of Indian Forensic Science Research. In J. Jeyasekar & P. Saravanan (Eds.), *Innovations in Measuring and Evaluating Scientific Information* (pp. 125–147). Hershey, PA: IGI Global. doi:10.4018/978-1-5225-3457-0.ch009

Jones, H. S., & Moncur, W. (2018). The Role of Psychology in Understanding Online Trust. In J. McAlaney, L. Frumkin, & V. Benson (Eds.), *Psychological and Behavioral Examinations in Cyber Security* (pp. 109–132). Hershey, PA: IGI Global. doi:10.4018/978-1-5225-4053-3.ch007

Jones, H. S., & Towse, J. (2018). Examinations of Email Fraud Susceptibility: Perspectives From Academic Research and Industry Practice. In J. McAlaney, L. Frumkin, & V. Benson (Eds.), *Psychological and Behavioral Examinations in Cyber Security* (pp. 80–97). Hershey, PA: IGI Global. doi:10.4018/978-1-5225-4053-3.ch005

Joseph, A., & Singh, K. J. (2018). Digital Forensics in Distributed Environment. In G. Shrivastava, P. Kumar, B. Gupta, S. Bala, & N. Dey (Eds.), *Handbook of Research on Network Forensics and Analysis Techniques* (pp. 246–265). Hershey, PA: IGI Global. doi:10.4018/978-1-5225-4100-4.ch013

K., I., & A, V. (2018). Monitoring and Auditing in the Cloud. In K. Munir (Ed.), *Cloud Computing Technologies for Green Enterprises* (pp. 318-350). Hershey, PA: IGI Global. doi:10.4018/978-1-5225-3038-1.ch013

Kashyap, R., & Piersson, A. D. (2018). Impact of Big Data on Security. In G. Shrivastava, P. Kumar, B. Gupta, S. Bala, & N. Dey (Eds.), *Handbook of Research on Network Forensics and Analysis Techniques* (pp. 283–299). Hershey, PA: IGI Global. doi:10.4018/978-1-5225-4100-4.ch015

Kastrati, Z., Imran, A. S., & Yayilgan, S. Y. (2018). A Hybrid Concept Learning Approach to Ontology Enrichment. In M. Lytras, N. Aljohani, E. Damiani, & K. Chui (Eds.), *Innovations, Developments, and Applications of Semantic Web and Information Systems* (pp. 85–119). Hershey, PA: IGI Global. doi:10.4018/978-1-5225-5042-6.ch004

Kaur, H., & Saxena, S. (2018). UWDBCSN Analysis During Node Replication Attack in WSN. In C. Pradhan, H. Das, B. Naik, & N. Dey (Eds.), *Handbook of Research on Information Security in Biomedical Signal Processing* (pp. 210–227). Hershey, PA: IGI Global. doi:10.4018/978-1-5225-5152-2.ch011

Kaushal, P. K., & Sobti, R. (2018). Breaching Security of Full Round Tiny Encryption Algorithm. *International Journal of Information Security and Privacy*, *12*(1), 89–98. doi:10.4018/IJISP.2018010108

Kavati, I., Prasad, M. V., & Bhagvati, C. (2017). Search Space Reduction in Biometric Databases: A Review. In M. Dawson, D. Kisku, P. Gupta, J. Sing, & W. Li (Eds.), Developing Next-Generation Countermeasures for Homeland Security Threat Prevention (pp. 236-262). Hershey, PA: IGI Global. doi:10.4018/978-1-5225-0703-1.ch011

Kaye, L. K. (2018). Online Research Methods. In J. McAlaney, L. Frumkin, & V. Benson (Eds.), *Psychological and Behavioral Examinations in Cyber Security* (pp. 253–265). Hershey, PA: IGI Global. doi:10.4018/978-1-5225-4053-3.ch015

Kenekar, T. V., & Dani, A. R. (2017). Privacy Preserving Data Mining on Unstructured Data. In S. Tamane, V. Solanki, & N. Dey (Eds.), *Privacy and Security Policies in Big Data* (pp. 167–190). Hershey, PA: IGI Global. doi:10.4018/978-1-5225-2486-1.ch008

Khaire, P. A., & Kotkondawar, R. R. (2017). Measures of Image and Video Segmentation. In N. Dey, A. Ashour, & S. Acharjee (Eds.), *Applied Video Processing in Surveillance and Monitoring Systems* (pp. 28–53). Hershey, PA: IGI Global. doi:10.4018/978-1-5225-1022-2.ch002

Knibbs, C., Goss, S., & Anthony, K. (2017). Counsellors' Phenomenological Experiences of Working with Children or Young People who have been Cyberbullied: Using Thematic Analysis of Semi Structured Interviews. *International Journal of Technoethics*, *8*(1), 68–86. doi:10.4018/IJT.2017010106

Ko, A., & Gillani, S. (2018). Ontology Maintenance Through Semantic Text Mining: An Application for IT Governance Domain. In M. Lytras, N. Aljohani, E. Damiani, & K. Chui (Eds.), *Innovations, Developments, and Applications of Semantic Web and Information Systems* (pp. 350–371). Hershey, PA: IGI Global. doi:10.4018/978-1-5225-5042-6.ch013

Kohler, J., Lorenz, C. R., Gumbel, M., Specht, T., & Simov, K. (2017). A Security-By-Distribution Approach to Manage Big Data in a Federation of Untrustworthy Clouds. In S. Tamane, V. Solanki, & N. Dey (Eds.), *Privacy and Security Policies in Big Data* (pp. 92–123). Hershey, PA: IGI Global. doi:10.4018/978-1-5225-2486-1.ch005

Korstanje, M. E. (2017). English Speaking Countries and the Culture of Fear: Understanding Technology and Terrorism. In M. Korstanje (Ed.), *Threat Mitigation and Detection of Cyber Warfare and Terrorism Activities* (pp. 92–110). Hershey, PA: IGI Global. doi:10.4018/978-1-5225-1938-6.ch005

Korstanje, M. E. (2018). How Can World Leaders Understand the Perverse Core of Terrorism?: Terror in the Global Village. In C. Akrivopoulou (Ed.), *Global Perspectives on Human Migration, Asylum, and Security* (pp. 48–67). Hershey, PA: IGI Global. doi:10.4018/978-1-5225-2817-3.ch003

Krishnamachariar, P. K., & Gupta, M. (2018). Swimming Upstream in Turbulent Waters: Auditing Agile Development. In M. Gupta, R. Sharman, J. Walp, & P. Mulgund (Eds.), *Information Technology Risk Management and Compliance in Modern Organizations* (pp. 268–300). Hershey, PA: IGI Global. doi:10.4018/978-1-5225-2604-9.ch010

Ksiazak, P., Farrelly, W., & Curran, K. (2018). A Lightweight Authentication and Encryption Protocol for Secure Communications Between Resource-Limited Devices Without Hardware Modification: Resource-Limited Device Authentication. In Y. Maleh (Ed.), *Security and Privacy Management, Techniques, and Protocols* (pp. 1–46). Hershey, PA: IGI Global. doi:10.4018/978-1-5225-5583-4.ch001

Kukkuvada, A., & Basavaraju, P. (2018). Mutual Correlation-Based Anonymization for Privacy Preserving Medical Data Publishing. In C. Pradhan, H. Das, B. Naik, & N. Dey (Eds.), *Handbook of Research on Information Security in Biomedical Signal Processing* (pp. 304–319). Hershey, PA: IGI Global. doi:10.4018/978-1-5225-5152-2.ch016

Kumar, G., & Saini, H. (2018). Secure and Robust Telemedicine using ECC on Radix-8 with Formal Verification. *International Journal of Information Security and Privacy, 12*(1), 13–28. doi:10.4018/IJISP.2018010102

Kumar, M., & Bhandari, A. (2017). Performance Evaluation of Web Server's Request Queue against AL-DDoS Attacks in NS-2. *International Journal of Information Security and Privacy, 11*(4), 29–46. doi:10.4018/IJISP.2017100103

Kumar, M., & Vardhan, M. (2018). Privacy Preserving and Efficient Outsourcing Algorithm to Public Cloud: A Case of Statistical Analysis. *International Journal of Information Security and Privacy, 12*(2), 1–25. doi:10.4018/IJISP.2018040101

Kumar, R. (2018). A Robust Biometrics System Using Finger Knuckle Print. In G. Shrivastava, P. Kumar, B. Gupta, S. Bala, & N. Dey (Eds.), *Handbook of Research on Network Forensics and Analysis Techniques* (pp. 416–446). Hershey, PA: IGI Global. doi:10.4018/978-1-5225-4100-4.ch022

Kumar, R. (2018). DOS Attacks on Cloud Platform: Their Solutions and Implications. In S. Aljawarneh & M. Malhotra (Eds.), *Critical Research on Scalability and Security Issues in Virtual Cloud Environments* (pp. 167–184). Hershey, PA: IGI Global. doi:10.4018/978-1-5225-3029-9.ch008

Kumari, R., & Sharma, K. (2018). Cross-Layer Based Intrusion Detection and Prevention for Network. In G. Shrivastava, P. Kumar, B. Gupta, S. Bala, & N. Dey (Eds.), *Handbook of Research on Network Forensics and Analysis Techniques* (pp. 38–56). Hershey, PA: IGI Global. doi:10.4018/978-1-5225-4100-4.ch003

Lapke, M. (2018). A Semiotic Examination of the Security Policy Lifecycle. In Y. Maleh (Ed.), *Security and Privacy Management, Techniques, and Protocols* (pp. 237–253). Hershey, PA: IGI Global. doi:10.4018/978-1-5225-5583-4.ch009

Liang, Z., Feng, B., Xu, X., Wu, X., & Yang, T. (2018). Geometrically Invariant Image Watermarking Using Histogram Adjustment. *International Journal of Digital Crime and Forensics, 10*(1), 54–66. doi:10.4018/IJDCF.2018010105

Liu, Z. J. (2017). A Cyber Crime Investigation Model Based on Case Characteristics. *International Journal of Digital Crime and Forensics*, *9*(4), 40–47. doi:10.4018/IJDCF.2017100104

Loganathan, S. (2018). A Step-by-Step Procedural Methodology for Improving an Organization's IT Risk Management System. In M. Gupta, R. Sharman, J. Walp, & P. Mulgund (Eds.), *Information Technology Risk Management and Compliance in Modern Organizations* (pp. 21–47). Hershey, PA: IGI Global. doi:10.4018/978-1-5225-2604-9.ch002

Long, M., Peng, F., & Gong, X. (2018). A Format-Compliant Encryption for Secure HEVC Video Sharing in Multimedia Social Network. *International Journal of Digital Crime and Forensics*, *10*(2), 23–39. doi:10.4018/IJDCF.2018040102

M., S., & M., J. (2018). Biosignal Denoising Techniques. In C. Pradhan, H. Das, B. Naik, & N. Dey (Eds.), *Handbook of Research on Information Security in Biomedical Signal Processing* (pp. 26-37). Hershey, PA: IGI Global. doi:10.4018/978-1-5225-5152-2.ch002

Mahapatra, C. (2017). Pragmatic Solutions to Cyber Security Threat in Indian Context. In R. Kumar, P. Pattnaik, & P. Pandey (Eds.), *Detecting and Mitigating Robotic Cyber Security Risks* (pp. 172–176). Hershey, PA: IGI Global. doi:10.4018/978-1-5225-2154-9.ch012

Majumder, A., Nath, S., & Das, A. (2018). Data Integrity in Mobile Cloud Computing. In K. Munir (Ed.), *Cloud Computing Technologies for Green Enterprises* (pp. 166–199). Hershey, PA: IGI Global. doi:10.4018/978-1-5225-3038-1.ch007

Maleh, Y., Zaydi, M., Sahid, A., & Ezzati, A. (2018). Building a Maturity Framework for Information Security Governance Through an Empirical Study in Organizations. In Y. Maleh (Ed.), *Security and Privacy Management, Techniques, and Protocols* (pp. 96–127). Hershey, PA: IGI Global. doi:10.4018/978-1-5225-5583-4.ch004

Malhotra, M., & Singh, A. (2018). Role of Agents to Enhance the Security and Scalability in Cloud Environment. In S. Aljawarneh & M. Malhotra (Eds.), *Critical Research on Scalability and Security Issues in Virtual Cloud Environments* (pp. 19–47). Hershey, PA: IGI Global. doi:10.4018/978-1-5225-3029-9.ch002

Mali, A. D. (2017). Recent Advances in Minimally-Obtrusive Monitoring of People's Health. *International Journal of Monitoring and Surveillance Technologies Research*, *5*(2), 44–56. doi:10.4018/IJMSTR.2017040104

Mali, A. D., & Yang, N. (2017). On Automated Generation of Keyboard Layout to Reduce Finger-Travel Distance. *International Journal of Monitoring and Surveillance Technologies Research*, *5*(2), 29–43. doi:10.4018/IJMSTR.2017040103

Mali, P. (2018). Defining Cyber Weapon in Context of Technology and Law. *International Journal of Cyber Warfare & Terrorism*, *8*(1), 43–55. doi:10.4018/IJCWT.2018010104

Malik, A., & Pandey, B. (2018). CIAS: A Comprehensive Identity Authentication Scheme for Providing Security in VANET. *International Journal of Information Security and Privacy, 12*(1), 29–41. doi:10.4018/IJISP.2018010103

Manikandakumar, M., & Ramanujam, E. (2018). Security and Privacy Challenges in Big Data Environment. In G. Shrivastava, P. Kumar, B. Gupta, S. Bala, & N. Dey (Eds.), *Handbook of Research on Network Forensics and Analysis Techniques* (pp. 315–325). Hershey, PA: IGI Global. doi:10.4018/978-1-5225-4100-4.ch017

Manogaran, G., Thota, C., & Lopez, D. (2018). Human-Computer Interaction With Big Data Analytics. In D. Lopez & M. Durai (Eds.), *HCI Challenges and Privacy Preservation in Big Data Security* (pp. 1–22). Hershey, PA: IGI Global. doi:10.4018/978-1-5225-2863-0.ch001

Mariappan, P. B. P., & Teja, T. S. (2016). Digital Forensic and Machine Learning. In S. Geetha & A. Phamila (Eds.), *Combating Security Breaches and Criminal Activity in the Digital Sphere* (pp. 141–156). Hershey, PA: IGI Global. doi:10.4018/978-1-5225-0193-0.ch009

Marques, R., Mota, A., & Mota, L. (2016). Understanding Anti-Forensics Techniques for Combating Digital Security Breaches and Criminal Activity. In S. Geetha & A. Phamila (Eds.), *Combating Security Breaches and Criminal Activity in the Digital Sphere* (pp. 233–241). Hershey, PA: IGI Global. doi:10.4018/978-1-5225-0193-0.ch014

Mbale, J. (2018). Computer Centres Resource Cloud Elasticity-Scalability (CRECES): Copperbelt University Case Study. In S. Aljawarneh & M. Malhotra (Eds.), *Critical Research on Scalability and Security Issues in Virtual Cloud Environments* (pp. 48–70). Hershey, PA: IGI Global. doi:10.4018/978-1-5225-3029-9.ch003

McAvoy, D. (2017). Institutional Entrepreneurship in Defence Acquisition: What Don't We Understand? In K. Burgess & P. Antill (Eds.), *Emerging Strategies in Defense Acquisitions and Military Procurement* (pp. 222–241). Hershey, PA: IGI Global. doi:10.4018/978-1-5225-0599-0.ch013

McKeague, J., & Curran, K. (2018). Detecting the Use of Anonymous Proxies. *International Journal of Digital Crime and Forensics, 10*(2), 74–94. doi:10.4018/IJDCF.2018040105

Meitei, T. G., Singh, S. A., & Majumder, S. (2018). PCG-Based Biometrics. In C. Pradhan, H. Das, B. Naik, & N. Dey (Eds.), *Handbook of Research on Information Security in Biomedical Signal Processing* (pp. 1–25). Hershey, PA: IGI Global. doi:10.4018/978-1-5225-5152-2.ch001

Menemencioğlu, O., & Orak, İ. M. (2017). A Simple Solution to Prevent Parameter Tampering in Web Applications. In M. Korstanje (Ed.), *Threat Mitigation and Detection of Cyber Warfare and Terrorism Activities* (pp. 1–20). Hershey, PA: IGI Global. doi:10.4018/978-1-5225-1938-6.ch001

Minto-Coy, I. D., & Henlin, M. G. (2017). The Development of Cybersecurity Policy and Legislative Landscape in Latin America and Caribbean States. In M. Moore (Ed.), *Cybersecurity Breaches and Issues Surrounding Online Threat Protection* (pp. 24–53). Hershey, PA: IGI Global. doi:10.4018/978-1-5225-1941-6.ch002

Mire, A. V., Dhok, S. B., Mistry, N. J., & Porey, P. D. (2016). Tampering Localization in Double Compressed Images by Investigating Noise Quantization. *International Journal of Digital Crime and Forensics*, *8*(3), 46–62. doi:10.4018/IJDCF.2016070104

Mohamed, J. H. (2018). Scientograph-Based Visualization of Computer Forensics Research Literature. In J. Jeyasekar & P. Saravanan (Eds.), *Innovations in Measuring and Evaluating Scientific Information* (pp. 148–162). Hershey, PA: IGI Global. doi:10.4018/978-1-5225-3457-0.ch010

Mohan Murthy, M. K., & Sanjay, H. A. (2018). Scalability for Cloud. In S. Aljawarneh & M. Malhotra (Eds.), *Critical Research on Scalability and Security Issues in Virtual Cloud Environments* (pp. 1–18). Hershey, PA: IGI Global. doi:10.4018/978-1-5225-3029-9.ch001

Moorthy, U., & Gandhi, U. D. (2018). A Survey of Big Data Analytics Using Machine Learning Algorithms. In D. Lopez & M. Durai (Eds.), *HCI Challenges and Privacy Preservation in Big Data Security* (pp. 95–123). Hershey, PA: IGI Global. doi:10.4018/978-1-5225-2863-0.ch005

Mountantonakis, M., Minadakis, N., Marketakis, Y., Fafalios, P., & Tzitzikas, Y. (2018). Connectivity, Value, and Evolution of a Semantic Warehouse. In M. Lytras, N. Aljohani, E. Damiani, & K. Chui (Eds.), *Innovations, Developments, and Applications of Semantic Web and Information Systems* (pp. 1–31). Hershey, PA: IGI Global. doi:10.4018/978-1-5225-5042-6.ch001

Moussa, M., & Demurjian, S. A. (2017). Differential Privacy Approach for Big Data Privacy in Healthcare. In S. Tamane, V. Solanki, & N. Dey (Eds.), *Privacy and Security Policies in Big Data* (pp. 191–213). Hershey, PA: IGI Global. doi:10.4018/978-1-5225-2486-1.ch009

Mugisha, E., Zhang, G., El Abidine, M. Z., & Eugene, M. (2017). A TPM-based Secure Multi-Cloud Storage Architecture grounded on Erasure Codes. *International Journal of Information Security and Privacy*, *11*(1), 52–64. doi:10.4018/IJISP.2017010104

Nachtigall, L. G., Araujo, R. M., & Nachtigall, G. R. (2017). Use of Images of Leaves and Fruits of Apple Trees for Automatic Identification of Symptoms of Diseases and Nutritional Disorders. *International Journal of Monitoring and Surveillance Technologies Research*, *5*(2), 1–14. doi:10.4018/IJMSTR.2017040101

Nagesh, K., Sumathy, R., Devakumar, P., & Sathiyamurthy, K. (2017). A Survey on Denial of Service Attacks and Preclusions. *International Journal of Information Security and Privacy*, *11*(4), 1–15. doi:10.4018/IJISP.2017100101

Nanda, A., Popat, P., & Vimalkumar, D. (2018). Navigating Through Choppy Waters of PCI DSS Compliance. In M. Gupta, R. Sharman, J. Walp, & P. Mulgund (Eds.), *Information Technology Risk Management and Compliance in Modern Organizations* (pp. 99–140). Hershey, PA: IGI Global. doi:10.4018/978-1-5225-2604-9.ch005

Newton, S. (2017). The Determinants of Stock Market Development in Emerging Economies: Examining the Impact of Corporate Governance and Regulatory Reforms (I). In M. Ojo & J. Van Akkeren (Eds.), *Value Relevance of Accounting Information in Capital Markets* (pp. 114–125). Hershey, PA: IGI Global. doi:10.4018/978-1-5225-1900-3.ch008

Nidhyananthan, S. S. A., J. V., & R., S. S. (2018). Wireless Enhanced Security Based on Speech Recognition. In C. Pradhan, H. Das, B. Naik, & N. Dey (Eds.), Handbook of Research on Information Security in Biomedical Signal Processing (pp. 228-253). Hershey, PA: IGI Global. doi:10.4018/978-1-5225-5152-2.ch012

Norri-Sederholm, T., Huhtinen, A., & Paakkonen, H. (2018). Ensuring Public Safety Organisations' Information Flow and Situation Picture in Hybrid Environments. *International Journal of Cyber Warfare & Terrorism*, *8*(1), 12–24. doi:10.4018/IJCWT.2018010102

Nunez, S., & Castaño, R. (2017). Building Brands in Emerging Economies: A Consumer-Oriented Approach. In Rajagopal, & R. Behl (Eds.), Business Analytics and Cyber Security Management in Organizations (pp. 183-194). Hershey, PA: IGI Global. doi:10.4018/978-1-5225-0902-8.ch013

Odella, F. (2018). Privacy Awareness and the Networking Generation. *International Journal of Technoethics*, *9*(1), 51–70. doi:10.4018/IJT.2018010105

Ojo, M., & DiGabriele, J. A. (2017). Fundamental or Enhancing Roles?: The Dual Roles of External Auditors and Forensic Accountants. In M. Ojo & J. Van Akkeren (Eds.), *Value Relevance of Accounting Information in Capital Markets* (pp. 59–78). Hershey, PA: IGI Global. doi:10.4018/978-1-5225-1900-3.ch004

P, P., & Subbiah, G. (2016). Visual Cryptography for Securing Images in Cloud. In S. Geetha, & A. Phamila (Eds.), *Combating Security Breaches and Criminal Activity in the Digital Sphere* (pp. 242-262). Hershey, PA: IGI Global. doi:10.4018/978-1-5225-0193-0.ch015

Pandey, S. (2018). An Empirical Study of the Indian IT Sector on Typologies of Workaholism as Predictors of HR Crisis. In V. Ahuja & S. Rathore (Eds.), *Multidisciplinary Perspectives on Human Capital and Information Technology Professionals* (pp. 202–224). Hershey, PA: IGI Global. doi:10.4018/978-1-5225-5297-0.ch011

Pattabiraman, A., Srinivasan, S., Swaminathan, K., & Gupta, M. (2018). Fortifying Corporate Human Wall: A Literature Review of Security Awareness and Training. In M. Gupta, R. Sharman, J. Walp, & P. Mulgund (Eds.), *Information Technology Risk Management and Compliance in Modern Organizations* (pp. 142–175). Hershey, PA: IGI Global. doi:10.4018/978-1-5225-2604-9.ch006

Prachi. (2018). Detection of Botnet Based Attacks on Network: Using Machine Learning Techniques. In G. Shrivastava, P. Kumar, B. Gupta, S. Bala, & N. Dey (Eds.), *Handbook of Research on Network Forensics and Analysis Techniques* (pp. 101-116). Hershey, PA: IGI Global. doi:10.4018/978-1-5225-4100-4.ch007

Pradhan, P. L. (2017). Proposed Round Robin CIA Pattern on RTS for Risk Assessment. *International Journal of Digital Crime and Forensics*, *9*(1), 71–85. doi:10.4018/IJDCF.2017010105

Prentice, S., & Taylor, P. J. (2018). Psychological and Behavioral Examinations of Online Terrorism. In J. McAlaney, L. Frumkin, & V. Benson (Eds.), *Psychological and Behavioral Examinations in Cyber Security* (pp. 151–171). Hershey, PA: IGI Global. doi:10.4018/978-1-5225-4053-3.ch009

Priyadarshini, I. (2017). Cyber Security Risks in Robotics. In R. Kumar, P. Pattnaik, & P. Pandey (Eds.), *Detecting and Mitigating Robotic Cyber Security Risks* (pp. 333–348). Hershey, PA: IGI Global. doi:10.4018/978-1-5225-2154-9.ch022

R., A., & D., E. (2018). Cyber Crime Toolkit Development. In G. Shrivastava, P. Kumar, B. Gupta, S. Bala, & N. Dey (Eds.), *Handbook of Research on Network Forensics and Analysis Techniques* (pp. 184-224). Hershey, PA: IGI Global. doi:10.4018/978-1-5225-4100-4.ch011

Raghunath, R. (2018). Research Trends in Forensic Sciences: A Scientometric Approach. In J. Jeyasekar & P. Saravanan (Eds.), *Innovations in Measuring and Evaluating Scientific Information* (pp. 108–124). Hershey, PA: IGI Global. doi:10.4018/978-1-5225-3457-0.ch008

Ramadhas, G., Sankar, A. S., & Sugathan, N. (2018). The Scientific Communication Process in Homoeopathic Toxicology: An Evaluative Study. In J. Jeyasekar & P. Saravanan (Eds.), *Innovations in Measuring and Evaluating Scientific Information* (pp. 163–179). Hershey, PA: IGI Global. doi:10.4018/978-1-5225-3457-0.ch011

Ramani, K. (2018). Impact of Big Data on Security: Big Data Security Issues and Defense Schemes. In G. Shrivastava, P. Kumar, B. Gupta, S. Bala, & N. Dey (Eds.), *Handbook of Research on Network Forensics and Analysis Techniques* (pp. 326–350). Hershey, PA: IGI Global. doi:10.4018/978-1-5225-4100-4.ch018

Ramos, P., Funderburk, P., & Gebelein, J. (2018). Social Media and Online Gaming: A Masquerading Funding Source. *International Journal of Cyber Warfare & Terrorism*, *8*(1), 25–42. doi:10.4018/IJCWT.2018010103

Rao, N., & Srivastava, S., & K.S., S. (2017). PKI Deployment Challenges and Recommendations for ICS Networks. *International Journal of Information Security and Privacy*, *11*(2), 38–48. doi:10.4018/IJISP.2017040104

Rath, M., Swain, J., Pati, B., & Pattanayak, B. K. (2018). Network Security: Attacks and Control in MANET. In G. Shrivastava, P. Kumar, B. Gupta, S. Bala, & N. Dey (Eds.), *Handbook of Research on Network Forensics and Analysis Techniques* (pp. 19–37). Hershey, PA: IGI Global. doi:10.4018/978-1-5225-4100-4.ch002

Ricci, J., Baggili, I., & Breitinger, F. (2017). Watch What You Wear: Smartwatches and Sluggish Security. In A. Marrington, D. Kerr, & J. Gammack (Eds.), *Managing Security Issues and the Hidden Dangers of Wearable Technologies* (pp. 47–73). Hershey, PA: IGI Global. doi:10.4018/978-1-5225-1016-1.ch003

Rossi, J. A. (2017). Revisiting the Value Relevance of Accounting Information in the Italian and UK Stock Markets. In M. Ojo & J. Van Akkeren (Eds.), *Value Relevance of Accounting Information in Capital Markets* (pp. 102–113). Hershey, PA: IGI Global. doi:10.4018/978-1-5225-1900-3.ch007

Rowe, N. C. (2016). Privacy Concerns with Digital Forensics. In R. Cropf & T. Bagwell (Eds.), *Ethical Issues and Citizen Rights in the Era of Digital Government Surveillance* (pp. 145–162). Hershey, PA: IGI Global. doi:10.4018/978-1-4666-9905-2.ch008

Sabillon, R., Serra-Ruiz, J., Cavaller, V., & Cano, J. J. (2017). Digital Forensic Analysis of Cybercrimes: Best Practices and Methodologies. *International Journal of Information Security and Privacy, 11*(2), 25–37. doi:10.4018/IJISP.2017040103

Sample, C., Cowley, J., & Bakdash, J. Z. (2018). Cyber + Culture: Exploring the Relationship. In J. McAlaney, L. Frumkin, & V. Benson (Eds.), *Psychological and Behavioral Examinations in Cyber Security* (pp. 64–79). Hershey, PA: IGI Global. doi:10.4018/978-1-5225-4053-3.ch004

Sarıgöllü, S. C., Aksakal, E., Koca, M. G., Akten, E., & Aslanbay, Y. (2018). Volunteered Surveillance. In J. McAlaney, L. Frumkin, & V. Benson (Eds.), *Psychological and Behavioral Examinations in Cyber Security* (pp. 133–150). Hershey, PA: IGI Global. doi:10.4018/978-1-5225-4053-3.ch008

Shahriar, H., Clincy, V., & Bond, W. (2018). Classification of Web-Service-Based Attacks and Mitigation Techniques. In Y. Maleh (Ed.), *Security and Privacy Management, Techniques, and Protocols* (pp. 360–378). Hershey, PA: IGI Global. doi:10.4018/978-1-5225-5583-4.ch015

Shet, S., Aswath, A. R., Hanumantharaju, M. C., & Gao, X. (2017). Design of Reconfigurable Architectures for Steganography System. In N. Dey, A. Ashour, & S. Acharjee (Eds.), *Applied Video Processing in Surveillance and Monitoring Systems* (pp. 145–168). Hershey, PA: IGI Global. doi:10.4018/978-1-5225-1022-2.ch007

Shrivastava, G., Sharma, K., Khari, M., & Zohora, S. E. (2018). Role of Cyber Security and Cyber Forensics in India. In G. Shrivastava, P. Kumar, B. Gupta, S. Bala, & N. Dey (Eds.), *Handbook of Research on Network Forensics and Analysis Techniques* (pp. 143–161). Hershey, PA: IGI Global. doi:10.4018/978-1-5225-4100-4.ch009

Singh, N. (2016). Cloud Crime and Fraud: A Study of Challenges for Cloud Security and Forensics. In S. Geetha & A. Phamila (Eds.), *Combating Security Breaches and Criminal Activity in the Digital Sphere* (pp. 68–84). Hershey, PA: IGI Global. doi:10.4018/978-1-5225-0193-0.ch005

Singh, N., Mittal, T., & Gupta, M. (2018). A Tale of Policies and Breaches: Analytical Approach to Construct Social Media Policy. In M. Gupta, R. Sharman, J. Walp, & P. Mulgund (Eds.), *Information Technology Risk Management and Compliance in Modern Organizations* (pp. 176–212). Hershey, PA: IGI Global. doi:10.4018/978-1-5225-2604-9.ch007

Singh, R., & Jalota, H. (2018). A Study of Good-Enough Security in the Context of Rural Business Process Outsourcing. In J. McAlaney, L. Frumkin, & V. Benson (Eds.), *Psychological and Behavioral Examinations in Cyber Security* (pp. 239–252). Hershey, PA: IGI Global. doi:10.4018/978-1-5225-4053-3.ch014

Sivasubramanian, K. E. (2018). Authorship Pattern and Collaborative Research Productivity of Asian Journal of Dairy and Food Research During the Year 2011 to 2015. In J. Jeyasekar & P. Saravanan (Eds.), *Innovations in Measuring and Evaluating Scientific Information* (pp. 213–222). Hershey, PA: IGI Global. doi:10.4018/978-1-5225-3457-0.ch014

Somasundaram, R., & Thirugnanam, M. (2017). IoT in Healthcare: Breaching Security Issues. In N. Jeyanthi & R. Thandeeswaran (Eds.), *Security Breaches and Threat Prevention in the Internet of Things* (pp. 174–188). Hershey, PA: IGI Global. doi:10.4018/978-1-5225-2296-6.ch008

Sonam, & Khari, M. (2018). Wireless Sensor Networks: A Technical Survey. In G. Shrivastava, P. Kumar, B. Gupta, S. Bala, & N. Dey (Eds.), *Handbook of Research on Network Forensics and Analysis Techniques* (pp. 1-18). Hershey, PA: IGI Global. doi:10.4018/978-1-5225-4100-4.ch001

Soni, P. (2018). Implications of HIPAA and Subsequent Regulations on Information Technology. In M. Gupta, R. Sharman, J. Walp, & P. Mulgund (Eds.), *Information Technology Risk Management and Compliance in Modern Organizations* (pp. 71–98). Hershey, PA: IGI Global. doi:10.4018/978-1-5225-2604-9.ch004

Sönmez, F. Ö., & Günel, B. (2018). Security Visualization Extended Review Issues, Classifications, Validation Methods, Trends, Extensions. In Y. Maleh (Ed.), *Security and Privacy Management, Techniques, and Protocols* (pp. 152–197). Hershey, PA: IGI Global. doi:10.4018/978-1-5225-5583-4.ch006

Srivastava, S. R., & Dube, S. (2018). Cyberattacks, Cybercrime and Cyberterrorism. In G. Shrivastava, P. Kumar, B. Gupta, S. Bala, & N. Dey (Eds.), *Handbook of Research on Network Forensics and Analysis Techniques* (pp. 162–183). Hershey, PA: IGI Global. doi:10.4018/978-1-5225-4100-4.ch010

Stacey, E. (2017). Contemporary Terror on the Net. In *Combating Internet-Enabled Terrorism: Emerging Research and Opportunities* (pp. 16–44). Hershey, PA: IGI Global. doi:10.4018/978-1-5225-2190-7.ch002

Sumana, M., Hareesha, K. S., & Kumar, S. (2018). Semantically Secure Classifiers for Privacy Preserving Data Mining. In Y. Maleh (Ed.), *Security and Privacy Management, Techniques, and Protocols* (pp. 66–95). Hershey, PA: IGI Global. doi:10.4018/978-1-5225-5583-4.ch003

Suresh, N., & Gupta, M. (2018). Impact of Technology Innovation: A Study on Cloud Risk Mitigation. In M. Gupta, R. Sharman, J. Walp, & P. Mulgund (Eds.), *Information Technology Risk Management and Compliance in Modern Organizations* (pp. 229–267). Hershey, PA: IGI Global. doi:10.4018/978-1-5225-2604-9.ch009

Survey, A. K. Balasubramanian & M. Rajakani (Eds.), *Algorithmic Strategies for Solving Complex Problems in Cryptography* (pp. 111–123). Hershey, PA: IGI Global. doi:10.4018/978-1-5225-2915-6.ch009

Tank, D. M. (2017). Security and Privacy Issues, Solutions, and Tools for MCC. In K. Munir (Ed.), *Security Management in Mobile Cloud Computing* (pp. 121–147). Hershey, PA: IGI Global. doi:10.4018/978-1-5225-0602-7.ch006

Thackray, H., & McAlaney, J. (2018). Groups Online: Hacktivism and Social Protest. In J. McAlaney, L. Frumkin, & V. Benson (Eds.), *Psychological and Behavioral Examinations in Cyber Security* (pp. 194–209). Hershey, PA: IGI Global. doi:10.4018/978-1-5225-4053-3.ch011

Thandeeswaran, R., Pawar, R., & Rai, M. (2017). Security Threats in Autonomous Vehicles. In N. Jeyanthi & R. Thandeeswaran (Eds.), *Security Breaches and Threat Prevention in the Internet of Things* (pp. 117–141). Hershey, PA: IGI Global. doi:10.4018/978-1-5225-2296-6.ch006

Thota, C., Manogaran, G., Lopez, D., & Vijayakumar, V. (2017). Big Data Security Framework for Distributed Cloud Data Centers. In M. Moore (Ed.), *Cybersecurity Breaches and Issues Surrounding Online Threat Protection* (pp. 288–310). Hershey, PA: IGI Global. doi:10.4018/978-1-5225-1941-6.ch012

Thukral, S., & Rodriguez, T. D. (2018). Child Sexual Abuse: Intra- and Extra-Familial Risk Factors, Reactions, and Interventions. In R. Gopalan (Ed.), *Social, Psychological, and Forensic Perspectives on Sexual Abuse* (pp. 229–258). Hershey, PA: IGI Global. doi:10.4018/978-1-5225-3958-2.ch017

Tidke, S. (2017). MonogDB: Data Management in NoSQL. In S. Tamane, V. Solanki, & N. Dey (Eds.), *Privacy and Security Policies in Big Data* (pp. 64–91). Hershey, PA: IGI Global. doi:10.4018/978-1-5225-2486-1.ch004

Tierney, M. (2018). #TerroristFinancing: An Examination of Terrorism Financing via the Internet. *International Journal of Cyber Warfare & Terrorism*, *8*(1), 1–11. doi:10.4018/IJCWT.2018010101

Topal, R. (2018). A Cyber-Psychological and Behavioral Approach to Online Radicalization. In J. McAlaney, L. Frumkin, & V. Benson (Eds.), *Psychological and Behavioral Examinations in Cyber Security* (pp. 210–221). Hershey, PA: IGI Global. doi:10.4018/978-1-5225-4053-3.ch012

Tripathy, B. K., & Baktha, K. (2018). Clustering Approaches. In *Security, Privacy, and Anonymization in Social Networks: Emerging Research and Opportunities* (pp. 51–85). Hershey, PA: IGI Global. doi:10.4018/978-1-5225-5158-4.ch004

Tripathy, B. K., & Baktha, K. (2018). De-Anonymization Techniques. In *Security, Privacy, and Anonymization in Social Networks: Emerging Research and Opportunities* (pp. 137–147). Hershey, PA: IGI Global. doi:10.4018/978-1-5225-5158-4.ch007

Tripathy, B. K., & Baktha, K. (2018). Fundamentals of Social Networks. In *Security, Privacy, and Anonymization in Social Networks: Emerging Research and Opportunities* (pp. 1–22). Hershey, PA: IGI Global. doi:10.4018/978-1-5225-5158-4.ch001

Tripathy, B. K., & Baktha, K. (2018). Graph Modification Approaches. In *Security, Privacy, and Anonymization in Social Networks: Emerging Research and Opportunities* (pp. 86–115). Hershey, PA: IGI Global. doi:10.4018/978-1-5225-5158-4.ch005

Tripathy, B. K., & Baktha, K. (2018). Social Network Anonymization Techniques. In *Security, Privacy, and Anonymization in Social Networks: Emerging Research and Opportunities* (pp. 36–50). Hershey, PA: IGI Global. doi:10.4018/978-1-5225-5158-4.ch003

Tsimperidis, I., Rostami, S., & Katos, V. (2017). Age Detection Through Keystroke Dynamics from User Authentication Failures. *International Journal of Digital Crime and Forensics*, *9*(1), 1–16. doi:10.4018/IJDCF.2017010101

Wadkar, H. S., Mishra, A., & Dixit, A. M. (2017). Framework to Secure Browser Using Configuration Analysis. *International Journal of Information Security and Privacy*, *11*(2), 49–63. doi:10.4018/IJISP.2017040105

Wahlgren, G., & Kowalski, S. J. (2018). IT Security Risk Management Model for Handling IT-Related Security Incidents: The Need for a New Escalation Approach. In Y. Maleh (Ed.), *Security and Privacy Management, Techniques, and Protocols* (pp. 129–151). Hershey, PA: IGI Global. doi:10.4018/978-1-5225-5583-4.ch005

Wall, H. J., & Kaye, L. K. (2018). Online Decision Making: Online Influence and Implications for Cyber Security. In J. McAlaney, L. Frumkin, & V. Benson (Eds.), *Psychological and Behavioral Examinations in Cyber Security* (pp. 1–25). Hershey, PA: IGI Global. doi:10.4018/978-1-5225-4053-3.ch001

Xylogiannopoulos, K. F., Karampelas, P., & Alhajj, R. (2017). Advanced Network Data Analytics for Large-Scale DDoS Attack Detection. *International Journal of Cyber Warfare & Terrorism*, *7*(3), 44–54. doi:10.4018/IJCWT.2017070104

Yan, W. Q., Wu, X., & Liu, F. (2018). Progressive Scrambling for Social Media. *International Journal of Digital Crime and Forensics*, *10*(2), 56–73. doi:10.4018/IJDCF.2018040104

Yang, L., Gao, T., Xuan, Y., & Gao, H. (2016). Contrast Modification Forensics Algorithm Based on Merged Weight Histogram of Run Length. *International Journal of Digital Crime and Forensics*, *8*(2), 27–35. doi:10.4018/IJDCF.2016040103

Yassein, M. B., Mardini, W., & Al-Abdi, A. (2018). Security Issues in the Internet of Things: A Review. In S. Aljawarneh & M. Malhotra (Eds.), *Critical Research on Scalability and Security Issues in Virtual Cloud Environments* (pp. 186–200). Hershey, PA: IGI Global. doi:10.4018/978-1-5225-3029-9.ch009

Yassein, M. B., Shatnawi, M., & l-Qasem, N. (2018). A Survey of Probabilistic Broadcast Schemes in Mobile Ad Hoc Networks. In S. Aljawarneh, & M. Malhotra (Eds.), *Critical Research on Scalability and Security Issues in Virtual Cloud Environments* (pp. 269-282). Hershey, PA: IGI Global. doi:10.4018/978-1-5225-3029-9.ch013

Yue, C., Tianliang, L., Manchun, C., & Jingying, L. (2018). Evaluation of the Attack Effect Based on Improved Grey Clustering Model. *International Journal of Digital Crime and Forensics*, *10*(1), 92–100. doi:10.4018/IJDCF.2018010108

Zhang, P., He, Y., & Chow, K. (2018). Fraud Track on Secure Electronic Check System. *International Journal of Digital Crime and Forensics*, *10*(2), 137–144. doi:10.4018/IJDCF.2018040108

Zhao, J., Wang, Q., Guo, J., Gao, L., & Yang, F. (2016). An Overview on Passive Image Forensics Technology for Automatic Computer Forgery. *International Journal of Digital Crime and Forensics*, *8*(4), 14–25. doi:10.4018/IJDCF.2016100102

Zhao, X., Zhu, J., & Yu, H. (2016). On More Paradigms of Steganalysis. *International Journal of Digital Crime and Forensics*, *8*(2), 1–15. doi:10.4018/IJDCF.2016040101

Zhou, L., Yan, W. Q., Shu, Y., & Yu, J. (2018). CVSS: A Cloud-Based Visual Surveillance System. *International Journal of Digital Crime and Forensics*, *10*(1), 79–91. doi:10.4018/IJDCF.2018010107

Zhu, J., Guan, Q., Zhao, X., Cao, Y., & Chen, G. (2017). A Steganalytic Scheme Based on Classifier Selection Using Joint Image Characteristics. *International Journal of Digital Crime and Forensics*, *9*(4), 1–14. doi:10.4018/IJDCF.2017100101

Zoughbi, S. (2017). Major Technology Trends Affecting Government Data in Developing Countries. In S. Zoughbi (Ed.), *Securing Government Information and Data in Developing Countries* (pp. 127–135). Hershey, PA: IGI Global. doi:10.4018/978-1-5225-1703-0.ch008

Zubairu, B. (2018). Security Risks of Biomedical Data Processing in Cloud Computing Environment. In C. Pradhan, H. Das, B. Naik, & N. Dey (Eds.), *Handbook of Research on Information Security in Biomedical Signal Processing* (pp. 177–197). Hershey, PA: IGI Global. doi:10.4018/978-1-5225-5152-2.ch009

About the Contributors

Ismini Vasileiou is an Associate Professor of Information Systems and Programme lead of the BSc (Hons) Digital and Technology Solutions at the University of Plymouth (including a Cyber Security Analyst pathway), with research interests including security education and technology-supported learning. She holds an EdD in Flexible Learning for Computing Degrees in Higher Education, and is a Senior Fellow of the Higher Education Academy. She is actively involved in academic delivery at both undergraduate and postgraduate levels, as well as the supervision of postgraduate research. She has previously published on topics including flexible learning, security education and technology-supported delivery, and has delivered a variety of invited presentations and keynote talks into relation to topics such as unconscious bias and stereotypes in STEM topics. Dr Vasileiou is currently the Chair of the STEM special interest group within the International Academic Peer Learning Leadership group, and is also actively involved in professional body activities for the computing sector, including current roles within the BCS South West Branch as the Chair, BCSWomen as the EDI officer, and the BCS Learning and Development SG.

Steven Furnell is a Professor of Information Security and leads the Centre for Security, Communications & Network Research at the University of Plymouth. He is also an Adjunct Professor with Edith Cowan University in Western Australia and an Honorary Professor with Nelson Mandela University in South Africa. His research interests include usability of security and privacy, security management and culture, and technologies for user authentication and intrusion detection. He has authored over 300 papers in refereed international journals and conference proceedings, as well as books including Cybercrime: Vandalizing the Information Society and Computer Insecurity: Risking the System. Prof. Furnell is the current Chair of Technical Committee 11 (security and privacy) within the International Federation for Information Processing, and a member of related working groups on security management, security education, and human aspects of security. He is also a board member of the Institute of Information Security Professionals, and chairs the academic partnership committee and southwest branch. He can be found on Twitter via @smfurnell and further details are at www.plymouth.ac.uk/cscan.

* * *

Matt Bishop received his Ph.D. in computer science from Purdue University in 1984. He is on the faculty at the Department of Computer Science at the University of California at Davis. His main research area is the analysis of vulnerabilities in computer systems, and he has done extensive work on data sanitization, elections and e-voting systems, policy, formal modeling, the insider threat, and computer and information security education. His textbook, "Computer Security: Art and Science", was published in December 2002 by Addison-Wesley Professional. He teaches software engineering, machine architecture, operating systems, programming, and (of course) computer security.

Diana L. Burley, Ph.D., is executive director and chair of the Institute for Information Infrastructure Protection (I3P) and full professor of human & organizational learning at The George Washington University (GW). Named one of SC Magazine's Eight Women in IT Security to Watch in 2017 and the 2017 SC Magazine ReBoot awardee for educational leadership in IT security, Dr. Burley is a global cybersecurity expert who regularly advises enterprises on strengthening their cybersecurity posture, managing cybersecurity risk, assessing human factors in the threat environment, and developing a robust cybersecurity workforce. She is a member of the US National Academies Board on Human-Systems Integration. Prior to GW, Dr. Burley led the CyberCorps program and managed a multi-million-dollar computer science education and research portfolio for the US National Science Foundation. Dr. Burley has written nearly 80 publications on cybersecurity, information sharing, and IT-enabled change; including her 2014 co-authored book "Enterprise Software Security: A Confluence of Disciplines." She has secured approximately $7 million in sponsored research support. Her honors include: 2016 Woman of Influence-Public Sector/Academia by the Executive Women's Forum in Information Security, Risk Management and Privacy; the 2014 Cybersecurity Educator of the Year; and a 2014 Top Ten Influencer in information security careers. She is the sole recipient of both educator of the year and government leader of the year awards from the Colloquium for Information Systems Security Education, has been honored by the U.S. Federal CIO Council for her work on developing the federal cyber security workforce, and served two appointments on the Cyber Security Advisory Committee of the Commonwealth of Virginia General Assembly Joint Commission on Technology & Science. She holds a BA in Economics from the Catholic University of America; M.S. in Public Management and Policy, M.S. in Organization Science, and Ph.D. in Organization Science and Information Technology from Carnegie Mellon University where she studied as a Woodrow Wilson Foundation Fellow.

Joshua Crumbaugh is an engaging and internationally respected cybersecurity subject matter expert, author, keynote and public speaker. During Joshua's ethical hacking career he has never encountered a single network that could keep him or his teams out. He has also accomplished a number of impressive social engineering feats, such as: talking his way into bank vaults, fortune 500 data centers, corporate offices, restricted areas of casinos and more. His experience in all things security led him to realize something had to change. This was the catalyst that led him to found PeopleSec where he is the CEO and Chief Hacker. Joshua is internationally recognized as one of the world's most accomplished social engineers and the world's leading expert on cybersecurity awareness.

Kevin Curran is a Professor of Cyber Security, Executive Co-Director of the Legal innovation Centre and group leader of the Ambient Intelligence & Virtual Worlds Research Group at Ulster University. He is also a senior member of the IEEE. Prof Curran is perhaps most well-known for his work on cyber security, blockchain and location positioning within indoor environments evidenced by over 800 peer review papers. He is one of the most interviewed technology experts in the UK with over 1000+ interviews in recent years https://kevincurran.org/interviews/.

Adele Da Veiga holds a PhD in Information Technology. She is employed at the University of South Africa in the School of Computing division. Her research projects relate to information security culture and privacy with related empirical studies in industry. She has publications in national and international accredited journals and in proceedings of peer-reviewed conferences. Prior to her academic career she was employed in the industry for 13 years where she specialised in information security, information security governance, audit, risk management and privacy. She holds a Certified Information Systems Auditor (CISA), a Certified Information Privacy Technologist (CIPT) certification and a Certified Ethics Officer (EthicsSA reg no. EO 572) certification.

Adrian Davis has a career spanning over fifteen years in information security. He has held various roles in the industry including Managing Director for (ISC)2 EMEA; Principal Research Analyst for the Information Security Forum, Governance Director for The Common Framework and most recently, Visiting Professor at Sunderland University. Over his career he has produced information security solutions for blue chip organisations; worked with professional bodies and academia to support cybersecurity education in UK degree programmes; created with professional bodies accreditation guidelines referenced by computing science programmes in the UK and across Europe; educational resources; contributed to the latest edition of Europe's eCompetence Framework (eCF), now recognised as a European Standard; and been appointed as an editor for the International Standards Organisation, leading the development of several information security standards within the ISO/IEC 27000 series on supply chain security, professionalism and cyber insurance.

Gurpreet Dhillon is a Professor and Head of Information Systems & Supply Chain Management at the Bryan School of Business and Economics, University of North Carolina, Greensboro. Previously he was at Virginia Commonwealth University where he directed and launched the Online MBA program. Professor Dhillon is a graduate of the London School of Economics and Political Science, the UK where he studied organizations and information. His research led him to explore aspects of information security, identity, and assurance. He has authored over 100 research articles that have been published in various journals. Professor Dhillon is also an author of over a dozen books, besides being the Editor-in-Chief of the Journal of Information System Security. He has been featured in the New York Times, USA Today, Business Week, among other popular press magazines and newspapers. He regularly consults with the industry and government and has been successfully completed assignments in the US, UK, UAE, Hong Kong, Portugal, India, Sweden, and Belgium.

Ludwig Englbrecht studied Business Information Systems at the University of Regensburg, Germany and at the Queensland University of Technology, Australia. His major field of study was IT-Security during his master studies. Currently he is a research assistant of Prof. Dr. Günther Pernul and Ph.D. student at the University of Regensburg. His research focus is on new approaches in IT-Forensics (Digital Forensics).

Peter Fischer has over 30 years' experience in Information Security. He is a Fellow of the Institute and chairs its Training Accreditation Committee In recent years he has led the review of the IISP Skills Framework which resulted in the publication of Issue 2.1 and has worked with The Tech Partnership to embed the Skills Framework into the standards for cyber security apprentices and degree apprentices.

Peter's previous roles include: Lecturer in IA at the National School of Government; Head of the Information Assurance and Certification Schemes at CESG; Head of the UK Common Criteria Certification Body; and Head of Information Security and Accreditation at GCHQ.

Lynn Futcher is currently an Associate Professor of the School of ICT, Faculty of Engineering, the Built Environment and Information Technology at the Nelson Mandela University based in Port Elizabeth, South Africa. She has a PhD in Information Technology. Her primary areas of research include Information and Cyber Security Education and Secure Software Development and as such is a key member of the Nelson Mandela University's Centre for Research in Information and Cyber Security (CRICS). She has been actively involved in the IFIP Working Group 11.8 (Information Security Education) since 2005 taking on several committee positions including Vice-Chair and Secretary. As current Chair of this working group, she aims to promote Information Security Education, Training and Awareness in academia, government and industry by encouraging collaboration and engagement amongst these key stakeholders.

Mark Harris is the Director of the Information Security Management program at the Augusta University Cyber Institute and School of Computer and Cyber Sciences. He has a Ph.D. in Information Systems Security from Virginia Commonwealth University, an MS in E-commerce and a B.S. in Information Technology from Old Dominion University. His research interests include behavioral factors of information security, mobile device security, security policy management, security awareness and training, and health security. He has authored many papers in well-respected refereed information systems security journals and conferences, such as the International Journal of Information Management the Journal of Information System Security. Before academia, Mark was a senior network engineer for a large university, where he oversaw an expansive network.

Karin Hedström, PhD, is professor in informatics at Örebro University, Sweden. Her research interest concerns the role of values for development and use of information systems. Hedström's reserach is mainly carried out within the areas of information security and eGovernment. Her research has been published in international leading journals such as Government Information Quarterly, Strategic Journal of Information Systems, Transforming Government: People, Process and Policy, Scandinavian Journal of Information Systems, Computers & Security, and Information Management and Computer Security, among others. Prof. Hedström is the current chair of IFIP TC 11 Working Group 1 - Information Security Management.

Alastair Irons is Academic Dean for the Faculty of Technology and a Professor of Computer Science at the University of Sunderland – where his subject interests focus on computer forensics and cybersecurity. Prior to joining the University in September 2008 he worked at ONE North East, Northumbria University and ICI having moved to the north east from Scotland after graduating in 1984 from Edinburgh University. Alastair became a National Teaching Fellow in 2010. Alastair's current teaching and research interests focus on cybersecurity and digital forensics – currently looking at threat sharing in cybersecurity, methods for digital investigations in "big data", digital investigations in journalism, gender issues in cybersecurity, as well as the role of computer forensics in South Africa. He serves on the management board of DYNAMO, the Advisory Board of the North East Digital Catapult and sits on the CPHC Committee. He contributes to the British Computer Society through a number of roles and is previous chair of the BCS Academic Accreditation Committee, chairs the BCS Cybercrime Forensics Special Interest Group and has recently been elected chair of the BCS NE England branch. In his spare time Alastair participates in karate where he is a 3rd Dan black belt in Shokokai Karate and is currently working towards his 4th Dan.

Sokratis Katsikas is a Professor with the Center for Cyber and Information Security, Norwegian University of Science and Technology, and Rector of the Open University of Cyprus. He has authored or co-authored more than 230 journal publications, book chapters and conference proceedings publications and he has participated in more than 60 funded national and international R&D projects in cyber and information security, and privacy.

Ronald Martin is a proud veteran of the U.S. Army. He has more than two decades of experience in network administration, analysis, engineering, and cybersecurity. He has extensive experience in information technology training, host-based and network-based intrusion detection systems, and corporate and government cybersecurity environments. Ron holds a BS Computer Science, a MS Computer Information Systems, and several leading industry and professional certifications, such as the CISSP, PMP, and CASP. Ron joined Augusta University in 2009 and is currently an assistant professor. He teaches graduate and undergraduate cybersecurity courses in the School of Computer and Cyber Sciences.

Abigail McAlpine is a Cybersecurity Ph.D. Researcher from Secure Societies Institute (SSI) at the University of Huddersfield and Bob's Business. Abigail has created a body of work around privacy and cybersecurity perceptions and is a writer and researcher for Bob's Business.

Nigel McKelvey (Ed.D., MSc., BSc., PGCE, MICS) is a lecturer in Computing at the Letterkenny Institute of Technology and specialises in teaching secure programming techniques at both undergraduate and postgraduate level. Other areas of interest include ethical gaming, performance-based programming and digital forensics. Nigel is an advocate of CoderDojos and encourages community programming initiatives.

Melanie Oldham has a background in events, IT and project management but she's always had a vested interest in information security. As founder of Bob's Business Ltd, she has gained 10 years experience in the industry and has become a reputable and well-respected force within the industry. Bob's Business provide Information Security e-Learning and Phishing Services. The products were developed to demystify the world subject of information security, often thought of as an inaccessible and dry subject. The use of animation and humour is key to the approach and is proven. In addition, as the founder and chair of the Yorkshire Cyber Security Cluster, Melanie is dedicated to reducing the amount of cybercrime within the Yorkshire region through working together within local information security professionals and academics to impart knowledge to those who ask for it.

Günther Pernul is full professor at the Department of Information Systems at the University of Regensburg, Germany. His research interests cover data and information security aspects, data protection and privacy, data analytics, and advanced database technologies and applications. He has wide research experience, has published more than 150 papers and participated and lead many National and European funded research projects.

Bart Preneel is a full professor at the KU Leuven. He heads the COSIC research group that is part of imec and that has 80 members. He was visiting professor at five universities in Europe. He has authored more than 400 scientific publications and is inventor of 5 patents. His main research interests are cryptography, information security and privacy. Bart Preneel has participated to more than 40 EU projects. He has served as president of the IACR (International Association for Cryptologic Research) and is co-founder and chairman of the Board of LSEC. He is a member of the Permanent Stakeholders group of ENISA and of the Academia Europaea. He has been invited speaker at more than 120 conferences in 50 countries. He received the RSA Award for Excellence in the Field of Mathematics (2014), the IFIP TC11 Kristian Beckman award (2015) and the ESORICS Outstanding Research Award (2017). In 2015 he was elected as fellow of the IACR. He frequently consults for industry and governments about security and privacy technologies.

Gerald Quirchmayr holds doctoral degrees in computer science and law from Johannes Kepler University in Linz (Austria) and currently is Professor in the Multimedia Systems Research Group of the Faculty of Computer Science at the University of Vienna. In 2001/2002 he held a Chair in Computer and Information Systems at the University of South Australia. He first joined the University of Vienna in 1993 from the Institute of Computer Science at Johannes Kepler University in Linz (Austria) where he had previously been teaching. In 1989/1990 he taught at the University of Hamburg (Germany). His wide international experience ranges from the participation in international teaching and research projects, very often UN- and EU-based, several research stays at universities and research centres in the US, Asia and EU Member States to extensive teaching in EU staff exchange programs in the United Kingdom, Sweden, Finland, Germany, Spain, and Greece, as well as teaching stays in the Czech Republic and Poland. International teaching and specialist missions include UN-coordinated activities in Egypt, Russia and the Republic of Korea. He has served as a member of program committees of many international conferences, chaired several of them, has contributed as reviewer to scientific journals and has also served on editorial boards. He is a member of the Austrian and German computer societies and a member of IFIP working groups. For his contributions to the international IT community he was received the IFIP Silver Core Award in 1995. His major research focus is on information systems in business and government with a special interest in security, applications, formal representations of decision making and legal issues. His publication record comprises approximately 150 peer reviewed papers plus several edited books and conference proceedings as well as nationally and internationally published project reports. In July 2002 he was appointed as Adjunct Professor at the School of Computer and Information Science of the University of South Australia. From January 2005 until January December 2010 he headed the Department of Distributed and Multimedia Systems, Faculty of Computer Science, at the University of Vienna and served as Vice Dean of the Faculty of Computer Science from October 2008 until October 2010. Since January 2011 he serves as deputy head of the Multimedia Systems Research Group group. In 2011 he was appointed as Deputy Director of the Doctoral Studies Programme Natural and Technical Sciences, served as the programs Director from October 2014 until October 2016 and then again as Deputy Director until October 2018. In January 2019 he was awarded a professotship by Ferdinand Porsche FernFH.

Thomas Schaberreiter earned his Master's degree in Telematics with distinction from the Graz University of Technology (Austria) in 2009. In 2013, he received his PhD as a double degree from the University of Oulu (Finland) and the University of Luxembourg. During his PhD studies he was working at the Public Research Centre Henri Tudor in Luxembourg. His PhD topic was centered around Critical Infrastructure Protection, with a focus on proposing an online risk monitoring and prediction framework that highlights the interdependencies among critical infrastructures and the diversity of critical infrastructure sectors. Thomas has been working at the Oulu University Secure Programming Group (OUSPG) as a postdoctoral researcher until 2016, and is currently working as a postdoctoral resarcher at the Multimedia Information Systems (MIS) research group of the University of Vienna Faculty of Computer Science. His current research interest lies in the security of complex systems and networks.

Kane Smith is Assistant Professor in the Department of Information Systems and Supply Chain Management at the University of North Carolina at Greensboro, USA. Research focus is on Information Privacy and Security, Decision Analysis and Developing Security Policy for the secure management of data within Organizations.

Shaun Smyth (BSc, MSc) has an educational background from Ulster University whose achievements include both a BSc in Computer Science and an MSc in Computational Intelligence. Shaun is currently involved in the research and writing of several papers and the collaboration with other lecturers and colleagues from the computing faculty on several papers on a range of different subjects with a view to future publication.

Qiang Tang is a senior researcher from the TSS (Trusted Service Systems) unit of the ITIS (IT for Innovative Services) department at Luxembourg Institute of Science and Technology. At the same time, he is an adjunct professor at the East China Normal University, Shanghai, China. His research interests lie in applied cryptography, privacy enhancing technologies, blockchain-enabled security design, and the security and privacy issues in machine learning and data mining (particularly recommender systems).

Teemu Tokola Has been teaching a variety of topics ranging from computer architecture, software development and embedded systems to cyber security at the University of Oulu, Finland, since 2004.

Index

E

F

G

H

I

K

L

M

O

P

Q

S

T

U

V

W

Purchase Print, E-Book, or Print + E-Book

IGI Global books are available in three unique pricing formats:
Print Only, E-Book Only, or Print + E-Book. Shipping fees apply.

www.igi-global.com

Recommended Reference Books

ISBN: 978-1-5225-2915-6
© 2018; 302 pp.
List Price: $245

ISBN: 978-1-5225-2190-7
© 2017; 133 pp.
List Price: $115

ISBN: 978-1-5225-2193-8
© 2017; 128 pp.
List Price: $120

ISBN: 978-1-5225-1016-1
© 2017; 345 pp.
List Price: $200

ISBN: 978-1-5225-1938-6
© 2017; 315 pp.
List Price: $190

ISBN: 978-1-5225-1088-8
© 2017; 372 pp.
List Price: $195

Do you want to stay current on the latest research trends, product announcements, news and special offers?
Join IGI Global's mailing list today and start enjoying exclusive perks sent only to IGI Global members.
Add your name to the list at **www.igi-global.com/newsletters.**

Publisher of Peer-Reviewed, Timely, and Innovative Academic Research

IGI Global
DISSEMINATOR OF KNOWLEDGE

www.igi-global.com Sign up at www.igi-global.com/newsletters facebook.com/igiglobal twitter.com/igiglobal linkedin.com/igiglobal

Ensure Quality Research is Introduced to the Academic Community

Become an IGI Global Reviewer for Authored Book Projects

The overall success of an authored book project is dependent on quality and timely reviews.

In this competitive age of scholarly publishing, constructive and timely feedback significantly expedites the turnaround time of manuscripts from submission to acceptance, allowing the publication and discovery of forward-thinking research at a much more expeditious rate. Several IGI Global authored book projects are currently seeking highly qualified experts in the field to fill vacancies on their respective editorial review boards:

Applications may be sent to:
development@igi-global.com

Applicants must have a doctorate (or an equivalent degree) as well as publishing and reviewing experience. Reviewers are asked to write reviews in a timely, collegial, and constructive manner. All reviewers will begin their role on an ad-hoc basis for a period of one year, and upon successful completion of this term can be considered for full editorial review board status, with the potential for a subsequent promotion to Associate Editor.

If you have a colleague that may be interested in this opportunity,
we encourage you to share this information with them.

IGI Global
DISSEMINATOR OF KNOWLEDGE
www.igi-global.com

Celebrating 30 Years of Scholarly Knowledge Creation & Dissemination

InfoSci®-Books

A Collection of 4,000+ Reference Books Containing Over 87,000 Full-Text Chapters Focusing on Emerging Research

This database is a collection of over 4,000+ IGI Global single and multi-volume reference books, handbooks of research, and encyclopedias, encompassing groundbreaking research from prominent experts worldwide. These books are highly cited and currently recognized in prestigious indices such as: Web of Science™ and Scopus®.

Librarian Features:

- No Set-Up or Maintenance Fees
- Guarantee of No More Than A 5% Annual Price Increase
- COUNTER 4 Usage Reports
- Complimentary Archival Access
- Free MARC Records

Researcher Features:

- Unlimited Simultaneous Users
- No Embargo of Content
- Full Book Download
- Full-Text Search Engine
- No DRM

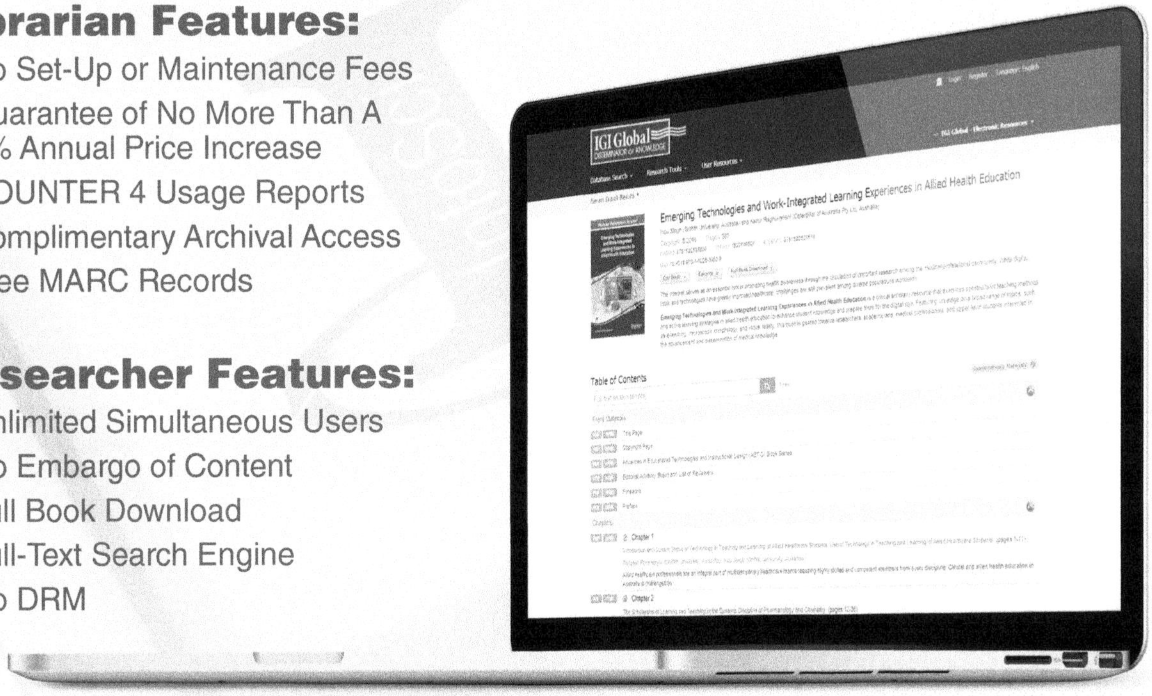

To Find Out More or To Purchase This Database:

www.igi-global.com/infosci-books

eresources@igi-global.com • Toll Free: 1-866-342-6657 ext. 100 • Phone: 717-533-8845 x100

IGI Global
DISSEMINATOR OF KNOWLEDGE
www.igi-global.com

IGI Global Proudly Partners with

eContent Pro International

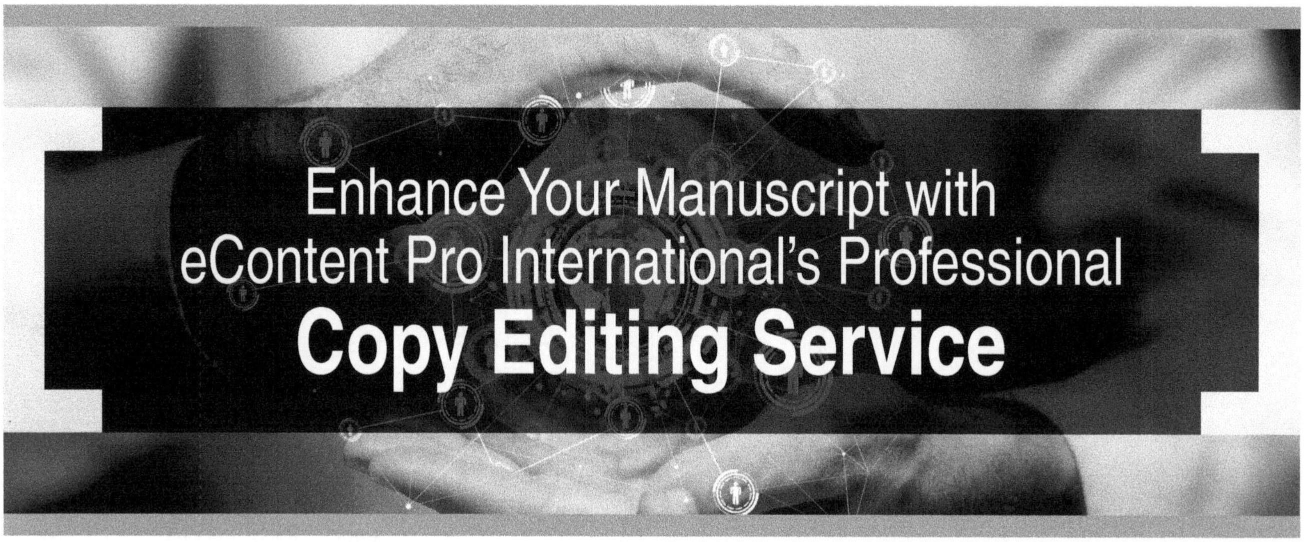

Expert Copy Editing

eContent Pro International copy editors, with over 70 years of combined experience, will provide complete and comprehensive care for your document by resolving all issues with spelling, punctuation, grammar, terminology, jargon, semantics, syntax, consistency, flow, and more. In addition, they will format your document to the style you specify (APA, Chicago, etc.). All edits will be performed using Microsoft Word's Track Changes feature, which allows for fast and simple review and management of edits.

Additional Services

eContent Pro International also offers fast and affordable proofreading to enhance the readability of your document, professional translation in over 100 languages, and market localization services to help businesses and organizations localize their content and grow into new markets around the globe.

IGI Global Authors Save 25% on eContent Pro International's Services!

Scan the QR Code to Receive Your 25% Discount

The 25% discount is applied directly to your eContent Pro International shopping cart when placing an order through IGI Global's referral link. Use the QR code to access this referral link. eContent Pro International has the right to end or modify any promotion at any time.

Email: customerservice@econtentpro.com

econtentpro.com

Are You Ready to
Publish Your Research?

IGI Global
DISSEMINATOR OF KNOWLEDGE

IGI Global offers book authorship and editorship opportunities across 11 subject areas, including business, healthcare, computer science, engineering, and more!

Benefits of Publishing with IGI Global:

- Free one-to-one editorial and promotional support.
- Expedited publishing timelines that can take your book from start to finish in less than one (1) year.
- Choose from a variety of formats including: Edited and Authored References, Handbooks of Research, Encyclopedias, and Research Insights.
- Utilize IGI Global's eEditorial Discovery® submission system in support of conducting the submission and blind-review process.
- IGI Global maintains a strict adherence to ethical practices due in part to our full membership to the Committee on Publication Ethics (COPE).
- Indexing potential in prestigious indices such as Scopus®, Web of Science™, PsycINFO®, and ERIC – Education Resources Information Center.
- Ability to connect your ORCID iD to your IGI Global publications.
- Earn royalties on your publication as well as receive complimentary copies and exclusive discounts.

Get Started Today by Contacting the Acquisitions Department at:

acquisition@igi-global.com

www.ingramcontent.com/pod-product-compliance
Ingram Content Group UK Ltd.
Pitfield, Milton Keynes, MK11 3LW, UK
UKHW050951290926
15470UKWH00005B/1760

9 781522 578475